A Social History of Twentieth-Century Russia

A Social History of Twentieth-Century Russia

Vladimir Andrle

University of York

Edward Arnold
A member of the Hodder Headline Group
LONDON NEW YORK MELBOURNE AUCKLAND

First published in Great Britain 1994 by
Edward Arnold, a division of Hodder Headline PLC,
338 Euston Road, London NW1 3BH

Distributed in the USA by
Routledge, Chapman and Hall, Inc.
29 West 35th Street, New York, NY 10001

British Library Cataloguing in Publication Data
A catalogue record for this book is available from the British Library

Library of Congress Cataloging-in-Publication Data
A catalog record for this title is available from the Library of Congress

ISBN 0 340 525150 (Pb)
ISBN 0 340 525169 (Hb)

1 2 3 4 5   94 95 96 97 98

Typeset in 10/11 Times by
York House Typographic Ltd.
Printed and bound in Great Britain by
Mackays of Chatham, PLC

To Jayne

Contents

Preface

In recent years, Western historical scholarship on Russia has rapidly been diversified by specialist studies written on 'social' or 'from-below' themes. This book offers a synthesis of these studies. It does not treat 'social history' as separate from politics; neither does it purport to define political events as shaped by sociological laws. The narrative describes 'society' in its various 'us-them' manifestations and its moments of change, and it explores the ways in which 'society' constituted the object and shaped the outcomes of political campaigns. In addition, it discusses the self-conscious identities and movements that, in certain periods, began to form a 'civil society' counterpart to the state – a public with its own agendas.

The book is intended to redress an imbalance in the range of texts that are available on Russian history. For the students interested primarily in political leaders, doctrines and affairs of state, there is plenty to choose from at all levels, from the introductory to the highly detailed and specialized. Students interested in economic problems, policies and developments are also well served by accessible introductions as well as specialized monographs. Those interested in social history, however, have had to make do without an introductory text written for them especially.

There is a reason for this. Social history represents a relatively recent development in historical studies in general and Western scholarship on Russia in particular. In Russia, developments over the past hundred years have been more obviously politically driven than in the major countries of the West; and Russians have lived under state regimes permitting little room for the kind of social movements and non-state public organizations that have been written about in many a Western social history. Besides, in so far as the topics of social history include concerns with social classes and the participation of ordinary people in processes of change, they are similar to the topics defined as significant by Marxist theory. There are of course several strands to Marxism, and it is perfectly feasible to be interested in social history without accepting any of them. The abstractions of Marxist sociology with its emphasis on class relations and 'laws of development', however, have been the stock in trade of Soviet historians whose accounts of the past have been notoriously obeisant to regime legitimation needs. Hence, Western historians who have tried to shift focus from political regimes, leaders and doctrines to more sociological topics have been at times accused by more conservative colleagues of peddling 'revisionist' apologies for what the Soviet regime has done to its people. Justifiably or not, the advent of social history in Western scholarship on Russia has been embroiled in polemics. I address some of the issues in Chapter 8, in the course of discussing the Stalin era.

I believe that, in general, writing a history of 'a society' is bound to be more difficult than writing a history of a government. The themes that social historians write about, the research techniques they employ and the issues of interpretation they face are more varied and less consensual than the themes and techniques of political history. The canvas is broader, the dangers of overgeneralization greater and the material more fragmented. The project is even more daunting when the subject is Russian society. Deciding what to include on the canvas and how subtly or boldly different the result should look from the contents of more conventional political histories of Russia is not easy.

The approach I have taken in filling the canvas refrains from broad brush strokes. It favours, in other words, offering insights through descriptive discussions of interactive processes rather then explanatory generalizations. My purpose is to provide the reader with 'a feel' for social situations, meanings and climates such as can be acquired from the available data. That, I believe, is the best way to understand social contexts and change. My approach even takes a step back from the premises and propositions of modernization theory. I show them in their use, for example in the role they played in the social perceptions, beliefs and actions of some of the groups I write about; but I do not use them as my own explanatory categories. In a similar vein, I refrain from assuming that categories like class reflect in an unproblematic way real social differentiation and identities. Sociological categories were labels and encodements of belief, used in certain types of discourse for a purpose; they tell us as much about the people who used them in their communications as about the people or behaviour they defined.

The intimate relationship between theoretical thought and social ideologies is a recurrent theme of this book, and so are their relations to the pragmatic reasoning involved in living the small-scale realities of everyday life. The reader will also find a continuity theme in the relations of the intelligentsia to the less educated classes on the one hand and political regimes on the other. Other themes that make a recurrent appearance in the narrative include gender relations, patron-client politics, family life and the demarcations between private and public spheres, management-worker relations, informal adaptations to bureaucratic controls, and generational differences. In addition, each of the historical periods under discussion has its own events, trends and phenomena that give it a distinctive characteristic. I hope it all adds up to a picture of the social contexts in which political developments took place. I offer it as being of interest in itself rather than as compelling some radical reappraisal of the motives and causes of political deeds and events that political historians have established or argued about.

Throughout the book is concerned with Russia – that is, *not* with the non-Russian lands of the tsarist and Soviet empires. Statistical data from all-empire censuses and surveys are occasionally used because Russian-only ones are not available; in such cases, the wider coverage is indicated.

Footnotes are only used to give sources of quantitative data and direct quotations. Each chapter has a further reading section in which I acknowledge the authors whose works I have used.

Special acknowledgements are due not only to the authors whose data, observations and insights I was able to draw on, but also to Christopher Wheeler, who persuaded me to embark on writing this book. I could not have wished for a more patient and understanding publisher's editor. Sarah Irwin, Neil Robinson, and Jayne Wilde read the whole manuscript and exercised their critical acumen to constructive effect, although they were under pressure of their own work. They helped to make the final version better than it would have been otherwise; but responsibility for any flaws that remain is my own.

Vladimir Andrle
York, 1994

1

State, Modernization, and Society in Tsarist Russia

The tsarist state was a self-confessed autocracy (*samoderzhavie*), an absolutist system of centralized rule in which decision-making about issues great and small was the personal prerogative of the monarch. The tsar was, of course, aided in his efforts to govern by a professional bureaucracy whose top-rank officials were on hand to give their advice. But while they were accountable to him, he was accountable to no body of men or laws. The central pinnacles of the state service were undergoing systematizing reforms that clarified the functions, jurisdictions, and appropriate operational procedures for government bureaux. However, such quests for administrative rationality were never allowed to reach a stage where the tsar's personal sovereignty over all matters of state might become subject to predefined limitations. It was only after the revolution of 1905 (of which more will be said in Chapters 3 and 4) that the tsar's top ministers formed a cabinet with a prime minister at its head. Even then, the monarchy remained the centre of imperial rule: the prime minister was not able to prevent his government colleagues from having direct access to the tsar and, during the First World War, Nicholas II (who ruled from 1894 to 1917) made a point of reasserting his powers by putting the armed forces under his personal command while his wife and her courtiers took control of civilian affairs. The ideological justification of this autocracy consisted of the notion that the tsar acted in a divine, blessed, spiritual union with the people of the Empire, hence ensuring that the state was never subjected to the self-interest of any particular group or section of society. The people could petition the tsar to advise on their problems, and we shall see below that certain corporate groups had institutionalized opportunities for influencing government decision-making through particular ministries. Nevertheless, the tsar had the sovereign right of last word on what was in the interest of the state and its people.

The provinces (*gubernii*) of the empire, which stretched from Poland and the Baltic in the west to the Pacific in the east, were under the control of governors accountable to the Ministry of the Interior in St Petersburg. The provinces were large territories, requiring regional divisions and elements of local government. Until the 1870s, local-authority functions were in the hands of corporate bodies of noble landowners in the countryside and merchants in the cities. The reforms under Alexander II (who ruled from 1855 to 1881) transferred the functions of local authority to elected councils, zemstvos in the rural countryside and dumas in the cities. The electoral system, however, was arranged to ensure noble majorities in the zemstvos (peasants were able to elect only about 10 per cent of the zemstvo members) and a majority of merchants, nobles, and educated professionals in the city dumas. The zemstvos and the city dumas were able to raise their own taxes to supplement the grants allocated by central government, and they had wide responsibility for developing local infrastructures, primary schools, hospitals, welfare institutions, cultural facilities, and advice agencies for economic moderniza-tion. Their decisions, however, were subject to veto by the provincial governors, and their deliberations were monitored by agents of the state security police. The state security police had been organized by Alexander II's predecessor, Nicholas I, as a branch of the Ministry of the Interior with a broad remit to collect information and take action to keep potentially destabilizing tendencies and events under control. In the late 1880s, another plenipotentiary of the central state, the land captain, was introduced into rural areas to supervise an element of peasant self-government that was exercised through village communes and peasant district authorities, the *volosti*.

Traditionally, the principles of tsarist autocracy had been shored up by its close association with the orthodox church. From the eighteenth century, however, these principles were in increasing tension with modernization ideologies. Peter I (who rules from 1682 to 1725) was the first tsar to introduce into statecraft the belief that, contrary to the medieval view of a fixed universe, the empire's strength was not just a matter of military conquests but also of developing economic resources by the application of science and technology. He encouraged the nobles to acquire a European education, he set up professional schools and the Academy of Sciences to make this learning available at home as well, and he organized an army of serfs to build St Petersburg. Making the brand-new naval city (which was an easy sail from Sweden, Prussia, and the West) into the empire's capital underlay the tsar's determination to make Russia a part of Europe's modernizing civilization. It was the Age of Enlightenment in Europe, and the nobles who travelled West to become educated returned as enthusiastic converts to its values. St Petersburg became a welcoming place for educated foreigners, while state service in both military and civilian ranks became organized on the basis of educational and professional merit. The Enlightenment ideas, according to which a good government was one that acted systematically in harmony with the scientific laws of nature, permeated educated Russia and entered the corridors of the imperial bureaucracy itself. Government should be rational and run by professionals who were trained in the values as well as the techniques of public service. The doctrines of the Prussian 'well ordered state' (*Polizeistaat*) exerted their influence, and, eventually, German legal theory that saw progress ultimately in the shape of the 'rightful legal state' (*Rechtsstaat*), in which a comprehensive, coherent, and impartially applied code of law would do away with all manifestations of individual caprice in the affairs of state. These visions of reformist progress were clearly at odds with the tsar's autocratic prerogative to exercise arbitrary power, and with the pre-

Enlightenment, mystical terms in which the prerogative was traditionally justified.

By the beginning of the nineteenth century, there was a great cultural gap between the overwhelmingly peasant Russia on the one hand and the educated, self-consciously enlightened, cultivated, europeanized Russia on the other. The Europeanized Russians lived in universities and academies, in the army officer corps, and in the bureaux of state service, in salons, discussion clubs, masonic societies, and in the editorial offices of publishing houses producing an expanding range of avidly read newspapers, literary 'thick journals', pamphlets, and books. Educated Russia lived in a spirit that found nourishment in Protestant pietism, romanticism, atheism, spiritualism, rationalism, and natural science, but rarely in the doctrines of the Orthodox Church. And educated Russia was at odds with the autocracy, its essence manifesting itself in acts of power which were not just repressive (for they could be benevolent as well) but also because they were, above all, arbitrary and, in that sense, irrational and unlawful.

The social groups that played a part in the developments of the nineteenth century included conservative and reformist bureaucrats, landed gentry, landless nobles, industrialists and businessmen, the professions, intellectual élites, workers and peasants. They played their parts under the influence of two main opposing forces: the autocracy and the radical intelligentsia. The core of the radical intelligentsia was born of the semi-clandestine circles and secret societies that, by the beginning of the nineteenth century, had an established tradition in high schools and universities, forming a strong subculture that drew varied degrees of commitment from students but that left few of them unaffected. As some of the graduates would not or could not find satisfactory placements in state service, they took this subculture with them into their adult lives, in preference to returning to their family origins. They lived in networks of intense friendships and intellectual commitment on the fringes of academia and polite society – both of which they were connected to by kin as well as educational background. These communities were quick to define their purpose in largely political terms, for it was the tsarist autocracy that, by its repressive actions, shaped and justified their sectarian and clandestine nature and that presented a visible as well as ubiquitous obstacle to intellectual, rationalist visions of progress.

By the middle of the century, the radical intelligentsia redefined its purpose: criticism or rebellion against the autocracy, in the name of Reason, was no longer justified, but service for 'the people' (*narod*), without whose awakening, it was now fervently believed, there would be no progress and the life of the cultured spirit would be sterile. Apart from the fact that it permeated the explosion of socially committed writing for which the creative intelligentsia of the mid-century generation became famous, and that it started the political history of revolutionary parties, this notion of service for 'the people' was notable in other respects. First, it represented a direct ideological challenge to the autocracy whose own legitimacy rested on the myth of the tsar's spiritual union with his people, whom he governed and protected with a wisdom born of paternal love and care. Secondly, 'service for the people' presented an interesting contrast to the 'service for the state' ethic of the nobility and officialdom. Thirdly, this notion enabled subsequent generations of the intelligentsia to identify the creativity of the best nineteenth-century writers with national awakening, and to give a new definition to Russian patriotism; here the ethics of 'being a true Russian' no longer consisted of loyalty to christian orthodoxy and the tsar but of an interest in, and a celebration of, what quickly became known as Russian classical literature.

The autocracy responded to this new ideological challenge with waves of repression and loud reaffirmations of its principles, which sounded hollow and plainly reactionary to many educated people. The Orthodox Church, isolated as it was from the challenge of Protestant reformation, did not even try to produce a fresh theology capable of meeting rationalist arguments on their own ground; besides, the recent expansion of the empire had brought into its realm peoples of other faiths, *vis-à-vis* whom the autocracy needed a legitimation that transcended religious differences. The concept of the tsar's spiritual union with 'the people' was also under pressure because 'the people' were now, almost by definition, on the other side of the cultural chasm from the educated Russia to which the autocracy – the tsar's, their families, the courtiers, and the bureaucracy – belonged, alongside the socially alienated intellectual radicals. This division became more visible in the second half of the century, when successive tsars exhibited an increasing need to separate their public selves from their private family lives.

Above all, however, the circumstances in which the autocracy operated during the nineteenth century never allowed modernization to disappear from the agenda. Alexander II was the greatest of these reform-minded tsars, and the changes he saw through included the abolition of serfdom, the introduction of an independent judiciary, new university charters, and the start of a railway-building programme, in addition to the already-mentioned zemstvos and city dumas. There was, however, something of this permanent reformist tendency within the state bureaucracy itself, which made its presence felt under less energetic or more conservative tsars. There were connections of thought – as well as of family and educational background – between the radical intelligentsia, the more moderate intelligentsia, and the reformist officials. The autocracy could be panicked by the radical intelligentsia into a reactionary stance while the body of its administration could not help but be influenced by what the radical intelligentsia had to say.

The intelligentsia, however, was also pulled in different directions. Soon after the abolition of serfdom, the radicals generated enthusiasm for pushing things forward by making their platonic links with 'the people' into real ones; one summer, they went into the countryside in their thousands to raise the peasants' consciousness. The peasants, however, appeared to greet the agitation of the young revolutionary populists (*narodniki*) with indifference. Many of the radicals returned disheartened, some deciding to make their impression on 'the people' by terrorist violence against the state. This widened the split between reformers and revolutionaries. The *Rechtsstaat*-seeking reformers went to the country to investigate peasant 'customary law' and to see how it could be incorporated into a single legal code. They were baffled by what they found (see Chapter 2). Back in the towns, they suffered a further setback when a self-confessed terrorist (Vera Zasulich) was set free by a jury to the cheers of the revolutionary sympathizers who packed the gallery, thus justifying fears that the independent judiciary would not be able to enforce the law. The *Rechtsstaat*-seeking reformers were thus thwarted, and many of them felt that the radicals were playing into reactionary hands.

The terrorist bomb that killed Alexander II took out of play the reform-minded tsar. Alexander III (who ruled from 1881 to 1894) and Nicholas II were mainly associated with autocracy's defensive face. Their period of rule was marked by a proactive state security police (Okhrana), who used ever wider special powers. The electoral procedures of the zemstvos were changed to make sure that the nobles who were large landowners pushed out the nobles whose connections with the intelligentsia were greater than their landholdings. Nicholas II did not conceal his sense of alienation from his educated subjects, who seemed to him treacherous – those who worked in government administration as well as those who did not. He oscillated between jealously guarded retreats into private family life and defiant attempts to demonstrate that he still had the affections and loyalty of the unsophisticated but truly Russian people. It was, however, only the temporary surges of patriotism at the beginnings of wars that brought him moments of gratification in this respect. They were followed by revolutionary surges. The war with Japan in 1904–5 brought no triumphs, only a swift and ignominious defeat. The revolutionary year of 1905 started when the tsar failed to dissociate himself from his guards: they had killed at least 130 men and women (this was the official estimate of casualties) who, led by a priest, were marching to his palace to deliver a petition. By October of that year, the tsar diffused the situation by setting up the state duma, an elective quasi-parliamentary institution that promised, at last, a shift to constitutional democracy. But the autocracy's prerogatives were reaffirmed by the dissolution of two dumas in quick succession, and the tsar did not dissociate himself from the lunatic fringe of counter-revolution that indulged in anti-Jewish pogroms.

The petition to the tsar that was stopped in January 1905 was one of the last in the centuries-old tradition in which sections of the population formulated their concerns or demands by addressing the monarch in floridly respectful terms. The profligate amounts of petitions and resolutions in which assembled groups of people articulated their demands during the following two years were mostly not addressed to the tsar at all, and of those that were – even the ones produced by assemblies of conservative nobles – pared the terms of the address to bare essentials. This in itself might not have meant that the autocracy was finally divested of all legitimating myth, but the tsar's hopes that 'the people', in contrast with the intelligentsia, still were 'genuinely Russian' and on his side could not have been encouraged by the thin and lukewarm crowds that lined the roadsides to watch the imperial cavalcade celebrate the tricentenary of the Romanov dynasty in 1913.

There was a surge of patriotism when Russia joined in the First World War, but the autocracy did not know how to take advantage of it without sinking even further into the xenophobia that had marked its policies towards ethnic minorities since 1905. The treatment of German-speaking peasants was a good example. Their ancestors had settled in the vicinity of the river Volga under the auspices of Catherine II (who ruled from 1762 to 1796), in other words, before the rise of German national consciousness. These peasants had never had any connections with Germany. They tilled their lands in egalitarian communes just like their Russian neighbours with whom they shared subsistence-level living standards, and over many generations they were above reproach as dependable subjects in times of both war and peace. But as the war with Germany approached, the right-wing press related imaginative tales about fiendish German colonists on the Volga exploiting Russian labour. As a result, the German-speaking peasants were disposessed of their lands by government edict.

After the Crimean War (1853–6) and the Japanese War, the First World War brought a third defeat to imperial Russia in less than six decades. The tsar did not reverse the early disasters on the battlefields by taking command at the front himself, and his reputation was not helped by the tsarina's way of deputizing for him in St Petersburg. She trusted the advice of a priest, Rasputin, who claimed to have magical powers more than she trusted the ministers of state. He seemed to her a real 'man of the people'. To the men in state service as well as the rest of educated Russia, the black-robed, bearded priest in the tsarina's entourage symbolized an autocracy that stepped back from rational modernity. Such misgivings might have been forgotten by the more conservative bureaucrats if there had been some success in the war, or at least in the policies of the interior. But there was none. When the hungry people of St Petersburg left their factory benches for the streets in February 1917, state officials advised the tsar to abdicate. By that time, even the tsar's brother-in-law publicly voiced republican opinions.

However, the autocracy's reactionary stance that was provoked by the radical intelligentsia, the revolutionary terrorists, and, in 1905–6, by the entry of urban workers and the peasantry on to the political stage, did not mean that the autocracy was altogether divested of its modernizing tendencies under the last Romanovs. In the late 1880s, the Ministry of Finance created an effective policy package of high tariffs, large grain exports, a strong ruble, and an organization of foreign and state investment that promoted rapid industrialization. A modern textile industry had grown impressively in central Russia under the auspices of indigenous entrepreneurs during the course of the century. The state sponsored the building of railways in the 1860s and 1870s, and then again with a much greater intensity from 1890 onwards. By 1905, there were nearly 32 000 miles of track, and more than 750 000 railway and telegraph workers were employed by state and private companies operating under the control of the Ministry of Communications. In 1890–1913, these railway-led industrialization policies developed a large mining industry, oil extraction, an iron-and-steel industry, and heavy engineering. Imperial Russia was counted in the top league of industrial producers (in terms of gross output) by the beginning of the war; and industry continuing to expand production into the third year of the war, registering an overall increase of 20 per cent in 1913–16.

Industrialization was accompanied by modernization programmes in non-economic spheres as well. During Nicholas II's reign, the number of primary schools doubled and the number of pupils tripled. The proportion of the population over four years of age that was literate increased from 20 to 40 per cent. Secondary schools were expanding even faster, with the number of pupils doubling every 10 years. By 1917, there were 90 higher education establishments, including 12 state universities, in the empire, with plans for establishing another 10 new universities waiting in the Ministry of Education pipeline.

It could not be said, however, that the autocracy was promoting an economic and social modernization through a unified strategy. The Ministry of Finance had a strategy in the 1890s, but was not able to protect industrial affairs from interference by the Ministry of the Interior, which was dominated more by fears of social unrest than by a commitment to industrial growth. The Ministry of the Interior was under the influence not only of its own officials and Okhrana chiefs but also the large landowners who were aggrieved by the Ministry of Finance tariff policy which threatened grain exporters by causing retaliatory tariffs abroad and by keeping the prices of industrial products high. Despite rationalizing improvements in the state service, there still was not a government cabinet within which the competing demands of different branches of the bureaucracy and the conflicting interests of different social groups could be moulded into a coherent strategy of modernization. The tsar remained the chief arbitrator and he was not a great strategist.

When the office of Prime Minister was set up, its incumbent, Stolypin (from 1906 until his assassination in 1911), introduced agrarian reforms whose aims included the replacement of communal ownership of peasant land by individual private ownership. The novelty of Stolypin's reforms was their intention to create for the state a new and large social base by turning the peasantry into a class of private property owners and entrepreneurs, whose interests the state would make it its business to protect and uphold. For the first time in the history of the Russian state, the government's legitimacy would consist not of a conceptual opposition between state interest and self-interest but of a fusion of state interest with the interests of a large property-owning class. Stolypin wanted to create a stable 'civil society' for the tsarist state. As we shall see in Chapter 3, however, the creation of landowning farmers was not the aim that became prevalent as the agrarian reforms took their course.

State, Society, Estate, and Class

In the eighteenth century, the autocracy regarded the empire's population as consisting primarily of two groups – the majority of poll-tax payers and the minority of tax-exempt servants of the state. Other than that, social policies took the form of *ad hoc* edicts applied to particular groups of the population. Thus Orthodox Jews were restricted to living in the Jewish Pale of Settlement (Poland, Lithuania, Bielorussia, Ukraine, and Bessarabia); they were allowed to move to Siberia, central Asia and the Caucasus, but not to Russia proper, unless, that is, they were entitled to reside anywhere because they were university graduates, members of merchant guilds, or prostitutes; but they could not join either of the two merchant guilds in Moscow, and their enrolment in state universities was subject to special quotas. These edicts were still in operation in 1913. In that year, the edict dispossessing Germans of agricultural land was applied to the Germans settled on the Volga but not to the ones settled near the Black Sea and in the Baltic provinces. These examples reflect not just ethnic prejudice but also the particularistic and *ad hoc* nature of law-making.

We saw in the previous section, however, that the state bureaucracy was influenced by the ideal of legal regionality, according to which government should take the form of laws which are not particularistic and *ad hoc* but universalistic (defining actions in generally applicable terms and addressing what people do rather than what they are) and systematic (logically related to one another). The push for administration by legal code went hand in hand with state efforts to capture the social differentiation of the empire's population in terms that went beyond the simple bifurcation of poll-tax liability, but that could facilitate a legal and systematic definition for the links between government bureaux and social groups. The *Digest of Law*, published in the 1820s and its revised edition published in the 1890s, therefore divided the population into social estates (*sostoianie* and *soslovie*). Everyone who carried a passport had his or her social estate stamped in it alongside his or her name and other personal identification data. One's *soslovie* could make a difference to the terms and channels through which one could transfer property, obtain credit from a state-owned bank, make a representation to a government ministry, take part in local government elections, or face the law when charged with an offence.

The concept of *soslovie* acquired a perjorative connotation in the writings of the intelligentsia in the mid-nineteenth century, who criticised it for giving Russian society a divided and closed 'caste-like' character. This criticism, however, exaggerated somewhat the rigidities of the social estates division. The social estates defined in the legal digest in fact varied with one another in their degrees of closure. The social estate that had the most rigidly ascribed membership and that gave its members the most distinctive legal status was the post-emancipation peasantry. The autocracy had decided that the state should prevent the peasants from sliding into the condition of landless proletarians, and so legislation on the peasant *soslovie* restricted its members by tieing them to the communes and preventing the communes from selling peasant land; at the same time, the autocracy had made no provisions for people of other social estates who might want to become peasants.

Alternatively, there was another social estate, the merchantry, in which membership was gained and maintained simply by the annual payment of fees to one of the locally based merchant guilds. The noble estate could be joined via high-flying careers in state service, while prominent non-noble scientists and professionals – whose achievements were made outside the state-service hierarchy – could be awarded membership by way of 'honoured citizen'. Membership in the state of the clergy was attained through seminary education, to which priests' children had a privileged but not exclusive access. The estate of 'townspeople' was something of a residual category for urban residents, and membership implied little in the way of distinctive legal status. To these social estates the general census added another category, 'aliens', which described the nomadic tribespeople of Siberia and central Asia, whose lifestyles kept them largely out of reach of state administration.

The Stolypin reforms were partly aimed as dissolving the system of social estates: peasants were to be separated from their communes and entitled to trade with their assets, including land, in the same way as all other property owners; the nobles were to be deprived of their privileged status that had guaranteed their dominance in local government; and there were to be wide-ranging changes in the legal code to make sure that, ultimately, all laws became 'all-estate' – applicable to everyone regardless of social status. But such changes were not unopposed, for the concept of social estate in Russian administration and political life was not an archaism but the result of relatively recent developments various groups considered beneficial. It reflected a system in which the precepts of rational policy-making required various state departments to seek corporate advice from certain social groups on matters of policy in which corporate interests were involved.

The Russian social estates did not have the autonomous self-organization and the independence from the state that had been the hallmark of their Western European counterparts. Their organizations were restricted to regional bases and they were subject to the attentions of provincial governors and state security policemen; crossregional assemblies of social estates delegates occurred only under the auspices of government ministers. It was, in fact, the ministries that articulated the interests of 'their' corporate groups: the Ministry of War spoke for the military; the provincial governors and the Ministry of the Interior for the landowning nobles; the Holy Synod for the clergy; and the Ministry of Finance for the merchants and industrialists. 'If society in Russia was to an unusual degree "bureaucratized" by the state, so too, conversely, was the state "socialized" by the interpenetration of bureau and estate.'[1] In 1901 this system was extended further by the state-security official Zubatov, who organized Moscow workers into trade unions and articulated their interests through the channels of the Ministry of the Interior.

At the start of the twentieth century, the concept of social estate that linked the branches of state bureaucracy to particular social groups still had two sources of vitality. First, most of the social estates defined in the *Digest of Laws* had privileges to lose if they were to be dissolved by a legislative shift towards all-estate laws and institutions, while the majority social estate, the peasantry, was more concerned about the availability of land to till than about equal status before universalistic laws. Secondly, the concept of *soslovie* was never exhausted by the *Digest of Laws* definitions: in autocracy's political practice, it could be used loosely to denote any social group or community that seemed to merit a differentiated approach in government policy. Stolypin's drive towards all-estate legislation, the coherence of which would have been based on a special-protected status for the laws of private property and private contract, would have appealed to an ideologically unified bourgeois class. But the merchantry was slow to give up a '*soslovie* mentality' while the majority of the intelligentsia, as well as the Ministry of the Interior, opposed the prospect of commercially minded self-interest becoming the hegemonic social ethic in the Russian state.

Most of the delegates speaking in the state dumas that were formed in the aftermath of the 1905 revolution introduced themselves by stating their social estate as it was in their passports, although there were many who referred to their social identity in terms of an occupation, ethnicity or property ownership. Most of them also used the term *soslovie* when speaking of social differentiation, for they were mainly moderates and the term 'class' was understood to belong to the vocabulary of Marxist radicals. But there could be little doubt

---

1 Freeze, G. 1986: 'The *soslovie* paradigm and Russian social history'. *The American Historical Review*, ix, 1, p. 25.

that the shock inflicted on the autocracy by the events of 1905–6 also shook the hold the *Digest of Law* categories of social estate had on personal identities. In this respect, Stolypin's drive for a dissolution of these categories in an all-*soslovie* legislation was quite realistic.

The loudest calls for the preservation of the social estates system in government legislation and policy came from the assemblies of nobles who argued that their *soslovie* was worthy of special consideration as a cultured community that knew how to be of responsible service to the state. But contrary to this claim, Stolypin's motive in seeking to end the nobles' privilege of forming local governments was to rid the zemstvos of nobles whose hearts and tongues belonged to the radical intelligentsia; the aim of a conservative consensus in zemstvo politics, he thought, would be better served by property qualifications than noble status.

Perhaps the validity of the noble assemblies' claims about their social estate to some extent depended on the degree to which they actually were a social group rather than a mixed-group category. This is discussed in more detail below.

The Nobility

According to the general population census of January 1897, 15 out of every 1000 of the tsar's subjects were nobles, and two-thirds of this majority were heredity nobles. In the St Petersburg province, 72 out of every 1000 residents were princes and princesses, counts and countesses, barons and baronesses. Every member of a titled family had the right to bear the title. Hereditary titles were transmitted by all the sons of a noble to all of their sons, the West European custom of primogeniture having never taken root in Russia. There were very few nobles who had large family fortunes going back as far as the eighteenth century; the 'old' families were in fact such a rarity that their members were instantly identifiable not by their titles but by their famous surnames.

The proportion of the total of agricultural land in the empire that was owned by nobles decreased from 35 per cent in 1877 to 22 per cent in 1905, and it plummeted still further after the peasant unrest of 1905–7 induced bouts of panic selling by the nobles.[2] By 1913, 90 per cent of all arable land was in the hands of the peasantry. By 1905, one-half of noble families owned no land at all, whereas only 15 per cent had been landless in the 1860s. The half of the noble families that still owned land in 1905 did so in rather unequal amounts: while just over one per cent of them owned more than 5000 hectares each, another 75 per cent had landholdings not exceeding 300 hectares (just over one square mile)[3] – typically orchards and bits of forest land surrounding rambling wooden houses in which the families resided during the summer. The small minority of nobles who were large landowners was quite well represented in the top four ranks of the state service. In 1905, one-third of the top bureaucrats

---

2 Shanin, T. 1985: *Russia as a 'Developing Society'*. London: Macmillan, appendix.
3 Hosking, G. and Manning, R. T. 1979: 'What was the united nobility?' In L. H. Haimson (ed.), *The Politics of Rural Russia, 1905–1914*. Bloomington Ind.: Indiana University Press.

owned on average more than 14 000 hectares. On the other hand, the remaining two-thirds of the élite echelon of the state service owned on average less than 100 hectares (one square kilometre).[4]

By the turn of the century, only a small minority of the nobles owned land in quantities that were large enough to provide a great deal of wealth. Similarly, only a small fraction of the nobles lived as substantial businessmen – nobles in fact accounted for only two per cent of the business élite that was earning profits in excess of 20 000 rubles in 1905; here they were outnumbered even by men of the peasant estate who made up 10 per cent of the business élite.[5] Many nobles possibly had some independent income from invested capital. The livelihood of the great majority of the nobles, however, depended on their ability to earn a salary or professional fees. Not surprisingly, the census of 1897 found that the 'noble estate' was by far the best educated, with 40 per cent of its males having completed secondary education and another 10 per cent being university graduates. Conversely, 71 per cent of the empire's university graduates were nobles, although this proportion would decrease rapidly with the expansion of higher education in the next two decades. More surprising, and a testimony to the social heterogeneity of the nobility was the opposite end of the educational statistics: the census found that 29 per cent of the members of the 'noble estate' aged over four were illiterate.

The top ranks of the state service were of course 100 per cent noble, for appointment to office at this level automatically conferred nobility on those appointees who were not already noble by birth. Below the top, however, the noble estate was quickly losing its numerical dominance. By 1897, only one-half of the military officer corps and 30 per cent of all civilian officials of the state were from noble families. In 1916, when the First World War admittedly necessitated a rapid replenishment of the army officer corps, 70 per cent of officer trainees were of the 'peasant estate', 26 per cent of the 'urban estates', and only four per cent were nobles.[6]

In the post-1905 decade, there were a few thousand noble families in the empire who still had a substantial stake in the affairs of the countryside as large landowners. There were also the tens of thousands of families who were holding on to their country residences in which much traditional socializing occurred during the summer and in the hunting season. Of the landless half of the 'noble estate', there were undoubtedly some who were regularly invited to country homes as guests. But these social circuits were in great part the bearers of a culture that had for long been blended by a pride in superior education and metropolitan careers at least as much as by any notions of squiredom. And while by no means all of the noble *soslovie* managed to transmit superior education, professional careers, or squiredoms from one generation to the next, it did not manage to maintain a near-monopolistic hold on the educated metropolis either. The special pleadings of the assemblies of

4 Manning, R. T. 1979: 'Zemstvo and revolution'. In L. H. Haimason (ed.), *The Politics of Rural Russia, 1905–1914*. Bloomington, Ind.: Indiana University Press.
5 Shanin, *Developing Society*, appendix.
6 Fitzlyon, K. and Browning, T. 1977: *Before the Revolution: A View of Russia under the Last Tsar*. London: Allen Lane.

nobles sounded less than compelling in the newly enlarged spheres of public life – to many of the nobles as well as the others who were there to hear.

The Merchantry

The other privileged 'social estate' named in the *Digest of Law*, the merchantry, was only one-third the size of the nobility in numerical strength, but it had a cogent economic characteristic in that it made up the élite of commercial people able and willing to pay hefty fees to the merchant guilds. These city-based guilds had by no means a monopolistic hold on trade: the tsarist state always permitted trade to be conducted by allcomers, and in pre-emancipation times even by serfs. Nevertheless, the fact that so many businessmen paid guild fees to maintain their membership in the merchant *soslovie* suggests that they found its corporate organization useful.

Until the 1870s, the 'merchant estate' had administrative responsibility for the collection of state taxes from the city populations, the organization of welfare for 'city artisans' and 'urbanites' as well as merchants, and the running of municipal services. The merchant guilds elected officials from among their members for the management of these responsibilities. Not many merchants relished these opportunities for public office – many regarded selection a personal misfortune to be avoided by bribes if necessary, for public office deprived them of time for their own business affairs and exposed them to the notoriously arbitrary mercies of provincial governors and other state officials. More attractive than the prospect of a term in municipal office was the fact that the corporate organizations of the merchant *soslovie* facilitated a regular contact with other important businessmen, that they were linked to other crucial organizations such as stock exchanges and trade fairs, and that they were able to convey their views to the Ministry of Finance.

When the functions of municipal government were transferred to the city dumas, the merchant representatives acquired a reputation for being passive and uninspiring local politicians compared to their colleagues from the ranks of the nobility and the intelligentsia. But when the dumas decided to launch substantial projects, such as the building of water and sewerage systems, paved roads, schools, and hospitals, the raising of finance and overall management tended to be done under the auspices of the merchant organizations. Although at times perhaps with taciturn reluctance, the merchantry was always involved in public affairs.

The criticism the merchantry incurred from the liberal intelligentsia (and subsequently from Western historians) consisted largely of the fact that not many of the merchant spokesmen seemed willing to challenge the autocracy. The merchant spokesmen held on to the *soslovie*-system etiquette of framing their petitions to ministers of the state simply as advice on what was the particular wish or interest of the people they represented, not as advice on what the government should do in the general interest of the state or humankind. In this respect the merchants differed from both the nobility, whose spokesmen had fewer inhibitions about formulating what was 'in the state interest', and the intelligentsia, for whose spokesmen it was a matter of pride to construct morally compelling arguments of a general nature and address them to the public at large. In the eyes of the liberal intelligentsia, the merchants' '*soslovie* mentality' amounted to shunning their responsibility of leadership in the development of a 'civil society' (*obshchestvo*) that could transcend the autocracy and put the state on the path of social progress.

It is not that the merchants did not have a grievance against the government and its bureaucrats, who often interfered with business enterprise in the arbitrary and *ad hoc* manner of the autocracy. The scientist Mendeleiev must have struck a chord when, in 1882, he addressed these words to a gathering of Moscow businessmen:

> . . . we, so to speak, are reaping the fruits of the past, when each *chinovnik* [state bureaucrat] was able to treat the factory owner and entrepreneur as the landlord treated the peasant. Factory matters were, it is true, considered with patience, but not really more than as the whim of the entrepreneur, and the factory owner was only able to consider himself free from various restrictions derived from the absence of a clear law when he was wealthy and made gifts.[7]

There were voices emanating from the business community which demanded that the state laws and regulations should reflect rather than fetter business interests. An anonymous textile manufacturer put it on record in the pages of an industrial journal in the following terms:

> In other countries they also have authorities for the affairs of trade and industry, but they have a different function. There they manage, i.e. satisfy the needs of industry and trade, and do not command those needs. This is a distance of huge measure, but all the same, it is necessary for us to bridge it.[8]

But the official spokesmen of the 'merchant estate' had reason for being slow to support the nascent public ideology of a business class. They knew that merchants had an image problem in Russian culture on which the *Polizeistaat* tendency of the autocracy could feed its distaste for commercial class interests. In Russian folktales as well as the influential *belles-lettres* of the mid-century intelligentsia, the Russian merchant was a narrow-minded, mean, and uncouth creature devoted to making money by cheating customers and keeping employees under a despotic and exploitative rule. This was, or at least had been earlier on, also the prevalent stereotype of the Russian merchant in the minds of modernizing reformers, which is reflected in the following description by a Western historian:

> Bearded, patriarchal, semi-Asiatic in dress and manner, and fully versed in the arts of haggling and swindling, the Russian merchants in the early nineteenth century not only lacked the distinctive urban ethos of the West, but also clung to their obscurantist cultural traditions.[9]

---

7 Mendeleev, D. quoted in Siegelbaum, L.H. 1983: *The Politics of Industrial Mobilization in Russia, 1914–17: A Study of the War-Industries Committees.* London: Macmillan, p. 3.
8 Quoted in Siegelbaum, *Industrial Mobilization*, p. 8.
9 Owen, T. C. 1981: *Capitalism and Politics in Russia: A Social History of the Moscow Merchants, 1855–1905.* Cambridge: Cambridge University Press, p. 1.

This description is based on respectable evidence and there is no doubt that the negative stereotype of the merchant, the *kupets*, in Russian culture had plenty of basis in living experience.

Rather than the Russian *kupets*, it was the modernizing state and non-Russian entrepreneurs who organized many of the industrializing activities. Foreigners who came at the state's invitation and assimilated in varying degrees (only the British almost never did) and the minority nationalities that the empire had acquired by virtue of its expansion westwards in the seventeenth and eighteenth century – Jews from the Pale, Germans from the Baltic provinces, Poles, and Ukrainians – played a prominent leading part in many of the developments that were putting the empire on the world industrial map. However, with the exception of the Jewish manufacturers in Poland, the non-Russian industrialists and financiers were closely bound up with the state capitalist activities of the Ministry of Finance. Their ethnic backgrounds blended well in the cosmopolitan melting-pot of the Western-oriented St Petersburg, but their corporations were largely dependent on state budgets and the good graces of ministry officials. On the issue of whether the autocracy should change its spots and rule the economy by the means of business-friendly legality rather than tutelage, they were not in the position to assert themselves as a coherent political force.

If there was a confident Russian bourgeoisie overdue to assert itself against tutelage by the autocratic state at the dawn of the twentieth century, it was the Moscow merchantry that looked destined to become its nucleus. This was perhaps ironic, for the stereotype of the patriarchal merchant with his 'semi-Asiatic' dress sense and 'obscurantist cultural traditions' fitted well the Moscow merchants of the first half of the nineteenth century. By their historic background, the Moscow merchants were at odds with the modernizing thrust of Peter I and the subsequent European-orientated tsars. They were Old Believers – in other words schismatics of the Orthodox Church who were offended by the modification of liturgy that had been introduced in mid-seventeenth century. Commitment to the Old Belief made the merchants, in their long coats and chest-covering beards, the carriers of old Muscovy traditions well into the nineteenth century. But it had also made them into a persecuted sect, which enhanced their commitment to the virtues of economic self-reliance and, the haggling and swindling stereotype notwithstanding, their ability to do business with each other on trust.

The Muscovy flavour of the milieu was evident in the nineteenth century in some of its contributions to Moscow's civic life, such as the Old Believer Cultural Educational Society devoted to driving out 'the German spirit' and replacing it with 'the Russian spirit' that was equated with the Old Belief and, as a secularizing tendency set in after mid-century, with pan-slavism and the patronage of what was regarded as traditional Russian art. The self-reliant style of business enterprise also meant that even the greatest of the fast-growing and industrializing firms eschewed impersonal corporate structures and remained under family control, thus providing an institutional basis for the persistence of strongly patriarchal values and practices. And in the political realm, the Moscow merchants were not below persuading the autocracy that it should protect their economic interests not only by high tariffs on textile imports but also by discriminatory restrictions on Jewish textile manufacturers who were developing a strong factory base in the Polish part of the Pale.

The economic base of the Moscow business milieu was the Central Industrial Region, the area around Moscow and the provinces to the north, where a growing population on relatively inferior agricultural land had led to an early development of rural crafts. The other traditional asset was Moscow's geographical position at the intersection of water trade-routes linking the Baltic with the Black Sea and the Caspian. This advantage was enhanced by the construction of the empire's railway network in the second half of the nineteenth century, of which Moscow became the hub. These were auspicious conditions for the development of light industries. The cotton fields that grew east of the Caspian provided the last ingredient for a textiles-led industrialization, an opportunity the Moscow merchants, enriched by a new blood of ex-serf entrepreneurs, were not slow to grasp. They imported technology from Western Europe and built large, modern textile mills. The most successful families, strengthened by some strategic intermarriages, managed to build up huge businesses which were well diversified but centred on textile manufacture and, in contrast to industrial capitalism in the rest of Russia, self-financed rather than state sponsored. Market led and self-generated, Moscow's capitalism was capable of facing St Petersburg's bureaucracy while standing on its own feet.

Some of the Moscow merchants would be seen reacting to the 1917 revolution by clutching icons. But such evidence of surviving archaism belied the extent of cultural self-transformation of the élite business milieu during the second half of the nineteenth century. The older generation, those born before the 1850s, distinguished itself by its philanthropic works. These expanded considerably in the second half of the century from the old merchant tradition of leaving legacies for religious and charitable institutions. Many of this generation devoted considerable time (as well as money) in their lifetimes to the setting up and running of philanthropic institutions, while the nature of the recipients of this largesse was becoming increasingly secular. By the end of the century, the Moscow merchant philanthropists had made a significant contribution to the development of social welfare and education in the city and in the industrial township, and as patrons of the arts. Many had travelled in the West during their youth, ostensibly to acquire industrial know-how, but, like the noble travellers of the previous century, they also brought back a commitment to the values of Enlightenment philosophy.

The Western influence became evident not only in the secular focus of these charitable works but also in its apparent motivation. This generation of philanthropic merchants did not simply leave legacies to religious orders on their deathbeds as if they wanted to save their souls – they devoted much of their lives to the setting up of civic institutions, which bore their names to posterity. Perhaps this was a 'quest for immortality', one of the traits of the European Renaissance. The social networks of the merchants' artistic patronage, in particular, suggest a further motive: to gain social acceptance from the intelligentsia, which the nobility had never gained. However, some of the art collections undoubtedly testify to the personal satisfaction the sons and daughters of the merchantry found in cultural and intellectual discovery.

On the whole, the generations born after the 1850s continued their families' involvement in business as well as philanthropy. Some of them, however, also continued the trend towards seeking personal satisfaction in creative pursuits, and they became famous as members of the artistic avant-garde that, at the beginning of the twentieth century, marked a new departure in Russian cultural history in its orientation to aesthetic modernism rather than social realism. Not that these merchant members of the intelligentsia were politically indifferent: some of them extended their largesse to revolutionary parties, including the Bolsheviks.

Others of this generation became leading politicians in the liberal movement. In 1901 they were set on a collision course with the autocracy by the city's chief of the state security police, Zubatov, who organized industrial workers into trade unions and encouraged anti-capitalist agitation as part of a policy which he explained in the following terms:

> For the above-class autocracy, 'divida et impera' is necessary. As a form of antidote to the bourgoisie, who feel proud and act impudently, and to create a balance of forces, we must favor the workers, thus . . . taming the bourgoisie and ideologists, and winning over the workers and peasants.[10]

The spokesmen for the Moscow businessmen at first responded to Zubatov by pointing out that their employees enjoyed better welfare provision and a higher standard of living than the peasantry. By 1905, some of the spokesmen conceded that there was a conflict of economic interest between industrial employer and employee, but argued that this was containable if only the employers could conduct their industrial relations without state interference. They supported trade-union legislation and the decriminalization of strikes. They criticized the arbitrary and irrational nature of autocratic officialdom, and they called for the rule of law. In 1906, the Moscow merchant families were the moving force behind the foundation of the Association of Trade and Industry, the first all-empire organization devoted to the promotion of business interests in the political arena.

In post-1905 politics, the Association had mixed success in asserting the legitimacy of capitalist class interests *vis-à-vis* both the autocracy and the radical intelligentsia. The leading lights in the Association were, to some extent, still divided between the old *soslovie* approach of petitioning the autocracy on matters of policy and the new ideological approach of pressurizing the autocracy to reform itself into a rule-of-law state. They were also unable to overcome the divisions of economic interest between different sectors of the business community and, in particular, between heavy industry, which was dependent on the state, and light industry, which operated without direct state patronage.

The Association took a step forward when it asserted the principles of capitalist self-organization during the First World War. Its argument was that industry's response to war requirements would be more efficient if government contracts for weaponry, munitions, and uniforms, etc., were channelled not by a select group of large industrial corporations that had always been the

---

10 McDaniel, T. 1988: *Autocracy, Capitalism, and Revolution in Russia*. Berkeley, Calif.: University of California Press, p. 69.

beneficiaries of state patronage but by territorially-based war industries committees of businessmen, professional engineers, and worker representatives. If the autocracy's essence was that its state bureaucracy did things by arbitrary fiat, state patronage of favoured monopolies was unlikely to lay the ground for economically rational practice. Rational practice, argued the Association, needed 'public organizations' rather than state bureaux to provide an institutional framework. And, in the context of war, an institutional framework for the rational management of the economy was a matter of vital patriotic interest.

When the language of social revolution gripped the political arena in 1917, the war industries committees were said by some to be 'class organizations' for the furtherance of industrial capitalists' interests. However, during the previous two years the great majority of committee members insisted that they were first and foremost 'public' or 'social' (*obshchestvennye*) organizations, this term having the pleasing double connotation of 'in contrast to the state' and 'in contrast to narrow class'. The active membership of the committees was, indeed, wider than just the industrial entrepreneurs. Nevertheless, it was often hard to convince other parties that a narrow class interest was not what the committees were about. Even the constitutional democrats' newspaper was sceptical in this respect:

> As always, questions of our economic development will be resolved by the industrialists in accordance with the needs of the whole country to the extent that this coincides with the interests of the large enterprises. In those cases when the interests of the country come into conflict with the class needs of the factory owners, preference will be given to the latter.[11]

Neither the Association nor the committees managed to persuade large enough sections of the intelligentsia that the values of patriotism, rationality, and social progress would be in safe hands when pursued by organizations dominated by businessmen.

The autocracy allowed the formation of the committees, but it did not allow them to assume strategic leadership of wartime economic development. Ministerial procurement officials continued to award the majority of state contracts to their long-favoured firms, leaving only the more difficult and less lucrative ones for the committees to distribute. The committees were never given sufficient authority to enforce their priorities for supplies of raw material and freight capacity, so that their subcontracting firms were unable to achieve a better production and delivery record than the monopolistic firms favoured by the state bureaucracy. The state also subjected the committees to numerous audits, some of which gave rise to allegations of bribery and mismanagement. In these circumstances, it was impossible for the committees to prove that 'public organizations' led by private entrepreneurs would be better at running the economy than the tsar's state bureaucracy. One of the side-effects of the mistrust between the state bureaux and the committees was that autocratic Russia achieved a markedly lesser degree of economic co-ordination during the war than any of its allies or enemies.

---

11 McDaniel, *Russia*, p. 42.

The scions of the Moscow merchantry who founded the Association and the committees did not succeed in establishing a basis for a capitalist-led 'civil society'. They were latecomers to the 'social public' (*obshchestvo*) that had grown to press the autocracy towards reform or revolution, and their advocacy of the virtues of private capitalist enterprise made only a faint impression on it. Taking into account the important role that intellectual and artistic élites had played in the cultural transformation of the Moscow business community in the second half of the nineteenth century, it would seem that, by the time of the empire's fall, the historical sum total of the influence the intelligentsia exerted on the capitalists was still greater than the capitalist influence over the intelligentsia. That raises the question of whether, in the context of a weak bourgeoisie and an embattled autocracy, the intelligentsia came close to becoming a hegemonic social class capable of shaping developments in post-autocratic Russia.

The Intelligentsia

When, earlier in this chapter, we discussed the creation of a cultured élite in the eighteenth century and the formation of the radical intelligentsia in the nineteenth century, we left off at the point where the radical core resorted to anti-state terrorism and thus parted political ways with the reformers, both in and out of state service, who were looking for a rule of law rather than a social revolution by any means.

This was neither the first nor the last difference in point of view within the ranks of the educated: there had been ideological conflict between Western-izers and Slavophiles over the issue of whether modernization should proceed with the help of materialistic individualism or the communitarian 'Russian soul' – an issue that continued to divide opinions without ever being resolved. The turn of the century saw further divisions. The introduction of Marxism, which happened to coincide with the drive for industrialization in the 1890s, expanded the range of revolutionary creeds. At the same time, the growth of the factories, educational and welfare institutions, zemstvos, and government bureaux brought about a substantial enlargement of the professional employ-ment sector, renewing a split between the radicals who chose to devote their life to revolutionary parties and those choosing to serve progress in salaried careers. The turn of the century also saw the rise of the Silver Age movement, which broke with the ideology of 'serving the people' in favour of serving art. Finally, atheism and positivistic philosophy lost their monopolistic hold on educated values as some members of the intellectual élite resuscitated an interest in religious themes: a response to the rise of Protestant movements and the beginnings of a new theological discourse within orthodox Christianity.

On the eve of the 1905 revolution, the hard core of the radical intelligentsia was divided between a number of revolutionary groups: the creative élite was divided between 'social realism' and a host of avant-garde aesthetic movements; the majority of the educated were increasingly differentiated and stratified in a pluralism of lucrative or humble career opportunities; and there were freelancers and the salariat, the Bohemians and the full-time revolutionaries. A shared pride in a superior education did not always expunge the differences of background between the nobles and other estates. After the 1905 revolution, the new freedoms of legalized political parties, trade unions, and professional associations, as well as the further expansion of economic opportunities emphasized the differentiation in educated life-styles even more. These were factors in support of the Marxist notion that the intelligentsia could never be a social class in its own right.

However, there were also factors pointing to the intelligentsia as a growing social group and a persistent historic agent. These start with nineteenth-century social and political vocabulary. Until the entry of the peasantry and the urban poor into politics in 1905, the term *obshchestvo* (i.e., the 'social public' or 'civil society' that formed attitudes and opinions outside the bureaux of the autocratic state) was virtually synonymous with the institutions and networks of the population's educated minority. The early nineteenth-century term *raznochintsy* (i.e., 'various-rankers') was coined to denote students and intellectual activists whose minds were formed by education and a commitment to Enlightenment values rather than by their social estate or their fathers' status within the hierarchy of state service. In the middle of the century, the term *intelligentsia* itself entered the language, denoting an articulate social group that made itself distinct by its shared outlook and activity. Finally, at the close of the century, the term 'third element' entered the political vocabulary, reflecting the contribution made to political life by the professional employees of the zemstvos, as distinct from officials of the central state bureaux ('the first element') and the elected officials of the zemstvos ('the second element').

A visible reminder of historical continuity in the relationship between the autocracy and the intelligentsia was the way in which schools and universities repeatedly re-emerged as the sites of oppositional politics. Throughout the nineteenth century they were the recipients of the lion's share of state security police attentions. In the late 1880s, students accounted for 25 per cent of all arrestees charged with political crimes, with the liberal professions and salariat contributing another 22 per cent.[12] At the turn of the century, schools and universities were often closed and reopened again after mass expulsions at the behest of the police – a procedure that did not prevent the murders of three government ministers by students between 1900 and 1904. The dramas of the 1905 revolution were enacted not only in the city streets, where striking workers marched, and on the country estates of absentee landlords, which peasants invaded to loot and burn, but also in the secondary schools and the universities, which the students, often with the connivance of their professors, took over and turned into centres of political discussion and organization.

Revolutionary events apart, the intelligentsia, which was about as strong in numbers as the noble estate (there was of course a large overlap of membership between the two categories), made a strong mark by its civic activities that tended to concentrate in the areas of cultural institutions and voluntary adult-education circles. At the turn of the century, two-thirds of Russian town-dwellings were still wooden, most of the streets were unpaved, and water and sewage were unpiped. The great majority of towns, provincial

---

12 Shanin, T. 1986: *Russia, 1905–1907: Revolution as a Moment of Truth*. London: Macmillan.

capitals included, still had no factories and no railway stations; rather more of them had military garrisons. However, three-quarters of the 900 towns had libraries and reading rooms, and all 50 provincial capitals had museums and theatres. Most towns had a good choice of locally published reading matter: 13 newspapers and 99 journals were published in Moscow in 1904, while the much smaller Siberian city of Tomsk (population 52 000) offered its readers 11 locally published newspapers and journals.[13]

As has already been said, the state industrializing activities went hand in hand with a fast expansion in schooling. In addition to the strides towards a universal basic-level primary education, in 1912 the four-year higher primary school was introduced to enable primary-school children to proceed to classical grammar schools without the benefit of special preparatory education. The broadening of educational opportunities at all levels naturally favoured social mobility. Whereas in 1880, 16 per cent of the students in university-level education came from the ranks of craftsmen, workers, and peasants, 40 per cent of the 120 000-strong student body came from these strata in 1915. By this time, the great majority of undergraduates were exempt from paying tuition fees and were in receipt of grants and bursaries.[14]

The Ministry of Education's efforts, however, never pre-empted the voluntary and often municipally sponsored social movement in which the men and women of the intelligentsia imparted basic literacy, science, geography, and the knowledge of Russian literature to 'the people' in adult 'literacy circles', 'Sunday schools', and evening classes. Prior to 1905, these activities were subjected to regular state-security surveillance and frequent, albeit temporary, bans. After 1905, the *okhrana* were too preoccupied with monitoring the revolutionary parties and the trade unions to spare the time for reporting on evening classes as well. Some classes grew into large and prominent institutions, such as 'peoples universities' and 'free universities'. One of them, the Shanyavski University in Moscow, grew to have 6000, mainly part-time, students. Not being a state university, it was unable to confer officially recognized degrees; its own diplomas, however, became documents of high prestige among the intelligentsia, especially after the Moscow State University teaching staff resigned their posts *en masse* in protest against restrictions on academic freedom in 1911, joining Shanyavski University instead.[15]

One-half of the Shanyavski University's students were women, although women made up only one-quarter of the undergraduates in state universities. Since women could not expect to have careers in the state bureaucracy, which had always been exclusively male and not about to change in this respect, there was perhaps less incentive for them to compete for state university places. But from the mid-nineteenth century if not earlier, self-fulfilment through education and cultural pursuits was a value that was passed on from mothers to daughters in many noble families. The actual level of education among the women of the educated nobility was higher than the level implied by the statistics that count formal certificates held by women as compared to men;

13 Shanin, *Developing Society*, appendix.
14 Fitzlyon and Browning, *Before Revolution*.
15 Fitzlyon and Browning, *Before Revolution*.

and, especially from the 1870s onwards, women were prominent among the leaders and martyrs as well as activists in the intelligentsia's social and political movements.

The intelligentsia's revolutionary wing was disdainful of the reformist and liberal ('bourgeois') values that favoured political freedoms under a *Rechts-staat* more than social equality, but it shared the conviction that there was a universally valid truth to be discovered and communicated about the laws that moved humankind. Populists, Marxists, or Russophiles – all thought that the revolutionary movement needed excellent theoreticians to lead it to success. The commitment to the superior value of theoretical knowledge lent an element of ambiguity to the notion of 'service for the people' (or 'service for the proletariat'). Intellectual leadership was the nature of the service, and its acceptance a moral imperative; but the masses were 'dark', 'unconscious', and frustratingly fickle in their duty to acquire culture, understanding, and morals. Thus the doyen of the mid-century generation of the radical intelligentsia, Chernyshevsky, vented his frustration: 'the mass of the population knows nothing and cares about nothing except its material advantages, and rare are the cases in which it even suspects any relationship between its material interests and political change.' And later the Marxist, P. Axelrod, went on record with the observation that 'even the most insipid liberalism of any intellectual still towers over the uncultured attitudes of the masses'.[16]

The attribution of moral superiority and high social significance in having an education and 'being cultured' was a belief the revolutionary intellectuals shared with the rest of the intelligentsia, and it was the key to the intelligentsia's sense of social identity. Educated knowledge and culture may have given those who possessed it career opportunities, and it may have enriched their lives by providing them with access to the personal pleasures of intellectual or aesthetic entertainment. But to the Russian intelligentsia, such considerations seemed crassly materialistic and frivolous. Knowledge and culture were above all serious, because they made the difference between social progress and backwardness. 'Being cultured' meant being on the side of social progress, and the ideological imperative of 'serving the people' often in practice meant a social activism geared to lifting the masses from their low cultural level to a higher one – teaching them, in other words, to appreciate the serious value of the scientific, ideological, and cultural output of the intelligentsia's creative élite. To the intelligentsia, 'being cultured' conferred social status, and being engaged in the 'struggle for the enlightenment of the masses' conferred social respectability.

The ideology behind this struggle hardly needed to be articulated when the majority of the 'dark masses' was illiterate and the provision of basic schooling a self-evidently urgent main task. By the beginning of the twentieth century, however, basic literacy was becoming quite common among the younger generation, providing a fast-expanding market for reading material. The intelligentsia's ideology of mass enlightenment responded to this growth in popular literature: literary critics and the growing ranks of pedagogues and propagandists condemned it with unanimous vociferation. This condemnation

---

16 Quoted in McDaniel, *Russia*, pp. 216 and 217.

was shared widely within the educated élite and also by the important stratum of the semi-educated – the million or so people with incomplete secondary schooling. Many of these people, however, were able enough and keen to make a point of reading the classics rather than popular literature. Upwardly mobile educators were especially prominent among the critics of the commercial reading matter. Condemnation was directed variously at portrayals of violence, salacious passages, and harmful superstition, at the omission of one or another set of enlightened ideas, and at the 'cynicism' with which the commercial stories apparently evoked materialistic desires.

The critics of popular literature wore diverse political colours, but the terms of their criticism shared an underlying commitment to the idea that peasant backwardness should be overcome by the promotion of a culture that was essentially unitary – that is, consistent in its hierarchy of values, moulded by the forms created by the mid-century 'classical' authors of Russian letters, and permeated by a scientific view of the world. The intelligentsia was united in an ideology of 'culturalism'. It had a strong belief in the power of the written word and the degree of influence exerted over an individual's character by what he or she read. Its social activism was in part geared to making sure that public libraries made available only edifying reading matter, and that this should be available to the book-buying public at heavily subsidized prices. The unitary conceptions of culturalism predisposed the intelligentsia towards striving for an anti-market monopoly over the means of enlightenment.

Another attitude that was widely shared among the intelligentsia was one that could be termed industrialism. The radical intelligentsia's anti-bourgeois stance did not extend to scepticism about the desirability of industrialization. Populists as well as socialists and liberals saw economic progress in the shape of large-scale, highly technological enterprises managed in accordance with the technocratic precepts of rationality. Capitalism was deemed essential to this progress only by some: the majority saw the essence of progress not in the flourishing of commerce but in the application of science to all aspects of production. This was especially evident in the revolutionary year of 1917, when the war industries committees busied themselves with the planning of large-scale projects in post-war industrial construction. The committees had always had a strong component of members who were professional engineers and managers rather than capitalist entrepreneurs. These members remained active even when businesses went bankrupt amid revolutionary chaos, laying the foundations for the state-planned economy of the next era.

In addition to its natural self-identification with intellectual values and life-styles, the intelligentsia also had a belief in its function in Russian society and history that could perhaps be summarized as consisting of three principal notions: the obligation of service to 'the people', culturalism, and industrialism. The obligation of service to 'the people' differentiated, on an ethical plane, the intelligentsia's attitudes from those of the state bureaucracy and the noble and merchant estates. Culturalism defined the intelligentsia's relationship to 'the people' as one in which the intelligentsia was responsible for producing a unitary culture and for channelling it to 'the people' so that they would become cultured instead of backward. And industrialism gave a leading role in the attainment of economic abundance to scientific and technological professionals rather than to the explicitly egotistical capitalist entrepreneurs.

The intelligentsia, having originally come into being as a result of the state's efforts to modernize Russia and having had the state-serving nobility as its social background, created a new social public that challenged the tsarist state for the mantle of progress, and that infused the intelligentsia's possession of education and culture with a modern sense of achieved nobility. It could perhaps be said that, at the beginning of the twentieth century, the intelligentsia more than any other social group had the attributes of a nascent social hegemony.

Further Reading

Marc Raeff, *Understanding Imperial Russia: State and Society in the Old Regime* (New York: Colombia University Press, 1984) is the source on which I have drawn for the discussion of the interplay between the autocracy, the radical intelligentsia, and the reformist tendencies within the state. This book covers the period from Peter I to the last tsarist decades and will reward a careful reading. Another book which provides a detailed analysis of the tsarist version of the absolutist state is Tim McDaniel, *Autocracy, Capitalism, and Revolution in Russia* (Berkeley, Calif.: University of California Press, 1988). This also offers an excellent account of the revolutionary movements in the last decades, including the relationship between their intellectual élites and working-class participants.

Gregory Freeze, *From Supplication to Revolution: A Documentary Social History of Imperial Russia* (Oxford: Oxford University Press, 1988) is an evocative compilation of translated petitions to the tsars.

Kyril Fitzlyon and Tatiana Browning, *Before the Revolution: A View of Russia under the Last Tsar* (London: Allen Lane, 1977) combines a lot of photographs with a highly readable and informative text on various aspects of life during Nicholas II's reign – a very useful introduction to the less political facets of the place and time.

The discussion of the Moscow merchantry in this chapter draws mainly on Jo Ann Ruckman, *The Moscow Business Elite: A Social and Cultural Portrait of Two Generations, 1840–1905* (DeKalb, Ill.: Northern Illinois University Press, 1984). Another good book on the Russian merchantry with its eye on the faltering transformation of the *soslovie* into a social class is Alfred J. Rieber, *Merchants and Entrepreneurs in Imperial Russia* (Chapel Hill, NC: University of North Carolina Press, 1982); see also William Blackwell, 'The Russian entrepreneur in the tsarist period: an overview', in Gregory Guroff and Fred V. Carstensen (eds), *Entrepreneurship in Imperial Russia and the Soviet Union* (Princeton, NJ: Princeton University Press, 1983), pp. 13–26. The best source on the capitalists' liberal movement is Lewis H. Siegelbaum, *The Politics of Industrial Mobilization in Russia, 1914–17: A Study of the War-Industries Committees* (London: Macmillan, 1983).

Jeffrey Brooks, *When Russia Learned to Read: Literacy and Popular Literature, 1861–1917* (Princeton, NJ: Princeton University Press, 1985) is the book whose arguments capture the culturalist aspect of the intelligentsia's social identity. The industrialist theme is discussed in Edward Acton, 'The Russian revolutionary intelligentsia and industrialization', in Roger Bartlett (ed.), *Russian Thought and Society 1800–1917: Essays in Honour of Eugene Lampert* (Keele: University of Keele, 1984), pp. 92–113. For intelligentsia women's attitudes, see Barbara Elpern Engel, *Mothers and Daughters: Women of the Intelligentsia in Nineteenth-Century Russia* (Cambridge: Cambridge University Press, 1983).

Finally, a great deal of insight into tsarist Russia is to be had from a focus on an ethnic minority: see, for example, James W. Long, *From Privileged to Dispossessed: The Volga Germans, 1860–1917* (Lincoln, NB, and London: University of Nebraska Press, 1988).

2

The 'Peasant Question' and the Rural World

In 1796, 96 per cent of the tsar's subjects lived in the countryside; in 1897, 87 per cent; in 1926, 82 per cent of Soviet citizens lived in villages. In quantitative terms at least, urbanization was an undramatic trend compared with the changes that took place in Russia during the nineteenth century and the first quarter of the twentieth century – the rise of an urban-based, educated 'society' (*obshchestvo*), the abolition of serfdom, the industrialization drive of the tsarist state, the revolution, and the subsequent establishment of the Soviet state. Ten years into the Soviet era, Russia was still very much a rural, agrarian country; – a land of the peasant.

This fact has subsequently been regarded as very important by historians. Soviet Marxist historiography celebrates Lenin's genius in achieving a partnership (*smychka*) of the working class with the peasantry, without which the October revolution could not have triumphed. 'A socialist revolution that took place in a sea of peasant backwardness' is also a recurrent theme in discussions of the revolution's fate by many Western historians. Of these, Moshe Lewin in particular accords the peasantry – its aspirations and culture – a pivotal role in the shaping of Soviet history. Unintentionally, the revolution and civil war brought about a social order in the vast countryside which was not unlike an archaic peasant utopia. And when the Soviet state eventually set out to transform this social order by its industrialization campaign in the late 1920s and early 1930s, its own bureaucracy, urban base, and political culture became infused with the peasantry's mental outlook and ways that it so ostensibly and violently defeated.[1] It would not be until the 1950s that Soviet society was firmly set on the course of qualitative urbanization, a trend which would eventually culminate in the pluralization of Soviet politics under Gorbachev in the late 1980s.[2]

---

1 Lewin, M. 1985: *The Making of the Soviet System: Essays in the Social History of Interwar Russia*. London: Metheun, introduction.
2 Lewin, M. 1988: *The Gorbachev Phenomenon: A Historical Interpretation*. London: Hutchinson Radius.

The purpose of this chapter and the next is to discuss the heritage the nineteenth century bequeathed to the twentieth century in the form of the 'peasant question' and the peasantry, and to discuss countryside politics from the eve of the 1905 revolution until the eve of the collectivization campaign in 1928. The discussion starts with a brief analysis of the notion that the conditions and culture of Russian peasant life may be in some ways comparable with other parts of the world.

The Peasantry in Sociological Theory

Sociological theory has tended to regard 'peasantry' as a general phenomenon, considering the conditions of peasant life and the characteristics of peasant culture to be shared widely across time and space – in other words, not unique to the histories of particular nations and localities. The peasant belongs to the world of face-to-face communities (*Gemeinschaft*) rather then impersonally organized society (*Gesellschaft*) (Ferdinand Tonnies); the peasant is part of a patrimonial rather than a bureaucratic system of authority; his or her thoughts and actions are bound by tradition rather than rational calculus and by customary obligations rather than by law (Max Weber).

But despite these premodern characteristics, peasant society is distinguished from other premodern forms, such as tribal order, by a history of relationships with city-based cultures. The tribal cultures that were found by social anthropologists in sub-Saharan Africa and the Pacific were home grown and in isolation from city-based influences: they were complete in themselves, though about to be crushed by the modern world's rapid globalization. Peasant society, on the other hand, is characterized by a history of relationships between a rural hinterland and the centres of literate organization, as well as by mutual contact between village communities. This sense of village relatedness to urban centres of power is emphasized, among others, by three protagonists of 'peasant studies': Robert Redfield, James Scott, and Teodor Shanin.[3]

Redfield writes of the distinction between Great Tradition and Little Tradition. The Great Tradition is based on literacy and specialized learning, and it is promulgated by political and religious rulers with their associated educated élites; the Little Tradition is promulgated by peasants who, subject to the legal control of the rulers, provide food for urban life and engage in some market exchange. Peasant culture has never been autonomous; it is a 'half-culture', a low counterpart to 'high culture': 'every peasant finds his self-respect, his contentment, qualified by the knowledge that he is poorer and ruder than the gentry, those people of the towns.'[4] The village 'half-culture'

3 Redfield, R. 1956: *Peasant Society and Culture: An Anthropological Approach to Civilization*. Chicago, Ill.: Chicago University Press; Scott, J. C. 1976: *The Moral Economy of the Peasant: Rebellion and Subsistence in Southeast Asia*. New Haven, Conn.: Yale University Press; Shanin, T., 1985: *Russia as a Developing Society*. London: Macmillan; Shanin, T. 1986: *Russia 1905–1907: Revolution as a Moment of Truth*. London: Macmillan.
4 Redfield, *Peasant Society*, p. 139.

lives by assimilating, distorting, and rejecting the pressures emanating from the cities. If a peasantry has had a long standing relationship with limited land and a little-changing gentry or élite, it becomes 'a recognizable and long-enduring human type'. Typically peasants revere their land, habitat, and ancestral ways. They derive their sense of personal worth from the labour they put into the land. Theirs is a sober and earthy ethic, in which endurance and hard work stands above entrepreneurial risk-taking, and the family and community above individual self-seeking. This emphasis on the acceptance of arduous labour, however, does not preclude the enjoyment of stopping when a necessary task is done. Peasants regard town life with 'a certain suspiciousness, mixed with appreciation', and believe that the rich should be generous while the powerful should not abuse their power.[5]

More recent students of the peasantry have criticized Redfield's emphasis on cultural factors for its implication that these in some way stand in the way of modern economic development. The peasantry's subjugation to metropolitan powers, they argue, is primarily economic in kind. The peasants are above all poor, and the more so as international capitalism creates ever greater disparities of wealth and power between the metropolitan centres and the rural peripheries. Scott points out that peasants are engaged primarily in subsistence farming, and on that basis explains peasant economic decision-making and a sense of justice. Subsistence farming is about minimizing the risk of one's family falling below the subsistence level. A new crop that has a track record of a higher-then-average annual yield than the traditional crop will not be introduced by farmers if it is more sensitive to weather fluctuations and therefore threatens to increase the frequency of below-subsistence harvests. Social status systems are also related to the estimated risks of below-subsistence years; smallholders tend to have higher status than peasants renting land and wage-labouring peasants, even if the wage-earners enjoy higher incomes in average and good years, for smallholding is seen as assuring a more secure subsistence base, relatively invulnerable to the vagaries of money economy.

The peasant sense of justice is based on the norms of reciprocity and the right to subsistence. Power relationships are accepted as more or less legitimate as long as the landlords and state officials appear to deliver on their obligation to help peasants in bad years. When they fail to honour the peasant's perceived right to subsistence, as they tend to do in commercializing, monetarizing economies, they become the object of peasant indignation. Peasant rebellions are based on this sense of moral indignation at the rich and powerful who have failed to meet their customary obligations. The rebellions are therefore conservative in their rhetoric and goals, and they are morally, rather than psychologically, driven by a pent-up frustration or perceived relative deprivation. Peasant communities tend to be egalitarian, but not in the sense that equality of status and income is accorded a high value *per se*: the high value is accorded to the norms of reciprocity and the right of every member to the means of subsistence.[6]

5 Redfield, *Peasant Society*, p. 140.
6 Scott, *The Moral Economy*, Chap. 1.

Shanin who, unlike the previous two authors, writes specifically about the Russian peasantry, shares with Scott the rejection of the view that peasants are of a culture which is yet to reach a stage of development that will permit its bearers the advantages of rational economic decision-making and autonomous political action. Like Scott, Shanin emphasizes the nature of farming, which is, by necessity, geared to securing subsistence rather than capital accumulation, and in that sense it is driven by a logic that values the possession of sufficient subsistence land above money. He seems to agree with Scott about the nature of peasant egalitarianism and sense of justice, which he sees well exemplified in the Russian peasantry. Also like Scott, Shanin is interested in the necessary conditions of peasant rebellions and revolutions, in which he sees peasants as acting deliberately rather than indulging in a Jacquery – i.e. an explosion of blind anger.

Shanin sees the advance of capitalism as a process that integrates all corners of the world into a single series of centre-periphery dependencies, in which the cost and benefits of economic development are unequally distributed. Underdeveloped economies become underdeveloped not simply because of some sort of cultural time-lag but because they become increasingly integrated into the world economy at the wrong end of the dependency chain, where increasing cash-flows tend not to bring about an all-beneficial economic 'take-off'. The rural majority become economically more threatened and therefore driven to a more desperate reliance on land smallholding for securing subsistence. At the same time, of course, land become more scarce as the population increases. Shanin demonstrates the peasant commitment to subsistence (i.e. non-entrepreneurial) farming in Russia by pointing out that, by the beginning of the twentieth century, peasants were buying and renting land at prices which precluded any hopes of profitability for a long time to come. With its Western-educated urban élites and subsistence-level rural masses, Russia in the nineteenth century became an early example of that phenomenon of twentieth-century capitalism – a 'developing society'. Shanin argues that the peasant participation in the 1905 revolution was a 'moment of truth' such as would be repeated not only in rural Russia in 1917 but also in large-scale peasant-based revolutionary movements in other parts of the twentieth-century world.

When we come to discuss the institutions and ways of Russian peasant life, it will be important to remember that the peasant was illiterate and not given to leaving on record an articulated view of him or herself and his or her world. Some peasants, of course, were not only literate but also socially mobile, joining the ranks of writers of historical records; but they took care to write in the idiom of their new milieu. Some of the most hackneyed descriptions of the peasant in Russian fictional literature were written by authors from peasant backgrounds. What is on record about peasant thoughts and action was written by members of the intelligentsia; this stands first and foremost as evidence of the ways in which the intelligentsia saw its world. The intelligentsia was identified intensely with the mission of modernity and cultural progress – an ideological world-view that transcended the narrower political ideologies and programmes. It is not just that the Russian intelligentsia were men and women of modern minds; the point is the broad and weighty significance they ascribed to this fact. What they wrote about the peasantry was overlaid by this significance, which was constructed as non-modernity.

The Peasant in Russian Literature

The reason for looking at the peasant in Russian literature lies not in the accuracy of the descriptions, for 'that, even in Russia, never was the business of literature'.[7] It lies in the fact that the fiction writers were an élite of the Russian intelligentsia, whose works were widely discussed in the 'society' media – the critical journals and political pamphlets. The peasant in literature therefore tells us of the history of the intelligentsia's attitudes to the peasantry. In the eighteenth century, peasant characters had walk-on parts in plays as comics. The ways of seeing the peasant in nineteenth-century writing, on the other hand, were invariably serious, but they varied in other respects. The range of views can be demonstrated by reference to the following writers: Radishchev, Turgenev, Uspensky, Tolstoy, Chekhov, and Gorky.

Radishchev made a lasting impact on the collective conscience of educated society when he wrote at the end of the eighteenth century his *Journey from Petersburg to Moscow*. The main subject of this book, however, is not so much the peasant as the serf-owning landlord who offends against all the values of the Enlightenment. He is corrupt, bereft of reason, human feeling, and sensitivity, deaf to the voice of nature, and without any compassion. The peasant is the victim of his cruelty. She (the most vivid descriptions are of a young woman) radiates innocence, natural beauty, and a capacity for pure love that shows the landlord's venality in the sharpest colours. She contrasts with the spoiled, 'syphilitic' nature of city aristocracy and invites the reader to luxuriate in tears while contemplating the social morals of serfdom Russia. There is no pretence to realism in Radishchev's portrayal of his peasant characters. Mindful of the literary conventions of his time, which required noble sentiments to be expressed in lofty language, he lets his peasants speak in feats of literary accomplishment. Peasants, then, were victims of social evil, who themselves exemplified the primordial goodness of human nature.

Writing some 50 years later, not long before the abolition of serfdom, Turgenev was the first writer who portrays peasants as individuals with the same range of attractive qualities as could be found among educated Russians. In *A Sportsman's Sketches* he describes with a convincing finesse a peasant who is a good rationalist administrator, another who is an idealist and a romantic dreamer, yet another who handles a moral problem, boys who are simply boys, an eccentric who speaks the language of birds, and someone who truly loves nature and life. This is a book of sketches of landscape and people encountered by a hunter during his sojourn in the forests. The peasants seem to be complex persons, but their lives are shown only in fragments and outside their normal village setting.

---

7 Fanger, D. 1968: 'The peasant in literature'. In Vucinich, W. S. (ed.), *The Peasant in Nineteenth-Century Russia*. Stanford, Calif.: Stanford University Press, pp. 231–62.

Uspensky wrote in the postemancipation period, when serfdom was no longer an issue, although the conditions and prospects of the peasantry were. What comes across is a form of human life on the other side of a social chasm. Uspensky's peasants are, above all, slaves of the land they till. The essence of peasant life is the impossibility of disobeying the commands of subsistence agriculture and earthbound survival. The peasant's spirituality consists in his acceptance of these commands, and his feeling that the earth that provides and receives him in death loves him. This is not a life of self-determination by moral choices. Nature commands and the peasant obeys. Take away the imperatives of subsistence on land and spiritual vacuity sets in. Peasants, argues Uspensky, do not have individual characters that could be developed in literary narratives of their lives. They live in a mass of humanity whose thought and will is embedded in the imperatives of their environment. 'To isolate a single entity from this mass of millions and try to understand it is an impossible task . . . Semyon Nikitich, the Elder, can be understood only in a heap of other Semyon Nikitiches.'[8]

Tolstoy accepted Uspensky's emphasis on the chasm between the peasantry and the intelligentsia, and endowed it with mystical significance. Whereas Uspensky saw alienation in the peasant's subjugation to the external imperatives of land-tilling existence, Tolstoy saw it in the educated individual's self-consciousness and his alienation from the concept of the natural necessity of death. He counselled the intelligentsia to learn spiritual wisdom from the earthy peasants – not because they were wise individuals but because their lives had the quality of humane acceptance of death, and because they were spontaneous, direct, and unselfconscious, their actions manifesting a sense of their own lives as a part of an organic whole. And, thought Tolstoy, there was a higher form of love for intellectuals to learn from their contact with peasants, as Pierre Bezuchov discovered from his acquaintance with the peasant Karataev in *War and Peace*:

> Attachments, friendships, love, in the sense that Pierre understood them, Karataev did not have at all; but he loved and lived lovingly with everything that his life brought him in contact with, and particularly with man – not with any particular man, but with those people who were there in front of his eyes.[9]

Tolstoy spent the last 40 years of his life on his country estate trying to learn these virtues from peasant neighbours.

What his neighbours taught Tolstoy is hard to know with certainty. What is certain is that a younger author, who also spent much of this time on his country estate, Chekhov, found there was nothing elevating to learn. Written in the closing years of the nineteenth century, his story 'Peasants' tells of mean, quarrelsome drunkards, thieves, and liars with few redeeming features other than the fact that, despite everything, 'they were people; they suffered and wept as people do; and in their lives there was nothing for which excuse might not be found'.[10] Chekhov's peasants were not necessarily so base because they were peasants but because they lived in a period of historical transition; there

8 Fanger, 'The peasant in literature', p. 232.
9 Quoted in Fanger, 'The peasant in literature',p. 253.
10 Quoted in Fanger, 'The peasant in literature', p. 258.

is an intimation in the story of a more dignified spirit that used to prevail in the village in the not-so-distant past.

Populist critics charged Chekhov with the blasphemy of forgetting that the peasant millions had 'the soul of a child'. But there was another writer, Gorky, who went even further than Chekhov in portraying peasants in the bleak colours of disenchantment. In his story, 'Chelkash', also written at the turn of the century, Gorky created a pair of main characters: Chelkash, a tramp and a thief, who was once conscripted from his village to the army and now chooses to wander in destitution rather than return to his village; and Gavrila, who is on his way back to his village after a period as a migrant labourer. While Chelkash feels driven from his peasant roots by a yearning for freedom, Gavrila is driven back to his by nostalgia and a yearning for security. Chelkash, himself a beggar of no morals, is eventually repelled by the apparently wholesome, good-natured Gavrila who turns out to be possessed totally by base materialistic greed that leaves no room at all for dignity in the soul. The story ends with Gavrila murdering Chelkash. There is no doubt where the writer's sympathies were: with the down-and-out who would not be seen dead back on his peasant land.

This was young Gorky. An older Gorky returned to the peasant question in 1922, in a pamphlet, *On the Russian Peasantry*. He wrote:

> Where, then, is that good-natured, thoughtful, Russian peasant, that tireless seeker after truth and justice, about whom Russian literature of the nineteenth century told the world so convincingly and beautifully? In my youth, I sought diligently for such a man through the villages of Russia – and did not find him . . . One can say now with assurance that, at the price of the ruin of the intelligentsia and the working class, the Russian peasantry has been reborn.[11]

This was a bitter comment by a writer of the revolutionary intelligentsia on the way the revolution was turning out: the Russian peasantry, he now thought, was the enemy that hijacked the revolution.

The Peasant in Russian Historiography

After the patriotic exertions of the war against Napoleon, the concepts of 'nation' and 'nationhood' (*narodnost'*) became important among educated Russians. This raised the question of whether it was adequate to know the past only through the recorded history of the state. 'Nationhood' carried the connotation of a form of civilized life developed by 'a people' rather than a state; to understand the essence of a national spirit and identity, a historian should recover the past of 'the people' as well as the state. Many of the Slavophiles and, in the second half of the nineteenth century, populists believed that a history of 'the people' by and large meant a history of the Russian peasantry. The earlier division of the intelligentsia into Slavophiles and Westernizers, and the later division between the populist movement and the other political creeds, to a degree (though by no means entirely) coincided

---

11 Quoted in Fanger, 'The peasant in literature', p. 261.

with differences among historians concerning 'the peasant question '. Westernizers' assumptions and the non-populist creeds tended to favour the historians who denied the viability of a history of the peasantry.

The peasantry, argued one of these historians, was a 'non-historic' social class; never having been a prime mover in historical developments, the peasantry in itself could not constitute a viable subject in history:

> History deals only with that which visibly moves, which acts and manifests itself, and thus history has no way of dealing with the popular masses; it deals only with representatives of the people, no matter in what form the government may express itself; and when the popular masses are set in motion, it is the directors of that movement, who are of primary interest and with whom history is and should be primarily concerned.[12]

This view gave rise to a 'statist' school of historians who argued that, in the case of Russia, historical initiative was always manifested primarily by the state, and that it would be impossible to write a history of anything without in fact writing a history of the state. The Russian peasantry was an 'ethnographic protoplasm', not a historical subject. The 'statist' school was self-consciously legalist in its approach, its focus the enactment of government decrees and laws. This was partly due to the pragmatically methodological fact that legislative matters were what most available records were about. However, the emphasis on legal history also fitted with that strand of Western-oriented thought which saw historical progress in terms of the evolution of *Rechtstaat* and a liberal constitution – that is, not in terms of a romantic self-realization of a tradition-rooted popular spirit.

The methodological advantage of the 'statist' historians in having relatively plentiful records for the pursuit of their subject was, the populist historians argued, a significant advantage only as long as it was assumed that the Russian state always was 'creative' in its legislative policies, that its legislative acts were more than a mere (and perhaps haphazard) confirmation of already-existing arrangements. If there was not a written record of something, was that sufficient proof that the thing did not exist? Thus the populist historians justified their recourse to ethnographic evidence, insights from the histories of other nations (notably German romantic historiography), and some speculation. The fact that government records were sparse on matters concerning the peasantry confirmed their view that peasant communities evolved from ancient to modern times autonomously from the formal organization of government.

Not surprisingly, methodological issues about the writing of history also concerned the interpretation of records in historical narratives. Here a notable contribution was made by L. N. Tolstoy, the novelist and the proponent of spiritual learning from the peasant. The occasion on which he discussed historical method concerned not the history of the peasantry as such but the history of the Napoleonic war encoded in his *War and Peace*. Tolstoy related how he had learnt of the falsity of historical records of battles when he was asked to collect reports about the fall of Sevastopol from 20 artillery

---

12 Solovyov, S. M. quoted in Petrovich, M. B. 1968: 'The peasant in the nineteenth-century historiography'. In Vucinich, W. S., *The Peasant*, p. 197.

officers. What these officers in the event reported were 'naive, unavoidable military falsehoods', because they wrote their reports not on the basis of what they themselves witnessed and experienced but on the basis of what they understood their superior officers expected to learn about the battle. The reports were framed in the conventions of military theory. It was a similar situation with reports he collected from participants in the battle of Borodino. Even the most 'lively and intelligent' cavalry officer framed his reports in terms of what he had learned about cavalry attacks from gullible historians rather than in terms of facts, such as that he had muddled through a chaos, fallen off his horse, sprained his arm, and run away from a Frenchman into a wood.[13] The validity of historical writing, thought Tolstoy, consisted in the degree to which it corresponded with the people's memory and the degree to which the narrative served to unite the people in a shared feeling. In that sense, in which a myth has an inevitable and positive part in the life of a people, a history quite properly deals in myth as well as written documentary evidence.

It is not known whether populist historians shared anything of Tolstoy's outlook on their craft. What is clear is that the major issue they took up with 'statist' historians was the origin of the Russian peasant commune, a topic that was poorly supplied by archival records while being richly overlaid by contested beliefs about the nature of the Russian people and its path to modernity. The Slavophile and populist historians believed the peasant commune to have had an uninterrupted lineage back into the first millennium, as a corporate body that regulated its members' affairs with only limited interference from the state or the landlord. It was a form of community (*obshchina*) that evolved, not unlike the 'civil society' (*obshchestvo*) of educated Russia that would evolve in the future, as an autonomous counterpart of the state, according to its own beliefs and principles of organization. The principles of peasant communal organization were those of communal control of land use. When further expansion of cultivated land became limited as it reached the boundaries of other communes or land that was at the personal disposal of the landlord, the commune resorted to land repartitions among its members in its own territory, to make sure that the available land was used productively. The scarcer the land relative to the demands made on it by peasant subsistence needs, the shorter the amount of time over which the commune allowed an allotment to remain unused. The commune was a form of control over land use which, having originated in times when land was plentiful and anyone could take as much as he could cultivate, continued to evolve without resorting to legal forms of ownership even as land became scarce. That the land was legally owned by the state or the landlord was not an issue; the issue was land use, and this the commune managed by a set of arrangements with the direct users – the peasant households. A more ancient institution than serfdom, the commune was a harbinger of a specifically Russian potential to progress from serfdom into modernity while avoiding a

---

13 Gifford, H. 1984: 'Tolstoi and historical truth'. In Bartlett, R. (ed.), *Russian Thought and Society 1800–1917: Essays in Honour of Eugene Lampert*. Keele: University of Keele Press, pp. 114–27, esp. 115–16.

Western-style system of private landownership. Or so thought the Slavophiles and populists.

The 'statist' historians argued that there was no evidence of direct lineage between the contemporary peasant commune and the organization of land settlement in the remote past. If there were communes of agrarian settlers in the early period of Russian history, as there perhaps were in the early history of the west Slavic and German lands, they were clan-based, patriarchal forms of organization belonging to the transitional period from nomadic to settled agriculture. But clan organization evolved into territorial state organization and henceforth it was the state that called the tune. The contemporary commune had its birth in the Muscovy state's way of imposing high obligations on its subjects, and the repartional commune was by and large forced on the peasants as a result of the poll-tax introduced by the modernizing Peter I. It was a device that helped the landlords to oversee the collection of tax and to make sure that every peasant could pay it. The state giveth and the state taketh; the contemporary peasant commune might remain as long as the state continued to administer the countryside in the way it did, but there was no moral lesson to be drawn from Russian history to the effect that the state should give up to the peasant commune its responsibility for changing the system of rural administration if such change was desirable for Russia's progress. The 'statist' historians and the Western-minded intelligentsia saw the peasant commune not as an organic, quintessential institution of the Russian people but as a temporal institution which was made and would be unmade in the process of Russian history. Viewed in any other way, the peasant commune was just a sentimental myth.

Intelligentsia's Views of Peasant Backwardness

At the risk of gross simplification, we identify some of the ways in which the peasant images created by writers and historians were reflected in the intelligentsia's ideological movements. In Radishchev's writing, the peasant characters were primarily a vehicle for an indictment of serf-owning nobility: they epitomized a Rousseauian view of the essential goodness of human nature, a wholesome and innocent victim of a corrupt, decadent, and brutal civilization. This would remain a romantic leitmotif of the radical movements seeking to overthrow the oppressors and build a civilization appropriate to the natural goodness of humanity. It was not necessary to take Radishchev's sentimental portraits of beautifully innocent peasant at face value. They spoke of the belief in the good, human essence. This was not a belief to be shaken by encounters with unattractive individuals from the peasant masses, for they only bore a testimony to their oppression. 'The people' were essentially good even if many people appeared to be bad. The belief could survive as an abstraction even when the peasantry came to be painted in bleak colours by later writers, and when the populists failed in their efforts to make a vital contact with the peasantry. It would appear again in an iconic form 100 years later, in the twentieth century, only this time the idealized image of simple, instinctive human wholesomeness would be clothed as an industrial worker.

We have seen that Turgenev was the only writer who put across not an image of 'the Russian peasant' but portraits of interesting individuals who happened to be Russian peasants. Here the implication was that the chasm between the humans of the city-based civilization and those of the old countryside was not as great as it was sometimes thought to be. Heart and reason could be found in the chests and behind the brows of the village people as well. Turgenev seemed to offer an optimistic view of the cultural difference – it was only skin deep; just take away the oppressive conditions and you will see. This kind of optimism was perhaps easier before the end of serfdom rather than after it. But it did survive in some ideological strands. It would live in the motives of some of the agronomists and health workers who chose country-bound careers at the beginning of the twentieth century, and in the beliefs of the constitutionalists and Stolypin reformers who sought to deliver the peasants from their communes and turn them into property-owning citizen farmers.

What of Tolstoy? He almost seemed to see the Russian peasant as a god-given opportunity for intellectuals to cultivate in themselves a religious feeling he thought they should have. His was the message of a spiritual sage: make yourself whole by welcoming your opposite into your heart as a positive value. Just as a mature adult makes the world better by laughing with children rather than at them, so the intellectual matures and makes the world better by partaking in the simple truth of peasant consciousness. Tolstoy tried to live as he preached and when he died the intelligentsia revered him as a saint. His message probably played an influential part in the motives of many of the 'go-to-the-people' populists and, later, the country-bound health workers and agronomists, for many of them endured hardships and exemplified devoted patience such as perhaps only the satisfactions of a religious sort of calling could explain. But the nature of Tolstoy's influence on the intelligentsia's attitudes to the peasantry is elusive, because his message was explicitly spiritual while the ideologies of the intelligentsia remained explicitly secular. There was no movement of educated Christians or mystics going to the countryside. Slavophile intimations of the soulful qualities of the Russian people notwithstanding, the populist, reformist, and revolutionary intelligentsia that sought contact with the peasantry primarily wanted the peasants to discard their superstitions and become modern.

To see how the descriptions of the peasantry by Uspensky, Chekhov, and Gorky tallied with the intelligentsia's ideological movements is much easier. Uspensky described in the Russian peasant the intelligentsia's nightmare of earthbound backwardness and gave it a humane and plausible materialist explanation. Chekhov and Gorky reaffirmed the view of the peasantry as a class in the process of dissolution by historical transition, which was propagated by the spread of Marxism among the intelligentsia at the turn of the century – the Marxist view of the 'idiocy of rural life' to be swept away by industrial capitalism and socialist revolution. Lenin wrote an economic history of Russia which emphasized its capitalist development with its attendant polarization of the peasantry into petty bourgeoisie and labourers, while the intentions of the government's Stolypin reforms appeared to prove his point.

The historians' debate about the peasant commune also culminated at the time when the Stolypin government set out to abolish the commune. The populist belief that the commune had developed indigenously despite the state rather than because of it, was transposed not into an ideology seeking to preserve customary peasant life as some sort of green utopia but into a vision of a Russian-style progress – a modernization under the auspices of technical know-how and egalitarian justice rather than capitalist egotism.

The intelligentsia was united in its perception of the peasantry as not just poor but also culturally backward and in need of modernizing enlightenment. The issue was whether this necessity could be achieved within the framework of the existing institutions governing peasant life. The commune was regarded as the main and most characteristic institution of the Russian peasantry, and the question was whether its continued existence was compatible with progress. The populist radicals and many government officials thought that it was, while the Western-minded liberals, Marxist socialists, and eventually the Stolypin reformers thought it was not. The Slavophile strands of opinion saw the Russian peasantry as a mass of undeveloped humanity with a progressive potential of its own. Western-oriented opinions saw progress in the peasantry dissolving into other social classes.

During the half-century between the end of serfdom and the First World War, government bodies and the intelligentsia's political movements expended not a little effort on collecting information about the peasantry. The questions the researchers asked and the reports they wrote were framed by their conceptions of the 'peasant question' – the question of where the peasantry stood *vis-à-vis* modernity, and how it should be led or what should be done to it so that Russia became more modern. Modernity was seen as the realization of reason in human affairs – a polity as a system of rights, an economy as a system of applied scientific knowledge, and a culture as a system of consciously chosen values. That which was just would come out of a system of legal or human rights; that which was productive and efficient would come out of a system of technological or economic laws; and that which was good would come out of a system of ethics. Modernity was a systemic cast of mind. The modern men and women who investigated the peasant ways were bewildered by what they found, for it denied their systemic conceptions of what made sense. 'What customs? We don't have any customs here', answered the peasants to the researchers' questions about peasant justice. The researchers fielded questions expecting answers in the form of logically coherent generalities such as would tell them about the peasants' system of rights and norms. The concept of 'custom' in the researchers' questions encoded an expectation of a system of customs. The peasants denied they had such a system. The researchers were bewildered. The Western-oriented ones despaired yet again at Russia's backwardness, while the Slavophiles went on looking for a system of customs which surely was there even if the people were still unconscious of it. But they all wanted the peasant to change, to become more systemic in his thoughts and actions, to become more like the way modern men and women saw themselves.

The Commune, the *Volost'* and the State

There was not a great deal of variation in the spatial arrangement of peasant life in Russia. The centre was the village – wooden cottages built alongside a dirt road in close proximity to one another. On the opposite side from the road, each cottage had a strip of land with sheds for poultry, animals, and storage, a bath-house, a vegetable garden and perhaps a small orchard – some two-thirds of an acre in total. Nearby was a river or a pond, often just at the back of the household lands. The cottage with its adjacent land and chattels was family property. By the turn of the century the average village consisted of some 70 households, although there was a considerable variation in size. Only the large villages had a church, a shop, and a tavern. Rather more villages, though by no means all, had their own primary school by the beginning of the twentieth century.

The village was surrounded by the village lands – the lands that were allocated by the emancipation reform to peasant use. They were controlled by the peasant commune. The majority of the communes – about two-thirds – comprised one village each. Some of the large villages were divided between two communes, and some communes controlled several small villages. The lands controlled by the commune were common lands – woods, meadows, and pastures – and plough lands. The plough lands were organized for three-field rotation farming: one field for autumn sowing, one for spring sowing, and one left fallow, the use changing around every three years. Each of the three fields was divided into parcels where each parcel was regarded as having a particular quality, in terms of the time and effort required to get a good harvest out of it. And finally, each of these parcels was divided into an equal number of narrow strips. On the basis of these divisions, the plough land was distributed among the households of the village for farming, each household having a certain number of the strips within each field and parcel. At the time of the emancipation, this number was determined in accordance with the size of the household, taking into account its number of able-bodied males and perhaps also its number of dependants. As the years went by and new families were formed by separation from the original households, the strips were redistributed by negotiation between the families concerned and with the approval of the commune. From time to time, if a village was subject to a great deal of demographic change which made further piecemeal redistribution of the existing strips difficult to negotiate, its commune might decide to redivide the plough land into a new set of parcels and strips, so as to carry out a new distribution among all the households. The majority of the communes in Russia (unlike the Ukraine, Bielorussia, and the Baltics) were 'repartitional' in this sense. It is not that radical redistributions were frequent, for they were a business of immense complexity; the point was that the peasants understood and accepted that their arable allotments were not theirs in perpetuity but subject to the communal right of repartition.

As the commune distributed its arable land among its families, so it distributed the obligation to pay taxes and redemption dues. (Redemption dues were the 50 annual payments due to the state to cover the cost of emancipation from serfdom – i.e. the cost of buying peasant land from the landlords.) The state had made the communes into its principal tax-collection points. Communes were assessed for tax and redemption dues on the basis of the arable land they controlled, and they were left to determine by themselves from whom and how to collect the money. It was common practice for communes to distribute this burden proportionally to the amount of land ploughed by each household, but in areas where agriculture constituted only a minor source of the villagers' income the commune might impose other ways of collecting money from its members, for example by charging villagers for permission to travel and to work outside the village. The commune also imposed some taxes and labour obligations of its own for the upkeep of local roads and other facilities.

The collection of taxes, the distribution of arable lands, and the management of the common land and communal facilities was not all the commune did. It also settled disputes between neighbours and acted as the police and judge for its members. The official police was thin on the ground in the rural areas and most villages never saw a uniformed policeman from one year to the next. It was the same with everything: the villages had to deal with fires in the dry seasons and with floods in the wet seasons, and they had to provide assistance for the victims of misfortune. Some of the assistance took the form of reciprocal arrangements between neighbours, but there was plenty that had to be organized on a wider basis.

That was not all. Although the farm tools and animals were the undisputed property of individual families, and the arable land was distributed among the families for their individual benefit, the communes played a dominant part in the management of agriculture. The three-field system of crop rotation and the interlocking spatial arrangements of the strips required farming to be done by common techniques and timing. It would not do for a family to delay its sowing, or to sow a slower-growing seed, because harvesting had to be done at the same time if crops were not to be trampled under foot, and because every family had the right to let its animals loose on the stubble. Mowing grass on the common lands, taking timber from the woods, grazing animals on the common pasture-land and on the fallow field – these were all things to be done in a co-ordinated fashion, so that every family could use its rights of access to the commons for its animals. There were additional reasons for the communal involvement in the agricultural process: for example, the commune had an interest in where and when the privately owned livestock was grazing, because the livestock was fertilizing the communal land as it chewed. Some communes took action to prevent farmers from improving bits of additional land they rented on a short-term basis from neighbouring private estates, if the improvement was to consist of cattle depositing their manure on the land belonging to the private estate rather than on the communal land. In any case, much of the additional land purchased or rented for peasant use from the neighbouring estates was purchased or rented by the communes rather than by individual peasants.

In the region around and to the north of Moscow, where the soil was poor but opportunities to earn cash outside agriculture were good, the communes took full advantage of their power to control the issue of passports to their members. The government had imposed passport restrictions on the freedom of movement within the empire, primarily so that peasants could not flee their obligation to contribute to their communes' payments of taxes and redemption dues. A peasant wanting to travel outside the boundaries of his country district (*volost'*) needed a passport, which the district office would issue only with the approval of the peasant's commune. The maximum duration for which a passport could be issued to a peasant was one year, after the expiry of which the passport holder had to apply to the commune for a renewal if he wanted to extend his stay away. Most of the passports, however, were issued for three- or six-month periods. Thus the villages kept their migrant labourers on a short leash. Moreover, some of the communes were themselves actively involved in the formation of migrant labour gangs, with whose temporary employers they made deals to the effect that the labourers' wages were paid in part directly to the communes, in defrayment of what the labourers' families owed their communes in tax and redemption contributions. As regards peasants who worked in towns on a less organized basis, who overstayed their passports and neglected to keep sending part of their wages to the people back home, it was not unknown for a commune to get the district office to sign a warrant and to send a policeman to bring the negligent son back.

It could be said that the communes exerted these kinds of control over individual peasants simply to safeguard the flow of hard-earned peasant cash into the coffers of the state. That, however, is only a partial truth, for the communes in effect also safeguarded the peasant's right to pay less tax than the state demanded, if the full amount exceeded what the peasant needed for subsistence. While making sure that no household or individual evaded their obligation to share the tax and redemption burden, the communes consistently paid less to the state than the required amounts – how much less depended on what the communes thought their members could afford to pay in any particular year.

Exactly what was this commune that seemed to have such a sway over the peasants' affairs? The intelligentsia called it an *obshchina*, but this was not a word the peasants often used. *Mir*, which also meant 'a world' or 'a universe', was the peasants' word for a village community; they tended to use it interchangeably with the other words for 'a village' – *selo* or *derevnya*. The commune was not a formal institution. It had no special buildings and no paid officials. The government did try to make it official, by insisting that every commune appoint its officers – the village elder, the tax collector, and two ranks of assistant policemen, one of the higher rank for every hundred households and one of the lower rank for every 10 households. These officials were subject to punishment if they failed in their duties to the state. They did not, however, have the uniforms or privileges of state servants. For the state, they were simply the bearers of the collective responsibility of the village for its duties to the state. The village appointed them for three-year terms, and it was rare for them to stand for re-election. They were, in other words, duties in which the senior men of the village commune took turns. They carried on with their normal lives while in office, for the office did not pay a salary and did not exempt them from their share of tax and redemption payment contributions.

Most of the big decisions of the village were taken by meetings of the *skhod*, a gathering of the male heads of the village families. They were by all accounts noisy and chaotic affairs, during which opinions were voiced one over another until suddenly silence descended and a decision was taken. Voting was rare, although the government was increasingly given to specifying the majorities (simple or two-thirds) by which important decisions should be carried. Rather, the commune seemed to strive for unanimous consensus, dissenting voices being answered by counter-arguments until they fell silent. Some opinions seemed to carry more weight than others in these gatherings, because of their bearer's age or some other quality that commanded a consensual respect within the community. But the more junior dissenters were not simply browbeaten into submission, for it mattered that the eventual decisions had the agreement of all. The intelligentsia's researchers often commented upon the fact that villagers tended to describe their actions and thoughts in the first person plural. Between the meetings of the *skhod*, communal decisions tended to be taken by the senior members, the elders of the village.

The ways of the commune reflected the weakness of state administration in the countryside. In the absence of rural uniformed firemen capable of quelling fires, state pension schemes and social security benefits that could help villagers in need, or of policemen that could uphold the state's laws against a vengeful neighbour, the people of the village were vulnerable to one another and obliged to rely on one another in difficulty. The village mattered – even to the peasant labouring in a town, for he, too, had nowhere else to go when accident, illness, or redundancy took away his earning ability. The individual peasant's security lay in keeping on the right side of village opinion and in being a part of a web of reciprocal relations with the village people. Being able to borrow cash from the rural people who had it (there were no other sources of credit other than the tavern keepers, shopkeepers, and the *kulaks* – the peasant families that currently did well enough to have cash to lend), and perhaps being able to repay the debt by a spate of free labour, was a lifeline for people who were seldom far above the bottom line of subsistence. Conversely, among the peasants who currently did well there were few in a position to secure their property and livelihood against natural misfortunes or against the ill-will of their neighbours – their security, too, lay in being able to call on the goodwill of the village. That is why disputes between neighbours, and their weddings, and their decisions to move out of extended-family households or to change their ways of making a living were all village affairs enacted in ways of symbolizing the witnessing and consent by the village community.

It would be a sentimental fallacy to conclude from these observations that communal life in the village was sweet. Opportunities for conflicts of interest were plentiful and multiplying as economic trends and state policies demanded ever more change from the peasant countryside. Consensus in the village was ever more difficult to maintain, and when the mechanics for maintaining a semblance of peace in the face of conflicting interests faltered, the resulting feuds could be violent and cruel, as could indeed be the communal ways of exacting conformity from individuals. Most of the time the communes maintained just enough peace for most of their members to go about their daily toil unmolested, to sow and reap a mean level of subsistence. As to whether the communal self-government and the webs of communal reciprocities offered other, positive compensations for the material harshness of peasant existence, the evidence is sparse and hard to interpret without help from the presumptions of either a romantic nostalgia or an urbane scepticism – the self-indulgencies of modern minds. What can perhaps be said is that, although instances of individuals taking their grievances to above-communal powers were increasing, they always remained outnumbered by the grievances settled within the village.

The next step up the ladder of authority were also seats of peasant self-government: the rural district (*volost'*) offices and magistrates. Here resided the full-time clerks who received communications from state offices, paid the salaries of rural teachers, wielded the stamps to print official permission into peasants' passports, administered the upkeep of rural roads, such as they were, and generally handled the business of rudimentary rural administration in their districts. They were answerable in part to the loftier organs of government with responsibilities for the peasant estate, and in part to elected peasant elders. The *volost'* office was also the seat of the rural magistrate, an elected peasant called upon to deal with crime and civil disputes in accordance with what legal experts called the 'peasant customary law'. Only peasants suspected of very serious crimes were referred higher up, to be dealt with by the state law. Like the commune elders, the *volost'* officials were subject to disciplinary powers of higher state administrators if they were considered to be negligent or venal in the discharge of their duties. But, like the village elders, they belonged to the peasant estate and were of the village rather than the city-based state.

The ultimate responsibility of the tsarist state administration for the rural hinterland was in the hands of provincial governors and their masters, the Ministry of the Interior. These seats of state power, however, were far away and, until the 1890s, they were represented locally by only a thin network of low-powered officials whose main function was to arbitrate disputes between peasant communes or district administrations. Somewhat closer to the rural districts and villages were the zemstvos – the semi-parliamentary institutions of local government in the countryside, in which the stratified system of selection gave the men and women of the peasant estate a minority representation. Some of the taxes collected in the villages went to the zemstvo budgets, which were sometimes enlarged further by grant allocations from central government. The zemstvos financed village schools and county hospitals, trained and employed peasant health workers to spread primary medical care into the villages, and agronomists to encourage peasants to introduce new crops and techniques into their farming. The zemstvos were the employing institutions of what came to be called, in the political language of the beginning of the twentieth century, the 'third estate': the professional intelligentsia dedicated to the modernization of the countryside. These specialists sought contact with the peasants at the grass-roots level to make a beneficial impact on them, but although they were numerous enough to be regarded as a liberal political force in the zemstvos and in capital-city politics, their numbers were spread thinly at the village level. Besides, some of the agronomists decided that a more effective way of introducing new techniques into agriculture was to concentrate their efforts on the large estates, in the hope of setting up successful islands of innovation which the peasant neighbours would gradually copy.

State presence in rural areas and its predilection for taking an active interest in peasant affairs increased substantially in the 1890s. The beginning of the decade saw the introduction of more than 2000 land captains into the rural hinterland of European Russia, to be followed shortly by similar officials in the rest of the empire. These officials were rather like the provincial governors in that they had a wide sweep of powers over their territories, while being answerable to the Ministry of the Interior. But whereas the provincial governors were far-away figures in the lives of most peasants, the land captains were close enough to visit 'their' villages from time to time, and unlike the rural arbitrators of earlier times, they were charged with the duty to interfere with village affairs whenever the decision of peasant self-government appeared to transgress some law or interest of the state. The land captains were all too soon overloaded with paperwork and bureaucratic reporting to have much time for strutting around the villages and ordering the commune elders to change their decisions. But they were high powered enough and close enough to the ground to signal the state's intention to carry out reforms in the countryside, in the first instance by extending the jurisdiction of state laws at the expense of peasant custom – in other words, by dissolving the peasant estate in a system of 'all-estate' legislation. They were also able to learn about the practicalities or rural life and to improve the quality of central government policy-making by the supply of relevant information. And last but by no means least, they were on the spot to adjudicate appeals from individual peasants against their communes. Their actual power to determine the course of events in the villages, however, was still limited crucially by the absence of effective law enforcement in the countryside. Most of the appeals by individual peasants against their communes were lodged by individuals who wanted to leave their villages and therefore no longer needed to keep on the right side of village opinion.

In the mid-1890s, a new government department, the Ministry of Agriculture, was set up for the purpose of modernizing Russian farming. The impact of this institution was in some ways similar to that of the zemstvos. The ministry employed an army of agronomists, surveyors, and other experts, and let them organize local councils of experts jointly with the zemstvos. These bodies claimed a wide range of authority on the basis of scientific knowledge, and they intensified substantially the previous zemstvo efforts to 'work with the grass-roots'. They thus strengthened the 'third element', the activist professional intelligentsia, and gave it an organizational base reaching into central government; these were the makings of a modernization movement that would come into its own under the auspices of the Stolypin reforms.

The Household and the Family

Households, not individuals, were the approved users of allotted strips of communal land, the bearers of the obligations exacted by the communes, and the owners of livestock, working tools, food stocks, kitchen gardens, and living quarters. Most of what a peasant did was done in the organizational context of a household. There has been some dispute among historians as to whether the household and the family were essentially the same thing in peasant society. Certainly, a family was hardly recognized as such by the village community if it did not have its own cottage, farmyard, chattels, and a kitchen garden, and most members of a peasant household were related to one another by blood or marriage. The school of thought that insists on the household and the family as separate concepts points to the evidence that an individual's entitlement to 'eating from the common pot' of a household was perhaps earnt by expending labour on the household economy rather than given by rights of birth; and, apparently, there were cases where customary law accorded working members of a household who were not family the same right to inherit a share of household property as other members who were family.

On the other hand, peasants did use the state's adoption laws to make sure of the inheritance entitlement of household members who were not blood relation. Such formal adoptions were particularly frequent among families with daughters and no sons; when the daughter of a sonless family married, she might bring her husband into her parental home rather than join his parental home as was normal custom, and her father would then legally adopt her husband as his son, the husband thus assuming his father-in-law's surname. In addition, it was extremely rare for natural sons to be disinherited by their fathers, although the threat of disinheritance was sometimes used against sons who did not do as they were told. On this evidence, the relations between members of a household were primarily defined as family relations, and only secondarily as the mutual relations of labourers earning their keep by working in and for the household. Finally, unlike the homes of merchants and artisans in the towns, village households rarely included among their residents hired servants or labourers. The peasant household was very much a family affair, and the conceptual distinction between 'household' and 'family' was not very clear in village-life. A peasant household was formed by a family, which was very much a unit of production as well as consumption.

Was the Russian peasant family typically an extended family? The general population census of 1897 found that the average family in Russia had 6.3 members. This was hardly an extended family size: a family of six or seven members was more likely to be a nuclear family of parents and children, perhaps with the addition of one or two other relatives. There were, of course, some families that were much larger than the average – and that were extended in their structure, comprising several conjugal pairs with their children. There is some evidence that such families tended to be less rare in the more remote rural localities, but the logic of the 6.3 average does not permit us to speculate that there were many of them. It was, however, commonly assumed by contemporary observers of the Russian peasantry that, if the typical family was no longer large and complex, it had been until recently. Thus thought a zemstvo statistician: ' . . . the essential fact is generally known, is banal. That families were larger before than now has long been known, of course, without any analysis of statistical data whatsoever.'[14] Most of the agrarian specialists regretted the passing of the big household, for they calculated that economies of scale applied to peasant production – the larger families being more productive per capita as well as in total.

But when did the trend from extended to nuclear family start? The specialists tended to assume that it started after the emancipation from serfdom. Interestingly, however, a landowner's lament at the passing of the big complex family had already been on record 100 years before emancipation. A belief in the passing of the extended family was long-standing and persistent among the commentators on peasant affairs, while the data were more ambiguous. The trouble was that, prior to the census of 1897, statistics of family size had been collected only in some localities. Some of these local data do support the view that, during the period from emancipation to the end of

---

14 Frierson, C. A. 1987: 'Razdel: the peasant family divided'. *The Russian Review*, xlvi, pp. 35–52.

the nineteenth century, when the population as a whole increased by 50 per cent, families became on average smaller. But there are other data which permit an altogether different view – that average family size had decreased only marginally since the eighteenth century.[15] One historian of peasant customary law dated the prevalence of the small family back to the sixteenth century.

What cannot be doubted is that the splitting of relatively large households into small ones was a long-established feature of peasant life. The equitable division of family property between sons of a patriarch on the patriarch's death had been the custom in Russia since time immemorial. By the second half of the nineteenth century, however, the vocabulary and the customs of the Russian peasantry suggested that it was also normal for a married son, who so desired, to set up an independent household for his own family, taking with him a part of the parental household property, even while his father was still in his prime. It was often said that the son was prompted to this step by his wife, who found it disagreeable to be subject to her mother-in-law's authority. But the available evidence also suggests that the splitting often occurred when the son and his wife decided that they were supporting too many dependants by their own labour within the old household, for example if the old household also included another son with his wife and a number of their children. Opportunities to earn wages outside the household also encouraged married couples to become independent. In other words, the patriarchal authority of the married son's father was not strong enough to keep an extended family together if one conjugal nucleus within it thought it was subsidizing the dependants of another conjugal nucleus.

When the members of an extended family decided they would rather split up, they notified the commune elders and set a date on which all the family members, some other relatives and neighbours, some of the commune elders, and the parish priest would gather in the original household's cottage. Here the decision to split the household would be affirmed against the elders' sceptical questioning, and the proposed property division would be reviewed. This could be a complicated affair as immovable property could not be divided into equal shares, requiring compensatory payments to be made by the head of the original household. Disagreements over the terms of the division would be settled under the elders' supervision, perhaps by drawing lots. The difficult part over, a literate elder might draw up a written notice summarizing the agreement and certifying that each newly formed household would form a viable economic unit, capable of subsistence and the payment of taxes. Then bread and salt would be broken into a number of pieces equalling the number of the newly formed households, the transaction would then receive a blessing from the priest, and vodka would be dispensed to the elders as a reward for their help. The communal assembly would later attend to the other part of the division – the division of the strips of arable land between the new households. Henceforth, the son that had branched off would join the commune assembly

15 Confino, M. 1985: 'Russian customary law and the study of peasant mentalites'. *The Russian Review*, xliv, pp. 35–43. For the data indicative of a downward trend in family size, see Frierson, 'Razdel'.

as a head of a household (*bol'shak*). The new household would build its cottage, backyard, and a kitchen garden either on a subdivision of the land adjacent to the original household or on a new piece of land at the edge of the village, allocated by the commune. Sometimes the whole package of agreements would be brought for confirmation before the assembly of *volost'* elders. Commune and *volost'* assemblies at times also approved household divisions that were opposed by the head of the original household, forcing him to accept the terms of settlement.

It could be said, therefore, that neither the extended family nor the nuclear family was typical, before or after emancipation. Both were common, and many people experienced periods of life in both. As sons grew up, married, and brought their wives into their parental homes, a family grew from nuclear to extended. Then it split, often forming one multigenerational family including the original parental pair, a married son with his family, his remaining unmarried siblings, and one or two small, nuclear families. The married son who remained in the original household with his parents could look forward gradually to taking over from his father as the head (*bol'shak*) of his household. This tended to be an informal transition, starting with the old man sending the son along to the commune assembly meetings as his proxy and ending with the heads of the other village households expecting the son to turn up at the assemblies rather than the father.

The intelligentsia's conviction that the Russian peasant family was in a process of transition from the extended to the nuclear family was in all probability based on histories of the transition from premodern to modern Western Europe rather than on evidence concerning Russian social history. The Russian social history does not provide a convincing picture of the past as belonging to peasant patriarchs lording it over households of a mini-commune size and complexity. Rather, the Russian way was to live under communal powers at the village level, and in households oscillating between a small extended and a small nuclear family. Be that as it may, educated Russia of the late nineteenth century was agitated at the supposed passing of the large extended family. Conservatives saw in it a dangerous breakdown of patriarchal authority, and tried to inhibit households splitting by ineffective legislation; populist economists were worried about the loss of economies of scale to peasant farming; populist radicals regretted what they saw as the infiltration of individualism into the ancient communalist peasant soul; and the Marxists saw a confirmation of their belief in the revolutionary effects of encroaching capitalism on the old rural order. In the meantime, however, if peasant Russia was at all changing in this respect, it was changing only marginally in the sense that perhaps rather fewer people than before were prepared to delay setting themselves up as independent families.

The Russian peasant family was patriarchal in the sense that the head of household (*bol'shak*) was male; the married couple's residence was patrilocal (i.e., in the man's home or village); the family's labouring tasks were divided between the sexes; husbands were expected to control errant wives by physical punishment; and the young men and women of the family were subject to different standards of sexual propriety. In addition, the symbolic rituals of village life reflected beliefs about women being prey to all-devouring sexual urges when young, young women being unclean and vulnerable to possession by evil spirits when bleeding, and having beneficial magical powers when post-menopausal; the nature of women, in other words, held the supernatural terrors as well as the life-giving powers of mother earth, while the nature of men was just being human.

But there were no rules that could not be broken on pragmatic and particularistic grounds. Since the commune elders felt responsible for each household's economic viability, it was not unknown for them to treat the household's mother as the head if she was demonstrably more competent than her husband. Within the household, the wife of the *bol'shak* had an undisputed authority over other women in the organization of the female tasks – looking after the domestic duties, tending the livestock in the backyard, and growing vegetables in the kitchen garden. The men's place was primarily in the allotment fields, although the women worked there as well, during the busy agricultural periods and at other times too if their men were earning their living somewhere else. Field work had its traditional notions of what were women's tasks and tools, although the precise division of labour varied from region to region and its 'rules' were often broken as necessity demanded. Where peasants were engaged in cottage crafts and industry, the work tended to be divided into men's and women's (and in some areas also children's), although some work was done in common. A female sphere of work vested a great deal of decision-making in the senior woman of the household and, since at the subsistence level of the economy there was no doubt that either sphere of work was equally important for survival, she had a respected place in the village community. The peasants' language had a special word for her, the *khoziaika*, which was a proud and equal counterpart to the male version, the *khoziain*. There is also some evidence that, when a family had to take an important decision that transcended the boundaries of male and female spheres of jurisdiction, it was often debated freely between the senior people of both sexes.

The patriarchal aspect of the peasant household was visible in the symbolism of the spatial arrangements of the one-room cottage, in which the senior man had his piece of the bench next to the icon corner, while the woman's place was diagonally across the room, next to the stove. When visitors entered the room, good manners requested that they bowed to the icon, and in so doing they also bowed in the direction of the *bol'shak*'s place. But the symbolism of these arrangements granted the woman's place a proximity to something equally important: she resided next to the stove, where lived the house spirit, a protector of the family welfare when he was not engaging in practical jokes, who had to be mollified by offerings of food. Symbolism apart, the patriarchal aspect of the peasant family resounded in the proverbs that enjoined the father to beat the devil out of his wife and not to spare the rod over his sons. It is impossible to generalize as to who suffered more from brutal patriarchs, whether their wives or their young sons, or how widespread the physical abuse was among the peasantry as compared with other social classes. There is no shortage of anecdotal witness accounts, and the evidence suggests that the village commune only rarely intervened in family affairs to protect people from wrathful husbands and fathers.

Otherwise, the evidence of proverbs and song lyrics confirms what could be inferred from the patrilocal marriage arrangements: the young wife, brought into her husband's family as a stranger, often had it difficult, especially if her husband was away from home on military service or as a migrant labourer. She was the most junior member of the family until she bore a healthy child, which gave her a more respected status. In the meantime, she was the one to do the most menial tasks at her mother-in-law's bidding while looking after the young children of the household, and the one to be laughed at when her ways seemed strange; sometimes, although again it is difficult to gauge how usual this was, she found herself in the no-win situation of having to fight off her father-in-law's sexual advances. There was a plausibility in the peasant belief that it was she who often pressed her husband to make an early bid for nuclear family independence.

An early marriage was not easily avoided by the young men and women of the peasant estate. Village culture encouraged semi-supervised socializing among the youth of both sexes, who often had their own gathering place in a cottage rented especially for this purpose. The village match-maker – usually a married woman of respected status in the community – set to work as soon as a matchable pair appeared to work on, to mediate in negotiations between the two families. The terms to be negotiated included the amount of the bride's dowry and the respective contributions to the costs of the wedding celebrations, which were elaborate community affairs lasting three days. If one of the pair decided to break off the engagement after a deal was struck, his or her family were often held liable to pay compensation to the other family. From time to time, couples circumvented the matching negotiations by eloping and eventually returning to ask for (and usual obtaining) their parents' forgiveness. The census of 1897 found that four per cent of male teenagers, 58 per cent of men in their twenties, and 90 per cent of men in their thirties were married, as were 15 per cent of female teenagers, 76 per cent of women in their twenties, and 88 per cent of women in their thirties. Peasant households, it seems, had an interest in marrying off their daughters to reduce their number of dependants, and in getting their sons to perpetuate the family line by begetting future labourers and heirs. The village community encouraged early marriages by intolerant attitudes to illegitimate births, and by allowing unmarried people some freedom of sexual play and courtship while expecting brides to enter their wedding nights as virgins; the traditional wedding rites included a triumphal public display of the bride's blood-stained nightgown.

Couples were expected to bear children from the beginning of their married lives, fecundity being considered good for economic prospects and generally a good omen, especially if the family did not have to wait long for its male progeny. But the peasant family was not child centred in the sense of lavishing much parental attention on the children's personal development. Infants were swaddled during a good part of their first year, fed some solid food within weeks after birth, then encouraged to learn to walk early, and, as toddlers, to graduate into the normal family diet and meal-times regime. As young children, they tended to be discouraged firmly from imposing much of their will and needs on the daily routines of the household. The family wanted its infants and children to be robust and, if they were not, it did not protect them much. The rate of infant mortality was still very high at the end of the nineteenth century, with some 25 per cent of infants not making it to their first birthday and another 25 per cent dying before the age of five. It was apparently not unknown for sick or weak babies to be killed by their parents, or left to die of deliberate neglect. There was an element in the treatment of infants and children which reflected a philosophy that they should be hardened for the harsh conditions of life, although ritual excesses that had scandalized earlier commentators on the peasant's ways, such as baptism of winter-born babies by full immersion in cold water in unheated churches, had become rare by the latter part of the nineteenth century.

Wives who were in a position to encourage their husbands to set up separate households for their nuclear family were mainly those whose husbands worked primarily on the land, or those whose children were already old enough to be a help around the farm. Many husbands were earning wages in off-farm employment at least during some parts of the year, but only some of them were able to combine their wage-earning activities with a continuous residence at home. Migratory labour was increasingly common. In 1890–1913, 60 per cent of peasant males of working age were taking some off-farm employment. In 1906–10, passports were issued annually to almost one-tenth of the total rural population of European Russia. This meant that a large proportion of men (only one-fifth of off-farm labourers were women, the great majority of them unmarried) spent some time away from their homes as migrant labourers. These were married men as well as single ones, for the statistics show that the percentage of men of all age-groups who were married was equally high for wage labourers as for the Russian male population overall, while being markedly lower for urban-born men. Some of the migrant employment was only for periods of two or three months at a time, but an increasing number of men ended up staying away in the industrializing towns and districts of Russia for years on end, returning to their family farms only during the busiest weeks of the agricultural calendar or for holidays, only permanently only in their late thirties or early forties. Many peasant women brought up their children and worked their family farms in the absence of their husbands, and this became the usual pattern in many villages of central and northern Russia by the beginning of the twentieth century. It may be difficult to say whether the 'typical' peasant family was extended or nuclear or something in between; but perhaps it can be said that, at the beginning of the twentieth century, the 'typical' peasant family was not necessarily one in which all its members lived together.

Material Culture

Russia is a large expanse of continental land, even if what concerns us is 'Russia proper', not the Ukraine, Bielorussia, Poland, and the Baltic lands to the south and west, nor the mountainous lands of the Caucuses between the Black and Caspian Seas, nor the lands of the Asian part of the empire stretching eastward from the Urals and the Caspian to the Pacific. Nevertheless, to traverse 'Russia proper' from St Petersburg in the north west to Tsaritsyn (later Stalingrad and later still Volgograd) in the south east is almost as far as an imaginary crow would have to fly to traverse Western Europe from Hamburg to Madrid – a matter of a few days after the advent of the railways, and a matter of weeks before then. It might be expected, therefore, that the provinces and districts of European Russia were inhabited by people of rather differing cultures, even if the focus of interest is only on the people of the peasant estate. Indeed, the folklorists of the nineteenth century found considerable variations in dialect and in the exact wordings of popular proverbs, tales, and songs. But the motifs and themes did not vary very much, even if the names of the characters populating folklore narratives may have done.

The ways of farming and the associated technologies of living were not very diverse either. This must have been in large part due to the fact that, unbroken as it is by any mountain ranges, there is not much variation in the basic climatic features. Another homogenizing factor also stems from the absence of mountain ranges: the north of the country is joined to the south by large rivers with many tributaries, which form natural routes for long-distance water transport during the summers but present no natural obstacles to overland travel during the winters, when the slow-flowing rivers tend to be under thick ice. Throughout the centuries, these conditions enabled people to migrate across large distances to claim new land for the farming they knew.

The Russian climate is continental, unaffected by the proximity of an ocean. Since there are no mountain barriers between the north polar cap and the Russian expanse of forests and steppes, cold air travels easily from the north, depressing winter temperatures even further below freezing than they would have been otherwise. Outside of the north-western corner there is not a great deal of rain. Snow cover is often not very deep during the winter, thus giving the land only a limited thickness of heat insulation, while post-thaw springs are all too often rainless; unfortunately, in many years a great deal more rain falls in late summer when the crops are ripe and liable to rot if not harvested dry. Finally, the changes between summers and winters are short and sharp, and the rapid spring thaw often causes floods. In sum, this is a climate which restricts farming by its long frost-biting seasons and it is vulnerable to spring droughts. This applies to the southern half of Russia as well as to the north; the average number of frost-bound days is lower further south, but this is a matter of degree rather than of difference in the natural limitations and hazards placed on agriculture. The variations in crops and farming techniques were consequently never very great. The staple product of field farming has always been grain – rye in the north and wheat in the south – while kitchen gardens everywhere were geared to providing a similar mix of basic root and leaf vegetables, although the range was wider in the south. Farming consisted of working with a similar range of tools on a similar range of tasks throughout the whole of Russia.

The great difference between Russian north and south is in the nature of the dominant wild vegetation and the soil type. The northern part, which extends roughly to 50 miles south of Moscow, is basically a land of coniferous forests with top soil that is light and shallow. Further south is the land of mixed woods and grass steppes, where the top soil is heavy and deep and much more fertile than in the north – the so-called 'black earth'. Ploughing in the south was the heavier job, calling for large metal instruments, while wooden ploughs, perhaps with small metal tips, were sufficient for the northern soil, with horses providing the main draught power in either case, although oxen were also used in some parts of the south. In the north, wood provided abundant fuel as well as raw material for building and crafts, while in the south timber was not so abundant, resulting in buildings that were less off-the-ground, often with earth floors and less extensive.

In the central region around Moscow, the proximity to trading routes and markets, combined with the fact that Russian cities had never gained monopoly rights over trade and crafts, led to the early development of village industries to supplement the modestly productive agriculture. The villages of this 'central industrial region' tended to specialize in particular crafts: some specialized in wooden furniture and utensils, others in the locksmith trades, yet others in the making of lace, etc. A textile industry, both cottage based and in large factories, developed in the rural parts of this region as railways connected it with the cotton-growing and wool-sheep farming of central Asia. Prior to that, the staple textile had been linen, with flax being grown in the north west. In eastern Russia, the busy trade transport on the river Volga provided another set of opportunities for peasants to supplement their incomes; north-western peasants found their wage opportunities shaped by the industries of St Petersburg; south-western peasants were influenced by access to the coal-mining regions; and in the Urals, by access to iron-smelting plants. In other words, the peasantry's material culture was subject to variation not so much within the agricultural sphere itself as in the sphere of crafts and in the type of opportunities provided by industrial development for migrant labour.

Most peasants were skilled in using a similar range of agricultural tools, plus some other basic tools, such as the axe, and in handling a similar range of poultry and animals. We have already noted that there was a great deal of similarity in the architecture of their homes. In the north the cottages were built with the shorter sides lining the broad village street; in the south, with the long side. The cottages were higher in the north, with more extensive outbuildings in the backyard, which were covered by a single roof. In either case, the typical cottage had one room with a large, flat-top, clay stove in the corner diagonally opposite the icon corner. The top of the stove served as a place for drying things and sometimes for sleeping on. Other sleeping places were on benches along the walls and, in the case of the northern cottage, also on a large bunk or half-loft near the stove. (In the summer, some of the outbuildings were used for more private sleeping arrangements.) Much of the wall-space in the cottage room was covered by shelves and cupboards. There was a table near the icon corner. The half of the room containing the stove was considered the women's place; in some cottages it was separated by a light partition or curtain. By the end of the nineteenth century, most cottages were equipped with chimneys, unlike the 'black cottages' common in earlier times. By this time, the usual form of lighting in the long, dark, winter evenings was the kerosene lamp. The cottage outbuildings included a steam bath, and most had their own well in the backyard.

Rites of Passage, Magic, and Religion

Populist ethnographers described the peasant world as animated by spirits that were behind everything that might (or did) affect one's fortunes, and for this reason they had to be managed by ritual observances. There was the house spirit behind the stove that had to be mollified by occasional offerings of food lest he decided to withdraw his protection; the surrounding forest was ruled by a spirit one had to keep on the right side of; and there was a whole array of other beings in the wilderness, evil as well as capricious, that were better kept at bay by digging little trenches around the village and its fields, and by whispering the right charms and performing the right gestures at appropriate times. The seasons of the year were seen off and welcomed in by elaborate communal rites; harvests were commenced by old women wading into the fields to clip the first few head of grain; cattle had their special day when they were sprinkled with water to ward off disease – there were symbolic actions to be performed throughout the agricultural year to make sure that the hard work was not laid waste by an angry nature spirit.

When the man of a house was dying, he might be helped along to a swift and painless end by someone sawing off a decoratively carved horse-head from the roof; the death accomplished, the body was taken out of the cottage through a window or a specially cut hole, so that the door remained closed to the evil spirits that wanted to rush in. The cottage was then ceremonially and thoroughly cleaned, the deceased's clothes disposed of, and all the water present in the pots and barrels duly replaced, because bad spirits had probably taken refuge in it. A mother who had just given birth was considered unclean and vulnerable to invasion by evil spirits, and consequently kept in isolation until her baby was baptized (usually three days after birth), and until she and the midwife carried out a rite of mutual handwashing on coming back from church. The marriage ceremony lasted three days, and its various elements marked not only the passage of the pair from one status to another within the household and the community but also, inevitably, it included bits of magic to ward off the possibility of infertility.

Illness and injuries tended to be regarded not as accidents but the results of someone casting an evil eye or in some other way mobilizing a malevolent spirit to do its work. The village community had its practically oriented bonesetters, masseurs and masseuses, and midwives, but also healers who did their business by whispering special secret charms as well as by administering mercury, quinine, herbal lotions, and blood-letting. Some of the village sorcerers and sorceresses were of the 'wise man' or 'wise woman' variety, who had had their magical secrets passed on to them by other sorcerers to whom they had been apprenticed. Others were believed by the villagers to be possessed of magical powers by virtue of being odd in some way, perhaps because they had a physical deformity, or simply because there was something in their character that marked them out as strange loners. They were believed to have made a pact with the forces of the underworld, which enabled them to cast spells, but also to undo the spells that had been cast. The sorcerers and witches tended to have specialized healing reputations, some being known as successful in dealing with fevers, others in reducing pain, in healing impotence and infertility, or in controlling chronic complaints, such as epilepsy. They were often called upon by healthy people for advice and fortune-telling, or for casting spells on third parties to alter their affections and thoughts.

The Russian peasantry was not unique in combining Christianity with pagan belief systems, as this kind of mixed religion was also common among the Roman Catholic peasantry in various parts of the world. In Russia, however, the pagan substratum of religious belief was arguably the stronger because the

Russian Orthodox Church had a number of weaknesses. First, its élite of monks and bishops bore the marks of long-standing intellectual isolation. Having cut itself off from the Greek Church after the fall of Constantinople in the sixteenth century, the Russian Orthodox Church became a subordinate part of the secular state in the eighteenth century. The state wanted to modernize itself and its economy, but it wanted the Church to serve as a bulwark against the possibly destabilizing influences of the West; the clergy was not to be exposed to Western influence like the secular servants. The state also deprived the Church of its lands, made the clergy into a hereditary social estate (although outsiders were encouraged to join it after 1869), but it did not find the money for making parish priesthoods into salaried careers. Seminary education was in the main poor in quality, and they were not its brightest and most inspired graduates who agreed to be ordained as parish priests. As modernization proceeded, the intelligentsia became secular and anti-Church, while within the Church there took place no closing of ranks between the black clergy (celibate monastic orders of mainly a mystical blend) and the white clergy (married parish priests, deacons, and sacristans). The parish clergy had to feed their families by tilling allotments of land alongside their peasant parishioners, and by charging them fees for their services. Educated society turned its back on the Church because it represented a pre-Englightenment, Old Muscovy culture; the monks looked down upon the parish clergy because they were not as devoted to mystical disciplines; and the peasants resented their priests who often seemed to them too insistent and greedy in charging for essential services. The priests, in other words, were in a weak position to provide strong religious leadership for their parishioners.

With the exception of national minorities such as the Volga Germans who were Lutherans (and whose priests were urban based and university educated), the Russian peasantry in its entirety belonged officially to the Orthodox Church. By the eve of the First World War, some 90 per cent of peasants still observed their basic duties to the Church; they took the communion and went to confession on a regular basis, as well as using the Church for baptismals, weddings, and burials. The peasants worshipped the icons in their cottages, went on pilgrimages, observed the holidays and the fasting prescribed by the orthodox calendar, and spent some 10 per cent of their budgets on religious artefacts and services. But their Christianity had long been criticized by urban-based commentators, and not only because it coexisted with pagan superstitions. The nature of the criticisms, however, varied with the critics' preoccupations: the peasants were thought to be insufficient in their piety in the early part of the nineteenth century, and insufficient in their knowledge and understanding of the Christian doctrine in the latter part of the century. The consensus, however, was that the strongest religious commitment was among the 10–15 per cent of the peasants belonging to dissident sects, of which by far the most numerous were the Old Believers – the followers of priests and monks who had rejected the mild adjustments to liturgy and dogma decreed by the Church Patriarchate in the seventeenth century. The Old Belief was even more orthodox than the official Orthodoxy in placing emphasis on fervent piety to be expressed through rigid adherence to prescribed liturgical forms. For the Old Believers as well as the majority adherents of the Official Church, salvation of the soul was to come through the magic of correctly carried out procedures of worship.

It did not matter if the worship was ministered by priests who were thought to be doubtful in their own morals or piety; what mattered was the procedural correctness and the uplifting aesthetics of religious service. There was little demand among the peasant congregation for the Church to provide moral guidance through sermons or any other forms of spiritual education, and the priests on the whole did not try to provide it. Until the advent of general primary schooling in the villages during the latter part of the nineteenth century, the Church had been the main institutional link between, to use Redfield's terminology, [16] the 'high' official culture of the cities and the 'low' peasant culture. But it was not a strong link. The 'high' part of the Church was itself isolated from the new city 'high' culture of modern enlightenment, while its 'low' part, the parish priesthood, was not in the position to have much impact on peasant beliefs and morals. These were shaped primarily by the pragmatics of nature-dependent survival within a loose cosmology of supernatural forces, and a more or less fervent piety such as was necessary to save the soul in the afterlife.

Customary Justice

Investigators of peasant customary justice found that the rulings of the *volost'* magistrates varied from one district to the next in comparable cases, in addition to which some of their informants denied the existence of any binding customs. The *volost'* court hearings tended to concentrate on who the alleged offenders and victims were by reputed character, what personal harm was done by the offence in question, and whether it was premeditated. Many cases that would have been heard before state courts as criminal cases were treated more like civil disputes by the peasant courts. Personal harm was an important criterion – it mattered whether a piece of stolen or damaged property belonged to someone who had invested a great deal of hard work in its acquisition or maintenance, and how easily that person could afford to lose it. Taking wood and poaching from a rich man's forest was hardly a crime at all in the peasant common sense. An offence committed in the course of a drunken revelry was often treated with mercy, but not if the alleged culprit was a habitual drunk of bad repute. It mattered whether a thing was stolen in hunger or in greed. The rulings of the peasant courts often commanded the culprits to compensate their victims rather then to submit to punitive sentences. Severe kinds of sentence, such as flogging, were often imposed on bad-character individuals who defaulted in their obligations to their communes. Some of these cases were referred to higher authorities with a recommendation that the offender be sent to exile. All in all, the peasant courts dealt with the cases before them on the basis of particular characteristics and circumstances, justifying their rulings simply as being "according to reason', 'according to justice', or 'according to man'.

---

16 Redfield, R. 1956: *Peasant Society and Culture: an Anthropological Approach.* Chicago: University of Chicago Press.

The majority of disputes and complaints were settled in the villages without ever reaching the *volost'* courts. The commune elders often tried to mediate between the conflicting parties to find a workable compromise, but if this proved impossible, they might persuade the complainant and the defendant to swear oaths on the truth of their case until one of them flinched. Many disputes were settled by the parties drawing lots and sealing the resulting arbitration with conciliatory drinks. Some offences, however, were dealt with in a more punitive manner by the village community. If a thief was a member of the village community, he or she might be subjected to ritual humiliation by being paraded through the village in a noisy procession, amid catcalls and much banging on oven doors, etc., perhaps harnessed as a horse and wearing the stolen item around the neck. If the offender was a woman, she would be stripped of her head scarf, and sometimes of her clothes as well. Culprits who tried to resist were beaten up. The parade would be concluded by the offender buying plenty of vodka for everyone.

Occasionally, village justice took the form of murdering suspected offenders after unspeakably cruel beating and tortures. This sort of ultimate vengeance tended to be inflicted on people who were outsiders, and suspected or convicted by the village community of a serious crime, such as horse theft. Horse thieves were the object of particularly venomous wrath because the horse was a highly valued chattel, as a draught animal and also as a symbol of well-being and potency. In the peasant's view, the state laws that could be used to punish horse thieves were disdainfully soft and totally inadequate as a deterrent. The lynchings of horse thieves were done in a scrupulously collective manner, to make sure that no member of the community could be a witness without taking a part, and with careful attention being paid to concealing the result from the authorities. However, lest it be thought that horse theft was an example of a crime to which the peasantry applied general moral rules, it was also known for some villages to keep their peace by consenting to pay protection money to horse-thief gangs, or to afford them refuge when needed; and some villages were long known as specializing in horse theft. As always, whether a dubious category of a person suffered villagers' vengeance or enjoyed their tolerance depended on the particular circumstances of the encounter. It was the same with wandering beggars, deaf-and-mute people, and people believed to be witches. Most of the time they were treated with kindness or at least with the sort of respect born of circumspection. But occasionally, when their appearance in a village coincided with some communal disaster, they were thought to be the cause; then they might meet the same horrible ends as the most heinous or unlucky of horse thieves. There was no apparent decline in these incidents after the 1890s.

The 'I', the 'We', and Abstract Concepts

One of Chekhov's short stories is about a peasant who is tried before a court on the charge of sabotaging a railway track by stealing a bolt from it. He does not deny that he took the bolt to use it as a weight for his fishing tackle. But he does not see why the theft should make him guilty of causing a train crash. The people of the village have been helping themselves to bolts from the tracks for years without causing any harm, for they have always taken care to take only some of the bolts, leaving other ones in place. It was not clear to the accused why he should be punished for something that was common practice, and why his theft of a particular bolt should be seen as the cause of a rail accident.[17]

Since the peasant in this story consistently used the pronoun 'we' ('we have been doing this', 'we understand that') in explaining his point of view to the court, the story illustrates two respects in which the Russian peasant was seen as culturally backward by his intellectual contemporaries, and in which he still continues to be seen so by many historians. First, the peasant was incapable of understanding the consequences of his acts, and his moral responsibility for them, because his consciousness of himself as an individual 'was only inadequately developed'.[18] Secondly, he was incapable of understanding modern scientific reasoning because it was alien to him to think in abstract concepts.

It is, however, also possible to give Chekhov's story a slightly different slant. Why believe that what some official experts say about track-bolts and train crashes is more true than what the villagers know about the track on their land and the trains that have safely passed on it? Unlike educated Russians, the peasant has no need to believe the modern system of authoritative truth more than the local knowledge that is based on personal experience and the opinions of people within the community, whose judgements on many things have been proven to be right in the past.

It was the same with the practice of landholding and the concept of area measurement. The peasants did not think about the land they tilled in acreages. The Stolypin land reformers wanted official surveyors to measure village lands in *desiatiny* (one *desiatina* being 2.7 acres) and to draw plans for official registers on which each head of household would have his property title marked out as boundary lines enclosing a consolidated area of the same, number of *desiatiny* as the sum total of the area of the scattered strips that were previously farmed by his family. The system of property holding was eventually to be one in which disputes over who owned a tree, for example, could be settled by surveyors determining the tree's exact location on the map and lawyers confirming one of the other of the disputants as having the legal entitlement to it. The justice of land consolidation would depend on the surveyors determining the right quantity of *desiatiny* for each property. But the peasants were reluctant to accept it, not because they were incapable of grasping that a long and narrow field could have the same area as a square one, but because no two fields were the same unless it had been proven by practice that they took the same amount of work to produce the same yield. The peasants knew their field strips as having particular practical qualities and it was irrelevant what a surveyor said about their area size. Besides, they knew that in practice their individual rights to land depended on the agreement of their fellow villagers; it seemed far fetched to believe that one's unfettered

17 Chekhov, A. P. 'Zloumyshlennik'. In *Sochinenia*, St Petersburg, iii, pp. 5–9.
18 Mironov, B. 1985: 'The Russian peasant commune after the reforms of the 1860s'. *Slavic Review*, xliv, pp. 438–67.

ability to use a piece of land could be guaranteed my maps and bits of paper in far-away offices.

Ultimately, the place of abstract concepts (area as quantity abstractable from a field of a particular shape and experientally known quality, cause and effect as physical laws abstractable from a particular experience of bolts, tracks, and passing trains) in the peasant mind depended on where the peasant thought the locus of social power was that shaped his fate in everyday practice. If this was within the village community, he knew local knowledge to be valid, for the community made it so by its practice – and local knowledge was particularistic and empirical. Abstract concepts belong to the realm of universalistic and theoretical knowledge; they have relevance only in the minds of people who have a reason to believe that the locus of social power in their world is or should be in an organization that is itself a reflection of a theoretical system.

To modern minds, the individual 'I' has its existence within a theoretical system of rights, within a monotheist theological system, within a system of psychological laws, within a system of literate discourse about thoughts and experiences, etc. The modern individual has the 'I' affirmed by a system of accreditation (exam certificates, bank balances, responses to written communications) which at the same time affirms the system within which the individual's acts and achievements are approved and make sense. This system of accreditation is additional to and to some extent autonomous of the affirmations of the 'I' that come from face-to-face encounters, because these encounters do not form the only locus of social power for the modern individual. The peasant had his or her individuality affirmed by the face-to-face community first and foremost. He or she may have also experienced him or herself as a body with a soul which had to coexist with a plurality of other spiritual forces. These forces were not so much a matter of a theoretical system as an empirical matter of coinciding events.

When an illness called for an intervention to restore health, a sorcerer with her mercury, whispered magical formulae, and an empirically based reputation was a better bet than a zemstvo physician with his mercury, a medical certificate, and no locally proven record of effectiveness. The peasant was pragmatic and empirically minded – he or she gave the physician his chance to prove his effectiveness on the same basis as the sorcerer and the witch. It was the same with the knowledge of the 'I': a matter of particular experience of suffering and joy, empirically attested recognition by personally known others, and the pragmatic ability to live with these others in their community. Self-consciousness was not for abstractive definitions, because there was no compelling reason to regard abstract concepts as having a higher validity.

An undeveloped sense of individuality and individual moral sense, a reluctance to accept abstract concepts as useful, and a belief in coinciding events being bound together by magical forces were the characteristics of peasant cultural backwardness in the eyes of educated, 'cultured' Russia. The peasant 'lack of culture' was regarded by modern people as a lamentable obstacle in the way of progress. But the ability to reason and to be self-conscious was perhaps not the main point of difference between the modern people and their country cousins. The main difference was that modern minds performed a leap of faith which endowed theoretical systems with a higher and more compelling reality than the pragmatics of working with empirically known facts in local contexts. The moderns did not see this leap of faith as something akin to a dogmatic suspense of reason for, on the contrary, they knew it as Enlightenment. In their world, the belief in theoretical systems of abstract concepts was displayed in words and actions that had their own local contexts and pragmatic uses as well, so that the business of worshipping theoretical systems above empirical manifestations of reality was in itself not dangerous; on the contrary, it could have its rewards. The peasant world was different. Here there was no living to be made by believing a theoretical system more than the empirical facts of common practice.

Schools, Literacy, and Folktales

Peasants became interested in providing basic schooling for their children at the time of the emancipation. Over the following decades, many communes and *volosti* set up their own primary schools in the localities where the Church and the zemstvos were slow to establish theirs. The government became committed to the principle of universal primary education in the 1890s, when the peasant free schools became incorporated into the state network, and the zemstvos and central government embarked on a programme of building new schools. Whereas in 1856 there was on average one primary school available for every 7762 inhabitants of the empire, there was one for every 3299 people in 1878 and one for every 1499 in 1911.[19] In 1911, a survey found that 65 per cent of the boys and 30 per cent of the girls of the relevant age-group (eight–11 years) were attending school. But these figures were an under-representation of the spread of basic primary education because the percentages were based on a three-year age-span while most peasant children attended school for two years rather than for the full-length, three-year course. Since school enrolment rates inevitably varied between different provinces and districts, it could be said perhaps that, in the relatively more densely populated and less remote regions, the goal of providing some basic schooling for every child was in sight by the time of the First World War.

Peasant interest in basic schooling was reflected in the fact that most schools received more applications for enrolment than they could accommodate. Although the average village schoolteacher was in sole charge of 44 pupils, discipline problems in the schools were few, and instruction in basic literacy and numeracy quite effective. But that was all that many peasant parents wanted from their children's schools. They were not interested in their children staying the full three-year course and acquiring the completion certificate, which was something the peasants regarded as more in the teachers' interest than their own; after all, the certificate no longer provided tangible benefits, such as exemption from military service. Most children attended school only for two years. This seemed to be by parental preference rather than because of economic pressures, since the drop-out rate was equally high

---

19 Eklof, B. 1986: *Russian Peasant Schools: Officialdom, Village Culture, and Popular Pedagogy, 1861–1914*. Berkeley, Calif.: University of California Press, p. 287.

for the children of better-off families as the poorest ones, and in any case very few children entered paid employment before they were 14 years old.

Many urban-based educators were disappointed by the fact that the spread of schooling into the peasant hinterland was not bringing about a fast and obvious transformation of the peasant culture. They had thought that the acquisition of literacy would turn peasants into modern individuals, but that was not how it turned out. The spread of literacy did not make peasants into rapacious seekers of theoretical knowledge, and it was not the case that the 140 000 schoolteachers became influential people within the village communities. In fact, they were a wretched lot. Their wages were very low, partly because the peasants resented paying school tax for the benefit of people who seemed to be paid for nothing during the long weeks of school holidays. Their job security was also low, as indeed were their general powers in the world of officialdom, for primary schoolteachers had neither the formal status of state service rank nor the informal status of the intelligentsia. To the peasants, teachers were outsiders who did not do 'real' work in the village and did not enjoy any useful powers outside it; their position commanded even less respect than that of the village clergy, or the zemstvo health workers, the *fel'dsheri*.

Literacy, however, did bring about the spread of popular literature into the countryside. This was distributed by pedlars who also sold icons and religious calendars. Reading matter was typically printed on single printers' sheets folded into 32 pages. It was quite an event in the village when a pedlar arrived to set up his bookstall. Apart from stories about saints, the peasants often bought stories about bandits for their entertainment. The earlier forms of this popular genre drew directly on oral tradition. The bandit story was typically about the adventures of an assertive and strong individual who, unlike his Western counterpart of the Robin Hood variety, was a rebel with no social justice motivation. He was an outlaw who spilled blood, looted property, and, with his cronies, took part in wild feasts. He also suffered the loneliness of a homesick outlaw. He might eventually redeem himself by taking up an opportunity to do a valiant service for the tsar. This might culminate in a heroic death, or it might be followed by the redeemed outlaw returning to his village as a modest man. Unlike the returnees from wilderness in Western literature, the homecoming Russian ex-bandit did not return from his travels spiritually enriched or empowered, although in some cases he was allowed to end his days in a modest material prosperity, if he had gained it by outwitting rich fools and foreigners. In cases where the bandit did not take up an opportunity to redeem himself in the tsar's service, he continued to suffer loneliness before a violent death put an end to his adventures.

There was a clear dichotomy in these stories between order and anarchy, a subordination of the individual (anarchy) to the community (order), and an identification of the powers of the community with those of the tsar. The reader's sympathy with the bandit was invited at points in the story where the bandit felt his loneliness or had to make his choice between repentance and punishment. At the beginning of the twentieth century, however, the tsarist state lost its monopolistic position as the redeemer of fictional bandits, for in some of the new stories the bandits were caught at the behest of private individuals, and some had their moments of redemption in the presence of civilian figures, such as physicians.

The bandit story was a direct descendant of orally transmitted folklore, in which the lawbreaker theme was often mixed with the belief that, unlike the stuck-up and corrupt landlords, rich men and officials, the tsar appreciated the peasant outlaw's wit and bravery. Hypocritical, avaricious, venal, and stupid middle-authority figures, including priests as well as landlords, officials and merchants, were also the butt of numerous satirical folktales. Here again the tsar or some high representative of his, such as a district military governor, often acted as a judge who took the side of the peasants against their supposed social superiors. The tsar in the folktales legitimated the peasants' wit and sense of justice while the middle-authority figures offended them.

Further Reading

The book that has been a particularly influential source of ideas and information in the writing of this chapter is George Yaney, *The Urge to Mobilize: Agrarian Reform in Russia, 1861–1930* (Urbana, Ill: University of Illinois Press, 1982). It is a detailed history running to 561 pages of main text, but well worth reading because it conveys not just the legislative facts but an insightful exploration of the ideas behind them and a vivid sense of the interactions between government officials, agrarian specialists, and peasants. It also defines two important themes of the modernization movement: the interplay between staff and line principles of administrative authority and, more directly relevant to understanding the 'peasant question', the commitment to a systemic view of the world and the activist motivation of the 'modern minds' that sought to change the peasantry. Besides, the text does not flinch from forthright judgements on its documentary sources and in some passages develops its arguments with exhilarating wit.

Less analytical in regard to the intelligentsia's modernization perspective but a very useful and stimulating introduction to the Russian peasant in Soviet history is Moshe Lewin, *The Making of the Soviet System: Essays in the Social History of Interwar Russia* (London: Methuen, 1985). This collection covers a number of other themes beside the peasantry and should be included in the short-list of any social historian looking for an introduction to Russian and Soviet history. It is no less valuable for being easy to read.

A very good collection of recent scholarly articles which have been used extensively as a source for a number of sections for this chapter is Esther Kingston-Mann and Timothy Mixter (eds), *Peasant Economy, Culture, and Politics of European Russia, 1800–1921* (Princeton, NJ: Princeton University Press, 1990).

As a general history of the peasantry in tsarist Russia, Geroid T. Robinson, *Rural Russia under the Old Regime* (New York: Macmillan, 1961) still holds its value for the serious student as one of the books to read at an early stage, although it was originally published in 1932. As regards the student who wants to extend his or her knowledge of the centuries before emancipation from serfdom, there is J. Blum, *Lord and Peasant in Russia from the Ninth to the Nineteenth Century* (Princeton, NJ: Princeton University Press, 1961).

In this chapter, the section dealing with the 'peasant question' draws in particular on the articles by Donald Fanger, 'The peasant in literature' and

Michael B. Petrovich, 'The peasant in nineteenth-century historiography', both in Wayne C. Vucinich (ed.), *The Peasant in Nineteenth-Century Russia* (Stanford, Calif.: Stanford University Press, 1968).

The section on the commune draws on Boris Mironov, 'The Russian peasant commune after the reforms of the 1860s', *Slavic Review*, 1985, xliv, 3, pp. 438–67; Moshe Lewin, 'Customary law and Russian rural society in the post-reform era', *The Russian Review*, 1985, xliv, pp. 1–19; Jeffrey Burds, 'The social control of peasant labor in Russia' and Timothy Mixter, 'The hiring market as workers turf', both in Kingston-Mann and Mixter, *Peasant Economy*. Also a good source is Roger Bartlett (ed.), *Land Commune and Peasant Community: Communal Forms in Imperial and Early Soviet Society* (London: Macmillan, 1990).

The discussion of the household and the family is based on the articles by Moshe Lewin, Christine D. Worobec, and Michael Confino published as a debate on peasant customary law in *The Russian Review*, 1985, xliv, pp. 1–43; Cathy A. Frierson, 'Razdel: the peasant family divided', *The Russian Review*, 1987, xlvi, pp. 35–52; William T. Shinn jr, *The Decline of the Russian Peasant Household* (New York: Praeger, 1987, The Washington Papers/124); Robert E. Johnson, 'Family relations and urban-rural nexus', in David L. Ransel (ed.), *The Family in Imperial Russia* (Urbana, Ill.: University of Illinois Press, 1978); Christine D. Worobec, 'Victims or actors? Russian peasant women and patriarchy', in Kingston-Mann and Mixter, *Peasant Economy*; Patrick P. Dunn, 'That Enemy is the baby: childhood in imperial Russia', in Lloyd deMause (ed.), *The History of Childhood* (London: Psychohistory Press, 1976). The discussion of the government agencies in the countryside draws on Yaney, *The Urge*, Chaps. 2–4.

The information about peasant customary justice is drawn from the contributions of Lewin, Worobec, Confino, and Yaney to the debate published in *The Russian Review*, 1985, xl; Stephen Frank, 'Popular justice, community and culture among the Russian peasantry, 1870–1900', *The Russian Review*, 1987, xlvi, pp. 239–65; and Cathy Frierson, 'Crime and punishment in the Russian village: rural concepts of criminality at the end of the nineteenth century', *Slavic Review*, 1987, xlvi, 1, pp. 55–69.

The discussion of the other aspects of peasant culture draws on Mary Matossian, 'The peasant way of life' and Donald W. Treadgold, 'The peasant and religion', both in Vucinich, *The Peasant*; Gregory Freeze, *The Parish Clergy in Nineteenth-Century Russia: Crisis, Reform, and Counter-reform* (Princeton, NJ: Princeton University Press, 1983); Samuel C. Ramer, 'Peasant medicine', in Kingston-Mann and Mixter, *Peasant Economy*; Maureen Perrie, 'Folklore as evidence of peasant mentalite: social attitudes and values in Russian popular culture', *The Russia Review*, 1989, xlviii, pp. 119–43; Jeffrey Brooks, *When Russia Learned to Read: Literacy and Popular Literature, 1861–1917* (Princeton, NJ: Princeton University Press, 1985); Ben Eklof, *Russian Peasant Schools: Officialdom, Village Culture, and Popular Pedagogy, 1861–1914* (Berkeley, Calif.: University of California Press, 1986); and Yaney, *The Urge*, Chap. 5.

3

Land, Politics, and the Peasantry, 1900–28

Living Standards and Conditions at the Turn of the Century

Between 1863 and 1897, the rural population of European Russia increased from 50 million to 79 million – in other words, by more than 50 per cent. The per capita share of allotment arable land fell correspondingly – a shortfall the peasants, acting both as individual households and as communes, tended to make good by renting or buying additional lands from their former landlords. But not surprisingly, land prices and rentals were rising, so that the investments in the additional land became ever more expensive relative to returns, if the introduction of more intensive farming methods was too slow to keep harvests improving apace. In addition, the industrialization drive of the 1890s increased the burden of taxation that was imposed on top of the allotment land redemption dues. The peasants thus became more impoverished, with an ever higher proportion of households falling below the poverty line. Added to this were runs of below-average harvests because of inclement weather, such as in 1889–92 and 1905–8. The peasant economic picture, therefore, was one of a long-term decline in living standards made worse by periods of actual famine. It is no wonder the peasants revolted – first in the Ukrainian provinces of Kharkov and Poltava in 1902 and then throughout European Russia in 1905–7. At least, this was the more or less standard thesis favoured until recently by the historians of Russian peasantry. There was also a Marxist version of this thesis, first outlined by Lenin himself, which added to the picture of impoverishment the complicating factor of a capitalist polarization of the rural economy, which created a contrast between increasing mass poverty and the accumulating riches of a small minority.

More recent scholarship is less broad-brush and unanimous. First, there is evidence of increasing living standards throughout the post-emancipation period, particularly during the last two or three decades of the tsarist empire. When building new cottages, many peasants built the 'white' ones rather than the 'black' ones – in other words, those with proper chimneys, in which people lived in smoke-free comfort but also at greater expense because keeping the heat in was less fuel efficient. Moreover, the cottages were being filled with manufactured furniture in addition to the rough-hewn fixed benches and shelves, and more peasants were seen wearing manufactured clothing and footwear rather than the traditional home-sown garb. The peasants also baked their bread out of wheat rather than the cheaper rye flour. When the government reduced direct taxes and replaced them by indirect taxation in the form of dues on vodka, sugar, tobacco, oil, matches, and imported goods, the peasants carried on buying these items despite the increased prices. The government also alleviated the hardship of the bad-harvest periods by providing interest-free loans for grain purchase to the worst-affected peasants; by postponing the collection of direct taxes and redemption dues in the early 1890s; by writing off accumulated tax and redemption debts in 1904; by abolishing redemption dues altogether in 1906; and by providing more relief in the form of interest-free loans in 1906–8. Finally, government relief measures apart, grain production statistics show that, despite the fluctuation in harvests, from the 1880s on the overall trend of grain production was rising even faster than the rural population, while more money was being earnt by peasants in off-farm employment.

The former thesis is thus challenged, but it does not fall down altogether when the economic time-series are considered in greater detail and separately for different regions. That per capita grain production was rising in the empire as a whole was due mainly to the healthy rise in productivity of the large farms of the south-west Ukrainian and the Russian south east (the New Russia steppes north of the Caucasus).[1] In the 'central industrial region' around and to the north of Moscow, and in the region around St Petersburg, per capita grain production was falling. These, however, were the provinces in which railway building, the development of manufacturing industry, and ease of access to commercial outlets for cottage crafts were providing plenty of opportunities for off-farm earnings. Interestingly, land prices were actually falling here for a while, although they started rising again after 1900 as if in confirmation of the fact that the family farm remained the main form of welfare insurance even for the industrializing section of the peasantry. However, the situation was different in the 'central agricultural region' (the black-earth lands to the south and south east of Moscow and the north of the Ukraine), and in the provinces along the middle and lower Volga. Here per capita grain yield was falling slightly while opportunities for off-farm earnings were much more limited; the districts to the north of the Ukraine were close enough for migrant labour to travel to the Ukrainian coal mines and farming estates, and there were trading centres on the Volga to provide labour opportunities for some districts, but this still left much of the peasant economy dependent solely on overpopulated farming. For many of the black-earth and the Volga peasants, living standards were subject to the long-term decline as advocated by classical overpopulation – impoverishment thesis.

1 Wheatcroft, S. G. 1990: 'Crisis and the condition of the peasantry in late imperial Russia'. In Kingston-Mann, E. and Mixter, T. (eds), *Peasant Economy, Culture, and Politics of European Russia, 1800–1921*. Princeton, NJ: Princeton University Press, pp. 128–72.

The evidence is less diverse on the polarization of the peasantry between rich and poor. By 1913, about 90 per cent of the empire's arable land was tilled by peasants, and peasants who employed full-time farm labourers were almost non-existent. The relatively prosperous peasant farms were the ones worked by extended families or nuclear families with sufficient working-age children. The poor families were the small ones and the ones with an unfavourable ratio of dependents to able-bodied working members. That is why the agrarian economists were concerned by the propensity of larger households to split. However, nuclear families with growing children looked forward to their situation improving again. The poorest families were the ones afflicted by misfortune, such as fires, chronic illness, alcoholism, and, most frequently, a failure to produce healthy children early enough in the reproductive cycle. Some of the small and poor families were, perhaps, the victim of unkind relatives, who forced them out of extended-family households. But the agrarian researchers did not find any evidence that the plight of the poorest peasants was due to exploitation by richer peasants, or that that was what the poorest peasants thought.

Although economic pressures were the worst on the Volga and the black earth, earning a living on peasant farms was hard everywhere – difficult enough for many peasants from all parts of Russia to brave miles of tangled red tape to separate themselves from their communes and move east to Siberia, where there was a promise of plentiful land. Many peasants cut through the red tape by leaving illegally; this often worked, for the Siberian authorities would rather help them find a suitable piece of land than go to the expense of sending them back under guard. Peasant colonization of the southern belt of Siberia stated with the building of the Trans-Siberian railway. Nearly 100 000 migrated in 1892, and the annual exodus increased steadily in the following years. The eastward movement peaked in 1907–9, when the government encouraged it by simplifying the bureaucratic procedures and by providing the migrants with concessionary rail fares. Nearly five million migrated to the promised land between 1904 and 1913. There was, however, also a reverse flow of returnees, amounting to some 15 per cent of the outflow, as not everyone managed to settle in new communes and new surrounding, and easily worked and accessible land was becoming hard to find towards the end of this period. All in all, however, the Siberian settlers did reasonably well; they tilled more land, bred more livestock, saved more cash, revolted less, and lived longer than the average peasant on the European side of the Urals, although less education and less health care was available to them. It should, however, in fairness be noted that they did not achieve their success at the expense of the native population; the government saw to it that they did not colonize traditional pasture lands and the native Siberian population increased during 1897–1911, from 870 546 to 972 866.[2] The settlement of Siberia was a relatively peaceful chapter in the history of a peasantry seeking new sources of cheap land.

---

2 Poppe, N. 1973: 'The economic and cultural development of Siberia'. In Katkov, G. *et al.* (eds), *Russia Enters the Twentieth Century, 1894–1917*. London: Methuen, pp. 138–51.

Peasant Uprisings in 1905–7

The Ukrainian peasants' rebellions in the provinces of Kharkov and Poltava that occurred in 1902 took the government by surprise. Since it was mainly the peasants in repartitional communes that were involved (a minority in the Ukraine), the main reason hitherto evoked by government conservatives in favour of retaining the commune-based system evaporated. The communes, with their collective responsibility for tax obligation, were believed to keep the countryside in order, but it now appeared that they could also act as bases for rebellious action. In 1903, the principle of collective responsibility was abolished and, from now on, redemption payments and taxes would be a matter between the state (mainly represented at the local level by the land captain) and the individual household. The state would no longer have the authority either to force the communes to reallocate debts among their members or to punish commune and *volost'* elders for other villagers' debts. Rural officials were also deprived of their power to impose corporal punishment on individual peasants. The following year, the tsar celebrated his heir's birth by writing off tax redemption arrears. The year 1904 was also the year in which many young village men were drafted into the army to fight the war against Japan. A great many peasants now travelled to towns on the railways and brought back newspapers to keep themselves up to date about the progress of the war. But there was no progress, only military humiliations to be registered alongside the hardships occasioned by the withdrawal of able-bodied men from the village economy. To the peasants, the government that was losing a war abroad and no longer seemed to have the stomach for enforcing collective responsibility in the villages seemed weak. This impression was reinforced by the news of Bloody Sunday and the strikes that followed in the cities during 1905. This same year also happened to be a bad-weather year for agriculture, threatening the peasants' subsistence. The peasants became interested in the zemstvos' political meetings, especially if such issues as taxation were on the agenda.

Those things that did come on the agenda were often connected with the fact that arable land held by peasants was assessed for local taxes at much higher levels than the forests and the meadows making up the former squires' private landholdings. The peasants knew these lands were a good economic asset for the landowners, whom they had to pay for the privilege of taking wood from the forests for their stoves and their buildings and for letting their animals graze in the meadows. The peasants never understood in the first place why so much of the forest belonged to the nobles and rich merchants when, by rights, it belonged to God: it was patent injustice that peasant land carried a heavier burden of local taxation than noble land. The peasants also resented having to pay rent to the private estates when they needed to cultivate more land than that allotted to them by the terms of emancipation. All in all, the boundaries between the land allotted for peasant use and the land that remained in private estates was a constant source of irritation, especially if peasant pastures and bits of woodland were much less easy to get to from the village than the privately owned forests and meadows. In 1905, like other years, most of the landlords were absent for most of the time; and since government authority wobbled, the peasants of one village after another, and one district after another, resolved to correct the injustices manifested by the land boundaries and by the tax and redemption obligations.

The peasants helped themselves to the woodland they needed from the landlords' forests and invaded the landlords' pastures with their cattle and horses. They stopped paying for their rented land and, when tax-collection time came in autumn, they resolved not to co-operate. More spectacularly, they also broke into the empty manor houses, took from them whatever they thought had some value, and set the rest on fire. In the northern half of the country, the houses were mainly of timber construction; they burnt well. After bathing the night sky in the glow of 'rural illuminations', they would not leave much on the ground to show that there ever was a landlord. The purpose of the fires indeed was to 'smoke the landlord out', to make sure that he never returned to claim his landed property. By the end of 1907, incidents of destruction of landlords' houses occurred in 54 out of the 75 districts (*uezdy*) making up the 'central agricultural region'; in 30 out of the 51 middle-Volga districts; in 19 out of the 39 New Russia districts (the south-eastern steppes); and in seven out of the 17 lower-Volga districts. In the 'central industrial region', the northern provinces and the Urals (in regions where farming was not the main source of income for the peasants), these extreme expressions of peasant rebellion affected only a very small percentage of the districts. Less spectacular acts of rebellion, such as illicit wood-cutting, occurred with more uniform frequency throughout all parts of European Russia. Some form of rebellion was on record in 242 out of the total 335 districts of the European part of 'Russia proper' – 4507 officially recorded incidents altogether, 7165 if the Ukraine, Bielorussia, and Lithuania are included in the count.[3] Most action violated landlords' property rights or denied compliance with state tax demands. Violence against people was rare, although some landlords and state officials did lose their lives. More lives, however, were lost when the authorities resolved to send armed guards into the countryside to restore order, for the peasants in some districts formed their own armed contingents to defend their gains.

The peasants usually took their action after meetings of the commune, but some things, such as the non-payment of taxes, were often co-ordinated at the *volost'* level. Zemstvo and the urban activists were often invited to these meetings to explain what was going on in towns. The role of 'outside agitators' in the disturbances, however, tended subsequently to be exaggerated by both conservative politicians and Marxist revolutionaries, who did not believe peasants capable of independent action. In fact, that peasants were on the political stage as an autonomous force could be seen in 1906, when they took full part in the duma elections. The revolutionary parties that sought to assume leadership in the countryside advised a boycott because the tsar's October Manifesto of 1905 set up the duma as only a semi-parliamentary body, with advisory rather than legislative powers. But the peasants used their

---

3 Perrie, M. 1976: *The Agrarian Policy of the Russian Socialist-Revolutionary Party from its Origins through the Revolution of 1905–7.* Cambridge: Cambridge University Press, p. 121.

vote and sent to the duma a large contingent of elected spokesmen, who made their due impact as the Labourite Group (*trudoviki*). Already during 1905, even before the duma elections issue came up, the peasants became visible as an organized political force when many of them, some hundreds of thousands, joined the All-Russian Peasant Union. This organization's fast rise eclipsed the Socialist Revolutionary Party, which always remained thinly scattered among the peasant grass-roots, despite its ostensibly propeasant populist heritage. The union activists included people of the zemstvo 'third element', such as teachers and agronomists; but the delegate composition at the union's national gathering in St Petersburg in November 1905, as well as the message of their resolutions, left no doubt that this organization was of the peasantry as well as for it.

The union resolutions and, later, of the duma Labourites, reflected peasant interest in a society in which land belongs to God and the right to use it to the people who work for their living on it. In contrast to the revolutionary groups of the intelligentsia, the rhetoric of the union and the duma Labourites was neither republican not atheist. However, it was not limited to expressing the right of labour to land: it also adapted the intelligentsia's notions of civil rights to the conditions in the countryside, in particular by calling for a democratization of rural administration which would do away with the plenipotentiary powers of the land captains and the nobles' hegemony in the zemstvos. Many of the resolutions also supported the intelligentsia revolutionaries' and liberals' aspirations in matters such as universal suffrage, the abolition of the death penalty, and more investment in education. Some of the union resolutions indicated that the peasant activists were drawn mainly from the younger age-groups – for example, the demand that commune decision-making should not be restricted to heads of households. Another recurrent feature of the resolutions' rhetoric was similar to the resolutions produced by urban workers in their gatherings; a generalized grievance against authority holders who were haughty, rude, arbitrary, and, above all, disrespectful towards ordinary people on whose labour they were parasitic. This reflected a crisis of authority which was in some ways more immediate and personalized than the structural crises articulated by the intelligentsia's liberal or socialist ideologies.

In keeping with the folktale motifs of popular monarchism, in which the tsar was on the side of the peasants against corrupt middle-authority figures, the rebellious actions that took place in the villages in 1905 were often started by false rumours about the tsar intending to give the noble lands to the peasantry. Interestingly, the actions that took place in the following two years tended to be preceded by rumours about the duma's decisions rather than the tsar's. In fact, such rumours came close to becoming true in the winter of 1905–6, when minister Witte pressed the government and the tsar to legislate a compulsory purchase of noble lands for reassignment to the peasantry. In the event, the tsar did not take Witte's advice, preferring instead the argument that such a land redistribution would undermine the institution of private property as well as encourage further anarchic pressures on the rural authorities. Nevertheless, the peasant rebellions paid off in other respects. The redemption payments for allotment land were abolished and, throughout 1906–8, the government compensated peasants for poor harvests by interest-free loans the repayment of which, unlike the repayment of the relief measures in the 1890s, it subsequently failed to enforce. In addition, the unrest in the countryside prompted the noble landowners *en masse* to sell their lands voluntarily, which the peasants were helped to buy by the government who set up a peasant bank especially for that purpose.

Whereas in the towns the revolution of 1905 was effectively diffused by the constitutionalist concessions offered by the tsar's October Manifesto, peasant direct action peaked again in the summer of 1906 and, to a lesser extent, again in the summer of 1907. The peasants in uniform on the whole remained loyal to the army which, together with the police and the newly established rural guards, eventually managed to restore a semblance of state authority in both town and country. In 1905 the Minister of the Interior, Durnovo, urged one of the provincial governors to 'take the sternest measures to bring the disorders to an end; it is a useful thing to wipe the rebellious village off the face of the earth, and to exterminate the rebels themselves without mercy, by force of arms'.[4] This sort of extremist advice was, on the whole, not taken up by the commanders of the punitive detachments, although they did impose extraordinary martial law measures in many rural districts. In 1905–8, the numbers of peasants who were executed or shot in action could be counted in thousands, and the numbers sent into Siberian exile perhaps in tens of thousands – a harsh repression, though not one on an overwhelming scale considering that the numbers of peasants who took part in the disturbances could be counted in millions. This did not mean that life in the countryside reverted to the picture of traditional rural backwaters: the government itself was trying to make sure that the Russian peasantry would be never the same again, by starting the most ambitious campaign of rural reform since the 1860s.

The Years of the Stolypin Reforms, 1906–13

The reforms that bear the name of the man who occupied the newly created office of prime minister, from 1906 until his death by an assassin's bullet in 1911, started officially with the issue of new laws and decrees in the autumn of 1906. Their start, perhaps, was speeded up by the revolutionary turn of events in the preceding year. However, a government reformist campaign on the peasantry had been brewing for decades, and in a tangible bureaucratic form at least since 1902 – the year in which the Ministries of the Interior, Agriculture, and Finance were brought together in high-powered joint committees set up especially for the purpose of instigating a radical agrarian reform.

The reformist ideas circulating through government bureaux reflected three types of respectable, radical preoccupation. First, there was the notion that all citizens should be subject to the same set of coherent, codified, and universally applicable laws: as long as the peasantry had its affairs regulated by mere customary laws and the archaic powers of communal assemblies, the majority

---

4 Quoted in Robinson, G. T. 1961: *Rural Russia under the Old Regime*. New York: Macmillan, p. 189.

of the population was living in a subcitizen status and a liberating legal reform
was essential. The second stream of ideas was a corollary of the first: advancing
the peasant to modern citizen status required that his rights to till or not till his
land be enshrined in legal forms of individual ownership. It was thought that
private property laws were needed to ensure both a stable political system and
the peasant's ability to modernize farming. Thirdly, it was thought that the
modernization of farming would be possible only if it took place on
consolidated, enclosed lands rather than on scattered strips. To educated
modern minds, a countryside of interlocking narrow strips of cultivated land
equalled medieval backwardness, while a countryside of large squares of land,
where each square was an individual productive unit under unfettered
ownership and management, meant technological innovation and economic
progress.

It is worth noting that this was a matter of modernist belief, first articulated
as a doctrine of agrarian progress in eighteenth century France, and not a
matter of empirical evidence. In fact, some Russian repartitional communes
entered the twentieth century by switching from three-field to four-field
rotation (the fourth field usually being animal fodder crops), by introducing
new industrial crops, improving irrigation, and bringing fertilizers into use,
etc. The communes did not rush into experimentation with new farming
methods but, if they decided to adopt something new, implementation would
be immediate on a village-wide scale. That each household farmed on
scattered strips did not mean that labour time was wasted in walking the
distance between them, as the agrarian economists thought, because the work
took place on different strips consecutively, not at the same time. In addition,
the narrowness of individual strips presented no physical impediment to
modern machinery if the farmers on neighbouring strips agreed to make joint
use of it. But the urban experts did not want the agrarian progress to depend
on such *ad hoc* arrangements between the tillers of narrow strips; agrarian
progress, they thought, was the application of science such as could properly
take place only on consolidated and enclosed fields. The shape of the future
was thought to be the *khutor*, the enclosed family farm where both household
premises and the fields were on the same large patch of consolidated land or,
failing that, at least the *otrub*, where the household premises remained in the
village but the arable land belonging to the family was consolidated and enclosed.

The decrees inaugurated in 1906 set up land settlement commissions at the
district (*uezd*) and provincial (*guberniya*) levels, gave the head of a household
the right to register the household's allotment lands as private property, and
the right to request of the commune that his strips of land be exchanged for
other strips to form a consolidated landholding. The decrees also enabled
comprehensive land consolidation to take place in one fell swoop across the
whole village if two-thirds of the households requested it. Land consolidation
projects were thus to be initiated either by an individual household that
registered its lands as private property, or by the villages acting on the basis of
majority consensus; the land captains and the land settlement commissions
would decide whether the projects should go ahead, the commissions providing
the surveyors and other technical assistants necessary for taking each project from
the initial negotiations through to the marking out of boundaries and the
registration of new landholdings with the provincial surveyor's office. The

commissions were also empowered to disburse grants to individual households to meet the expense of moving out of the village into a *khutor*. The peasant bank was also to assist the process of new land settlement by lending money to peasants for the purchase of ex-gentry land in consolidated parcels.

Some limitations on the rights of private ownership in land were never lifted. Peasants were not allowed to sell their household plots to members of other social estates, and financial institutions remained banned from issuing mortgage loans against ex-allotment land, even if its holder had registered it as his private property. The greatest fetter on private property rights, however, became the Stolypin reform itself, or rather the land consolidation aspect of it. If an individual peasant succeeded in getting the land captain and the land settlement commission to approve his proposal for creating a consolidated landholding for his household, the project required other villagers to exchange their strips, regardless of whether or not they had registered them as private property. To make the matter even more complicated and ambiguous from the point of view of private property rights, some of the strips that had to be exchanged in the course of consolidation projects were in fact not ex-allotment lands but strips purchased by individuals as additional land from noble landowners or the peasant bank. Moreover, if another individual or group subsequently had another consolidation project approved, some of their neighbours' strips might be subjected to the mêlée of compulsory exchanges again. Property title, in other words, did not make a piece of land immune from involuntary reallocation. It was the same when the village decided to engage in a comprehensive reorganization of landholdings by a majority vote – the minority had to comply regardless of whether they thought themselves to be the legal owners of their strips. Nobody was supposed to lose out overall in these exchanges, unlike in previous communal reparations, but we have seen that the equivalence of these exchanges was easier for the surveyor to believe in than for the peasants. In addition, it is possible that some of the village-initiated projects did hide within them an element of redistributive intent as well as the lauded desire to farm in large consolidated squares instead of in narrow, scattered, and interlocking strips.

At the beginning of the reforms, the land captains played a key role in spreading information about the new laws as well as in approving peasants' land-consolidating proposals because, being Ministry of the Interior officials in charge of maintaining peace in the countryside, they tended to discourage initiatives that threatened to cause too much trouble and strife. The law gave them the power to reject proposals on the grounds that they were not in harmony with wider interests, or to let projects proceed only as and when a workable degree of consensus was achieved among the villagers involved. However, the land captains' as well as the land settlement commissions' performance was assessed to some extent by the number of consolidation projects that were proposed, approved, and implemented. The annual numbers of projects in the pipeline duly rose to hundreds of thousands.

Only a minority of the projects, however, were initiated by individual households. The majority were initiated by villages or by groups of households, and comparatively few in Russia proper resulted in the establishment of fully enclosed individual farms. In the first instance, many of the village-initiated projects involved the straightening out of boundaries with the fields belonging to neighbouring villages. Otherwise, consolidation was only partial, resulting in each household farming a handful of scattered, chunky oblongs instead of dozens of scattered narrow strips. The group-initiated projects sometimes involved not the creation of a consolidated square of land for each household of the petitioning group but a parcel of land for the group as a whole, which the individual members proceeded to subdivide among themselves in the traditional manner of open-field interstripped farming. Far from a streamlined progression from the traditional repartitional commune to the fully enclosed yeoman's *khutor*, the projects reflected a wide variety of practical compromises between the authorities and the peasants. Perhaps the peasants responded to the 1906 laws by submitting village-level or group projects to preclude dissenting individuals from disrupting their neighbourhoods by their petitions for consolidation. And the authorities accepted the collectively proposed projects even if they fell short of the fully-fledged *khutor* ideal, because implementing these projects would not require them to protect independent-minded peasants from the wrath of aggrieved neighbours.

By 1910, the role of the land settlement commissions in the land reforms increased at the expense of the peasant bank and the land captains and, within the commissions, the role of surveyors and agrarian experts increased at the expense of gentry and government officials. From the state side, the thrust of the reform became distinctly technocratic, oriented to achieving land reorganization such as was deemed by the experts to be helpful for the introduction of new farming methods. The original aim of institutionalizing the legal rights of private property among the peasantry was eclipsed by the goals of physical land consolidation.

New decrees issued in 1910–11 speeded up the process. Comprehensive village-wide land reorganization could henceforth be initiated at the request of a simple majority of households in non-communal villages, and any village that had not carried out a general repartition of land in the previous 24 years was now regarded as non-communal. In communal as well as non-communal villages, partial reorganizations imposing new land settlement on unwilling neighbours could be initiated by a mere one-fifth of the households. The new projects over-ruled any property rights: they subsumed privately bought, mortgaged, or rented strips as well as ex-allotment ones, and this time no veto powers were envisaged for the land captains if they thought that implementing a project might provoke too much controversy. The new decrees also put paid to the earlier ideas of entrepreneurial property owning by imposing a limit on the amount of ex-allotment land a household was allowed to have. The agrarian experts wanted to see a movement towards streamlined, efficient farms of medium size that could be operated by the households without recourse to using wage labour, and they wanted the farmers to form co-operatives for the buying of grain, fertilizer, and machinery; they were opposed to the capitalist spectre of *kulak*-labourer division in the countryside. The land settlement commissions assumed wider powers in modifying peasant project proposals and in settling disputes between peasants by ordering some cash compensation to be paid to project-injured parties. The peasants lost their right to appeal the commissions' decisions to the courts.

The peasants, however, did not lose their ability to persuade the commission experts that conditions in particular villages made desirable various types of land settlement, not just the fully enclosed and individualist *khutor* and *otrub*. And powerful though the land settlement commissions seemed to be, they were not able to bring projects to conclusion with any great speed. By the time the First World War put the land reforms on hold, a majority of the peasant households in European Russia were possibly involved in the projects that were still in the pipeline, but only one in ten already farmed a concentrated landholding and only one in a hundred set up a new home in a *khutor*.[5]

The Stolypin reforms made it easier for peasants to leave their villages for good by converting their allotment lands to private property and selling them to their neighbours. Peasants could also move more freely by virtue of no longer needing the permission from the heads of their households so that they could be issued with passports. When in town, peasants became subject to the same laws and courts as the rest of the urban population. But otherwise the legal differences between the social estate of the peasantry and the other social estates did not disappear. The Stolypin reforms failed in their original purpose of putting the legal rights of private ownership into the heart of the farmland economy. The main force of the reforms became increasingly focused on the physical consolidation of individual farm landholdings, which ran counter to any legal property rights that might have been vested in the various bits of interstripped land. The land consolidation projects tended to be initiated by village communes or by groups of households rather than by strongly individualist peasants wishing to separate their farms from their villages. They bore the stamp of compromise between village politics and the urban visions of efficient farming yeomanry.

There was another phenomenon besides Stolypin reforms that, by all accounts, became prominent in Russian rural life during the prewar decade: hooliganism. In the cities, hooliganism was acknowledged by a consensus of policemen, criminologists, and lawyers as nothing new. After 1905, however, the experts were worried about what seemed to them a sweeping rise of the phenomenon in the villages. The Ministry of the Interior set up a special commission to report on the subject in 1913, and much of the learned discussion at a national congress of criminologists in the following year grappled in particular with rural hooliganism. Landowners publicly worried about it in their conferences, the duma heard speeches about it, and, already in 1910, police officials recorded their opinion that hooliganism presented a graver threat in the countryside than peasant rebellion.

By 'hooliganism' was meant a wide range of acts – from petty theft and disturbances of the peace to rape, arson, and murder – that were committed with no apparent motive or prior organization by groups of rowdy young men who liked a drink. It was associated in particular with the villages of Russia proper and had a number of special characteristics. First, the victims were mainly people who looked educated, wealthy, or of noble birth, and people such as the village clergy. Peasants in *khutory* also seemed to be the regular butt of the rowdies' sense of humour, although it is difficult to say whether they were vulnerable because of their physical isolation from potential help or because the process of land consolidation had made them generally unpopular

---

5 Willetts, H. T., 'The agrarian problem'. in Katkov, *Russia Enters*.

and fair game. Secondly, the rural hooligans enjoyed a measure of protection from their neighbours, who appeared to be generally unwilling to inform on them, especially if the victims were outsiders to the village community. Thirdly, the hooligans by most accounts seemed to come especially from the ranks of the young men of the village who spent a part of their year away in industry as seasonal labourers. Their daredevil escapades, it seemed, were often performed as a display of urban sophistication, although they were apparently performed in the villages more often than in the towns. Finally, rural hooliganism went largely unpunished because police were still extremely thin on the rural ground and, despite their scarcity value, they were unpopular with the locals. Peace and quiet was mostly enforced by the village officials, which they achieved by increasing the number of arrests and fines from 90 000 to 132 000 between 1910 and 1913. Nevertheless, according to the experts this was just the small tip of an iceberg, for the rural officials were reluctant to apprehend errant young men who enjoyed a measure of loyalty from their kith and kin.[6]

The War Years, 1914–17

In the summer of 1914, 3.9 million men were called up to the army to fight under the Russian flag in the First World War, and the number of draftees rose to 15 million by 1917. The war effort also requisitioned some 20 per cent of horses from the village economy, and a commensurate proportion of carts. Interestingly enough, this massive withdrawal of labour power and other resources from the agricultural economy did not result in a substantial decline in grain production during the war years. By 1917, the total sown area dropped to 91.5 per cent of what it had been in the peak production year of 1913, and the crop was almost 90 per cent of the 1909–13 average.[7] Little is known about the ways in which the depleted peasantry continued to keep production at levels that should have been sufficient to feed the bourgeoning army and war industry. What is clear, however, is that the overall relationship between the food producers and food consumers was marked by uncertainties on both sides and increasingly fraught as the war years went by.

The responsibility for grain procurement was given to the Ministry of Agriculture and, at the ground level, to the same surveyors and agronomists that had constituted the activist corps of the Stolypin land settlement commissions. The agrarian specialists involved themselves in the new work quite willingly because, like the land consolidation movement, the grain procurement responsibilities granted them an opportunity to exert influence on the peasantry in the name of science and modernization. Also, their new tasks made them exempt from serving in the army at the front. Their visionary

---

6 Weissman, N. B. 1978: 'Rural crime in tsarist Russia: the question of hooliganism, 1905–1914'. *Slavic Review*, xxvii, p. 233. I have rounded up the figures reported here to the nearest 1000.

7 Yaney, G. 1982: *The Urge to Mobilize: Agrarian Reform in Russia, 1861–1930*. Urbana, Ill: University of Illinois Press, p. 409.

sight was set on the spectre of creating a nation-wide system of production and distribution that would benefit everyone by its rational efficiency in the peaceful long term, as well as meet the immediate wartime needs of army and industry. In practice, however, there was nothing to stop army colonels from buying supplies for their regiments in an *ad hoc* fashion during the first year of the war. Since nobody believed that an orderly system of procurement and distribution would be set up in time to assure the supplies necessary for the immediate needs of the newly mobilized soldiers and defence industry workers, everyone who was in the position to do so took care to build up stocks for his own little sub-empire of the war machine. The sabre-rattling purchasers of grain had the cash to outbid each other, grain prices went up, and the rising prices encouraged further buying and hoarding. This created local shortages that confirmed initial fears of famine and generated suspicions that the nation's fate was falling into the hands of unscrupulous speculators.

After the first year of the war, the tsar restricted direct military participation in grain procurement to the war-front zones. In the interior, grain procurement was henceforth to be organized by the surveyors and agronomists working under the centralized direction of the Ministry of Agriculture. The enforcement of centralized authority in the countryside, however, was undermined by the tsar's decision to take personal command of military operations at the front. His absence from Petrograd (the capital's name had been Russified when the war began) meant that he could no longer arbitrate when ministerial bureaux produced conflicting policies. The result was a flow of ministerial edicts concerning grain prices, financial subsidies, and the selling of grain across provincial boundaries, etc., which lacked the consistency of a single strategy. The administrative powers of grain procurement in effect devolved on the surveyors and agronomists, who were neither willing nor able to use any strict enforcement measures against the peasantry. The specialists tried to develop a system of surveying grain-producing capacities while making sure that peasants sowed and cultivated their lands to capacity, despite the different degrees to which individual households were affected by the loss of labour to the war effort, and they tried to operate a system of grain purchases according to a plan of local state-procurement quotas. In continuation of their favoured policy of prewar years, they liked to encourage farmers to set up credit co-operatives that would act as the main purchasing agents *vis-à-vis* individual producers. But they did not succeed in fulfilling the procurement quotas, which did little in the way of calming the urban and military fears of famine. In their dealings with the peasants, the specialists were handicapped by the facts of monetary inflation and the decline in the availability of urban-produced goods that the peasants might want to buy for their cash.

But the prices and conditions under which the state wanted to buy its grain were not the only source of uncertainty in the villages. It is not clear how or whether the specialists tried to persuade households to redistribute their lands to make sure that the families most depleted by military call-ups did not leave a substantial portion of their allotments uncultivated. If such a process did take place, it was probably done with the help of restoring communal powers and land repartition at the expense of the land settlement and the attribution of private property titles such as had been achieved under the Stolypin reforms. But even if the prewar achievements of the land settlement commissions remained unaffected by the exigencies of wartime economy, any uncertainties about the rights of land use must have been made worse for two other reasons. First, in 1915, when the Germans occupied the western provinces of the empire and looked poised to further their advance eastwards, the tsar gave his backing to a strategy of scorched-earth retreat to deny grain to the enemy, which would involve a large-scale evacuation of the peasantry from the scorched areas to the regions further east. Secondly, right at the beginning of the war, the generals promised to reward the best soldiers with new land when peace broke out: a widespread rumour arose that the state would give new land to all soldiers on their return from active service. The Stolypin reforms had never progressed as far as to sort out the claims that might be made on communal land by people who had been absent from their villages for a time but unofficially remained members of their peasant communities. Now there were also rumours that new claims on village lands might be made by refugees from the western regions and by demobilized soldiers.

After the abdication of the tsar in February 1917, the specialists continued their procurement work under the auspices of a new Ministry of Food Supplies. The provisional government also set up a new central agency for land settlement. Some of the specialists thus continued work as procurement plenipotentiaries while others returned to the longer-term tasks of land reform. But the procurement work was becoming even more difficult than it ever had been. The thousands of purchasing co-operatives the specialists had helped to set up dissolved as peasants turned their backs on state-organized grain procurement and on tax and debt obligations in general. As regards the new land settlement committees, there is no evidence that they accomplished anything during the revolutionary year. Some of the specialists tried to preserve their credibility with the peasants by joining them in new repartitions and in the taking of land from neighbouring private estates. Some specialists were chased away and many lay low in their district offices, leaving the peasants to sort out their land among themselves for the time being. The powers of the local zemstvos, the land captains, and the state procurement agencies collapsed while the administration of the countryside was taken over by peasant assemblies – the village communes and the *volost'* and district soviets.

The Years of the Civil War, 1917–21

One thing the peasant assemblies did in 1917–18 was to organize and seek legitimacy for the takeover by peasant communes of land belonging to private estates and the state. This could not have amounted to a substantial addition of plough land to peasant holdings because about 90 per cent of the total arable land was already under peasant cultivation by 1916. The gentry and the state-owned estates were mainly woodlands, meadows, and fallows. But the peasants had a strong interest in free access to these resources – they had always resented having to pay someone for timber that was grown by nature and felled by themselves, or for letting their cattle graze in the meadows. When the Bolsheviks came into government in the autumn of 1917 and passed their decree on the nationalization of all land, the peasants interpreted it as confirming the rights of their communes to the meadows and woodlands in their vicinity. Some of the business transacted by the rural soviets during the revolutionary period concerned the division of these rights between neighbouring villages. The peasants also stopped paying rents and mortgages for the arable land they had acquired from the neighbouring gentry and the peasant bank and, in this as well, they felt vindicated by the land nationalization decree. The months of unfettered peasant rule in the countryside also saw some looting of gentry property and some violence against unpopular state administrators, but the evidence of these incidents would hardly justify the description of what happened in the rural Russia as a violent rising of the land-hungry poor against the landowning gentry and capitalist farmers. Some 100 000 rural gentry families were still resident in the countryside and farming in the mid-1920s.[8] Many of them had to give up some of their land, cattle, and other resources to their peasant neighbours during the revolutionary year, but the amount of property that was left to them was usually based on fairly generous calculations as to what a family needed to make a decent living from farming by its own labours. It is doubtful that violent looting and burning of gentry property approached anything like the scale of the disturbances in 1905–6.

It has been claimed by many historians that the Russian peasantry took advantage of the breakdown of state administration in the countryside to sweep away the Stolypin land reforms and resurrect with a vengeance the ancient ways of open-field, interstripped farming under repartitional communes. 'Black repartition' is a term often used to describe this movement, which is interpreted as a practical expression of a belief that land belongs equally to all those capable and willing to till it. A dose of caution is needed here. The bulk of the evidence from the revolutionary period consists of pronouncements by non-peasant politicians and revolutionaries about what the peasantry believed, wanted, and did. The evidence of what the peasants actually did with their lands, and why, is sporadic, and it points in various directions. A great deal of repartitioning of land did take place in the villages, and much of this included strips and consolidated fields to which private ownership titles had been issued during the Stolypin years. But we have seen that the institution of private ownership had been a prime ambition of the reforms only in their beginnings and not in the way the reforms were implemented by the land settlement commissions; the reforms became a movement of land consolidation in the interest of farming efficiency rather than in the interests of privatization, and land consolidation took various forms besides the setting-up of fully enclosed farms.

The fact that in 1917–21 many repartitions included supposedly privately owned parcels of land does not in itself testify to a rejection of the Stolypin reforms, for the Stolypin projects had been doing that as well. Some of the repartitions that took place in 1917 and after, including ones that were hailed by some revolutionary politicians as signs of a spontaneous movement towards

8 Channon, J. 1987: 'Tsarist landowners after the revolution'. *Soviet Studies*, xxxix, 4, p. 584.

farming co-operatives, looked like the group settlement projects that had been started before the war. Some of the post-1917 village repartitions were aimed at switching from three-field to four-field crop rotation – again something that had started to be introduced in many localities under the auspices of the land settlement agronomists during the pre-war years. Interestingly, the army of surveyors and agronomists that used to work for the Stolypin land settlement commissions became employed by the new People's Commissariat for Agriculture, which set up local land settlement committees and, in 1919, armed itself with land reform legislation that bore a striking resemblance to the laws of 1910–11. This enabled a comprehensive land consolidation project to be started by a simple majority of the village assembly, and gave minorities the right to separate their lands from the rest of the village even if this required changes in the village's pattern of landholding. The commissariat soon reported a shortage of qualified surveyors for this work; but no surveyors at all would have been needed by peasants interested only in the sort of repartitions that had been done in the villages for centuries without any professional help.

Many of the repartitions that took place in 1917–21 did end up in households farming a proliferation of very narrow strips; many of the peasants who had moved out of the village into enclosed farms moved back into the village and allowed their enclosed lands to become a part of the communally partitioned fields again; and in many villages readjustments to the strips and their distribution were done almost on a year-by-year basis during the civil war period. But it is not necessary to assume that the peasants in these villages were motivated by die-hard enthusiasm for repartitional commune traditions, which in any case never included frequent repartitions. Their actions can be more plausibly explained by immediate circumstances. These were the years in which the urban economy collapsed and drove millions of town inhabitants to the rural countryside in search of survival. The capital cities lost half of their populations to the villages during the civil war years. In 1917–18, the army also demobilized its millions, and they were often stranded in the middle of nowhere by a railway system that was breaking down along with the rest of the industrial sector and as bridges and tracks were blown up by the combat regiments of the civil war. Hundreds of thousands of destitute people, many of them armed, set up camp in the vicinity of the railway tracks, looking for the means to keep body and soul together. The increasingly desperate Soviet state itself organized marauding bands to requisition grain for the cities, in competition with the civil war combatants who raided villages for horses as well as food. These were not circumstances in which even the sturdiest of yeoman farmers could hope to cultivate their isolated enclosed *khutor* without being plundered into starvation. Safety, such as it was, was living in the village and working on interstripped fields in a huddle with one's farming neighbours. Farming efficiency was not important in any case, because surplus grain would be taken away by a procurement gang of one sort or another.

The *khutor* farmers returned to their villages, and so did long-lost urban cousins and soldier sons. The peasant assemblies spent much time deliberating which returnees constituted compelling reasons for the households that received them to be given extra allotments of land. The assemblies no longer consisted of heads of households; many of the returning soldiers were armed with weapons as well as revolutionary ideas about the nature of freedom and democracy. The communal assemblies became one-man-one-vote institutions (and they would be soon asked by state legislation to extend suffrage to women as well). A great deal of positive decisions about the returnees land claims naturally meant more repartitions. As regards the people in the migrant encampments, the villagers tried to stave off their claims. But many of these people were also armed with guns and the alleged backing from the new powers-that-be, and they had the time to attend the assemblies of the *volost'* and district soviets. Often a compromise was reached with the villages. The villages would let the immigrants take some of the arable and fallow lands that had recently been taken away from nearby estates, or some of the more distant village lands. Some of the new settlements would soon try to gain aid from the new state by declaring themselves to be state farms or socialist communes.

Not all the immigrants, it should be said, forced new agreements to be made about land boundaries and distribution. Many had useful industrial craft skills which could be put to good use, as the supplies of the things the peasants needed from the factories dried up. They set up shop in the rural areas and produced things that could be bartered with the peasantry for food and raw material. This, of course, did not help the state's efforts to requisition grain – the peasants bartered more of their supplies within the local rural economy, and they were diversifying what they grew to provide not just surplus grain but also other things that could be consumed or used as raw material for rural industries, such as potatoes, millet, flax, sugar beet, sunflower oil, and tobacco. These switches towards rural self-sufficiency also occasioned some reorganizations of landholdings. In sum, the resurgence in land repartitional activities among the villagers were caused not so much by the Russian peasants' traditional preference for the ways of the egalitarian repartitional commune but by the exigencies of subsistence in a context of a collapsing urban economy, an influx of urban population into the rural areas, and visitations by grain-requisitioning gangs.

Grain requisitioning was at the core of the relationships between the peasant village and the outside world. In 1917, the agronomists working for the Commissariat of the Food Supplies were supposed to operate the state's monopoly over grain trade. But they were ineffective, for the roubles payable to the peasants for grain were fast losing their value – the provisional government was printing too many of them while the things the peasants could buy were fast disappearing from the market. A more effective means whereby food was conveyed from the villages to the cities came in the form of the bagman – the thousands of urban men who crowded into rural-bound trains with bags filled with things that could be exchanged for grain. They remained important in the civilization-sustaining exchange between town and country throughout the civil war years, despite the repeated attempts by government authorities to ban the 'speculators', but not as important as the gangs of men with swords and guns were during 1918–21. Some of them were just desperadoes raiding the rural grain stores for their own benefit, while the others were soldiers procuring for their regiments. An increasing number were workers sent by the factories to supply the works canteens. The main body of the requisitioning gangs, however, quickly became constituted by urban workers and demobilized soldiers enforcing the state monopoly over grain surpluses under the auspices of the People's Commissariat for Supplies. There were tens of thousands of them, roaming the grain-producing regions in armed detachments of 20 to 30 men. Since they were allowed to keep one half of any hidden stocks of grain they found for themselves, there was no shortage of volunteers for the job.

The gun-point methods of food procurement were not a Bolshevik invention. Many an officer of the tsarist army supplied his regiment by these means in the panic-stricken year of 1915, and the provisional government also resorted to forced seizures of grain hoardes in the summer of 1917, when the pacific methods of state officials appeared to be failing. The first incidents of violent retaliation by the peasant villages against armed procurement agents occurred while the provisional government was still in office. The Bolsheviks inherited an urban economy that was already on a fast slide towards calamity, and they were not the only politicians who were short of ideas for a peaceful settlement to the food-supply problem. What they were not short of were hungry workers and ex-soldiers with guns and, in the circumstances, it probably seemed a constructive idea to organize them into a state agency of procurement rather than let them join the ranks of anarchic banditry.

Needless to say, the peasants impeded the raid gangs brandishing paper warrants in the same way as they defended their property against other marauders: they pleaded that they were already plundered clean, hid their stocks, led the visitors by the nose as long as they could, delayed the grain-collecting process by revealing only unthreshed stocks, and occasionally ambushed the visitors to give them the lynching treatment traditionally administered to horse thieves. The Bolshevik leaders soon understood that the commissariat gangs (*otriadniki*) needed some rural-based organization to provide them with local support. Peasant resistance, they proclaimed in the summer of 1918, was happening because the village communes and *volost'* soviets were kulak-dominated institutions. The revolution had to foment the class struggle in the countryside, which it would henceforth do by working with the poor landless peasants. The established village economy in most grain-producing areas did not have many landless peasants, but there were the new migrants from the cities and the ex-soldiers in their shanty encampments whom the village communes were slow to welcome with bread and land. They were the 'landless and poor peasants' from whose ranks the *otriadniki* recruited local committees of poor peasants (*kombedy*). Many of the *otriadniki* themselves settled in the rural localities to form the corps of the *kombedy*. Thus was formed a rural embryonic organization of the new state power. Although occasionally they were able to take advantage of village feuds, on the whole they did not succeed in penetrating the peasant communes. But they established themselves as an armed organization in the large villages and small rural towns that were the seats of *volost'* and district soviets. In 1919 they organized new elections to the local soviets and duly installed themselves as the full-time executives of the district soviets.

The formation of the *kombedy* in the summer of 1918 and of the new district soviets in the following year marked the end of peasant self-administration that had come into being in the winter of 1917–18. However, relating the story in this way makes the developments in rural administration seem orderly and uniform when in fact they were not. The grain requisitioning was never anything other than an anarchic chaos of plunder and defence of the peasant economy, which was complicated further by the attempts of provincial soviets to stop the export of requisitioned grain from their areas. In addition, large areas of rural Russia were near the shifting front lines of the civil war, successively falling under the military control of different Red and White commanders; and in 1920–1, many districts were also under the intermittent control of the Greens – the numerous bands of armed peasants of whom some were little more than bandits while others had a political programme aimed against the Reds as well as the Whites. Not surprisingly, peasant armed uprisings reached the largest scale in the grain-producing regions which saw the worst of the plunder by the civil war armies and the state's requisitioning gangs: the central black-earth region, Tambov province, and the mid-Volga.

Perhaps some caution should be applied to the conventional wisdom that accords the eventual success of the Red Army in the civil war to the peasantry supporting it in preference to the Whites. Some of the White generals were strongly monarchist and of the landowning gentry; their attempts to restore the prerevolutionary order in the zones they occupied presumably did little for their popularity among the peasants. Others, however, fought under he banner of the provisional government and the right to power of the Constituent Assembly – the parliament that was duly elected in 1917 and dissolved by the Bolsheviks as soon as it met in January 1918. Besides, the Whites had only their battalions to feed by grain requisitioning, and their hinterland consisted of grain-surplus producing regions; they did not need to collect enough grain to feed the civilians in industrial areas and the cities as well. They were probably quite impatient and hamfisted in their ways of finding food, for they did not need to entertain thoughts about the economy's civil administration; logic suggests, however, that they had the need or opportunity to impose particularly exploitative visitations only on some peasant districts while leaving others alone. The requisitioning gangs working for the Bolshevik state, on the other hand, were supposed to collect enough grain to feed not only the Red army but also the civilian inhabitants of the capital cities and the normally grain-importing areas of the central industrial region and the north, and they had to collect it from a much reduced grain-surplus zone – the central black earth and mid-Volga because the south east, Siberia, and the Ukraine were behind enemy lines. The Red Army managed to recruit its soldiers from the rural areas as well as the capital cities, but this was in all probability due less to the appeal of their propaganda than the promise of full stomachs to the migrants in the shanty towns near the rural railway stations. As for village recruits, many of them deserted as soon as their battalions started to move further afield, or when the agricultural season called them back home. Besides, some of the recruiting was done simply at gun point.

By 1921, the Bolshevik grain-requisitioning campaigns were even extended to the grain-importing regions around Moscow and Petrograd, where few peasants ever produced more grain than the amount needed for their own consumption. In the central black earth and the mid-Volga, the relationship between the peasants and the state grain collectors was an affair of unremitting bitterness. Here it should be noted that the pressure from the capital-city masters on the requisitioners was becoming increasingly desperate, as the capital cities were increasingly short of bread, but this was not simply because the peasants were successful in hiding their stocks. The infrastructure – the flour mills and, mainly, the railways – was crumbling. The peasants had to queue for days to deliver their grain to the state collection points, and much of what they delivered stuck somewhere along the chain and, if it was not stolen, it went to rot.

In the provinces of the Volga, a drought combined with the increasing violence and determination of the requisitioning agents to produce an epic-scale famine in 1920–2. In Petrograd and the other capital cities, periods of high mortality associated with an inadequate diet had been evident since 1919; that is why the requisitioning was becoming desperate. After dry weather had caused a thin harvest in 1920, the requistioners, fired by the conviction that the kulaks were hiding the precious stuff, collected even much of the grain that the peasants needed to feed themselves and their animals and the grain they needed to sow for next year. Consequently, the harvest was bad again in 1921 while animal produce plummeted. The government owned up to the famine and appealed to the West for aid in the summer of 1921. By the time the American relief agency set up the delivery of aid grain to the provinces of the Volga, they found death on a mass scale, from simple starvation as well as epidemics of infectious disease to which starving people had no resistance. They also found direct evidence of people who tried to buy their time by resorting to cannibalism.

It has been estimated that the Russian empire lost population of about 16 million people to premature death during 1914–22. About two million soldiers died in action on the battlefields of the First World War, and to these military casualties should, in all probability, be added the number of soldiers who were killed by infectious disease in the crowded conditions of prisoner-of-war camps in Germany, Austria, and Turkey. This fate also undoubtedly befell some of the civilians who were displaced by the war into equally crowded refugee camps. The civilian population in the Russian hinterland, however, suffered only its normal prewar mortality rate during the First World War. The majority of the aforementioned 16 million premature deaths, therefore, must have occurred during 1918–22.[9] The military engagements of the civil war were on a small scale compared to those of the First World War, and it is unlikely that they claimed as many battlefield casualties. It was the civilian population that bore the brunt of untimely deaths during the civil war. Famine was the main cause, and peasants constituted the majority of its casualties.

The Years of the New Economic Policy, 1921–8

While the armed forces of the new state were mopping up the Green 'bandits', and just after they quelled the highly symbolic mutiny of the sailors in the island fortress of Kronstadt opposite the shores of the capital city, the tenth congress of the Bolshevik Party inaugurated the New Economic Policy. There were to be no more forced requisitions. Instead, the peasants were obliged to

---

9 Wheatcroft, S. 1981: *Famine and Factors Affecting Mortality in the USSR: The Demographic Crises of 1914–22 and 1930–33*. Birmingham: University of Birmingham, Centre for Russian and East European Studies, SIPS 20.

pay tax (in grain at first and in cash from 1924 on) and were free to sell the rest of their surplus food in open markets.

The terms of the new peace also returned to peasant villages a substantial measure of administrative autonomy under the guise of a dual power between the rural soviets and communal assemblies. The communal assemblies were recognized by the Russian Republic land law of 1922 as 'land societies,' whose jurisdiction extended over all matters of village land organization. Rural soviets were to look after all other matters of public administration. But the rural soviets covered larger territories than the communes and, their budget allocations from central government being very small, their activities were dependent on the communal assemblies' power to raise taxes for the financing of local services and projects. The new rural soviets had annual elections of deputies, which were subject to the state's rules: universal suffrage but no vote for priests, policemen, landowners, and kulaks of the old regime. They also had full-time officials on their executive committees, who were answerable to their superiors up the lines of the soviet government command structure and to the committees of the Bolshevik Party. But the party was very small in rural Russia and virtually non-existent below the level of the *volost'* towns. Deputies of the soviets attended their meetings relatively infrequently, and then only to listen to proclamations of state policies on a broad variety of subjects and to rubber stamp the practical decisions of the 'land societies'. The land societies, on the other hand, met often, although attendance rates were low too, which suggested the old practice of communal assemblies according to which only heads of households were expected to attend. The main practical preoccupation of the soviet executives was to collect state taxes for the government, which they did, like the officials of the tsarist government before them, by negotiating with the communal assemblies.

The repartitional commune and the family household thus remained the prime institutions of peasant life. This did not mean, however, that village life sank back into some sort of timeless traditionalism. In fact the peasants were busy interacting with the agronomists and land surveyors employed by the Commissariat of Agriculture. The number of specialists working in the countryside rose from about 7000 to 17 000 in the course of the 1920s, the later figure exceeding the height of specialist presence in the countryside during the Stolypin reforms.[10] They paid lip-service to Bolshevik desires for collective farms while negotiating with the peasants whatever land consolidation measures seemed conducive to increasing farming efficiency in local conditions. Since the major variable in the specialists' theoretical thinking was still the distance a farmer had to travel in the course of cultivating his fields, the fully consolidated and enclosed *khutor* was still the theoretical ideal of an efficient farm. But the specialists were happy to compromise with local interests and realities just as they had been during the Stolypin reforms. In practice the group land settlement projects continued to be popular, taking groups of households out of their communes to form a consolidated and enclosed patch of land between them; the group was then free to farm their land either in the interstripped form of a new minicommune or to farm it

---

10 Yaney, *The Urge*, p. 538.

collectively in one piece or to divide it into individual consolidated farms – whatever seemed the most practical to them. Thus it was possible for the specialists to help set up individual *khutora* or *otruba* and report to the authorities the birth of a new co-operative farm. Unlike the Stolypin reforms, such consolidated farms could not be converted into private property, but it was understood that henceforth they would not fall under any repartitional projects of the original communes.

In some regions the most popular kind of land settlement was a transition from three-field to multifield crop rotation with the widening of individual strips. (Some influential politicians, including the Moscow party chief, Bauman, took this movement up as their particular banner of progress.) Many communes carried out land settlement projects which combined traditional interstripped farming with the collective cultivation of some of the fields, the proceeds from which were used to finance communal spending on further agricultural improvements, schools, welfare, etc. In fact the variety of land reorganization projects was immense and a testimony to the flexibility with which the agrarian specialists adapted their technical advice to the conditions of local economy and village politics. Overall the number of projects and land area covered by them substantially exceeded the land reform achievements of the Stolypin era. The projects were initiated either by peasant communes or by groups of peasants wishing to consolidate their lands out of their communes; the specialists could offer their services only when called upon to do so by the peasants.

The countryside was also changing in other respects. The average family size fell from 6.1 in 1917 to 5.1 in 1924 and 4.5 in 1929.[11] Birth rates, on the other hand, quickly went up to prewar levels during the 1920s. The falling average family size was therefore due to a combination (or either) of two things: more young adults of the households went to towns to look for work, and extended-family households tended to split sooner rather than later. Some of the land reorganization activities probably involved the traditional business of dividing household allotments. The specialists carried on advising against the creation of very small farming units but, on the other hand, as is discussed below, peasant families had every reason not to appear to be of above-average prosperity. The countryside also lost its 'landless proletariat', the urban folk and the ex-soldiers who left the cities during the civil war hunger years; they went back to the towns in the hope that the trade unions there would recognize them as workers entitled to be helped to find work. The countryside, in other words, was becoming less overpopulated by working-age adults while increasing in its population of children. Another numerical change was in the number of communes, which tripled from the prewar level of about 100 000. The splitting of large communes into smaller ones took place both during the civil war, when many of the returned soldiers set up separate communes rather than return under the authority of their fathers, and in the course of the group land settlement projects during the 1920s.

---

11 Shinn, W. T. jr 1987: *The Decline of the Russian Peasant Household*. New York: Preager, The Washington Papers, 124.

The year 1922 brought a very good harvest. The state authorities, however, were disappointed with the amount of grain that was finding its way into the state's storage depots from whence it could be exported. They party congress in 1923 was told of a 'scissors crisis' – that is, a crisis of procurement caused by grain prices being too low relative to the prices of industrial goods. The peasants preferred to hold on to their produce because they knew that the grain prices would eventually rise. How to close the blades of the scissors – in other words, bring the relative terms of trade between agricultural and industrial goods into a balance such as would motivate peasants to sell their produce in ever increasing quantities – would be the political-economic issue during the years that followed. The government tried to handle it by imposing price ceilings on industrial goods and state-purchased grain in various combinations. In 1925 the harvest was also good and this time grain prices were high relative to industrial prices, but again the peasants held on to some of their grain – because the low-priced consumer goods disappeared from the market before the peasants could buy them. Feeding the urban population was not a problem, for there was enough food on sale in the town markets. The problem was for the state to buy grain cheaply and in large quantities to trade it abroad for industrial investment goods. The resumption of industrialization, on which the party had decided at its conference in 1926, seemed to depend on the state's ability to export agrarian produce. The free-trading peasant seemed a fickle factor in the industrial development plans.

The academic branch of the agrarian specialists came under fire for being 'neopopulist' from younger scholars, who called themselves 'agrarian Marxists'. While the neopopulists believed that the peasantry was economically more or less homogeneous and concentrated their researches on helping the peasants and their communes to make their farming more productive, the Marxists thought they could detect the beginnings of a capitalist polarization between rich and poor in the countryside. The specialists, they thought, should be concentrating on helping the poor and 'middle' peasants form proper collective farms with large-scale fields and industrial production methods, instead of helping kulaks and the communes dominated by them to form individual farms under the guise of co-operatives. The specialists' practice of working with the peasant communes in disregard of the incipient class structure reflected the old populist belief that the Russian peasant commune, however backward, could be a harbinger of a socialist future. But the path to a real socialist future lay in forming collective farms with advanced technology and division of labour, which would have to assert themselves against the peasant communes, for they would never grow out of them.

Many Bolshevik politicians in any case always suspected that the troubles with grain procurement were due to 'kulak speculators'. In 1926 the government passed a punitive law (confiscation of property and up to five years in prison) against grain-hoarding for the purpose of causing price rises, and it anticipated the Marxist researchers' discoveries of a kulak class by making taxation strongly progressive so that the poorest third of peasants could be exempt from the agricultural tax while the richest had to pay a surtax not only on the basis of their landholding but also on all their supplementary income. The idea was to tax likely hoarders of grain heavily enough to force them to sell their stocks. It is not clear how this differentiated approach to the peasantry worked in practice, because not even the most committed agrarian Marxists were producing much in the way of convincing empirical evidence that the villages already had their class of rich kulaks.

The best evidence of peasant differentiation came from the provinces of the Urals and western Siberia, where the earlier generation of settlers tended to be better off than recent immigrants. By coincidence, these were also the provinces reporting a good harvest in 1927, at the end of which a party congress inaugurated the first five-year plan of industrialization. But in 1927 the government decreed very low ceilings on grain prices; the peasants were therefore slow to sell their harvest, preferring instead to use much of it for breeding more livestock. That was the occasion on which Stalin and his friends in the party leadership turned against the New Economic Policy (NEP) by direct action, and started an offensive against the pro-NEP 'rightists' in the party central committee. He organized a force of urban party militants and led it to the Urals and west Siberia to take grain. The plenipotentiaries helped the provincial and district soviets work out procurement targets. At the same time, they decreed that peasant assemblies were quorate with only one-third of the membership present and jointly responsible for meeting the village targets. This enabled the targets to be approved by the poor peasants' vote, who would help identify the households from whose stores the targets could be met. In April the central committee would decree that the poor peasants could keep for themselves one-quarter of the hoards they helped to find. This did not go smoothly – about 700 cases of rural violence were recorded and 300 plenipotentiary requisitioners lost their lives in the course of the campaign.[12] It is not known how many peasant casualties there were, but the success of the campaign was measured by the speed with which it corrected the shortfall in grain procurements. Violence, however, was not the main form of peasant response to the new regime. The relatively well off households hurried to split up into smaller ones (as many had been doing in response to the post-1926 progressive taxation measures) and sowed less grain for the next season. This augured a smaller harvest in 1928 and put on the agenda another round of 'administrative measures' to make sure that the government's granaries would fill up to the degree required by the first five-year plan in 1929.

Further Reading

The discussion of peasant living standards draws on P. R. Gregory, 'The Russian agrarian crisis revisited' in R. C. Stuart (ed.), *The Soviet Rural Economy* (Totowa, NJ: Rowman & Allanheld, 1983) and S. G. Wheatcroft, 'Crises and the condition of the peasantry in late imperial Russia', in E, Kingston-Mann and T. Mixter (eds), *Peasant Economy, Culture, and Politics of European Russia, 1800–1921* (Princeton, NJ: Princeton University Press, 1990). The revolution of 1905–7 is treated in depth by T. Shanin, *The Roots of Otherness: Russia's Turn of the Century, Volume 1: Russia as a 'Developing Society'*, and *Volume 2: Russia, 1905–1907: Revolution as a Movement of Truth*

---

12 Yaney, *The Urge*, p. 549.

(New Haven, Conn.: Yale University Press, 1986), but see also the review article by J. Bushnell, 'Peasant economy and peasant revolution at the turn of the century: neither immiseration nor autonomy', *The Russia Review*, xlvi, 1987, pp. 77–88; another source is S. J. Seregny, 'Peasants and politics: peasant unions during the 1905 revolution', in Kingston-Mann and Mixter, *Peasant Economy*.

The discussion of the Stolypin reforms is based on G. Yaney, *The Urge to Mobilize: Agrarian Reform in Russia, 1861–1930* (Urbana, Ill.: University of Illinois Press, 1982), Chaps 6–9; and E. Kingston-Mann, 'Peasant communes and economic innovation: a preliminary inquiry', in Kingston-Mann and Mixter, *Peasant Economy*. The Siberian migration is treated by N. Poppe, 'The economic and cultural development of Siberia', in G. Katkov *et al.* (eds), *Russia Enters the Twentieth Century, 1894–1917* (London.: Methuen, 1973); and hooliganism by N. Weissman, 'Rural crime in tsarist Russia: the question of hooliganism, 1905–1914', *Slavic Review*, xxxvii, 1978, pp. 228–40.

The story of the First World War and the civil war period draws on Yaney, *The Urge*, Chaps 10–11; O. Figes, *Peasant Russia, Civil War: The Volga Countryside in Revolution (1917–1921)* (Oxford: Clarendon Press, 1989), and O. Figes, 'Peasant farmers and the minority groups of rural society', in Kingston-Mann and Mixter, *Peasant Economy*. The discussion of the NEP period is based on Yaney, *The Urge*, Chap. 12; D. Atkinson, *The End of the Russian Land Commune, 1905–1930* (Stanford, Calif.: Stanford University Press, 1983), Chaps 14–18; T. Shanin, *The Awkward Class* (Oxford: Clarendon Press, 1972), Chaps 9–10; S. Gross Solomon, *The Society Agrarian Debate: A Controversy in Social Science, 1923–1929* (Boulder, Col.: Westview Press, 1977); and T. Cox, *Peasants, Class, and Capitalism: The Rural Research of L. N. Kritsman and his School* (Oxford: Clarendon Press, 1986).

4

Workers and Townspeople, 1890–1917

The purpose of this and the next chapter is to describe the uncertain and changing structures of the urban population, the conditions and institutions of urban life, and the contribution and responses of urban residents to political events. The period under discussion in these two chapters starts with the tsarist industrialization drive in the 1890s, ends on the eve of the Soviet industrialization drive, and includes the revolutions of 1905 and 1917. This subjectmatter is further complicated by the fact that, although large concentrations of industrial labourers were undoubtedly among the more visible new social phenomena that marked a transition from peasant society, not all the large industrial plants were built in the vicinity of urban centres or with the intention of forming the nuclei of new cities. Industrialization did not mean urbanization for everyone involved, at least not immediately.

Although not all the new industrial workplaces were urban, most were and industrial growth had an urbanizing impact. In 1861–1912, the urban population trebled while the rural population 'only' doubled. Here it is worth while reminding ourselves that the thriving provincial town had never been a strong item in the historical legacy of Russia, especially not in Russia proper. Over the centuries, Russian tsars had tended not to grant lucrative trade monopolies to city-based guilds or to grant political autonomy to urban patricians. Hence, not many Russian towns were important, long-established economic and cultural centres in their own right. Many were, first, military garrisons, secondly, local outposts of state administration, and little else besides. The all-empire general census of 1897 counted 932 towns with 16·2 million residents (13 per cent of the total population). Only 17 towns had more than 100 000 inhabitants, and 12 of them were outside Russia proper, in the provinces of Poland, the Baltics, and Ukraine. The great majority of Russian towns were very small, semi-rural backwaters, and many of them remained so. Urban growth took place mainly in the large towns. The largest five per cent of towns increased their share of the total urban population from 27 per cent in 1861 to 53 per cent in 1897. In Russia proper, the constellation of towns was very much dominated by the two largest cities of the empire, St Petersburg and Moscow. The population of St Petersburg grew from about 500 000 in 1860 to over one million by 1890, and to 2.2 million by 1914; Moscow grew from 450 000 in 1860 to 900 000 by 1890, and to over 1.5 million by 1912.

The question that dominates the writings of Western social historians on the last decades of the tsarist era, the revolution and the first decade of Soviet rule is one of popular participation in the political developments, and in particular the nature of the relationship between the Bolshevik Party and industrial workers. Western social historians on the whole do not accept the version propounded by Soviet official historiography published from the 1920s to the 1970s, according to which the Russian industrial proletariat became ever more politically conscious and united under the leadership of its most advanced elements, who were effectively organized by Lenin's Bolshevik Party. But to some extent influenced by their colleagues' writings on the labour movements and social conditions in Western countries, Western social historians of Russia have been concerned to rescue these themes from neglect or dismissal by those historians who describe the Bolsheviks' ascent to power in the exclusively political terms of authoritarian ideology, an unscrupulous will-to-power, and effective conspiratorial organization.

According to this latter school of historians, it was exactly the undeveloped nature of the urban, modern sector of Russian society that made it possible for the Bolsheviks to hijack the popular revolution of February 1917 by manipulating street mobs, organizing the *coup d'état* in October, and building up a repressive, totalitarian state. The lack of modern social structure and identities among the mass of the people in the cities meant a lack of a shared popular sense of democratic political legitimacy and civic responsibility in the cities in which the structures of politics were shaped; this dealt a weak hand to liberal and moderate politicians, which the Bolsheviks were simply first off the mark to exploit. The Bolsheviks' talk of working-class interests, workers' revolution, and a workers' state was but an ideological cloak that historians ought not to have confused with historical realities.

The purpose of this and the following chapter is not to settle the dispute about the nature of the politics that saw the demise of tsarist and, eventually, the establishment of Bolshevik rule. It is simply an attempt to describe 'the social' in terms other than those used to describe, explain, or justify political acts. But inevitably, like the information on the Russian peasantry, such information does not come to historians unmediated by the writers of historical sources who had their own purposes and a discourse to attend to in their writings. Unlike the source materials on the Russian peasantry, the ones on the working class and the labour movement do include workers' memoirs which Western, as well as Soviet, social historians have drawn upon. However, they were published (mainly in the 1920s) under undoubtedly political auspices and with the benefit of partisan hindsight perspectives on the prerevolutionary labour movement and the revolution. The interpretation of such materials that is reflected in this chapter is informed not so much by an interest in the differences between party political visions that may be evident in the sources as by an interest in the deeper preoccupation with backwardness and modernity that the Russian producers of historical sources on urban social conditions and the working class may have shared. Like the peasantry, industrial workers and the urban poor tend to be made visible primarily in the intelligentsia's relationships to them. The next chapter also deals with sections of the intelligentsia directly, alongside other groups that were discernible in the social landscape of the early Soviet period.

St Petersburg and Moscow at the Turn of the Century

The two big cities were in some obvious physical respects quite different from one another. St Petersburg was founded by Peter I at the beginning of the eighteenth century as a modern European capital city. The city centre, which was then built quickly, surpassed Moscow in the number of stone and brick buildings, their scale, and the straightness of their lines. True, construction over the next two hundred years was anarchic during boom periods and, despite official policies favouring stone, brick, and mortar, much new construction consisted of cheap wooden houses that wrote no proud message on the skyline – in 1900 timber buildings still made up 40 per cent of the total. These were, however, mainly in the suburbs; in the centre, the vistas still told the tale of a city erected as a message of modernity: 'a city of bold and firm outlines rather than of warm color and picturesque detail . . . it is a sketch, an outline, a general statement', wrote an American travel writer.[1] In Moscow, on the other hand, wooden buildings made up two-thirds of the total, and haphazard, one-floor structures with little orchards and bits of waste land were very much in evidence in the city centre, as were dirt-track, intertwining side-streets and back lanes. Moscow was an anarchic and low-profile sprawl offering plenty of rural retreats in its nooks and crannies. Although long established among the 10 largest cities of the world, Moscow was known to be 'a big village' by the metropolitan sophisticates of St Petersburg. It was only now, in the first years of the twentieth century, that the visual character of the city centre was becoming coherently defined by four-floor buildings lined up along straight, paved streets.

The architectural and town-plan differences that were evident between the two cities, of course, reflected their different histories; Moscow was 600 years older and had suffered a number of major fires in its time but, above all, its growth was always organic and a matter of individual enterprise. By the end of the nineteenth century Moscow was a major centre of large-scale factory production just like St Petersburg, while at the same time retaining a major component of small-scale artisan workshops. Moscow was only just acquiring a coherent, modern city façade, but it did not altogether lack in metropolitan trappings: in 1904, Moscow had 19 theatres, nine museums, a permanent circus, 94 hospitals, 201 pharmacies, 973 educational institutions of all levels, and 13 newspapers, in addition to seven cathedrals, 18 monasteries, 522 taverns, and 316 beer halls.[2]

Both cities could be said to be numerically dominated by migrants rather than by settled families. To simplify presentation, the statistics that follow pertain to Moscow only, because directly comparable statistics such as are available also for St Petersburg are very similar. In 1882, only 26 per cent of

---

1 Williams, H. W. 1915: *Russia of the Russians*. New York, p. 399, quoted in Bater, J. H. 1976: *St Petersburg: Industrialization and Change*. London: Edward Arnold, p. 322.
2 Bradley, J. 1985: *Muzhik and Muscovite: Urbanization in Late Imperial Russia*. Berkeley, Calif.: University of California Press, p. 42.

Moscow residents had been born in the city; in 1912, 29 per cent. Of working-age males, 12 per cent had been born in the city.[3] Of the total population in 1902 as well as in 1882, 15 per cent had been resident in the city for less than a year, 42 per cent for more than 10 years; the proportion of long-term residents was not rising because it was common for wage labourers, especially the male ones, to retire from the city on reaching middle age. There was a substantial annual outflow as well as inflow of migration: it has been estimated that every year about 100 000 people left Moscow while 150 000 moved in.[4] Throughout the nineteenth century, men were the majority sex in Moscow but the female part of the population was rising, from 41 per cent in 1871 to 46 per cent in 1911.[5] The population consisted mainly of working-age adults; in 1897, only 22 per cent of the city's inhabitants were under 16 years of age and 11 per cent were older than 50.[6] Women of child-bearing age outnumbered children. Although the majority of the adult Moscow population were married, only just over one-third of the city's total population were living with their own families.[7] The trend towards urban family living was slow; between 1882 and 1912, the proportion of dependants in the total Moscow population – the people supported by their families rather than earning their own living – rose from 29 per cent to 35 per cent.[8] Of the children living in Moscow, 23 per cent were illegitimate, compared to two per cent in Moscow province as a whole.

The Moscow census of 1902 collected information on the occupations of self-supporting residents. The returns showed a population making a living in hundreds of different occupations which were not easy for the analysts to sort into broader categories with much certainty or consistency. According to a recent analysis, the census found that over three per cent were major proprietors, managers, bureaucrats, and officers; two per cent were modern professionals – teachers, engineers, doctors, etc.; another two per cent were semi-professional – clergy, nurses, medical technicians, draftsmen, entertainers; over eight per cent were small proprietors and low-ranking managers and officials; over six per cent were clerks of various sorts; and five per cent were students, pensioners, and other non-working white-collar people. Some 18 per cent were craftsmen and skilled manual workers; 31 per cent were semi-skilled and service workers; 16 per cent were unskilled labourers and menial service workers; and eight per cent were unemployed, on poor relief, in hospital, and other marginal categories.[9] Over the following 10 years, the white-collar and skilled-manual categories would increase their share only very slightly. The people in the manual classes made up almost three-quarters of the population and, within the manual classes, skilled workers formed a minority of less than one-quarter. The skilled occupations were probably

---

3 Bradley, *Muzhik and Muscovite*, p. 103.
4 Bradley, *Muzhik and Muscovite*, p. 104.
5 Bradley, *Muzhik and Muscovite*, p. 34.
6 Crisp, O. 1978: 'Labour and industrialization in Russia'. In Mathias, P. and Postan, M. M. (eds), *The Cambridge Economic History of Europe*, vii, Part 2. Cambridge: Cambridge University Press, pp. 308–415.
7 Bradley, *Muzhik and Muscovite*, p. 217.
8 Bradley, *Muzhik and Muscovite*, p. 146.
9 Bradley, *Muzhik and Muscovite*, App. A, pp. 359ff.

overcounted, as the questionnaires asked for 'occupations' rather than current job descriptions, and there were many people claiming a skilled trade who were in fact earning their living in semi-skilled and unskilled jobs. The census made an unconvincing attempt to count the people in some illegitimate occupations, finding 313 male and 462 female 'beggars and thieves'. But the legal twilight zone was large by all other accounts. For example, it is unlikely that in Moscow prostitution was much less widespread than in St Petersburg, where the number of prostitutes was estimated as between 30 000 and 50 000 in 1905, more than five per cent of the total female population.[10]

Women formed one-third of Moscow's self-supporting population as a whole, but less than one-tenth of the clerks, one-sixth of the skilled manual workers, and one-quarter of small proprietors and managers. On the other hand, women made up more than one-half of the pensioners and students as well as of the people who were unemployed or on poor relief; they formed almost one-half of the semi-professionals (many were nurses, medical technicians, and lower church personnel), more than one-third of the semi-skilled and unskilled manual workers (many were textile workers, cooks, governesses, and domestic servants), more than one-third of the professionals (the majority of teachers were women) and almost one-third of the major proprietors and managers (most of the landowners and rentiers were women).[11] Three-quarters of the Moscow men and one-half of the women were literate.[12]

Muscovites as well as the inhabitants of St Petersburg lived mostly within walking distance of their workplaces. The privileged classes lived in the city centres, although many of their number owned additional homes or dachas in the woodlands outside the city boundaries, in which they would seek refuge from the heat and dust of the summer months. The city centres were not occupied exclusively by the better-off classes; it was common for city-centre buildings to house wealthy residents in spacious first-floor apartments and their poor neighbours in overcrowded garrets and cellars. City centres hosted artisan workshops and small factories as well as shops, offices, and banks; and some of the large factories built in the nineteenth century were close to the city centres as well. Large factories also defined the character of many of the areas spreading away from the city centres, and here there were large concentrations of factory workers and other labouring people.

In Moscow a sizeable number of people lived in employer-provided accommodation, but they were a decreasing minority, making up over 20 per cent of inhabitants in 1882 and 15 per cent by 1912. In 1912, another relatively small group lived in lodging houses, but 75 per cent of the total population lived in privately rented apartments. In St Petersburg, almost 90 per cent of the total housing stock belonged to the privately rented sector by 1900. In both cities, however, the great majority of the population lived in multi-occupied

10 Glickman, R. L. 1984: *Russian Factory Women: Workplace and Society, 1880–1914*. Berkeley, Calif.: University of California Press, p. 68.
11 Based on Glickman, *Russian Factory Women*.
12 Engelstein, L. 1982: *Moscow, 1905: Working-Class Organization and Political Conflict*. Stanford, Calif.: Stanford University Press, p. 45.

apartments, because only very few could afford not to share the rent costs. In St Petersburg in 1900, the average number of residents per apartment was 7.4 and per room 1.7. In Moscow in 1912, the average apartment housed between eight and nine residents, of whom less than one-half were in any way related to each other.[13] In Moscow only seven per cent of the population enjoyed the luxury of living in an apartment where the number of rooms was at least equal to the number of residents. For 31 per cent of the population the number of people in a dwelling exceeded the number of rooms so that there were up to two people to a room; for 57 per cent, there were between two and four people to a room and for under five per cent, there were five or more residents to a room.[14]

Moscow was a late starter in building that marker of modern urbanism, a comprehensive water and sewerage network. In 1882, only 22 per cent of housing units were plumbed in and, by 1912, 40 per cent of the population still lived in houses without this amenity. The situation was better in St Petersburg, where 90 per cent of apartments with three or more rooms had running water and water closets by 1900. It was, however, St Petersburg that particularly suffered from epidemics of typhus, presumably because the piped water was taken from the river Neva without adequate filtration. At the turn of the century, there were 165 cases of typhus occurring per 10 000 of population in St Petersburg, compared to 21 in Moscow. In 1908, 7700 people had typhus in St Petersburg, during which year the disease claimed more deaths in the city than in all German cities. Of all deaths in St Petersburg, 47 per cent were due to infectious disease in that year. The epidemic at last moved the civic authorities to commit themselves to a construction project that would supply the city residents with clean water from Lake Ladoga; work on the project started in 1914.[15] In both cities, the city dumas were dominated by men with an interest in real estate who were answerable to electorates limited by property and other qualifications to about two per cent of the male populations. As an American traveller observed in 1915, in St Petersburg 'something like civic spirit' was a very recent phenomenon.[16]

St Petersburg was a particularly unhealthy place to live, but other cities had their epidemics too. There was a serious outbreak of cholera in Moscow as well as in St Petersburg in 1909. Typhoid claimed its victims in recurrent bouts in all big cities, although its rates were, again, substantially higher in St Petersburg than in Moscow. Another disease that thrived in the cities was syphilis. Nearly seven per cent of railwaymen were treated for venereal infections in 1905 alone, a rate that was much higher than the national average but in line with the metropolitan areas.[17] The most common chronic problem afflicting the urban population, however, was tuberculosis. At the turn of the century, Moscow

13 Bradley, *Muzhik and Muscovite*, p. 200–1; Bater, *St Petersburg*, p. 329.
14 Chase, W. J. 1990: *Workers, Society, and the Soviet State: Labor and Life in Moscow, 1918–1929*. Urbana, Ill.: University of Illinois Press, p. 186. It is possible that some of the multi-occupied rooms were subdivided by thin partitions to provide a modicum of privacy.
15 Bater, *St Petersburg*, p. 352.
16 Williams, *Russia of the Russians*, quoted in Bater, *St Petersburg*, p. 367.
17 Reichman, H. 1987: *Railwaymen and Revolution: Russia, 1905*. Berkeley, Calif.: University of California Press, p. 103.

had an average annual mortality rate of 24 per 1000 which was only four per 1000 lower than it had been in the 1860s. The rate was slightly higher in St Petersburg, having been much higher than Moscow's in the 1860s. The Moscow rate was only slightly lower than the national average, but it was very high, and St Petersburg's even higher when it is considered that these two cities were mainly populated by the physically most robust age-groups.

By the late nineteenth century, the metropolitan educated circles came to regard epidemics as evidence that municipal action was needed to safeguard public health, and that public health was endangered by urban squalor and poverty as well as by an inadequate water and sewage infrastructure. A well publicized focus for the new concern in Moscow was the Khitrov market near the city centre – a concentration of privately owned lodging houses surrounding a time-honoured place for the hire of casual labour. Since this was where gainful employment could be found on a casual basis, it was here that many immigrants arrived and sought lodgings they could afford. By the turn of the century, Khitrov was a teeming slum with its own service economy and artisan production of cheap, recycled goods, a criminal underworld, and a skid-row culture that many found impossible to leave. The police were worried about the criminal subculture and its effects on the newly arriving and, as yet, innocent migrant labourer. The social reformers were worried that the slum, with its overcrowding, lack of hygiene, and unwholesome living, was a hothouse of infectious disease that threatened to spread to all areas of the city. Since it was soon realized that owners and residents connived to evade the enforcement of sanitary regulations, the provision by municipal authorities of alternative lodgings for migrant labourers came on the agenda. The municipal authorities had long resisted being involved for fear that such provision would only increase Moscow's attractiveness to vagrants, but at the beginning of the century they established several large subsidized dormitories and cafeterias for people willing to accept institutional regimes designed to promote sober and hygienic living. Similar public establishments were set up in St Petersburg as well. As with the less restrictive and less sanitary private lodging houses, they became long-term home to people with steady but poorly paid jobs as well as temporary shelter to transitory migrant labourers.

However limited in its scope and effectiveness, the involvement of charitable institutions and municipal authorities in the provision of subsidized shelter for immigrants, and their general concern about the most notorious slums, marked the beginnings of a new public welfare policy. First, subsidized accommodation for the homeless was available to anyone with a valid passport, including peasants; previously, municipal authorities explicitly excluded peasants from their concerns on the grounds that their welfare was the responsibility of their village communes. Secondly, the Khitrov slum problem was defined as one of poverty, overcrowded housing, and the real or imagined moral depravities of slum living – conditions known to apply to much broader multitudes of metropolitan inhabitants than just the vagrants, orphans, and destitute old-aged people that made up the traditional concepts of pauperism. It was now thought that neither incidental generosity to beggars, nor poor relief administered through orphanages and almshouses, nor anti-vagrancy laws were adequate ways of dealing with the social pathologies and public health hazards represented by the Khitrov slum. The thoughts of the metropolitan educated circles thus turned to rational, municipally co-ordinated policies of poor relief and public health measures that would reform the urban poor as well as aid the survival of the most indigent unfortunates. The belief grew that the dangers of urban squalor needed to be combated by sanitary plumbing and clean flop-houses, and also by the promotion of sobriety, thrift, industriousness, hygienic habits, education, and culture.

The new thinking wanted the municipal administration to co-ordinate the aims of long-established charities and poor-relief institutions with the aims of newer, late nineteenth-century voluntary associations such as the Temperance Society, the Society to Disseminate Useful Books, and the Society for the Encouragement of Industriousness; and it wanted the municipal administration to lead the development of a systematic, rational administration of poor relief. It was a reformist movement in three senses. First, it criticized the work of long-established institutions of poor relief, such as the Imperial Foundling Home and the Moscow Workhouse, seeking to change them and to create new, additional municipal institutions. Secondly, as we have seen, it sought to reform the poor by promoting what were considered as the essential virtues of urban modernity among them. And thirdly, in emphasizing the role of municipal administration in the creation of a systemic social policy, it sought to enlarge the autonomy of city government from the tsarist autocracy and its imperial bureaucracy; in so doing, it aligned a sense of civic virtue with a liberal political ideology. In Moscow this kind of municipally oriented liberal reformism was more pronounced than in St Petersburg.

The Imperial Foundling Home, founded by Catherine at the end of the eighteenth century, occupied one of the more impressive buildings in central Moscow; at the beginning of the twentieth century, the Home was taking into its care about 10 000 infants every year. The infants were wet-nursed in its dormitories for an initial three-week period before being placed in peasant foster homes outside Moscow. But a high proportion died while still in the home, and of those who survived long enough to be found foster homes, almost 40 per cent died before reaching adulthood. Once a showpiece of imperial charity towards indigent children, the Home was highlighted by the new reformist opinion in Moscow as another example of what was corrupt and ineffective in the old ways of poor-relief provision. But since the Home was run by an imperial foundation rather than a city-based authority, the reformists could exert only an indirect pressure on its administration. By contrast, the Moscow Workhouse was a municipally controlled institution which became the subject of large-scale reform in the mid-1890s. Subsequently, it administered separate almshouses for paupers who were unable to work, and for those who were able to work a network of vocational training centres ('centres for the love of labour') as well as a large hostel with a library and a hall for public readings, concerts, and dramatic productions. Having been an almost moribund place of detention for the relatively few vagrants apprehended by a sporadic enforcement of anti-vagrancy laws, the Workhouse became a large institution dispensing poor relief with reformist intentions to some 15 000 people per year. About one-half of the Workhouse wards were referred by the police, while the other half sought admission to the Workhouse voluntarily; there were many more who applied but were turned away.

Another institution established in the mid-1890s as a flagship of the new civic reformism was the Moscow Guardianship of the Poor. The Guardianship worked through district offices with small numbers of professional staff who solicited voluntary cash contributions from the wealthier inhabitants and organized volunteer social workers. The social workers had systematic rounds, visiting the poorest parts of their neighbourhoods to identify individuals with the most pressing needs, referring them to appropriate charities, or recommending them for aid out of the district office funds. Three-quarters of this aid was dispensed in cash hand-outs, although the preferred policy was to arrange payments in kind to prevent mis-spending on drink. The volunteers also endeavoured to get to know their needy clients well enough personally to be able to give self-improvement advice. The volunteers' other function was to build up a systematic dossier of the needy and their problems for another new institution, the Council of Charities; there were 25 000 individual welfare cases on file in the information office of the Council by 1908, alongside a library of material on charities and voluntary associations. The purpose of the Council and its information office was twofold: to co-ordinate the work of different charities with the Guardianship activities, and to prevent abuse of welfare provision by professional scroungers.

The Workhouse, the Guardianship, and the Council were municipal institutions of a rationalist, secular social policy. They made Moscow renowned as a pioneering centre of welfare reformism in Russia. But the city authorities stopped short of attempting to raise the amount of tax revenue that would be needed to make the intentions of welfare reformism effective. The vocational centres of the Workhouse were, in the event, unable to provide the sort of self-transformative work experience and occupational training they intended. The ranks of the Guardianship volunteer social workers were thinning as the years went by. In the foundation year of 1895 they numbered 1700, evenly balanced between men and women; in 1910, there were 1100 volunteers, predominantly women.[18] The loss of volunteers was in part thought to be due to demoralization in the face of overwhelming indigence and squalor, but mainly due to the fact that the volunteers had no voice in the Guardianship's policy decisions. The municipal authorities insisted on an authoritarian management structure – perhaps because they were authoritarian by inclination or because they shrank from facing down the imperial autocracy's fear of civic movements.

Nevertheless, Moscow's social reformism provided another ingredient to the emerging social structure of modernity, in addition to the time-honoured preoccupation of the educated classes with the significance of Enlightenment culture and the peasantry's lack of it. The Muscovites' perceptions of threatening culture gaps may have started with the obvious presence of peasant migrants and ragged vagrants in the city's streets, but they developed to take in the fact that the city conditions themselves generated their own, urban kind of 'dark mass'. After all, many of the most troublesome elements in the Khitrov slum or in the workhouse tended to be people of the urban artisan estate, not just migrant peasants. The gap was between the realities and values

---

18 Bradley, *Muzhik and Muscovite*, p. 327.

of urban slum living on the one hand and the ideals of modern urban social respectability on the other. The social reformers believed that indigent slum dwellers could be reformed into an industrious, self-reliant, and upwardly mobile working class. To the Russian intelligentsia's emphasis on modern social respectability as the possession or at least appreciation of high Enlightenment culture, the social reformers added a notion of respectability as the possession of work ethic, sanitary habits, marketable work skills, and a desire for self-improvement. They created a rationalist philanthropic movement wherein they portrayed themselves as an enlightened civic middle class striving to have a respectable working class for a neighbour. This was perhaps the main significance of the new definition of pauperism as an urban social problem.

Factory Workers and the Labour Movement before 1905

The Moscow civic middle-class movement was but one strand of the Russian intelligentsia's self-consciousness. This, as we have seen in previous chapters, was much preoccupied with the contrast between peasant backwardness and cultured modernity. Marxism arrived in Russia just as the tsarist state was making its push for industrial capitalism in the 1890s, and it caught the imagination of the Russian intelligentsia. Marxism's emphasis on industrial manufacturing as the bearer of technological progress, its systemic sociology, and its teleological, redemptory vision of history appealed to the Russian intelligentsia's faith in theoretical thought and political radicalism. The concept of the working class as a modern and important social agency thus acquired wide currency among educated Russians before it had a chance to become a significant source of identity among industrial workers themselves. Even some tsarist police officials saw a new social force of ambivalent potential lurking in the shadows of the factory smokestacks. For the Western-oriented sections of the intelligentsia, the factory represented technological progress and, at the same time, an important locale of cultural transformation in which the sons and daughters of backward peasant Russia were destined to join the progressive world. From this vantage point, the intelligentsia anticipated factory workers' cultural qualities to be influenced in particular by two variables: the kind of work a factory worker was doing and the degree to which he lost personal connections with the peasant world.

The kinds of factory work were judged by the intelligentsia in terms of their similarity or dissimilarity with preindustrial peasant and artisan work: the more dissimilar, the better, for the industrial activity would be taking the worker's habits of thought further away from what Marx called 'the idiocy of rural life'. Skilled workers in the printing trade were clearly an epitome of urbane culture, because their work was an integral part of the printed-word domain that made and sustained the intelligentsia itself. But print works tended to be small establishments. The dominant image of industrial progress took the form of a large engineering factory; even before the mass-produced automobile arrived to put an unmistakable historical stamp on the twentieth century, engineering production had come to symbolize many of the things that made modern industry different from premodern industry. Engineering factories worked on iron and steel by means of mechanically powered machine-tools capable of producing precision components that made up engines and machines; they differed from peasant artisan workshops by their dominant raw material, their high-powered machines, and the kind of knowledge that informed both the products and the production process. The prevalence of iron and steel in the raw material and the equipment of an engineering factory was in itself a marker of progress. Iron and steel was the image of the new age. Pictures of newly opened hospital wards were taken in such a way as to leave no doubt in the viewer's mind that the beds had metal frames – iron bedsteads communicated hygiene, efficiency, and the benefits of science in a way that wooden-frame beds could not. Engineering and metal-working ('metalist') plants in general were further away from the preindustrial past than, say, textile factories. Textile factories used mechanically produced energy to drive fast-working machines, but their raw material, their product, and, indeed, the processes of spinning and weaving, did not seem in their very nature to be so different from the industries already known and understood in the premodern, peasant world. By the same logic, the labourers in, say, brickworks were expected to differ hardly at all from backward peasants. Skilled engineering workers, on the other hand, worked in a Promethean iron-and-steel world in which they had to read blueprints and, in some cases, even trigonometric tables to set up their machine-tools; they were used to abstract thought and the application of general principles to particular cases; and, therefore, they were expected to share with the intelligentsia and the print workers the virtues of modern cultured consciousness believed to be absent from the peasant mind: a sense of individual self, an ethic of self-discipline and responsibility, a regard for moral principle and legal right, and a personal interest in political theory and social progress. The conviction among the intelligentsia that this kind of reasoning was valid was widespread and unshakeable. This is how a liberal journalist put it in his treatise on the *Psychology of the Russian Worker Question* published in 1911:

> Workers in machine production are always in the forefront of every movement. They are aristocrats, the progressivists . . . developed people with a well-formed sense of individuality . . . . In the form of their conversation and even their language, they are almost indistinguishable from our intellectuals.[19]

These virtues of 'developed people with a well-formed sense of individuality' were thought more likely to take root among workers who were 'fully committed' to urban industrial life than among workers who are still peasant migrants. In the Western-oriented intellectual's perception of the peasantry, it was axiomatic that the difference between peasant and modern humanity was much more than skin deep; for liberals as well as Marxist socialists, the working class could hardly be expected to realize its progressive qualities to the full while its members were still involved with the rural peasant world. The intelligentsia looked forward to a truly non-peasant working class and

---

19 Quoted in Mandel, D. 1983: *The Petrograd Workers and the Fall of the Old Regime: From the February Revolution to the July Days, 1917.* London: Macmillan, p. 13.

measured progress by counting the percentages of factory workers who were themselves the children of factory workers, who no longer entertained any claims to allotments of peasant land, and who no longer kept their dependants in the villages. The fact that such differentiation of factory workers from the peasantry was a slow and unsmooth trend did little to challenge the Marxist intelligentsia's beliefs in the working class: should workers be found failing in living up to the high expectations held of their class, this would be easily explained away by the contaminating presence of the peasant element.

The peasant element was indeed strong. In fact, much of the industry was in rural locations. The cities of St Petersburg and Moscow were the most industrial in Russia proper, but they hosted fewer than one-fifth of the empire's factory workers. There were modern textile mills in the 'central industrial region', the area around and to the north of Moscow where agricultural land was poor and the peasantry accustomed to supplementing their incomes by other kinds of work. Some of these factories were in small towns but others were strategically positioned between villages from which labour could be drawn locally. There were long-established metallurgical plants in the open spaces of the Urals countryside, where the first generation of workers had actually been given land allotments to lure them there. By 1900 the typical worker still lived in a village, and some plants closed production as a matter of course in the summer so that the workers could get on with their harvests. There were newly opening mines and steel-works in the empty steppes of eastern Ukraine and southern European Russia, where the conditions were hardly suitable for any other than strictly migratory labour, but some of the employers tried to combat the problems of high labour turnover by building family housing for their workers rather than barrack dormitories. Some new factories were growing in old ports and trading centres along the Volga, others in the countryside along the new railway lines, and a few isolated islands of modern industry were cropping up even in the small district towns lost in the depths of the fertile 'black earth', hitherto firmly agricultural regions.

In other words, in the early 1900s industrialization still had an uncertain relationship with urbanization. Some factory workers walked to work across fields from their peasant homes or lodgings; some lived in company compounds, in otherwise rural locations, or on the outskirts of towns; and some lived in multi-occupied city apartments, hostels, and flop-houses; very few lived in city apartments with their own families. Most Russian factory workers were the first ones within their own families to experience factory work, although second- and third-generation workers were already quite common in the longer-established plants. But the second- and third-generation workers tended to be, just like their parents, rural-born migrants living apart from their families while working in the factory and expecting eventually to return to their home village. The intergenerationally transmitted pattern was one of peasant wage-labour migration. Even the skilled print workers who lived in Moscow city centre on relatively high wages were still found to have strong personal connections with their peasant backgrounds by a survey carried out in 1908: 90 per cent were sending money to their relatives on a regular basis and almost half still had immediate families directly involved in peasant farming.[20] Such connections with the peasant countryside were rather less prevalent in St Petersburg, where people migrated greater distances than was the case in Moscow, so that it was less of an option for married workers to keep their immediate families in peasant homesteads. In St Petersburg in 1908, 32 per cent of single workers and 12 per cent of married workers were involved in peasant farming, although one-half of the singles and one-third of the married ones still maintained their entitlements to peasant land allotments.[21]

The majority of Moscow and St Petersburg factory workers were under 30 years of age, while only 20 per cent of the men and 14 per cent of the women were over 40.[22] As was the case with the metropolitan population as a whole, the great majority of factory workers in Moscow and St Petersburg were born outside the city boundaries and belonged legally to the social estate of the peasantry. But in 1902 more than one-half of the Moscow factory workers had been resident in the city for more than five years, and over one-third had been there for more than 10 years; on the other hand, almost one-fifth had been in the city for less than two years. The pattern was one in which people, mainly men but increasingly also women, migrated from the villages to factory employment in the urban areas on reaching their late teens, so that the adult experience of most factory workers in the metropolitan areas consisted of just that – earning a living in a city. In that sense, they were perhaps workers first and peasants second.

The question on the intelligentsia's commentators' lips, however, was how many of the factory workers wished or expected to return to village life at a later stage. In Moscow at the turn of the century, it was still very common for the men to leave factory employment and to return to their village homes on reaching 40 years of age. There were good practical reasons for this: the wages were not high enough to afford family housing in the city, good pension schemes such as could provide for city-based retirement were still very rare for manual workers, and becoming free of village communal obligations and getting cash from the sale of communal land allotments was not easy prior to the Stolypin reforms. For those who had a peasant family to return to, a return was the easiest way of facing up to the prospects of middle and old age. The pattern was not quite the same for women. Most women factory workers were married, but their husbands were with them in the town rather than left behind in the village homestead, although their children often were left to be brought up by relatives in the village until they were old enough to join the urban labour force. Those women who stayed in factory employment beyond their youngest adult years were more likely than their male counterparts to stay in the city for the rest of their years. The Moscow population of the over-forties had a female majority, contrary to the younger age-groups.

The industrial workforce was young, largely peasant by background, with a substantial contingent of recent arrivals from the countryside, and it was not

20 Shanin, T. 1985: *Russia as a Developing Society*. London: Macmillan, appendix.
21 Smith, S. A. 1985: *Red Petrograd: Revolution in the Factories 1917–1918*. Cambridge: Cambridge University Press, p. 18.
22 Glickman, *Russian Factory Women*, p. 93.

quick to burn the bridges connecting it with the peasant hinterland. The migrant flavour of much of the labour force was emphasized by the fact that many factories recruited their immigrant labour from particular localities, partly on purpose, if it was believed that certain rural areas had artisan traditions that produced good-quality workers, and partly by default, as many new workers were recruited by the personal recommendation of existing workers who had come from the same village.

The immigrant flavour of the factory workforce reflected the migrant nature of the metropolitan population as a whole. When the relatively privileged young men arrived in the metropolis from the provinces to study at the university, the first thing they did was to join a student *zemlyachestvo*, a mutual help club for students hailing from the same district. The locality of background thus defined solidary networks which enabled new arrivals in the city to find accommodation, cheap food and drink, sources of cash loans if needed, and convivial company that taught the newcomers the ropes in the university and city. Factory workers, especially the male ones, did the same. *Zemlyachestvo* was historically the first kind of metropolitan-based organization that many factory workers joined and managed for their own mutual benefit. It confirmed its members' immigrant identity and, at the same time, their new occupational identity, while helping them to adapt to new surroundings both in and out of the workplace. Since these organizations were ones in which new immigrants were in a sense expected to learn from and emulate the longer-established immigrants, they conferred a social status to those who already were skilled and experienced in the ways of the factory or city: they were taught to appreciate the contrast between being a naive bumpkin and a man of the new world. Although not every immigrant worker joined a *zemlyachestvo*, the newcomer status was an issue everyone had to deal with in order to become materially and socially more comfortable. Young factory workers' holiday sojourns in their villages were occasions for celebration of both the home reunion and the contrast between old and new identities.

The Western-oriented sections of the intelligentsia saw the fact that the cities and the factories were largely populated by people from peasant backgrounds as socially highly significant, because they regarded the peasantry as profoundly lacking in culture in general and modern social virtues in particular. They did not see the students' organizations of *zemlyachestvo* as a phenomenon testifying to the importance of countrymen's provincialism in the university's student culture. The student *zemlyachestvo* was seen as a phenomenon of student life in the metropolis first and foremost, not as a phenomenon of backwoods provincialism. But why not view the workers' *zemlyachestvo* in the same way, as serving the needs of young adults who worked and lived in the city away from their families? Common location of birth was a pretext for membership; but what the organizations were essentially about was not the locality of origin but the trials and tribulations of independent existence in the city or the factory. It is possible to view the city-located factory from this perspective as well. The socially distinctive feature of it, perhaps, was the industrial work itself and the fact that the workers were predominantly young, living away from family home, and having an awareness of themselves and their peers as being at some stage of the passage from the status of a newcomer to that of an experienced old hand. The cities and the city-based factories were places that were numerically dominated by more or less settled immigrant workers – that much can be seen from the known demographic facts. As to exactly what importance peasant backgrounds had for the behaviour of factory workers always was and still is a matter of speculation based on beliefs about 'the peasant mentality' and its supposedly inert qualities.

The radical intelligentsia's theories, which considered the type of industry and the social distance from the peasantry to be powerful influences on workers' consciousness, were not supported by the evidence concerning strikes, although the radicals considered militancy as a natural outcome of advanced consciousness. Although never legal, strikes were fairly common from the latter half of the 1880s. They occurred among all types of workers in all kinds of industry and location. The 'metalists' were in fact less strike-prone than many other kinds of worker, and urban-located factories were no more strike-prone than rural ones. Both skilled and unskilled workers were involved, women as well as men. Some strikes spread from one factory to another via the agency of *zemlyachestvo* networks, or through an informal exchange of information about the conditions in different factories that took place during workers' holiday sojourns in their villages. Contrary to the then prevalent theoretical expectations, it was not the case that the strikes by the more peasant and less 'developed' types of worker were necessarily less organized and disciplined, more 'spontaneous', violent, and irrational than the strikes of the 'metalists'. Prior to 1905, the great majority of strikes were local disputes about pay and conditions which took place without the involvement of revolutionary party activists; most were settled within a day or two.

The government tried to defuse the dangers of widespread labour unrest by legislation curbing employers' excesses. In the early 1880s, child labour was outlawed and the Factory Inspectorate was set up for the supervision of labour conditions in all establishments using mechanical power and employing at least 50 workers. In 1897, during an industrial boom and a peak in strike activity, further Factory Acts were passed, which among other things limited the working day to 11 hours. By 1905, most of the large factories had a 10-hour working day with somewhat shorter Saturdays, although some workers worked overtime and it was not always clear whether they did so voluntarily. Provision for injury and illness was made compulsory in all factories in 1903, but not pension schemes nor redundancy compensation. About one-third of the factory labour force were covered by pension schemes, mainly those working in state-owned concerns, the railway companies, and the steel-making plants in the Urals and the south.

The Factory Acts perhaps made the conditions of work across industries somewhat more homogeneous than they would otherwise have been, and perhaps on the whole better than the conditions in many artisan workshops, which were not subject to any government supervision. But apart from the fact that factory work was often very unhealthy and dangerous, the quality that stands out with regard to industry is its heterogeneity. We have already seen that industrial establishments were in all kinds of location. They also varied in many other respects. There were plants run on very paternalistic lines, where the owners and senior managers made serious efforts to know every worker by

name, even when large numbers made this difficult. There were also plants
where the relationships between workers and managers were quite impersonal
– including plants where many of the managers were foreigners who could not
speak Russian. Some factories were distinguished by the fact that they were
run like total institutions, providing work, sustenance, accommodation, and
recreation, so that the worker hardly ever needed to step outside the company
premises; many large companies had their own police forces, gaols, and sober-
up stations as well as clinics and hospitals. There were companies where labour
turnover was high, others where the workforce was very stable, and yet others
where the workforce was two tier, consisting of a transitory day-labourer
component and a stable long-contract component. Work organization, too,
varied from one factory to the next and indeed from one shop to the next
within the same factory. In some places the basis of work process organization
was the *artel'*, a gang of workers who were often migrants from the same
village, whose leader subcontracted jobs from the management and kept the
work process under the control of the gang itself. In some places skilled
workers had the subcontractor's authority over hired hands. In many factory
shops most aspects of managerial authority were centralized in the hands of
foremen while in others the foreman had to share authority over particular
aspects with various engineers and administrators.

The kind of work done on many factory shopfloors was not in fact very
different in its character and organization from the work done in preindustrial
artisan workshops. The pattern of investment in many Russian industries was
influenced by the availability of cheap labour and the expectation that the
product did not have to be of high quality to find extensive home markets.
Highly productive machines coincided with a reliance on crude labouring jobs
within the same production processes, and machines were often valued for
their adaptability to do different tasks rather than for their precision and
efficiency within a specialized range of operations. Even the most glamorous
'metalist' factories of St Petersburg included many a shopfloor corner and yard
where the atmosphere was artisan rather than industrial. It was perhaps only in
the most modern cotton mills that the production process was unremittingly
machine paced and technologically streamlined; on most other factory floors,
the work went on in job series, the pace and detailed implementation of which
was not predetermined by technological design.

Across industries, production workers tended to be paid by piece rates, most
workers were on renewable one-year contracts, and all workers were subject
to extensive company rule-books which specified various penalties for
misdemeanours. Theft of company property seemed to be something that
many employers felt compelled to combat; workers were commonly subject to
personal searches at exit gates, and some factories set up workers' 'comradely
courts' for the trial of apprehended offenders, in the hope that the shame of
peer-inflicted public punishment would be a more effective deterrent than
penalties imposed by the management. Fines were the most usual form of
punishment; corporal punishment was a rare practice by the early 1900s.
Companies varied in the readiness with which their managers felt able to deal
with difficult workers by dismissal or redundancy. In some state-owned and
state-subsidized heavy-industry plants, there was evidently a general expectation that managers should avoid jeopardizing workers' job security. In the

Urals steel-works, for example, it was common practice to respond to shortages of orders by putting all workers on shorter weeks rather than making some of them redundant; difficult workers were sometimes induced to leave by lump-sum insurance payments when they were injured in accidents or fell ill, in preference to putting them through dismissal procedures. Accident rates were high in many jobs, although the greatest health hazard to workers across many industries were chronic respiratory illnesses caused by high air pollution in poorly ventilated workplaces.

By the early 1900s, over 90 per cent of the factories employed their labour all the year round, without making a general provision for workers to return to their villages at harvest times. Many factories, however, had to institute extra 'sticks and carrots' to prevent substantial numbers of workers from taking an extended leave in the summer. This was often cited as evidence of the workers' continuing commitment to their peasant backgrounds. On the other hand, it should be remembered that workers did not have annual entitlements to vacation leave and going back to the villages to help with the agricultural high season was the only way they could afford having a prolonged break from the factory and city. They were not the only ones who showed a need for this, as taking prolonged summer breaks in the countryside was customary among the professional and white-collar classes of the metropolitan population as well. Factory calendars, however, included a good sprinkling of religious holidays, and the rule-books of some factories institutionalized workers' right to go on leave for special family occasions. The average Russian factory worker worked 264 days in a year – almost 19 days fewer than his counterpart in the Protestant-dominated state of Massachusetts.[23] Some of the most modern textile factories in St Petersburg, however, were soon to start introducing fuller work years.

The heterogeneity of factory conditions across industries was complemented by diversified group identities. Workers saw themselves and one another as belonging to this or that company, and as belonging to a particular shop within a company, and perhaps also as belonging to a *zemlyachestvo* network. The minority in skilled jobs requiring an apprenticeship training very much identified with their craft. Production workers who worked with machines tended to derive some pride from that, even if the work they did was classed as semi-skilled and requiring only a short period of training. The lowest of the low were the numerous ranks of unskilled auxiliary labourers. Occupations, jobs, and work groups were segregated between the sexes, and male workers looked down upon female workers and 'female jobs', although the lines of segregation were changing, with some previously 'male jobs' becoming 'female'. Womens' wage rates were one-half to two-thirds of mens', and it would take the First World War for the labour movement to incorporate equal pay for equal work among its demands.

In the cities, native-born urbanites and the longer-established immigrants considered themselves superior to the newcomers. It is not clear how workers managed to acquire a skill or to progress from auxiliary labouring to machine production jobs. Few companies operated any special training schemes. Much presumably depended upon personal recommendation and the good graces of

23 Crisp, 'Labour', pp. 308–415.

foremen, and perhaps also upon extraneous qualities, such as literacy and general education attainment. In the case of apprenticeships for skilled crafts, it also depended upon the willingness of the young recruits to put up with the low wages and the general deprivations of apprentice status. It does not seem to be the case that workers of the peasant estate were discriminated against in favour of members of the urban-artisan estates in these respects. The urban artisans were found among the unskilled labourers, while peasants were found among the skilled craftsmen. In a sense, the factory floors belonged to the peasant estate, unlike urban non-industrial work places, such as shops and offices, where the non-auxiliary employees tended to be 'urbanites' by social estate.

The Marxist intelligentsia's yearning for a 'conscious' working class was still some way from finding any reflection in reality. The preferred term of Marxist theory for factory workers, the 'industrial proletariat', meant nothing to them. The theoreticians' other preferred term, 'a worker' (*rabochii*) was too close to the term commonly used for the low-status auxiliary labourers (*chernorabochii*) to gain quick acceptance as a self-applied collective label. If they had to refer to themselves as a large category, some factory workers were still happy to say they were 'peasants', for that was what the official stamp said in their passports and the word shared a root with the word for Christians. Otherwise, workers were quite happy to refer to themselves as 'toiling people', although this was an all-inclusive old term for everyone who did manual work for a living, regardless of whether or not the work was in factory employment. But collective self-designations by the name of the company for which one was working, or the word for an industry ('metalist', 'textilist'), an occupational title, or craft trade were much more common.

We have already noted that most of the strikes were about wage-related issues. Some of these were not so much about the wage rates themselves as about issues arising from the calculation of piece-rated earnings or from conditions the workers felt prevented them from doing well on piece-rates that were not their own fault. For example, the workers in some shops felt they should not have suffered lowered earnings if their productivity decreased when they had to work on low-quality raw material or with unreliable machines. Some disputes were about what the workers believed were arbitrary impositions of disciplinary fines. In addition, there was an interesting residual of disputes where the workers' grievances appeared to focus on foremen or supervisors who were generally capricious or rude.

In fact, deference and dignity appeared as issues of personal conflict between workers and supervisory or white-collar employees in a variety of evidence from the factory floors. Some company rule-books included clauses requiring the worker to show deference to managerial ranks, for example by removing his cap when talking to a superior. It was common practice for the managerial ranks to address workers by the familiar form of second-person singular while expecting to be addressed by the polite form of second-person plural. Such expectations of ritual deference to managerial authority had a dubious legitimacy among ex-peasant workers. Peasants were used to interacting with the nobles in this manner, but such interactions were not very frequent in their lives; most of the time, they lived among their own kind and did their work without any interference from supposedly superior outsiders. On the factory floors, however, the men who expected deferential treatment from the workers did so on a daily basis, while supervising the work process and taking decisions that affected the workers' earnings and working conditions. They were not nobles and much of what they did was not based on relevant technical expertise, for this was largely held by the skilled manual ranks. Their claims on the workers' deference were resented by the workers who often saw the supervisory and white-collar ranks as people whose practical contribution to the work process was obscure and possibly just parasitic. The supervisory ranks, however, often felt that their capacity to supervise or manage the work process was seriously threatened if what they perceived as insolence on the part of some workers remained tolerated. Stemming from a transference of traditional principles of hierarchical authority to industrial settings, this conflict led to many workers coming to share a general resentment of 'little white hands' (*beloruchki*), – non-manual employees – even before some workers became educated in the socialist outlook on industrial capitalism and its exploitation of labour.

The first workers who became exposed to articulate political opinions were a handful of individuals who joined the underground discussion circles of the radical intelligentsia in the late 1880s and early 1890s. These 'conscious' workers tended to be rather unusual in their personal characteristics, in that they were even younger than average, unmarried, and given to puritanical commitments, such as teetotalism, as well as to bookish self-improvement. They tried to emulate the personal tastes of respectable educated society, and shared the intelligentsia's disdain for the lack of culture and moral principle among the 'mass workers'. 'He hated all the workers and therefore it was empty near his workbench, as if it were a place infected by the plague', said a 'mass' worker about a 'conscious' worker of his acquaintance.[24] Such 'conscious' workers were clearly limited in their ability to lead the 'mass' workers into political struggles. The Marxist revolutionaries were initially not much more successful in enlisting an active and effective worker support than earlier radical underground circles had been. Manual workers were a small minority among the party membership, and not all of them had any special access to the factory floors, because they worked in small artisan workshops. Besides, the secret police were vigilant and quick to nip in the bud any beginnings of agitational effectiveness on the part of the underground organizers by sending them into exile.

As has been already noted in Chapter 1, the first organized labour movement that articulated factory workers' discontents on a broad basis was initiated by a Moscow secret police chief, S. V. Zubatov. His strategy of 'police socialism' was aimed at giving a new lease of life to tsarist autocracy by drawing on the traditional peasant belief that God and the tsar were essentially on the side of the poor against greedy property owners, corrupt officials, and jumped-up petty despots. The traditional yearning of the poor was for *pravda*, truth and justice, in one vague but powerful concept. Zubatov's workers' associations were started in 1901, which coincided with the onset of an economic

---

24 Quoted in McDaniel, T. 1988: *Autocracy, Capitalism, and Revolution in Russia*. Berkeley, Calif.: University of California Press, p. 179.

depression that followed the industrial boom of the 1890s. Apart from organizing public lectures, the associations helped workers to draft petitions stating their demands to employers and encouraged them to lodge complaints against managerial abuses with factory inspectors. The number of workers' complaints about beatings and coarse treatment registered by the factory inspectorate in the Moscow province shot up from 161 in 1901 to 2146 in 1902.[25] This provided a basis on which Ministry of the Interior officials, city governors, and police chiefs could intervene with employers on workers' behalf, thus making the powers of the autocracy to be seen to be on the side of the *pravda*. But for workers the upshot of an activated aspiration to the *pravda* was the sympathy strike motivated by solidarity with the workers in other disputes as well as by purely local grievances. The year 1903 saw a wave of such strikes in Moscow and several other cities; in the Ukrainian city of Odessa, it almost reached the proportions of a general strike.

Strikes remained illegal, although the legalization of economic strikes was considered desirable by some government ministers, including the influential S. Witte. Zubatov was politically embarrassed within the government and removed from Moscow where the associations were henceforth allowed only sporadic, low-profile and heavily policed activity. In the capital, however, he was able to provide patronage to G. A. Gapon, a charismatic priest who, in 1903, established the Assembly of the Russian Factory and Mill Workers of the City of St Petersburg. Gapon's rhetoric could not have been more different from that of the Western-oriented radical intelligentsia. It was very Slavonic, rich in resurrectionary Christian imagery, and effective in moving the crowds in packed public halls to frenzied oaths of martyrdom in a just and holy cause. The demands of the holy cause, however, were very radical and modern in their content. They included a minimum wage, an eight-hour day, elected worker committees to have joint powers with company boards in the handling of workers' grievance and disciplinary matters, the right to form trade unions, the involvement of worker representatives in the drafting of social-insurance legislation, an introduction of progressive income tax instead of indirect taxes and land redemption payments, a comprehensive education system, the freeing of political prisoners, constitutional guarantees of civil rights, cessation of the war with Japan, and the ministers of government to be made accountable to a constituent assembly elected by universal franchise. Gapon's strategy was to present the well publicized demands as a petition to the tsar by his most devoted and peaceful subjects who had a complete faith in his paternal wisdom and his resolve to take the side of the people against corrupt bureaucrats and exploiters.

The petition was drafted and publicized in public meetings and the press during 1904, when the disastrous military defeat by Japan brought to a head the dissatisfaction of educated society with the autocracy. The liberal press was now gaining readership among the workers, and Gapon's petition was reflecting the liberal intelligentsia's aspirations as well as the specifically working-class concerns. The petition was in effect inviting the tsar to save his rule by embracing democratic reforms rather than letting the atheist and

---

25 McDaniel, *Autocracy*, p. 80.

republican movements of the radical intelligentsia dictate the terms of political change. At the same time, Gapon's movement was successful in wooing the support of liberal and socialist activists as well as religious-minded people, Zubatov's police socialists, and 'mass' workers. When several workers were dismissed from the large Putilov works after a dispute with a generally unpopular foreman in the autumn, Gapon took up the case as one of principle, since the dismissed workers were assembly members. The Putilov managers would not negotiate and the city's industry became engulfed in a larger-than-ever strike wave.

The petition's delivery to the tsar was set for Sunday, January 9, 1905. The arrangements were publicized well in advance, to give the tsar an opportunity to make his arrangements for receiving the petition at the Winter Palace, in front of which the workers would congregate after marching from the industrial suburbs via several routes. The fact that the authorities refused a permit for the gathering did not deter the organizers, for there was always a hope that the tsar would in the event over-rule his officials. Between 50 000 and 100 000 workers took part in the march, many bearing icons, wearing their Sunday best, and bringing their children along to signify peaceful intent. But the tsar elected to be in his other residence for the day, and some of the military detachments posted to stop the march from reaching the palace opened fire on the marchers. The first public demonstration of an organized labour movement thus became Bloody Sunday, an event that shocked public opinion in Russia and across the world. The popular belief that the tsar was essentially on the side of the people turned its opposite, and all authority structures became engulfed in a deluge of discontent. The radical intelligentsia's atheist and anti-autocracy language became the dominant medium for the political articulation of workers' discontent; the traditional rhetoric that identified the Russian soul with Christian orthodoxy and the tsar became a medium used primarily by die-hard conservative zenophobes.

The Year 1905

The day after Bloody Sunday the authorities banned the assemblies and ordered the police to busy themselves with suspected strike fomenters. Thousands of workers were arrested and promptly sent into exile, but the clamp-down did not prevent workers' protests and strikes spreading quickly. In January and February, strikes became a daily occurrence in regions that had never seen any before and the overall number of strikes in Russian industry exceeded in those months the annual records of previous peak years. Workers often walked out first and formulated their demands later. Disputes with foremen that were previously settled without walkouts were enough to precipitate strikes in the general climate of outrage at the injustice of Bloody Sunday. The demands that striking workers formulated almost always included higher wages, but increasingly also shorter working hours, with the eight-hour day becoming a generally adopted slogan, negotiating rights for elected workers' representatives in cases of conflict with management, and the end to management arbitrary disciplinary powers. Deference and dignity issues were articulated in striking workers' resolutions with increasing frequency. Workers demanded that they may pass through factory gates without personal searches, that managers address them in the polite second-person plural, and that particularly offensive bosses be dismissed. In some cases where the employers refused to be dismissed, workers forced unpopular foremen to resign by humiliating them in a fashion reminiscent of the peasant village charivari: foremen were manhandled into wheelbarrows and ceremoniously paraded out of the factory premises. There was some violence – against unpopular bosses, against workers who refused to join a strike, against workers brought in from the outside to break a strike, and against policemen or armed guards if they tried to intervene. There was also some looting of property and vandalism. The majority of the strikes, however, took their course without any damage to persons or property. Employers were often quite willing to negotiate with the strike committees and make concessions.

In February the government set up a special commission to investigate St Petersburg workers' grievances. The Shidlovsky Commission was to have elected workers' representatives on it. Ballots were organized on factory floors to elect delegates to a college of electors, who would then elect the commission representatives. The electoral process involved many factory workers (almost 150 000 voted) in many meetings in which workers articulated their interests on a supra-local basis and established their expectations of democratic representation. The government lost its nerve and aborted the commission when the college of workers' electors demanded the immediate freedom for arrested workers and a lift of the ban on Gapon's assemblies. Over 50 000 workers went on strike when they learnt that their elected representatives would not be consulted by the government after all. But the Shidlovsky Commission left behind a longer-lasting legacy: a body of elected workers' representatives as well as the experience of providing a mandate by a democratic process. The electoral college and the relationships between its members and their electors formed a basis for other institutions that came into being during the months that followed: trade unions, interfactory strike committees, and, in the autumn, the St Petersburg Workers' Soviet.

The strike movement and actions, such as the Shidlovsky Commission elections, got under way without much political leadership from the supposedly proletarian revolutionary parties. Both factions of the Social Democratic Party, the Mensheviks and the Bolsheviks, as well as the Social Revolutionary Party and the anarchist groups, were aiming for an armed uprising against the tsarist state rather than for an institutionalization of workers' power in industrial bargaining. They thought workers' strikes to be of limited value if they were just 'spontaneous' protests against the management or if they voiced 'merely economic' demands. The Bolsheviks altogether refused to have anything to do with the Shidlovsky elections, and throughout the eventful year the decisions of the revolutionary organizations to involve themselves in workers' struggles could rarely be seen to make much difference to what actually happened, when the workers went on strike and when they went back to work. But when workers voted for strike committees or for delegates to bodies such as the Shidlovsky Commission, they tended to elect many who were either already self-declared supporters of the revolutionary parties or who would become so after entering the wider political process in their worker delegate capacity. Workers tended to elect people who spoke the best at their meetings and who seemed articulate enough to hold their own in the political world outside the factory floor; and the most articulate workers now tended to be drawn into a political discourse in which the radical intelligentsia's ideological vocabularies prevailed. This was a time of political-opinion polarization between autocracy and revolution, in which it was not easy for new entrants into the political arena to articulate a group interest and couch it in moderate or pragmatic terms. The revolutionary parties were gaining worker membership, although they were never to control the ebb and flow of the workers' strike movement.

The outrage at the events of Bloody Sunday also led to a wave of protest in the traditional bastions of political radicalism, the universities and secondary schools. Again, the protest was about particular student grievances as well as the brutalities of political repression. Students occupied classrooms to demand curriculum changes, parents demanded a say in the running of schools, and academic staff demanded autonomy from government interference in appointments and teaching. In March the government closed the universities.

Another avalanche of middle-class politicization was precipitated in February, when the government invited the institutions of 'society' (the zemstvos, the city dumas, and professional associations) to formulate opinions on how the state could be improved. There always seemed to be a contradiction between this policy of wooing the educated society and the repeated proclamations of the autocracy that its principles were not negotiable. The hundreds of conferences convened by the established institutions of 'society' produced a flood of petitions advising that the principles of autocracy be replaced by those of a constitutional government based upon an elected legislative assembly. Many of the establishment liberals were happy to retain the tsar as a constitutional monarch, but there was a leftward trend in the contents of the petitions as the months went by. By the summer, it was common for the petitions to advocate a general franchise and social legislation as well as basic rule-of-law principles.

Even more radical were the unions of professional people that were being set up alongside workers' trade unions. Lawyers, engineers, accountants, agronomists, veterinarians, statisticians, medical personnel, pharmacists, academics, teachers, office workers, railway employees, and writers established their unions without waiting for police permission to do so. Most of these professional unions had radical liberal leaderships, but few were as large as the Union for the Equality of Women (6000–8000 members) and the Union for Jewish Equality (7500 members).[26] In May the educated unions formed the Union of Unions, the leadership of which declared its aim for a political general strike to overthrow the autocracy. Moderate liberals favouring gradual reforms were becoming isolated while the radical professionals leaned towards the revolutionary parties.

---

26 Ascher, A. 1988: *The Revolution of 1905: Russia in Disarray*. Stanford, Calif.: Stanford University Press, p. 143.

It was not just developments in Russia proper that were rocking the state. The largest and best organized radical party in the empire was the Jewish Bund, which operated in the cities of the Jewish Pale of Settlement, that is in the Baltics, Poland, and Ukraine. Militancy was also high among the Polish workers and intelligentsia. The Mensheviks had particularly strong grass-roots support in Georgia, the only place in the empire where a Marxist party found support among the peasantry as well as urban workers. Outside Russia proper, the erosion of tsarist authority was giving rise to nationalist and ethnic as well as liberal and socialist aspirations.

The Bloody Sunday procession and the unrest among workers, students, and the professional intelligentsia that followed turned the streets and public meetings halls of the cities into a stage for a newly enlarged political public. Groups of people came on it to demonstrate their identity and political opinion, and there were spectators who joined them or formed an alternative opinion and self-identity in response. The events of the political street theatre were reported and commented upon in the press, thus reinforcing the participants' sense of being a historical actor and witness. But it was not every day of the year in 1905 that the city streets were a scene of political demonstrations. The erosion of the regime's authority allowed the political theatre, but it also had another consequence: life in the cities became menaced by violence. This was so not only during the moments of political spectacle, for example when the police or Cossacks tried to disperse a meeting, but also more crucially outside these moments, in the course of normal everyday life.

The tsarist state had a rather weak police force. It always relied on mobile Cossack and army units to quell major disorders, but much of the army was now in Manchuria and the remainder was overstretched as disorders multiplied in the vast countryside as well as in the cities. The police was demoralized; it could not cope and it could not rely on firm and consistent backing from a government whose legitimacy was being questioned with an unprecedented intensity. The police found themselves exposed to ridicule when they were seen to back down from attempts to enforce bans on public assemblies, and to hatred when they persisted. Besides, they were exposed to assassins' bullets, for the anarchist wing of the revolutionary movement considered them a regular target for its terrorist campaigns. From the early weeks of the year, the police ventured into the streets only in large formations, which left them unpoliced for much of the time.

The cities' criminal element quickly became very large and intrusive. Individuals scuttled about their business in fear and with a growing sense of frustration. When in groups, they were increasingly given to taking the law into their own hands. The streets became the scene of impromptu lynching parties to avenge street-crime outrages, and vigilante groups were formed by shopkeepers, workers, and residents to hound down suspected criminals. The criminals in turn formed their own armed gangs. The distinctions between law-abiders and law-breakers were becoming blurred. While many people experienced the ecstasies of social solidarity and liberation during the moments of political street theatre, many also became prey to feelings of fear and animosity outside these moments, which they tended to focus on the people in their own surroundings rather than on the remote autocracy. In some cities, groups of workers were given to menacing with violence not only suspected criminals but also any passer-by who looked educated or well heeled; some young men formed gangs to loot affluent people's apartments; groups of revolutionary supporters dealt out violence to suspected police informers; other groups, to students or to suspected revolutionaries. The violence associated with the breakdown of authority was multiplied by the violence of the backlash. Within a few weeks, the reactionary forces were able to use zenophobia and anti-semitism to get mobs into the streets, and to vent a hatred under a sort of tsarist banner.

The pogroms on Jews, foreigners, and suspected revolutionaries was in a large part organized by the Black Hundreds, an ultraconservative organization which was known to have supporters in high places and rumoured to have the sympathies of the tsar. Police passivity began to look like a sinister conspiracy in many of the cities where the police witnessed the pogroms but did absolutely nothing to prevent them or to bring the perpetrators to justice. The appearance of the Black Hundreds mobs on the scene served to shift the balance of attitudes among the newly enlarged political public further to the left. Its other historical effect was to propel large numbers of the Jewish population to emigrate from the cities of the Pale overseas, in particular to the USA, and to shift the balance of progressive opinion among the Russian and ex-Russian Jewish population in favour of the Zionist version of socialism.

The Black Hundreds counted some industrial workers among their supporters; many more workers, however, were joining newly formed trade unions, workers' co-operatives, and workers' clubs which had connections with the revolutionary parties and also the parties themselves. There were more than 60 workers' unions in Moscow and more than 50 in St Petersburg by the end of the year. From the early spring on, workers who were on strike led their leaders to formulate political, mostly liberal-constitutionalist demands as well as the demands reflecting more specific workers' interests.

In May and June the liberal and socialist majority of the political public followed with interest developments in the textile city of Ivanovo-Voznesensk, where a strike of over 30 000 workers stopped production in all the city's factories. The strikers' 24 demands were mainly economic and otherwise notable by the fact that they included pregnancy leave and the provision of nurseries; until then, workers' struggles records hardly ever reflected the substantial presence of women in the factories. But what particularly caught the imagination of the wider public was the election of an assembly of delegates that put the strike under a single organization, which, for a while, virtually controlled the whole city. The strikers originally elected the assembly in response to a suggestion from a factory inspector who thought that such a representative body would be useful for a speedy and peaceful settlement. But since the factory owners were slow in coming to the negotiating table, the assembly found itself organizing a prolonged struggle; it published its own bulletin to keep the strikers informed of developments and, to protect them from the Black Hundreds, it organized a militia. The assembly thus became known as the first instance in which insurgent workers set up their own self-government on a city-wide basis; in other words, the first-ever soviet of workers' deputies. The workers started the strike in a peaceful and disciplined manner, but eventually responded with bouts of violent rampage to the employers' refusal to grant substantial concessions and the state authorities' refusal to recognize the militia or to permit further mass meetings. When the employers did make concessions, the workers refused to call off the strike unless arrested strikers were released. The strike lasted two months and ended in the workers' defeat.

In the summer the moderate constitutionalist section of the intelligentsia was frustrated by the tsar's apparent inclination to follow mainly conservative advice in his response to reformist proposals. On the other hand, the government granted greater autonomy to the universities and permitted them to reopen at the beginning of the new academic year. The new autonomy made it safe for political meetings to be conducted on university premises without police permission. Radical students campaigned for the universities to open their doors to all members of the general public who wished to convene or attend meetings. The student body in most institutions backed this proposal, subject to the proviso that public meetings should not be allowed to jeopardize normal teaching. Although there were many revolutionary activists among the students who advocated the suspension of the normal academic programme, the majority of students were concerned to resume their academic progress towards graduation. Most students were living on the breadline, but also in the knowledge that they were almost certain to get very well paid and secure jobs immediately after graduation. In the event, the universities quickly became busy political meeting places for workers and everyone else, as the radical students wanted. And, as the radicals hoped, the heady atmosphere of the meetings spread outside the lecture halls to create a climate conducive to a general strike against the autocracy.

The snowball towards a general strike started when Moscow printers stopped work to demand higher wages, walked out, and gathered in the vicinity of the university. The mixed crowd of printers and students refused to disperse when asked to do so by the police, the mayhem became violent, and the Cossacks who came along to restore order killed 10 people. Printers in St Petersburg and other cities stopped their presses rolling. The Cossacks caused another outrage among the educated classes when they arrested students who lingered after the mass public funeral of the Moscow university rector, a nationally prominent leader of the liberal movement. The snowball became an avalanche when the railway workers' union declared a general strike on the railways, demanding a constituent assembly as well as economic improvements. Some railway workers were already on strike because of economic grievances, and it did not take the union long to persuade the rest to follow. The railway strike included telegraph operators. Telephone and postal workers followed, as did almost everyone else from ballerinas and bank clerks to weavers and waiters. Sporadic unrest spread almost to the armed forces, especially to the soldiers in Manchuria who wanted to get home and who found themselves stranded by the railway strike. By mid-October, the economy was stopped, and striking workers in the cities elected their soviets. The general strike was a moment of unity under a liberal, that is, constitutionalist and anti-autocracy, banner. Even some of the employers supported the strike, by agreeing to pay striking workers' wages or by raising money for their support. The Moscow business community was especially prominent in aligning itself with the liberal cause. Municipal authorities demanded an autonomy from central government; in particular, they wanted to put the police forces under their control.

The tsarist government had to do something to detach reformist liberal opinion from the revolutionaries and to detach the professional intelligentsia from the workers. On October 17 the tsar issued a hastily drafted manifesto which proclaimed for his subjects 'the principles of real personal inviolability' and the 'freedom of conscience, speech, assembly, and union'; this also reaffirmed an earlier promise to set up an elected parliamentary body, the state duma, with a wider franchise than had been mooted in the summer. The terms of power-sharing among the tsar, the council of ministers, and the state duma were vague. It would soon transpire, however, that the prime minister and his cabinet were to be appointed by the tsar rather than the state duma, and that initiative in the legislative process was to be with the prime minister rather than the duma. Franchise was only to be given to males aged 25 years or more, and was to be organized via electoral colleges tied to the social estates system so that the privileged would be better represented in the duma than the rest; the ratio of voters to deputies was even more detrimental to the urban workers than the rural peasantry. The tsar would have the right to dissolve a duma if its majority came to a deadlock with the government. And last but not least, there was little in the manifesto or in the subsequent pronouncements of the tsar and his ministers that promised a revocation of emergency powers which provincial governors could wield to quell discontent by the use of police repression. In fact, the number of provinces and regions that were under emergency powers was already large and still growing – the autocracy felt unable to dispense with the despotic instruments of repression.

The October manifesto ended the general strike, but not strikes or unrest in the streets; neither did it lead to the dissolution of workers' soviets. On the contrary, the St Petersburg Soviet organized a 6000-strong militia and, amid a general confusion among state and municipal officials, enjoyed considerable influence over the affairs of the city until it was suppressed two months later. The soviets exerted plenty of political initiative in other cities as well, and the St Petersburg Soviet soon began to try to put its provincial counterparts under its own leadership. The St Petersburg Soviet was dominated by metal workers, partly because they were numerically dominant in the capital's industry and partly because they were concentrated in several very large firms where the elections of deputies could be organized quickly. It also reserved a certain number of places for revolutionary party nominees. Its dominant political colours were left liberal and Menshevik socialist. The Bolsheviks had been slow to involve themselves in the general strike or the soviet, neither of which ever proclaimed support for an armed uprising. But they increased their profile in the workers' movement along with the other revolutionary parties during the two months following the October manifesto, when revolutionary parties did not need to keep their activities within the limits of a conspiratorial underground.

The post-manifesto strikes put an end to the broad cross-class alliance between liberal and working-class aspirations. The workers' movement was impatient for major social legislation and the eight-hour day in particular. In the capital, the industrialists formed their own organization and agreed to be firm in not conceding what they considered industry could not afford. Strikes and workers' attempts to introduce the eight-hour day by stopping work after eight hours were followed by lockouts. The employers responded by establishing a solid common front, refusing to compensate workers for the wages lost through stoppages. The St Petersburg Soviet attempted to organize another general strike at the beginning of November, but with no more than mixed success. A gap was developing between, on the one hand, the militant mood on the factory floors and the left-wing rhetoric in the soviet and, on the other, the workers' waning ability to endure starvation while striking without financial support.

In the streets and the meeting halls of the cities, the October manifesto propelled the political theatre of 1905 into its most intensive action. The radical liberals and socialists thought the terms of the manifesto to be inadequate, while the conservatives, whose numbers probably increased in the course of a year plagued by violent and uncomfortable social unrest, were upset that this unrest apparently forced the tsar into making a concession. The radicals took to the streets with anti-tsarist satire and they defaced the tsar's portraits. The Black Hundreds also took to the streets in large numbers to attack the radical processions and to carry out pogroms on Jews and other suspected infidels; if they overpowered their victims, they forced them into ritual kneelings before undefaced portraits of the tsar. In Moscow another large political funeral, this time of a Bolshevik revolutionary murdered by a Black Hundreds worker, resulted in several thousand mourners coming under attack from the Black Hundreds as well as from the Cossacks. The rhetoric of street politics had a momentum that allowed no cues on which moderate characters could speak their conciliatory lines and be heard.

In December in Moscow, the revolutionary parties – the Menshevik Social Democrats as well as the Bolsheviks and Social Revolutionaries – decided to start an armed uprising. They heard only the high notes in the messages given by the bearers of news about soldier mutinies and the political theatre in other cities. They had a pledge of support from the militants in Moscow's white-collar trade unions and from groups of textile workers. The tactic was to defeat the army and the Cossacks by small, mobile groups of armed insurgents. But the army brought big guns and used them to destroy the buildings in which the insurgents sought cover. The uprising was over in a few days. Some barricades were built in the streets during the days of the warfare, which suggested a broader Muscovite involvement. But in themselves, the barricades stood as evidence to active participation in the uprising by no more than a small proportion of the city's population. The streets were, on the whole, empty, and it is not clear what the people who stayed away were thinking.

There were armed uprisings and mutinies in other cities as well, although not in St Petersburg. The government responded by a campaign of repression throughout the empire, which lasted well into 1906. Thousands of people were killed in violent confrontations with military units and in martial law executions. Tens of thousands of strike leaders and revolutionary activists were arrested and sent into exile. Radical members of the professional intelligentsia were sacked from government jobs. The soviets were dispersed and the revolutionary parties driven underground once more.

The Last Years of the Tsarist Era

The revolutionary parties failed to retain the active support they had gained during the 'days of liberty'. This was so not only because of police repression. The broader ranks of the radical intelligentsia remained anti-autocracy in their attitudes, but the experience of 1905 reinforced their belief that social progress was hampered by the masses' 'lack of culture'. The terms on which the regime honoured the freedom of association promised by the October manifesto made it much easier than before to organize culture clubs, libraries, and evening or Sunday classes for the masses without police interference and, as has been already noted in Chapter 1, this was where the main thrust of the 'serve the people' impulse was directed. Apart from voluntary work in the popular education movement, many of the socially minded intelligentsia sought their self-realization in employment in workers' consumer co-operatives, and many more in the rapidly expanding state employment sector as teachers, doctors, and agronomists, etc. Those willing to join the underground revolutionary parties were few. The remaining party activists sneered at these attitudes of the 'bourgeois intelligentsia', proclaiming their satisfaction with the 'proletarianization' of their own ranks. But the recruitment of working-class activists was not nearly sufficient to sustain underground cells in more than a handful of industrial work places. Besides being well penetrated by the secret police, the revolutionary parties were consumed by sectarian ideological quarrels (this was the particular forte of intellectual leaders in foreign exile), by struggles for organizational control between the leaders abroad and the activists at home, and by social tensions between educated and uneducated members.

The trade unions also atrophied. New laws that permitted their existence did so only conditionally. Trade unions had to register with special city commissions headed by policemen, and they were banned from activities that could be construed as preparing for strikes. Going on a strike was not illegal, but being a 'ring-leader' of one was. Employers were not prevented by law from sacking striking workers and rehiring only those deemed not to be ring-leaders. Many employers refused to recognize the trade unions as their negotiating partners; and the employers had all the bargaining power, because the pacification of the country did not put an end to economic depression. The great majority of the trade unions founded during 1905 no longer existed in 1909. The number of strikes that occurred in 1907–10 was relatively low, and strikers were hardly ever victorious. The employers quickly clawed back the gains workers made in 1905; the work day was restored to at least nine hours, fines for labour indiscipline and gate searches were reimposed, punch clocks were installed to eradicate tardiness, disciplining, hiring and firing again became an undisputed managerial prerogative, and efficiency measures were introduced on many factory floors to increase productivity and reduce wage costs.

The restoration of the status quo on the factory floors did not remove the problems of legitimacy of managerial authority and the sense of grievance that workers had about pay and conditions. The frequency of strikes assumed an upward curve once more as soon as the prewar industrial boom started. In April 1912, an event horribly reminiscent of Bloody Sunday occurred in the Lena goldmines in Siberia, where troops killed 172 marching miners. As in

1905, popular indignation at the massacre precipitated a veritable strike movement. The number of strikes officially recorded by the factory inspectors throughout the empire rose from 466 in 1911 to 2032 in 1912, 2404 in 1913, and 4098 in 1914.[27] An increasing proportion of the strikes were classified by the factory inspectors as 'political' rather than just 'economic'. Workers in many factories took to commemorating by one-day strikes the labour May Day and the anniversaries of Bloody Sunday and the Lena massacre. Emancipation from serfdom was also commemorated in this manner. Where employers tried to punish these strikes by fines or sackings, more strikes followed out of solidarity. Strikes also occurred in response to events in the state duma, and in protest against court trials of workers and soldiers.

Statistical compilations of 'economic' and 'political' strikes in 1912–14 show a marked concentration of political strikes in St Petersburg, where employers were particularly belligerent. In Moscow, the bastion of liberal businessmen, the textile factory owners included labour May Day in the list of official holidays; hence there were no 'political' strikes there on that day, and no follow-on strikes in solidarity with workers who were fined for May Day absence from work. In St Petersburg, the 'metalists' were well represented among strikers, but so were the workers of textile, food-processing, woodworking and printing industries. Not all 'metal' industry was affected, however. Some engineering plants, both large and small, were altogether bypassed by labour militancy. Action was concentrated in several privately owned firms that were neighbours to one another. It is difficult to infer from such data strong sociological causes of labour political militancy in the form of a male, skilled, and thoroughly urbanized engineering worker. Such 'advanced worker' types were found among the non-militants as well as the militants. The skilled worker who joined one or other of the revolutionary parties was as often an artisan baker or silversmith as much as an engineering factory worker; and some factory recruitment took place via *zemlyachestvo* networks – that is, among immigrant workers rather than urban natives. The cells of revolutionary party activists in the factories were in any case small, and their influence on the strike movement was hardly decisive. Anti-capitalist slogans were notable by their absence from the 'political' strikes, as was anything else that could be traced back to specific party policies, even after both the Bolsheviks and Mensheviks had started to publish in 1912 daily newspapers for a wide worker readership (*Pravda* and *Luch*). However, when the police closed the newspapers in the following year, thousands of workers went on strike in protest. *Pravda*'s editorial policy was independent of the Bolshevik leadership in exile, and it took care to cultivate a broad working-class rather than a narrow Bolshevik appeal. *Luch* actually had a policy of criticizing the strike movement for being too 'spontaneous' and politically undirected.

---

27 McKean, R. B. 1990: *St Petersburg between the Revolutions: Workers and Revolutionaries, June 1907–February 1917*. New Haven, Conn.: Yale University Press, p. 193.

Popular Culture and Civic Movements

Prior to 1905, the great majority of urban working men and women spent their leisure time socializing in their living quarters, in alehouses, and on walks. Men also spent some of their money gambling on organized fist-fights. Women presumably spent rather more of their time in their living quarters, judged by the fact that women factory workers spent more money on relatively more comfortable accommodation, although their wages were lower than men's. After 1905 pastimes became a little more varied. Mass-produced commercial literature, which has been already been discussed in Chapter 1 as the object of the intelligentsia's disapproval, became even more popular. The number of low-brow books – mainly the adventures of the detectives, Holmes and Pinkerton (by Russian writers, not translations from English originals), and romantic novels – that were printed annually increased from under 457 titles and under 9000 copies in 1901 to 2394 titles and almost 29 000 copies in 1912.[28] But most popular fiction was published in serial form in tabloid newspapers. The St Petersburg daily tabloid had a circulation of 250 000 (compared with *Pravda*'s 30 000). Another new form of popular entertainment, which also met with disapproval from the educated classes, was the cinema. In 1911, there were 100 cinemas in the capital alone showing newsreels and imported films. The most popular imported film was a tale about Don Cossacks produced by Pathe specifically for the Russian market. The first Russian-made feature film was shot in 1908, and several popular titles were produced every year from then on. Sports entertainment became more varied with the advent of football clubs.

This is not to say that the intelligentsia's efforts to promote high culture among the working classes was altogether in vain. Workers' educational societies in St Petersburg had thousands of members, as did their Moscow counterparts. Although the formal education of the majority of members did not exceed two years of primary schooling, the societies' libraries had plenty of borrowers for the classics. Club members were mostly young, single, male, skilled, and on above-average wages. The busiest clubs were city-centre ones catering for a variety of occupations rather than those situated in the exclusively industrial suburbs. These clubs were not the only places where educational self-improvement opportunities were available: public libraries, temperance societies, and municipally run 'people's universities' were but a few of the wide range of institutions that organized adult education schemes for the benefit of the working classes. There were also special Sunday classes for young women workers run by women's organizations.

In 1912 the government passed legislation obliging private industrial employers to set up sickness insurance organizations (*kassy*) run by joint boards of managers and elected workers' representatives. State enterprises were not included in this legislation, presumably because the biggest ones, such as the railways and the steel plants in the Urals, had already relatively advanced welfare schemes. By 1905, the railways had a network of hospitals,

---

28 Brooks, J. 1985: *When Russia Learned to Read: Literacy and Popular Literature, 1861–1917*. Princeton, NJ: Princeton University Press.

clinics, and midwife stations catering for 2.5 million employees and their dependants. By the outbreak of the war, the 1912 legislation resulted in 64 new *kassy* covering almost 90 000 workers in St Petersburg and 190 new *kassy* covering almost 230 000 workers in Moscow.[29] Some of the *kassy* formed consortia to set up their own medical centres and hospitals. Most of the *kassy* voted for levying the highest deductions from the workers' wages permitted by the law (two per cent) to provide the highest possible benefits. Despite the efforts of the revolutionary parties to influence the elections, most worker representatives elected to the boards were unconnected with any political group. Nevertheless, in St Petersburg the committees' work was often reported as being fraught by mutual mistrust between management and worker representatives.

The Wartime Strike Movement

The war against Germany and Austria that Russia entered in July 1914 naturally brought about an expansion of defence-related industries and a contraction of peaceful ones. The number of 'metalists' in Petrograd more than doubled between 1914 and 1917, increasing their share of the capital's factory workforce from 40 to 60 per cent. Overall, the factory labour force increased by 40 per cent in Moscow and by 60 per cent in Petrograd during the war. This did not, however, mean that immigration into the cities accelerated: the population of Petrograd grew by about 10 per cent between 1914 and 1917. Expansion of the labour force was achieved by recruitment from other parts of the urban population as well as by immigration from the countryside. Many women joined factory workforces, increasing their proportion from one-quarter to one-third in Petrograd industries, from three to 20 per cent in the Petrograd metal factories, and from 58 to 68 per cent in the Russian textile industry. Men of draft age (20–40 years) joined the ranks of 'metalists' from other occupations in the knowledge that they were thus increasing their chances of avoiding the draft; less than a half of male draft-age metal workers had to leave the bench for the trench.

There were relatively few strikes in Russian industry during the first year of the war, although many workers had to work harder and longer hours in return for wages which did not keep up with rising prices. Only skilled workers in defence-related industries were receiving inflation-beating pay rises. By 1916, however, all workers suffered unprecedented hardships as the overstretched economy could no longer sustain a steady supply of raw material for the factories and fuel and food for the towns. A new wave of strikes was started by the textile workers of Ivanovo-Voznesensk in mid-1915. The number of strikes registered by the factory inspectors throughout the empire rose from 68 in the second half of 1914 to 1034 in 1915 and 1576 in 1916, when almost a million workers took part.[30] Bloody Sunday was once more commemorated by large-

---

29 McKean, R. B. 1990: 'Social insurance in tsarist Russia: St Petersburg, 1907–1917'. *Revolutionary Russia*, iii, 1, pp. 55–89.
30 McKean, *St Petersburg*, p. 406.

scale strikes in January 1917. On February 23 textile workers from the traditionally militant Petrograd district of Vyborg walked out to demand 'bread'. (It was International Women's Day, but it is not clear whether this had much to do with the strike's timing.) Half the capital's factory workers were on strike the next day, four-fifths by February 27. On that day service-sector workers and the professional classes were in the streets as well, and the general strike also took hold of Moscow and other cities. Troops refused to interfere, and the crowds invaded public buildings and forced prison gates to open. The tsar dealt with the crisis by prorogating the state duma. Instead of going home, the duma deputies elected ten of their number to form a provisional government. Three days later the tsar abdicated, his brother declined to succeed him, and the tsarist state came to an end.

Further Reading

The discussion of Moscow and St Petersburg at the turn of the century is based on J. Bradley, *Muzhik and Muscovite: Urbanization in Late Imperial Russia* (Berkeley, Calif.: University of California Press, 1985) and J. H. Bater, *St Petersburg: Industrialization and Change* (London: Edward Arnold, 1976). Bater's treatment is an urban history in a social geography mould, while Bradley's is an excellent social history concentrating on the rise of municipal welfare reformism. Both books provide a wealth of social data on the cities and their development.

The discussion of the 1905 revolution draws mainly on A. Ascher, *The Revolution of 1905: Russia in Disarray* (Stanford, Calif.: Stanford University Press, 1988). There is much to be said for the view that, if one were to single out one particular year as the turning point in Russian history which separated old tsarist Russia from the modern era, that year would be 1905. Ascher's account is very readable, vivid, and well balanced in its insights into the intelligentsia's, as well as labour's, movements. Accounts that concentrate on the workers are G. D. Surh, *1905 in St Petersburg: Labor, Society, and Revolution* (Stanford, Calif.: Stanford University Press, 1989); L. Engelstein, *Moscow, 1905: Working-Class Organization and Political conflict* (Stanford, Calif.: Stanford University Press, 1982); and H. Reichman, *Railwaymen and Revolution: Russia, 1905* (Berkeley, Calif.: University of California Press, 1987). Interesting information on students is provided by J. Morrison, 'Education and the 1905 revolution', *Revolutionary Russia*, i, 1, June 1988, pp. 5–19.

There is a whole batch of books worth reading on factory labour in tsarist Russia. An introductory text on the tsarist period, which is very clear and informative while also being something of an exception in taking care to treat the tsarist industrial policy and employers fairly, is O. Crisp, 'Labour and industrialization in Russia', in P. Mathias and M.M. Postan (eds), *The Cambridge Economic History of Europe*, vii, Part 2 (Cambridge: Cambridge University Press, 1978), pp. 308–415. A classic treatment of the peasant–worker connection during the early industrialization years is provided by R. E. Johnson, *Peasant and Proletarian: The Working Class in Moscow in the Late*

Nineteenth Century (Leicester: Leicester University Press, 1979). T. McDaniel, *Autocracy, Capitalism, and Revolution in Russia* (Berkeley, Calif: University of California Press, 1988) gives a comprehensive account of tsarist labour legislation as well as a wide range of analytically careful insights into the processes of social-class formation. R. L. Glickman, *Russian Factory Women: Workplace and Society, 1880–1914* (Berkeley, Calif.: University of California Press, 1984) is the only book about labour that focuses on women, although this is certainly not its only merit. My discussion of the labour movement in the last tsarist decade is based mainly on the detailed study by R. B. McKean, *St Petersburg between the Revolutions: Workers and Revolutionaries, June 1907–February 1917* (New Haven, Conn.: Yale University Press, 1990). An article giving a wealth of information on welfare provision and pre-war reforms is also by McKean, 'Social insurance in tsarist Russia, St Petersburg, 1907–17', *Revolutionary Russia*, iii, i, 1990, pp. 55-89. Other useful accounts of the labour movement under the old regime are provided by V. E. Bonnell, *Roots of Rebellion: Workers' Politics and Organizations in St Petersburg and Moscow, 1900–1914* (Berkeley, Calif.: University of California Press, 1983); V. Bonnell (ed.), *The Russian Worker: Life and Labor under the Tsarist Regime* (Berkeley, Calif.: University of California Press, 1983); and R. Zelnik, *A Radical Worker in Tsarist Russia: The Autobiography of Semyon Ivanovich Kanatchikov* (Stanford, Calif.: Stanford University Press, 1986).

Finally, there is a review article to recommend to those embarking on a study of the Russian working class before and during the revolution: M. Perrie, 'The Russian working class 1905–17', *Theory and Society*, xvi, 1987, pp. 431–46. Perrie draws attention to the tendency of Western historians to accept somewhat uncritically the theorizing which saw workers as generally more or less 'developed' or 'conscious' and skilled metal-bashers with no peasant connections at the top of the proletarian quality ladder.

5

Urban Classes under the New Regime, 1917–28

As in the October days after 1905, the cross-class social unity of the general strike soon came under strain from a rising tide of factory workers' militancy. Workers again wanted an eight-hour day and did not wait for management agreement to practise it, and they demanded higher wages and a say in who was hired or fired. They also revived the 1905 custom of putting unpopular managers in sacks and driving them out in wheelbarrows. They continued to use strikes to press for their demands, although this was no longer the only means at their disposal for gaining concessions. Industrial militancy was concentrated in the early part of the year in the capital cities, among the 'metalists' in particular, but spread more widely as the economy deteriorated and politics became more polarized. In the early part of the year, militant workers were under some pressure from other workers as well as the general public to restrain themselves and refrain from jeopardizing the supplies of much needed clothing and ammunition to soldiers at the front. This particular source of restraint relaxed, however, after the June offensive's failure caused public opinion to swing against the continuation of war.

Also in the early part of the year employers quite easily made concessions to workers' demands because they knew the political situation would not allow them to assume a tough stance. Workers dominated the soviets without whose backing the government was not able to supply police or troops to support lockouts or strike breaks. In any case, the employers were staking their hopes of restoring industrial peace on the long-term policy that had been adopted in previous years by the war industries committees and their labour groups: to recognize workers' organizations as regular negotiating partners and to create management–worker arbitration chambers for handling disputes. This policy was supported by both the new government and the soviets. Neither the government nor the soviets, however, were able to find a permanent and workable solution to conflicts over the division of authority between managers and workers' factory committees.

Like the city soviets, factory committees were the immediate result of the February revolution. When the provisional government issued a law in an attempt to limit their powers, they were even formed in those factories that did not yet have them. The legislated limits on the factory committees' powers did not hold because the government had no practical means of enforcing them. The committees were meant to have powers of supervision over managerial decision-making in matters of procedure concerning dismissal and the hiring and the disciplining of workers, in addition to organizing activities for the workers' benefit which did not encroach on the management prerogative. The first conflicts occurred in factories whose managements wished to reinstate staff who had been wheelbarrowed out by the workers. They became more widespread and protracted when price inflation cancelled the value of workers' wage rises and, in particular, when managers tried to lay off workers or close down a factory as cash-flows and the supplies of fuel or raw material faltered. In both Petrograd and Moscow the socialist press gave a great deal of publicity to several cases of factory owners allegedly concealing stocks of raw material to justify closures. The factory committees demanded access to all accounts and information to prevent such 'counter-revolutionary sabotage' by the capitalists. They did not regard a loss of profitability as a legitimate reason for lay-offs, and this attitude was widely shared in the political theatre although at this time (late spring) the immediate overthrow of capitalism was not really on revolutionary politicians' agendas. The factory committees insisted on ever wider powers of veto over management decisions and, in cases where the management refused to co-operate, they attempted to take full control. In the autumn the factory committees held a congress at which they discussed the expansion of workers' control from individual factories to the economy as a whole.

The factory committees were always in something of a dilemma as to whether their purpose should be a militant defence of workers' interests or whether they should accept some of the responsibilities of management. By the summer some factory committees accepted responsibility for deteriorating labour discipline and productivity, in response to which they voted to restore elements of the old order they had overthrown, such as piece-rates and incentive bonus payments, the levying of fines for disciplinary infractions, and personal searches at factory exits; in Petrograd they also published lists of errant workers in the city's press. Some factory committees also tried to organize supplies of food and heating fuel for their workers (we saw in Chapter 3 that shortages were becoming serious), and many took over or set up culture clubs to advance workers' 'consciousnesses'. Some of these clubs were run under puritan philosophies that saw entertainment as frivolous and only enlightenment as serious. Last but not least, an increasing number of the factory committees organized their own militias – to protect workers from violent crime, food stores from looters, and the revolution from the expected counter-revolutionary attempts.

The factory committees were not the only organizations formed for the pursuit of workers' interests. As in 1905, trade unions mushroomed – over 70 were set up in Petrograd and over 50 in Moscow by the end of the year. Both cities also had their trade-union councils. Most of the unions were organized on an industrial rather than craft basis, and they tried to negotiate wage contracts including systematic tariffs graded by skill, work-conditions, and the worker's age. Some of the contracts contained 'no strike' clauses and allowed for the reintroduction of piece-rate payments. Most of the unions also had equal-pay clauses for women, although this was more of a gesture than a practical step in the majority of factories where jobs were segregated between the sexes.

Workers were of course well represented in the soviets. The Moscow Soviet of Workers' Deputies, for example, consisted of 625 deputies, 80 per cent of whom were workers; most of them were elected in the factories on the basis of one deputy per 500 workers, the rest being elected by workers' co-operatives. (Non-worker deputies were mainly nominees of the revolutionary parties.) It is unlikely that the lower-level soviets elected in eight of the city's districts during the spring were any less working class in their composition than the Moscow Soviet. In addition, workers' interests could be hardly ignored by the politicians who stood for elections to the city duma in June and the district dumas in September; universal suffrage (men and women over 18) made the city's factory workers into a powerful constituency in democratic elections.

The privileged classes, on the other hand, were too small to form a significant constituency in universal suffrage voting, and they were, of course, excluded altogether from the Soviet stage of the political theatre. Their best hopes lay in the provisional government holding out until a general election to the Constituent Assembly and a constitutional government which, although dependent on the votes of the poor, might be able to take the path of social reformism such as would leave space for legal rights of free contract, property, and enterprise. An alternative hope lay in the chaos and hardships of the revolutionary period leading to a popular backlash and a military coup, which would postpone universal franchise government until the masses became prosperous and cultured. The signs of popular counter-revolutionary backlash were not too auspicious for the moment, although the disagreeable aspects of the collapse of tsarist authority (crime, general breakdowns in services) were as much in evidence as they had been in 1905, and the economic slide towards hunger was worse. Conservative forces, however, lost their rallying symbol when the tsar abdicated, and the Black Hundreds were no longer on the scene (although anti-semitism and xenophobia did not disappear). Conservative hopes boiled down to epaulettes on horseback. Increasing numbers of the old regime's privileged strata were taking the option of waiting it out abroad.

The provisional government had the loyalty of the officer corps at the front and, until early summer, it had the promise of support from most of the actors in the domestic political theatre, including all three revolutionary parties (Social Revolutionaries, Mensheviks, and Bolsheviks). But the revolutionary leaders had trouble containing the impatience with which the workers expected the new democracy to deliver them tangible gains. The workers were not alone in entertaining such a heightened expectation of political change. In February, sophisticated liberal politicians believed that military and economic failures would turn into success once the autocracy was out of the way, just as in October Bolshevik leaders thought that the economy would improve soon after the provisional government was swept away. The provisional government's home-front problem was that it was unable to enforce its laws. When the factory committees exceeded the powers delimited for them by the April law, for example, there was no way in which the government could police the owners' and managers' prerogatives. The factory committees, after all, had their own armed militias and the soviets had their own Red Guards to stand against the government-controlled police.

The political theatre was in fact filled with a plethora of organizations which claimed authority that had vague and overlapping jurisdictions. Thus in Moscow the following bodies were among those involved in running public affairs in the city: the Committee of Public Organizations, made up of 150 representatives of war industries committees, trade unions, co-operatives, political parties, and old city administrators (until June); the plenipotentiary of the provisional government; the elected city duma (from June); 17 elected district dumas (from September); the Moscow Soviet of Workers' Deputies; eight district soviets; and the Moscow Soviet of Soldiers' Deputies. The soviets had executive committees, joint committees, and numerous special commissions to deal with urgent problems, such as food supplies. (We have seen that the factory committees also had special commissions to deal with food-supply emergencies, and all these commissions competed with the regular government procurement agencies, co-operatives, and private traders for the shrinking supplies of food.) In addition there were 'social organizations' which expected privileged access to the Soviet, such as the Council of the Trade Unions, or to the government, such as the employers' associations. Men under arms were organized in the army, the police, the factory committees, and the soviets as well as in anarchist groups, criminal gangs, and citizens' vigilante groups. Some provincial cities declared themselves independent republics, but this was a relatively small addition to problems that prevented the provisional government from wielding the powers of effective control.

As in 1905, the three socialist parties that emerged from the underground increased their membership rapidly, and the great majority of workers elected to the factory committees and the soviets belonged to or were about to join one of these parties. Thus some of the factory committees were mainly Menshevik, others were mainly Bolshevik, and some were Social Revolutionary. At the beginning of the year the differences between the parties were obscure, and a Bolshevik-dominated factory committee was not necessarily any different in its policies from a Menshevik-dominated one; both had to be responsive to the aroused aspirations of their 'constituencies' and neither was in receipt of any practical industrial policy directives from their parties. It was the same for the worker deputies in the soviets: they had some sort of mandate to represent the interests of their electors in the factories, which they combined with a fairly free and confused voting for a great many political resolutions of an often rather general and esoteric nature. The notable characteristic the worker deputies of all party colours shared was that they were skilled male workers of the 'conscious' variety: the ones willing to join in the socialist intelligentsia's political discourse. They were also happy to act as a conduit for general party-political statements to workers' meetings; thus after worker assemblies had decided the practical business on the agenda, some remained a little longer to vote on general political resolutions proposed by party groups, to enable the parties to claim mass working-class support for their general slogans.

In Moscow the first test of public opinion about the respective parties was the June election to the city duma, in which the electorate was asked to vote for party slates of candidates rather than for individuals. The election returned the Social Revolutionaries (SRs) as by far the strongest party, with Kadets (liberal constitutional democrats), Mensheviks, and Bolsheviks trailing far behind. The Kadets were strong only in the city centre, where the professional classes lived. In the factory districts the SRs had only a slight advantage over the Mensheviks and Bolsheviks. Whereas the SRs and the Mensheviks enjoyed a measure of cross-class support, the Bolsheviks only obtained their votes in the factory districts. Another difference between the Bolsheviks and the other socialist parties was in the kinds of men they presented as candidates to the working-class voters. Bolshevik candidates were a very homogeneous group: they were almost exclusively young and working class. By this time the Bolsheviks were quite clearly differentiated from the other parties in their policies in that they had refused to join an all-party coalition within the provisional government and, instead, called for the transfer of 'all power to the soviets'.

In July, when the provisional government was shaken by the latest defeat in the war and by news of increasing desertions of soldiers from the battlefields, the Petrograd Bolsheviks tried to ride the rising wave of anti-war opinion by calling a general strike and starting an armed uprising. They had no success and the government closed down their press and issued warrants for the arrest of their leaders. The episode made few new friends for the Bolsheviks among the workers, although many disapproved of the government's repressive measures. A shift of working-class support from the SRs and the Mensheviks to the Bolsheviks occurred in August, after an army general (Kornilov) attempted a *coup d'état* that failed. The provisional government was damaged by rumours according to which it was itself involved in the conspiracy; and since the government coalition included the SRs and the Mensheviks, they were damaged by the rumours also. In Moscow the September elections to the district dumas, although marred by a low turnout, gave a clear victory to the Bolsheviks; the Kadets were the second largest party, with the SRs and Mensheviks falling far behind. Politics were polarized. While the victorious Bolsheviks' campaign was under the slogan of 'all power to the soviets', the Kadet voters could be presumed to wish 'all power to the provisional government' until the Constituent Assembly elections. The SRs' and the Mensheviks' advocacy of preserving the status quo between the provisional government and the soviets until the general election lost its appeal.

In September the Bolsheviks became the majority party in the Petrograd Soviet. They formed a Military Revolutionary Committee of the Soviet to take charge of the Red Guards, ostensibly to stave off any further attempts by the provisional government to turn to the army for help. Recruitment to the Red Guards accelerated after the Kornilov affair, and some of the factory committees' militias pledged their support as well. When the government attempted a further repression of the Bolshevik press, the Red Guards prevented it and, on October 25, retaliated by taking over the strategic points of the city and putting the provisional government under arrest, just in time for the opening of a national congress of the soviets. This *coup d'état* had been made possible by the Bolsheviks gaining a wide working-class support for the 'all power to the soviets' slogan. But the military committee did not ask the congress of the soviets to form a new government; instead, it asked the delegates to ratify a new government in the form of the Council of People's Commissars, a body consisting of Bolsheviks led by Lenin with a minority addition of left-wing SRs (who would resign several months later). Moderate socialists (most of the Mensheviks and SRs) walked out of the congress in protest. During the following days other socialists, including the leaders of the railwaymen's union and several prominent Bolsheviks, attempted to persuade Lenin and his central committee to accept a formula for a broader-based socialist government such as could claim some political legitimacy; they met with a rebuff.

Many of the workers' meetings which had passed resolutions in favour of 'all power to the soviets' had also affirmed their support for a government based on the election of the Constituent Assembly. Despite the growing disaffection with the provisional government, the idea that a universal franchise constitutional government should be the eventual outcome of the revolution continued to command wide belief. The Bolsheviks, left-wing SRs, and anarchists always articulated ideas to the effect that in Russia the revolution should bypass 'bourgeois democracy' and hand power directly to the proletariat and socialism. Many of their working-class supporters, however, evidently saw the call for 'all power to the soviets' as being against the (unelected) provisional government rather than against a universal franchise democracy. The new Bolshevik government did not dare to put a stop to the general election which had been scheduled for November. The election gave a clear victory to the party with the longest spectrum of opinion between its right and left wings – the SRs. The Bolsheviks came a poor second, although they did well among the urban working class. The Constituent Assembly met in January 1918; when it refused to ratify the Bolshevik government, the Red Guards dispersed it and arrested the leaders of the SRs and the Kadets. The Bolshevik *coup d'état* was completed, the Kadet Party was outlawed, its presses closed down, and the era of the 'dictatorship of the proletariat' started. The SR and Menshevik Parties were driven underground and destroyed soon after by police terror.

The Civil War and NEP Years, 1918–28

As we saw in Chapter 3, the years 1918–22 were a catastrophe for the economy and the population in general. But they were a success for the Bolshevik government, which managed to emerge from the chaos with a state that had the territories of the tsarist empire (except Finland, the Baltics, and Poland) under its administrative control. The economic collapse was perhaps an unintended but nevertheless important factor in this success. Hunger aided recruitment to the armed forces of the new regime – the Red Army, the grain-requisitioning squads of the Commissariat for Supplies, and the state security police (cheka) – which formed the nucleus of the new state and an indoctrination school for its new cadres. The military adventures and victories over 'the counter-revolution' cloaked this nucleus in a heroic revolutionary mythology. Industrial collapse drove the capitalist owners from their factories, and the workers invited 'their' state to take charge to preserve their livelihoods (industry was nationalized in June 1918). Hunger drove the people who had a chance of finding subsistence in the peasant countryside away from the cities; the population of Moscow was reduced by a half and that of Petrograd by more than 60 per cent. The depleted ranks of workers and city dwellers were glad to accept food obtained from the guns and bayonets; the Bolsheviks were successful in organizing their armed men and in extending their control over the urban civilian institutions whose men and women were dependent on the armed men (i.e., on the state's patronage) for the delivery of their survival rations.

However, the formation of the new state power in the urban-industrial sector was not plain sailing. Its only claim to legitimacy rested on the notion of a 'dictatorship of the proletariat', a 'homogeneous socialist government' decisive enough to save the revolution for the working class. But it did not take long for the relationship between the new regime and the industrial workers to come under strain. The workers had given substantial political support to the Bolsheviks in late 1917, but the Bolsheviks had seldom been able to control the workers' militancy. Indeed, they had hardly tried to control it, being content instead with gaining the workers' political support in return for giving an unqualified approval for the workers' economic and anti-management demands. Now the Bolsheviks were in charge of the state while the workers' living standards were dropping quickly.

The workers' strikes and protests had their peaks in early summer 1918, in early 1919, again in summer 1919, and finally in the winter of 1920–1, which culminated in the Kronstadt uprising and the Bolsheviks' replacement of the policies of 'war communism' by the 'New Economic Policy' (NEP). Few of the strikes were directed against the factory management: the demands were addressed to the political authorities, usually the soviets. In 1918 the economic demands included higher wages, but from then on hyperinflation and the collapse of the ruble transformed these demands into ones for particular material goods (in some factories their own produce) which could be either consumed or bartered. In 1918 some of the demands were also about jobs as the metal industries in particular sought to scale down defence-related production at a time when the word war was at an end and the civil war was yet to start (late in that year). All the strikes and protests were about food rations. In this respect they acquired an increasingly evident political flavour as the protesting workers often blamed their hunger on corrupt or inefficient authorities, and demanded that their food rations be brought up to parity with those of the Red Army, communist administrators, or 'bourgeois specialists'. Striking workers also demanded an end to limits on the amount of food they were allowed to procure in the countryside by personal barter, and they wanted free travel on the trains for this purpose. Some also demanded the lifting of the ban on free trade with peasant produce, and some advocated the transfer of procurement functions from the state agencies to workers' co-operatives. Many strikes started as a result of indignation at broken promises and at the strong-arm methods used by the authorities to quell discontent. From 1919 many of the strikers' demands included explicitly political points: against the compulsory draft to the Red Army, against the rigging of elections to the soviets, against the suppression of the soviets and factory committees that had been elected with non-Bolshevik majorities, against the repression of the SR and Menshevik parties, and also against the civil war and the Bolshevik dictatorship in general. Some striking workers called for a transfer of power to freely elected soviets, and some endorsed the calls, made by the White Armies as well as the SRs, for the reconvocation of the Constituent Assembly.

The presence of anti-Bolshevik opinion among workers became evident in spring 1918 when virtually all the provincial industrial centres elected soviets with SR or Menshevik majorities. The Bolsheviks dispersed these soviets, outlawed the non-Bolshevik parties, closed down their presses, and arrested their leaders. In the autumn of that year, workers in some of the large heavy-industry plants elected slates of candidates standing for the illegal socialist parties to the Petrograd Soviet. The Mensheviks and SRs were legalized at the beginning of 1919, to be banned again after several weeks during which their leaders proved very popular speakers at striking workers' rallies. In the spring, workers in many factories elected SR and Menshevik majorities to their factory committees. These too were suppressed by the Bolsheviks, who reverted to the methods of the Red Terror that had been employed in the summer and autumn of the previous year. But the SRs and the Mensheviks did not control the workers' protests any more than the Bolsheviks had done during 1917. (As in 1917, the Mensheviks were actually against strikes.)

Right from the beginning of their rule, the Bolsheviks declared strikes an illegitimate form of protest harmful to the workers' state. They explained their occurrence as stemming from backward workers' susceptibility to counter-revolutionary sedition by White Guardists, Black Hundreds, anarchists, SRs, and Mensheviks in factories where Bolshevik grass-roots organization was weak or faulty. The reference to 'backward workers' coincided uncomfortably with the fact that many of the strikes occurred in engineering plants, traditionally the supposed breeders of 'conscious' workers, and also in factories that had been known to be Bolshevik strongholds in 1917. But the Bolsheviks had a favourite explanation for this: the proletariat was becoming 'declassed' because its best cadres were the first ones to volunteer for the armed forces of the revolution, or they were joining the Bolshevik Party, which was promptly siphoning them off from the shopfloor to 'other posts in the revolutionary struggle' – that is, to administrative positions. The administrative posts to which the Bolsheviks felt the need to appoint reliable proletarian cadres mushroomed quickly, and such cadres had to be found among the workers who joined the party; very few of those who joined remained 'at the factory bench' for long. The Bolsheviks shifted the definition of the 'conscious' worker in this chain of reasoning, in that they identified the paragon of true proletarian virtue with membership of their own party. Workers who remained on the factory floor were not in the party and therefore were an 'unconscious' element needy of intensive political education. This reasoning saved the Bolsheviks any qualms they might have had about using force to suppress strikes and workers' protests.

The coercive methods used by the authorities to suppress strikes included lockouts, mass dismissals followed by selective rehiring, and, in strategically significant work places, the deployment of armed forces to keep the work going; some strikers were threatened with confiscation of their ration cards, and suspected ring-leaders were arrested. There was not really much consistency in the authorities' actions – much depended on the judgement of local bosses. All railway workers, however, were put under a military court martial regime (and the Bolshevik leaders considered but rejected making the 'militarization of labour' a general policy).

As in the tsarist pre-war years, there were strikers' rallies which ran into violent confrontations with the Bolshevik armed forces. The first known incident of this kind occurred in Kolpino, near Petrograd, in May 1918 when a number of workers were killed by troops during a protest march on the local soviet about food and jobs. News of this incident contributed greatly to the wave of indignation that was already under way in Petrograd. The largest violent confrontations involving rebellious workers, however, occurred in provincial industrial centres. In March 1919, the city of Astrakhan on the lower Volga was engulfed in several days of bitter fighting when striking metallurgical workers were attacked by loyal government troops but joined by mutinous soldiers. Several thousand insurgents were killed during the fighting and hundreds were subsequently executed by the new regime's security police, the Cheka. Like most of the large-scale incidents that occurred in the provincial industrial centres, they were known in the capital cities only through rumours because the Bolshevik authorities controlled the press. As we have seen in Chapter 3, far from being a straight war between the Red Army and the White Armies, the civil war consisted of thousands of violent skirmishes between the Bolshevik armed forces and various groups of rebels in civilian clothes as well as regular White Army recruits. This kind of violence swept through not only the peasant countryside but also some of the industrial centres.

It is doubtful, however, that the industrial strikes of the civil war period ever approached the scale of the strike movements in 1905–6, 1912–14, and 1916–17. The new regime was more ruthless than its predecessors in repressing opposition and keeping any news of it under its censorship. It was also quick to instigate a propaganda effort which could take advantage of the fact that radical socialist impulses were widespread among the Russian population, so that the task was simply to persuade enough people that Bolshevik dictatorship was socialism's best chance in the inevitably difficult circumstances of war and revolution. The new regime was also creating a large structure of authority into which ambitious members of the working class were co-opted. And last but not least, workers' strikes were hardly an effective method of protest against privations when industry was collapsing anyway for a whole host of reasons. As the civil war months and years went by, the paramount issue was felt in stomachs, and workers could talk about it in factory meetings just as well as in strike rallies. The factory authorities let them do that in work time – there was not enough raw material and fuel to keep production going in any case. The logic of the petitions to higher authorities was that they should centralize the economy to make sure the workers' jobs were saved and rations delivered, and that they should not forget the particular factory or locality where the meeting took place. The factory authorities were sympathetic, as indeed were the representatives of the higher powers that came along to the meetings. They promised to do their best, and sometimes they managed to be seen doing their best by getting something delivered. Relationships of political patronage were thus developing between industrial work places and men of political authority.

The factory authorities could also be seen to be understanding and benevolent by letting workers be absent from work when they needed to be – by the end of the civil war it was normal for one-third of the workforce to be missing from the factory floor every day – and by letting them use factory equipment for making things for their own food barter as well as for official factory output. Metal workers were making products like kerosene lamps and cigarette lighters to put in their bags to exchange for foodstuffs on their trips to the countryside, and textile workers could take cloth and so on. Thus in the

Moscow textile factories the number of workers on the payroll in 1919 was almost 70 per cent of what it had been in 1913, while their official output amounted to under 13 per cent of what it had been in the pre-war year.[1] It is not known for sure what the workers did in the work time made spare by faltering production lines, but in the centralized industrial authorities, complaints that factory managers let the factory produce go to the workers rather than to the state distribution agencies were rife, and the 'bagmen' crowding into country-bound trains with things to barter with peasants were a proverbial mass phenomenon of the civil war years.

Workers were hungry and cold, but possibly not quite as hungry and cold as their urban neighbours who were not in factory employment. For an urban dweller, having an industrial job was better than not having one. Industrial workers were officially accorded better rations than the majority of the people in the towns; their factories were sometimes able to use political patronage to secure greater reliability of ration deliveries for their workers than that which could be ensured by the state distribution network for the general population; and the factories could provide a privileged access to useful equipment and materials under conditions of slackened labour discipline. In short, workers were not subjected to factory closures and a loss of entitlements when proper production could not continue. This was not a formula for lasting industrial peace, but perhaps it was just sufficient to help the new regime keep outbursts of working-class hostility local and at bay while the civil war lasted. The terms on which workers could be made politically loyal or quiescent and also economically productive would have to be faced later by the new state.

The new regime's relationship with the educated strata was even more complicated. One facet was the Red Terror. This started as a retaliation against the oppositional activities of (mainly) the Social Revolutionary Party, but quickly became loosely organized persecution of 'enemies of the people' who were defined so as much on the basis of what they had been under the old regime as on any proof of personal involvement in some 'counter-revolutionary' activity. Tens of thousands lost their lives under the auspices of the Red Terror, other tens of thousands were put in concentration camps, while many of the rest were disenfranchised and deprived of food rations as well as dispossessed of their property. About a million emigrated by 1921.

The people at risk of being treated as 'enemies of the people' were landowners and business people, tsarist officials and policemen, priests, and also members of the intelligentsia. Some of the intelligentsia were caught up in the regime-sponsored proletarian enmity because they were known or suspected supporters of non-Bolshevik parties, but others simply because, at times, it was enough to look educated, appear haughty, or to have coveted goods to be labelled contemptuously as *burzhui* (a bourgeois) and face instant proletarian justice. This was a climate in which the educated profession that had been particularly renowned for its radical political orientation before the war – the medical profession – lost 25 per cent of its practitioners to

---

1 Husband, W. B. 1990: *Revolution in the Factory: The Birth of the Soviet Textile Industry, 1917–1920*. Oxford: Oxford University Press, p. 93.

emigration.[2] Relatively few members of the intelligentsia welcomed the Bolshevik coup. The Bolshevik faction of the socialist movement had never had wide support among the intelligentsia compared to the socialist and liberal movements overall; its unconditional support of labour militancy during 1917 was disapproved of as irresponsible demagoguery by the majority of the educated public, and its October *coup d'état* as downright offensive. In that sense there was an element of political logic in the leather-jacketed Red Terrorists' tendency to equate being educated under the old regime with being a 'bourgeois' enemy.

But that was only one facet of a complex and contradictory relationship. Another was the new state-builders' pragmatism, which told the Bolshevik leaders that they needed the support of technical expertise to succeed. Within months of October, military expertise was recognized as indispensable, and army officers were recruited to build the Red Army. The civilian professions were also enticed to stay at work under the new regime. There was in fact more to this than just short-term pragmatism; after all, retaining professional engineers in the factories did not prevent industrial collapse as the civil war went on, and yet the policies of paying 'bourgeois specialists' high salaries and privileged rations to keep them in their factories prevailed despite opposition within the Bolshevik Party itself. Their millennarian belief in a working-class revolution notwithstanding, the Bolshevik leaders still had something in common with the long-established values of the Russian intelligentsia: a vision of social progress as the attainment of (high) culture by the masses and the development of a science-driven, rational, and technological civilization.

The pro-Bolshevik faction of revolutionaries that came closest to challenging the old equation between social progress and culturedness were the self-professed promoters of proletarian culture (*proletkul't*). They argued that the revolution's fate depended on its ability to leave the old 'bourgeois' culture behind and to develop a truly revolutionary culture instead. But what they attacked in the old culture was primarily the aesthetic they saw as cultivating the myths of individualist subjectivism. The answer lay not in finding a folkloric culture within the working class and establishing its hegemony over the high culture of the pre-revolutionary era; rather, it lay in inventing a new culture for the proletariat and making that hegemonic. The *proletkul't* movement's art was above all avant-garde, its mission to teach such aesthetics and ethics to an uncultured mass as would be appropriate for the building of a new civilization. It substituted a robust collectivism for the 'bourgeois' humanist preoccupations with individual character and motivation, but it did nothing to change the relationship of tutelage between the artist and his or her audience, or the notion that special training and skills were indispensable for effective art performance. Finally, the vision of the new civilization that the robust collectivism was to serve had the sleek shapes of a superb machine, a rational objectivist universe. But this vision was not peculiar to the proletarian culture movement; the radical avant-garde novelty consisted of the claim that the achievement of reason in human affairs would be quicker and purer with

2 Williams, C. 1991: 'War, revolution and medicine: the case of the Petrograd Doctors, 1917–1920'. *Revolutionary Russia*, iv, 2, pp. 259–87.

people unburdened by the classical achievements of high enlightenment culture – a claim Lenin and his supporters in the Bolshevik leadership did not accept.

The political defeat of the proletarian culture movement was a defeat of an ideological stance against the new regime's search for a *modus vivendi* with the educated strata. At the same time, it released the machine utopia as a vision of progress which many of the non-Bolshevik professional intelligentsia could share with many of the Bolshevik revolutionaries. The machine utopia was reflected in Lenin's belief that society's administration would eventually be so well tuned by a scientific organization of its tasks that 'every cook' could take a turn at being one or other of its precisely defined cogs. It was also reflected in the slogan 'communism equals electrification plus Soviet power' and in making the experts of the war industries committee to work on future industrial development in the new state's offices of centralized planning and economic high command. It inspired further avant-garde movements in the performing arts, where time-and-motion 'laws of mechanics' of the human gesture were studied to teach actors pure, truthful expression and the audience a new, higher-plane humanity. 'The actor on the stage must first of all become an automaton, a mechanism, a machine . . . . The new Taylorised man has his own new physiology. Classical man, with his Hellenic gait and gesticulation, is a beast and savage in comparison with the new Taylorised man,' wrote a film-maker in an article called 'The industrialization of gesture'.[3] The inspirational 'Taylorised man' was an allusion to the teachings of Frederick W. Taylor, whose ideas of 'scientific management' of factory production, based on the assumption that all work activities should be studied analytically, redesigned, and taught with a view to ridding them of any dysfunctional movement and energy expenditure, had become popular among Russian engineers before the war, and they now had the backing of Bolshevik leaders as well.

Culturalism, industrialism, and machine utopia provided a bridge between the traditional modernizing aspirations of the intelligentsia and the intellectual leaders of the new regime. The new regime reinstated engineers in managerial posts and backed the authority of their technical expertise against the claims of 'workers' control' within the factories. In the longer run, it hoped that the rationality of Taylor-inspired 'scientific organization of labour' (NOT) would resolve the problem of legitimacy of managerial authority and thus provide terms on which workers could be both politically loyal and economically productive. While production in the factories was grinding to a halt, institutes of NOT research sprang up and gained political backing to set about the task of creating a new, supremely efficient 'production culture'. Non-Bolshevik professors of fundamental and applied science were invited to resume the work of their academies. By the mid-1920s, scientific research would claim a higher proportion of the gross domestic product in Russia than in most Western

---

3 Sokolov, I. 1922: 'Industrializatsiya zhesta'. *Ermitazh*, x, July, p. 6. Quoted in Yampolsky, M. 1991: 'Kuleshov's experiments and the new anthropology of the actor'. In Taylor, R. and Christie, I. (eds), *Inside the Film Factory: New Approaches to Russian and Soviet Cinema*. London and New York: Routledge, p. 49.

countries.[4] The universities had more students during the civil war than ever before, although many of the staff opposed the new government requirement that access to higher education be broadened to include workers lacking in grammar-school qualifications. Amid the hunger of the civil war years, educational activities also thrived at the grass-roots level where there appeared to be no shortage of young people willing to take part in new literacy campaigns.

The new regime also offered some patronage and grounds for new-era optimism to cultural élites. Classical music, opera, ballet, and theatre continued to perform to full houses throughout the civil war, and many of the artists probably found it an agreeable new phenomenon that their audiences now encompassed a wider social range. New schools were set up for film-makers, avant-garde theatre found its political sponsors, and houses of the arts were established to provide a meeting place and a modicum of survival comforts for members of the creative intelligentsia. Literary people were able to form bookshop and publishing co-operatives to organize an outlet for their non-political work and, like scientists, they were sought after as speakers in workers' clubs and government-sponsored enlightenment societies. The new regime made no secret of its policy to make culture serve 'the revolution', but its criteria for judging this service were still vague and in some respects not altogether different from the old intelligentsia's aspirations to raise the general cultural level of the masses. Like scientists and engineers, writers and artists could form their own unions through which they could channel their views on professional matters to the government, and their numbers included presti-geous figures who had personal access to powerful Bolshevik patrons. For those who could acquiesce in the Bolshevik hijack of the revolution, the civil war years held some promise as well as threat.

Many of the people who survived the civil war years with an optimistic focus on the new-era promise were disappointed after the inauguration of the NEP in 1921. Extreme-left revolutionaries were disappointed because, far from leading directly to a moneyless socialist economy, the hyperinflation of the civil war years was to be replaced once more by a strong currency and money trade; Bolshevik working-class militants were disappointed by the ban on factions within the party and by the reimposition of hierarchical management in the factories; industrial managers as well as workers were disappointed that they had to get industry going under conditions of budgetary stringency; artists and cultural activists were disappointed that financial stringency curtailed the state's patronage of their work; and all 'mental workers' had to contend with earning their government salaries under conditions in which their professional autonomy was subject to increasing political controls. The last open stand by a professional group for autonomy was a strike by university academics in Moscow and elsewhere in 1922. Soon after its defeat, a large group of intellectuals were sent into exile abroad. The intelligentsia that remained began to learn the arts of living in a politically controlled bureaucracy.

The NEP was introduced by the Bolshevik leaders as necessary and

---

4 Lewis, R. A. 1972: 'Some aspects of the research and development effort of the Soviet Union, 1924–35'. *Science Studies*, ii, pp. 153–79.

temporary backward step, a 'state capitalist' detour on the road to socialism. Apart from allowing peasants to sell privately the produce surplus to state delivery quotas, the authorities issued trade licences to would-be entrepreneurs, leased small nationalized factories and workshops to them, and even made a legal provision for the formation of joint-stock companies. In addition, the state put its own sector of the economy under budgetary discipline and tried to refrain from making deficits up by printing money. The policy succeeded in bringing about a fast economic recovery. After the good harvest of 1922, the supplies of food to the cities became plentiful enough to warrant the abolition of rationing, the cities' population grew by a new flow of rural–urban migration, and industrial output was restored to pre-war levels by 1926. In that year, Moscow's population (since 1918 the capital city) reached 2.2 million.

Apart from vague hopes of foreign investment, however, the terms on which the NEP was introduced did little to indicate how the industrial economy was to expand beyond its prewar levels. The strategy for further industrialization became a matter for political battles within the party and government, which in the event resulted in the abandonment of the NEP in 1928. In practice, however, it was clear right from the beginning that the 'nepmen' (the private entrepreneurs) would have no part in the economy as capitalists who invest their profits to expand their businesses. The state taxed their profits at a 50 per cent rate, discriminated against them in the provision of credit and in supplies of state-produced goods, and local authorities often taxed them further by treating them as 'former people' who were disfranchised and as such also liable to surcharges on rents and the price of public utilities. Even more ominously, a licence to trade apparently gave the licencee no right to engage in 'speculation', and the laws reserved for state authorities the power to declare private business contracts null and void if they were 'against the interests of the state'. The leases and licences were renewable annually and often revoked. Thousands of businesses were forced to close down in the winter 1923–4, for example, when the authorities carried out one of their clamp-downs on 'speculators'. In addition, many nepmen found themselves on the receiving end of secret police attentions. Business time horizons were short and the name of the entrepreneurial game was survival rather than expansion, and the ability to stay on the right side of the authorities rather than the ability to accumulate capital and make good investments. Nepmen's investments consisted of not much more than spending on basic stock renewal; when an extra ruble was made, it was better to spend it in a bout of conspicuous consumption in a city fleshpot.

The majority of nepmen were in the distributive trade, and most were street pedlars and market stallholders; only one-quarter of licensed traders had shop premises with solid walls, compared with two-thirds in the pre-war years. Trading establishments employing more than five workers numbered 15 600 in the whole of the Soviet Union in 1923, about three per cent of the total.[5] As regards the private manufacturing sector, the number of factories peaked at 2000 in 1923; on average they employed 21 workers, one-tenth of the average

5 Ball, A. M. 1987: *Russia's Last Capitalists: The Nepmen, 1921–1929*. Berkeley, Calif.: University of California Press, p. 91.

state-owned factory. In addition, over 200 000 licences were issued to small artisan workshops, over 80 per cent of which employed fewer than four workers. Two-thirds of these workshops were located in the countryside.[6] Another two million or so people supplemented their incomes or eked out a living by making saleable articles in their homes. The flagships of the capitalist component in the 'state capitalist' formula, the joint-stock companies, amounted to 76 in the whole of Russia in 1926; more than 70 per cent of their shares were owned by state trusts.[7]

This was hardly a private sector that merited the label 'capitalist'. The nepmen included disfranchised 'former people' who had little hope of state employment, but the great majority were pedlars and petty producers. They helped to revive a moribund economy by a myriad of shoestring operations under conditions determined by a state bent on preventing them from becoming capitalists. Some nepmen did make money to flaunt in taverns and theatres, but not even the richest nepman had the powers of a capitalist if he was not able to choose where to invest his money. Nevertheless, the political discourse was full of dark allusions to the private sector of the economy as a breeding ground for a potentially hegemonic capitalist class, and the press was full of venomous satire featuring fat nepmen in furcoats being horribly greedy at the expense of decent working people.

Most press venom was directed against private traders rather than manufacturers, as were indeed most of the forced closures of allegedly errant businesses. The machine-utopia image of a future socialist economy as a giant super-efficient factory reinforced the view, traditional among the peasantry as well as the intelligentsia, that saw productive labour as virtuous and trading with the products as parasitic. The realities of low-technology manufacture in small private factories and artisan workshops may have offended the eye that was firmly fixed on a machine-utopia future, but they were seen as doomed by the productive strength of the industry that was owned and administered by the state. The trading nepmen, on the other hand, were clearly more than a match to the state-run networks of goods distribution, and people who needed things had to depend on them. The nepmen were weaving their profit motive into the tapestry of everyday social life – a threatening thought to those who saw the profit motive itself as a capitalist menace. Besides, if shortages and high prices were irritating the population, it could be politic to blame them on 'kulaks and nepmen', and to exaggerate the 'class-enemy' dangers they posed to the 'workers' state'.

To the state-owned industry, the NEP brought a requirement that it become productive again, and that it puts the unit costs of production on a downward-sloping curve. This was not easy as the revolution had won the coveted eight-hour day for the workers – a reduction of some 13–20 per cent – and the equipment's mechanical condition was no longer what it had been before the war. In addition, restoring reliable supplies of raw material to the factories was

6 Ball, *Russia's Last Capitalists*, pp. 133–6.
7 Ball, *Russia's Last Capitalists*, pp. 156–7.

proving a protracted process which, in 1923, caused the 'scissors crisis' and an occasion for Trotsky and his supporters to break ranks with the rest of the party leadership over the question of the terms of trade between the industrial sector and the peasantry. The metaphorical scissors had their blades open. Textile production in particular was inadequate and expensive (three times as expensive as in 1913), while the peasant production was already recovered and its prices were down to prewar levels – a market situation which threatened that the peasants might shrink back from increasing their participation in it. The economic logic of closing the blades demanded that the consumer-goods industry increase its production and decrease its prices, and the left opposition was unhappy about the political implications of asking industrial workers to carry the burden. In the long run, everyone agreed, industry would have to grow by new investment, but the Marxist way of posing the question as to where the money for investment should come from was asking whose labour should be exploited the most. The industrial sector was too small for its workers to afford sufficient capital accumulation, went the argument. Should 'a tribute' be exacted from the peasantry to finance further industrialization? That was against the terms on which the NEP had only just pacified the peasantry, and the left opposition was not pressing this argument for the time being, as it was still holding on to hopes of a 'permanent revolution', a domino-theory scenario in which the Russian revolution should inspire the proletariat in the developed West to take power and then offer development aid to its eastern comrades. But this hope looked unrealistic by this time. As Trotsky lost his bid for the party leadership after Lenin's death in January 1924, the politburo put building 'socialism in one country' on the agenda: a Russian industrial development without the help of a socialist Germany or England.

This should be a state led, planned development, everyone in the party leadership agreed, and there were already plans in hand for the construction of a large network of power stations. Beyond that, the question for the planners was to decide whether the state exports of grain should finance investment in the consumer-goods industry first, or in the capital-goods industry. The logic of the NEP, based as it was on the goal of motivating the peasantry, favoured consumer-goods industry. Grain could be exchanged abroad for up-to-date technology for the consumer-goods factories, which would then generate more capital by tapping the potential mass market the peasantry constituted. An alternative logic was to develop 'sector a' first – the capital-goods industries (steel, engineering, etc.) that would then make home-made machines for other industries including the consumer-goods, 'sector b' products. This approach promised a faster and more comprehensive industrialization, albeit at the expense of making the expansion of consumer markets initially slower while requiring greater amounts of cash to be spent abroad at the beginning – importing heavy-industry technology would be more expensive than light-industry equipment – thus making more acute the question of how to get the peasantry to deliver more grain. The consumer-goods argument had the upper hand at first, but this argument assumed international peace; in 1927, however, diplomatic relations with the West hit a new low and a veritable war scare swept through domestic politics. The heavy-industry argument looked stronger if a need to make guns, tanks, and aeroplanes came on the political agenda. The five-year plan of industrialization announced to a party congress at the end of 1927 reflected heavy-industry priorities.

Neither side of these high-policy disputes, however, had much direct relevance to the question of how to get industrial workers to co-operate with the task of raising their labour's productivity. Perhaps three strategies could be discerned as coinciding with one another. One was, of course, the NOT. Its institutes were busy doing fundamental time-and-motion research on the norms and procedures of scientifically efficient working, and on the methods of instructing workers in them. The second approach was also inspired by NOT. This concentrated attention on propagandizing the virtues of time discipline and efficiency among workers rather than on laboratory research on work processes by scientists and engineers. Thus a League of Time was founded in 1924 for the purpose of promoting a clock-brained 'production culture'. The third approach was political: to charge the trade unions with a care for productivity as well as their members' interests, to make the factory committees organize 'production conferences' in which shopfloor workers could exchange ideas with management on production matters, and to recruit workers into the party (and its youth branch, the *komsomol*) in large-enough numbers to form a core of highly motivated and disciplined political activists on every shopfloor.

None of these approaches yielded quick results. It was a long and laborious task for the NOT scientists in their research institutes to create a concrete version of the machine utopia that could be introduced into the diverse, custom-ridden, and altogether messy real worlds of existing industry. The League of Time movement could likewise hold only a long-term promise of creating a civilization in which methodical regimen schedules permeate souls and everyday life. The production conferences came alive mainly when they turned into bargaining sessions between workers and managers; they had some use then but not quite what was intended. The recruitment of workers into the party and the *komsomol* proceeded well from the first 'Lenin enrolment' in 1924, so that roughly every tenth shopfloor worker was in by 1928; but a mass party base was not much better than a small one when it came to translating a political allegiance into a practical and effective concern for improving shopfloor work standards. From 1926 the *komsomol* started organizing well publicized 'shock work brigades', but they were a mixed blessing for production rationalization since what they were doing amounted to offers of youthful brawn and demands for the reallocation of best machines and raw material from senior workers to themselves, in order to bust the rates.

The practical policy adopted for immediate effect was to impose budgetary stringency on the factories. This was not enforced with an unrelenting uniformity; since the industrializing vision's conventional wisdom believed in economies of scale, small plants that were forced by financial losses to close down or make labour redundant were allowed to do so while large plants in a similar situation were sometimes helped with loans and subsidies. As a result, the proportion of the factory workforce employed in establishments with more than 500 workers increased from over a half in 1914 to almost three-quarters in

1927.[8] Nevertheless, industrial workers could be made redundant and, by 1923–4, they took over from former white-collar workers as the largest category on the unemployment register. Another policy of raising labour productivity was to pay as many workers as possible by piece-rates, and to set up in the factories time-study bureaux for the purpose of introducing rationalization measures and revising the piece-rates. In 1925, textile factory managers were simply ordered by the government to make workers operate three weaving machines simultaneously if they had hitherto operated just two. The workers started strikes which were settled by larger-than-planned wage raises and by local back-pedalling on the rationalization measures. Another concession made to the workers in that year was to allow again more or less democratic elections to the factory committees. (Since 1920, the committees had been subordinated to the trade-union bureaucracy which nominated the committee candidates.) In 1927 the government-decreed rationalization campaigns resumed and, on the occasion of the tenth-anniversary October celebrations, the party asked the textile industry to rationalize further so that the workers could work a seven-hour day without a loss to their daily output. This was introduced as a package with three-shift working, and experiments were encouraged with split shifts where a worker did his or her day in two stints of three and a half hours each with a break of that length in between; the hope was that that way the worker could work more intensively more of the time, although opinions about this varied. About a quarter of the textile workers supposedly worked a seven-hour day by the early 1930s, although by this time overtime working was common.

It is not clear whether the rationalization campaigns could be credited with the fact that the average hourly productivity of labour in 1927 was about 10 per cent higher than in 1913. Other relevant policies were in operation, such as the standardization of products so that production lines could work longer without changes of set-ups, in addition to which some factories received new imported machinery. The rationalization campaigns had a mixed success in regard to their goal of keeping increases in wages slower than increases in labour productivity, since this was achieved in only two of the NEP years. The official faith in the untapped potential of NOT, however, was unshaken and played a part in the increasing optimism that was formented politically among the industrialization drive's planners. Another effect of the rationalization campaigns was to increase the tensions between workers and the 'bourgeois specialist' engineers who had to be in the front line of the shopfloor rationalization struggles; this was probably unintended at the time, but it made 'bourgeois specialists' a convenient scapegoat alongside 'kulaks and nepmen' in the 'left turn' politics of 1928–31, of which more will be said later.

Few politicians expressed much concern about unemployment at the time, although the Stalinist ones and their propagandists would castigate the NEP for it afterwards. Neither the NEP nor, for that matter, the industrialization campaign that followed it were expected to produce full employment – not in

8 Davies, R. W. 1985: 'From tsarism to NEP: continuity and change in the industrial economy, 1913–1927'. Unpublished paper presented to Soviet Industrialization Project Seminar, University of Birmingham, November, p. 17n.

the near future at least, because it was generally believed that the peasant sector was overpopulated to such an extent that migration from it would continue to exceed the available urban-sector jobs for a long time to come. The politicians were concerned that Red Army men should find jobs on returning from civil war duties, and ordered factory managers to give them priority in their hiring policies. Another concern was voiced by the women's department of the party (*zhenotdel*) about women taking a disproportionate share of redundancies, and occasionally by the *komsomol* about the difficulties faced by urban youth in finding secure employment. The number of employed industrial workers in 1926 was higher than in 1913, but lower than in the war-industry peak year of 1917. Women munitions workers were vulnerable to losing their wartime jobs, and women were losing their jobs when financial stringencies led to periodic slim-downs of clerical staffs in administrative institutions. The new jobs of bureaucratic authority were presumably less vulnerable to redundancies, as state administration was growing, but they were very much a male preserve (as were, indeed, elected posts in factory committees, trade unions, etc., and also party membership). Overall, the Soviet workforce was growing in 1921–8, and so did the number of employed women, although not their share of the growing total, which was similar to what it had been in 1902; women made up 30 per cent of the employed population in Russia in 1929, and 36 per cent of Moscow's economically independent population in 1926.[9] The women's share of the unemployment register was higher than the men's, and their average stay on it was longer. The *komsomol* concerns about urban youth were reflecting the fact that factory committees and trade unions put pressure on managements to favour returning workers in their hiring policies. There was a varied but, on the whole, fairly high rate of voluntary labour turnover in the factories, and we have seen that workers were not afraid to strike or drive wage bargains during the rationalization campaigns; this was a pattern of industrial behaviour which suggested that the existence of the unemployed outside the factory gates did not make those who were in employment particularly fearful of losing their jobs.

It is difficult to gauge from the available data whether the urban social problems of slums and pauperism, so well described by the social reformists during the prewar years, were better or worse in the mid-1920s. Overall, the housing situation could not have improved; Moscow's population, for example, was 700 000 larger in 1926 than it had been in 1912, but new house-building was yet to reach the prewar rates of activity, while the existing housing stock deteriorated in quality during the civil war years in particular, when nothing was repaired and many of the wooden fittings that could be ripped up and burned were used for fuel. The superior apartments that were vacated by the privileged strata's emigration or appropriated by the new-regime authorities did not amount to a housing stock that could make a difference to the overall housing shortage; they became very overcrowded if 500 000 workers were moved into them during the civil war, as the Moscow authorities

---

9 Johnson, R. E. 1991: 'Family life in Moscow'. In Johnson, R. E. (ed.), *Family Life in Moscow During NEP*. Indianapolis, Ind.: Indiana University Press, p. 113.

claimed.[10] (Many of the rehoused 'workers' were probably new government officials taking residence in Moscow after it became the capital in March 1918.) As in the pre-war years, the big cities had their criminal underworlds, street hustlers, and homeless migrants. They also had a well publicized though unquantified problem of children left parentless by civil war dislocations, who roamed the city-centre streets in criminal gangs. Drug-trafficking was rife, especially in cocaine, morphine, and opium, as was prostitution.

The evidence of the 1926 census, however, showed an important difference from the demographic patterns of 1880–1913. Moscow was no longer a city of migrants living apart from their own families, in accommodation units shared with people who were not family relatives. The pattern now was to live in small families. The number of family-based households in Moscow was 550 per cent higher than in 1897, while the city's population was 100 per cent higher. In 1926, 83 per cent of Moscow inhabitants were living in family-based households, with the average household having just 3.5 members. That many Moscow residents now lived in their own nuclear families is also indicated by the rise in the proportion who were dependent on another breadwinner's income, from 35 per cent of the total population in 1912 to 46 per cent in 1926; the dependants included housewives – just over one-half of the Moscow women aged 15 or more were not self-supporting (compared to eight per cent of the men) and 65 per cent of them were the principal breadwinners' wives.[11] Of the city's population, 51 per cent were female in 1926. The number of women of child-bearing age exceeded the number of children by an even greater margin than in 1912, but women were no longer going back to the countryside to have their children, preferring instead to adjust to urban conditions by limiting fertility. Urban family living was not comfortable. Households lived in tiny separated parts of rented apartments, having to share kitchens and bathrooms with other households, and relatively few of those that relied on a single breadwinner could have had much cash to spare after providing for basic necessities. That made the break from the old migrant pattern of urban wage-earning and rural family-raising only more impressive. Whether this was a natural culmination of long-term prewar trends or an effect of the revolution is not clear. But be this as it may, the NEP was a period in which migrants were arriving in the cities to stay.

Questions of Social Class

Social class and class membership became important facts in the lives of the urban population under the new regime. Establishing one's origins as working class brought personal opportunities, while being accused of originating from the 'exploiting classes' spelt personal dangers. But since prerevolutionary society had been far from neatly divided between 'pure proletarians' and 'bourgeois exploiters', the questions of class origin that people had to answer

---

10 Chase, W. J. 1990: *Workers, Society, and the Soviet State: Labor and Life in Moscow, 1918–1929*. Urbana, Ill.: University of Illinois Press, p. 29.
11 Johnson, 'Family life', pp. 106–24.

on the frequent occasions they needed to provide a curriculum vitae were not ones of undisputable fact. It was the same with what people could say of their actions and allegiances in 1917 and during the civil war. Only a minority were either Red or White, for the civil war was too chaotic to make the political categories of personal survival clear-cut. Current class position was also something that could hardly escape a person's awareness; 'nepmen' and 'bourgeois specialists' were subject to political vigilance while 'workers' (in political administration as well as in the factories) were often able to claim a solicitous treatment from the state when standing before the courts or in the queues for housing or ration coupons. Before the revolution, 'class' and 'class consciousness' had been theoretical terms used mainly by Marxist revolutionaries, and they had had some social reality (albeit not quite the same as that predicted by the theory) among the intelligentsia and factory workers. Under the new regime, class consciousness was made an inescapable fact of life by the rhetoric of political administration.

Further Reading

An introductory collection of short readings emphasizing workers' importance in the politics of 1917 is D. H. Kaiser (ed.), *The Workers' Revolution in Russia, 1917: The View from Below* (Cambridge: Cambridge University Press, 1987). S. A. Smith, *Red Petrograd: Revolution in the Factories, 1917–1918* (Cambridge: Cambridge University Press, 1983) is informative and insightful without being excessively long. Another account of workers and the revolution in the capital is provided by D. Mandel, *The Petrograd Workers and the Fall of the Old Regime: From February Revolution to the July Days, 1917* (London: Macmillan, 1983) and D. Mandel, *The Petrograd Workers and the Soviet Seizure of Power* (London: Macmillan, 1984). My discussion of 1917 is based mainly on Smith, *Red Petrograd*; D. Koenker, *Moscow Workers and the 1917 Revolution* (Princeton, NJ: Princeton University Press, 1981); and W. G. Rosenberg, 'Understanding strikes in revolutionary Russia', *Russian History*, xvi, 1989, nos 2–4, pp. 263–96. A more general discussion of the social underpinnings of the revolutionary politics is offered by L. H. Haimson, 'The problem of social identities in early twentieth century Russia', *Slavic Review*, xlvii, spring 1987, no. 1, pp. 1–20 and W. G. Rosenberg, 'Identities, power, and social interactions in revolutionary Russia, *Slavic Review*, xlvii, spring 1987, no. 1, pp. 21–8. See also, however, the review article by M. Perrie, 'The Russian working class 1905–17', *Theory and Society*, xvi, 1987, pp. 431–46.

Information on industrial strikes after the Bolshevik seizure of power is provided by W. G. Rosenberg, 'Russian labour and Bolshevik power after October', *Slavic Review*, xl, summer 1985, no. 2, pp. 213–38; V. Brovkin, 'Workers' unrest and the Bolsheviks' response in 1919', *Slavic Review*, xlix, 1990, no. 3, pp. 350–73; and M. McAuley, *Bread and Justice: State and Society in Revolutionary Petrograd 1917–1922* (Oxford: Clarendon Press, 1992). S. Fitzpatrick, 'The Bolsheviks' dilemma: class, culture and politics in the early Soviet years', *Slavic Review*, xlvii, 1988, pp. 599–613, is an insightful discussion of the *proletkul't* and the Bolshevik sociological theorizing about workers after October.

The relationships between the Bolsheviks and the intelligentsia during the civil war years are discussed ably by McAuley, *Bread and Justice*, and by C. Read, 'The intelligentsia and the experience of the revolution: some non-Bolshevik responses, 1917–21' (an unpublished paper presented to Soviet Industrialization Project Seminar, University of Birmingham, June 1985). D. J. Raleigh (ed.), *A Russian Civil War Diary: Alexis Babine in Saratov, 1917–1922* (Durham, NC, and London: Duke University Press, 1988) chronicles the everyday life and thoughts of a non-Bolshevik provincial university teacher.

The policies of the new regime on the 'bourgeois specialists' and the ideological commitments to a machine utopia are discussed in the following: K. E. Bailes, *Technology and Society under Lenin and Stalin: Origins of the Soviet Technical Intelligentsia, 1917–1941* (Princeton, NJ: Princeton University Press, 1978), Chaps 1–2; K. E. Bailes, 'Alexei Gastev and the Soviet controversy over Taylorism', *Soviet Studies*, xxix, July 1977, no. 3, pp. 373–94; M. R. Beissinger, *Scientific Management, Socialist Discipline, and Soviet Power* (London: Tauris & Co., 1988), Chaps 1–2; and R. Stites, *Revolutionary Dreams: Utopian Vision and Experimental Life in the Russian Revolution* (New York and Oxford: Oxford University Press, 1989). M. Yampolsky, 'Kuleshov's experiments and the new anthropology of the actor', in R. Taylor and I. Christie (eds), *Inside the Film Factory: New Approaches to Russian and Soviet Cinema* (London: Routledge, 1991), pp. 31–50, is a specialized but fascinating detailed account of the penetration of machine utopia into an avant-garde cultural theory.

A wide range of interesting information on the NEP society is provided by W. J. Chase, *Workers, Society, and the Soviet State: Labor and Life in Moscow, 1918–1929* (Urbana and Chicago, Ill.: University of Illinois Press, 1990), although the narrative at times rather strains to provide a social explanation for the political decision to abandon the NEP. Another wide-ranging source is E. Johnson (ed.), *Russia in the Era of NEP* (Indianapolis, Ind.: University of Indiana Press, 1991). The best book on workers and industrial relations during the NEP, which I have drawn upon in my discussion of the 1920s' rationalization campaigns, is C. Ward, *Russia's Cotton Workers and the New Economic Policy: Shop-floor Culture and State Policy 1921–1929* (Cambridge: Cambridge University Press, 1990). A useful article on the political aspect of NEP relations between Bolsheviks and workers is J. Hatch, 'The "Lenin levy" and the social origins of Stalinism: workers and the Communist Party in Moscow, 1921–28', *Slavic Review*, xlvii, 1989, no. 4, pp. 558–77. A good source on the policies of state formation during the first 12 years of the new regime is P. Kenez, *The Birth of the Propaganda State: Soviet Methods of Mass Mobilization 1917–1929* (Cambridge: Cambridge University Press, 1985). The best book on the 'nepmen' is A. M. Ball, *Russia's Last Capitalists: The Nepmen, 1921–1929* (Berkeley, Calif.: University of California Press, 1987). Information on the unemployed and the policies on employment is provided by J. C. Shapiro, 'Unemployment and politics in NEP Russia' (an unpublished paper presented to the Soviet Industrialization Project Seminar, University of Birmingham, December 1988). The literature on the economic policy disputes during the NEP is immense and perhaps rather tangential to the subject of this book: E. H. Carr and R. W. Davies, *Foundations of a Planned Economy*, i, Parts 1 and 2 (London: Macmillan,

1969) is still a classic, documenting the transition from the NEP to a crash industrialization campaign. A usefully brief and clear assessment of NEP economic performance is provided by R. W. Davies, 'From Tsarism to NEP: continuity and change in the industrial economy, 1913–1926-7' (an unpublished paper presented to the Soviet Industrialization Project Seminar, University of Birmingham, November 1985).

As most histories of urban Russia before and after the revolutions, this chapter mainly concentrates on the two main cities. This is inevitable in an introductory text, for Moscow and St Petersburg were dominant in terms of size, industrial concentration, and political action. But the conditions and the course of events in the provinces should not be assumed to have been just a backwater reflection of those in the capital cities. R. Pethybridge, *One Step Backwards Two Steps Forward: Soviet Society and Politics in the New Economic Policy* (Oxford: Clarendon Press, 1990) provides a useful counterbalance to the metropolitan bias.

Finally, two more items provide two different kinds of insight into the NEP period: J. Brooks, 'Public and private values in the Soviet press, 1921–28', *Slavic Review*, xlviii, 1989, no. 1, pp. 16–35, and E. J. Dillon, *Russia Today and Yesterday* (London: J.M. Dent and Sons Ltd, 1929), which is a memoir by a Russian émigré, a former high tsarist official, of his visit back to Russia during the 1920s.

6

The 'Great Breakthrough' and Collectivization, 1928–39

The decade that started in 1928–9 is often referred to as 'a revolution from above'. It saw the break-up of peasant communes, rapid industrialization, mass migration to the cities and industrial settlements, a great deal of social mobility, a famine, mass-scale deportations to exile settlements and concentration camps, executions and show trials, purges of the party and state apparatus, zig-zags between radical and conservative themes in culture and social policy, and a deification of the leader, to name but some of the many trends and phenomena in a complicated historical process. When the dust settled at the end of the decade, state bureaucracy, its political patterns, and the social structure were of the type which became synonymous with 'Soviet-type socialism' or 'Stalinism'.

It may be useful to think of the eventful decade as consisting of several subperiods. The years 1928–31 were the ones of the 'great breakthrough' and the crash campaigns of collectivization and industrialization; the dominant rhetoric in public life was uncompromisingly civil-war-like and it was laced with radical socialist 'cultural revolution' themes. The years 1932–3 were years of famine in the countryside and a deep economic crisis in the industrial sector; radical left rhetoric that had not died down was silenced, and the party leadership struggled with whether it should make a U-turn in its economic strategy. Economic development resumed in 1934–5 under more moderate and better balanced plans, and living standards began to rise. The 'great terror' or 'yezhovism' (*yezhovshchina*), when purges and a police terror swept through the ranks of the regime's own cadres, occurred in 1936–8; public rhetoric was extremely denunciatory and the frenzied witch-hunt atmosphere was spiked with spectacular show trials of famous party leaders. In 1939–40, the repressive police apparatus was mainly busy with the populations and social élites of eastern Poland and the Baltic states, which were annexed by the Soviet Union under the auspices of a peace treaty with Germany. As is often the case with periodization in history, these subperiods are pots that leak some of their content into one another; but it is useful to bear in mind that the 'revolution from above' was not a one-act drama.

The most significant campaigns whereby the state effected social changes on a large scale were those concerned with the reorganization of the peasant countryside into a system of collective farms, and those concerned with industrialization. They are described in this and the next chapter. First, however, we turn our attention to some of the events and processes of the political break that started the main campaigns.

The Left Turn

The commitment to rapid industrialization made by the party congress in 1927 may have implied a strain on the New Economic Policy (NEP) framework of trade between the peasantry and the industrializing state sector, but the assumption was that the NEP would basically remain in place. The government economists who laboured on the drafts of the first five-year plan also shared this assumption. The congress decision, however, had the political effect of neutralizing the 'left opposition' within the party, many of whose members transferred their allegiance from the exiled Trotsky back to the ruling politburo, since now they saw a policy they could identify with. This made it politically feasible for Stalin to initiate a split with the man with whom he had been obliged to share the pinnacle of party hierarchy, and who was the chief ideologue of the NEP, Bukharin.

Stalin's first major step in this direction was his emergency grain-finding campaign (the 'Urals-Siberian method' already mentioned in Chapter 3), which brought the grain in but also antagonized the most productive farmers and broke the peasants' trust in the government's intentions. It seemed expedient to repeat the method on a countrywide and more systematic basis in the following agricultural year, to make sure that the 'kulak does not go on strike' again. Bukharin's difficulty in preventing this was that it was possible to argue theoretically that the 'Urals-Siberian' method was within the existing NEP laws and party policy, because it merely coerced 'kulak speculators' and left the trading rights of the 'middle peasant' alone. Many in the party central committee knew that, in practice, this was not so, but not all of them dared to protest; after all, many of those who were employed by the party apparat were the general secretary's – Stalin's – appointees and protégés.

Other steps soon followed. In March 1928, Stalin initiated a campaign for 'self-criticism' and 'party democracy' within the party, which invited party and *komsomol* (party youth organization) members to bring to account any party member or official in their locality whose conduct in office seemed stale or in some way corrupt. This was ostensibly a campaign against 'bureaucratism' and 'party degeneracy' rather than against the NEP, but it so happened that one of the first *cause célèbre* cases was about a group of officials in Smolensk province. These officials had hobnobbed with kulaks and former landowners, whom they had helped to form a collective farm. They protected the farm's prosperity by granting tax concessions and state credits, and as of late, by stalling on the freshly recommended 'Ural-Siberian method' of grain procurement. The indictment did not allege that the favoured collective farm was inefficient, or indeed that the rural district for which the officials were responsible had a below-par record of grain-marketing. Apart from the hobnobbing with the kulaks, some venality, and the fact that one of the officials had married a former landowners' daughter, it alleged drinking bouts and sexual orgies. The

Local OGPU (security police) chief had apparently been reporting the officials' misdemeanours to the provincial party and law-enforcement offices since 1925, but the reports were always shelved – such was the mutual protectionism of the local power élite. It was only when he took his dossier to the central committee at the beginning of 1928 that a full investigation started. The 'Smolensk scandal' publicity that followed associated the NEP ways of encouraging highly productive farms, and Bukharin's theory of prosperous farmers' 'gradual growth' (*vrastanie*) into socialism, with 'party degeneracy' and bureaucratic corruption. As with the 'extraordinary measures' of grain collection in Urals-Siberia, the 'Smolensk scandal' signalled that the NEP was suspect without giving Bukharin a chance to defend it in public argument.

Another significant step towards 'the great breakthrough' took place at about the same time: the arrest and subsequent show trial of 53 mining engineers charged with deliberately misusing their expert decision-making powers over the past six years to cause accidents and low productivity. Eleven were sentenced to death and 38 received prison sentences. Party resolutions followed which, while acknowledging that not all 'bourgeois specialists' were necessarily bent on wrecking socialist industrialization, exhorted vigilance against those who still acted as class enemies under the cover of their professional expertise. Bukharin and his allies in politburo and government opposed neither the trial nor the campaign for 'class vigilance'. However, since the 'bourgeois specialists' were generally pro-NEP and moderate in their beliefs as to what kind of production-growth plan targets were feasible, allegiance to NEP principles and moderation in economic planning became associated with class-enemy suspects and their 'bourgeois conservatism'. 'Bourgeois specialists' were purged from the government planning offices and the five-year plan was redrafted upwards as rival groups of economic planners outdid each other in their displays of revolutionary optimism. The five-year plan inaugurated in July 1928 was already much higher than previous drafts, its targets were upgraded further in the following year, and, at the end of 1929, the central committee decreed that it be completed not in five years but in four. The intellectual key to the target amplification was the overthrow of the 'economic conservatism' which had insisted on intersectoral balances between growth targets, empirical methods of estimating productive capacity, and sound money. The 'economic conservatism' failed to take into account what could be achieved if the proletarian masses were mobilized politically – went the 'left turn' argument. The pre-NEP 'war communism' theories that socialist dynamism should eventually lead to a moneyless economy came back.

The campaigns against 'party degeneracy' and 'bourgeois specialists' provided a platform for young communist radicals in all manner of institutions and walks of life to attack moderate officials for 'rightist deviation' if not 'bureaucratism', and established professional élites for 'bourgeois conservatism' if not for wrecking. We have already seen in Chapter 3 the generational division between prewar professionals and young Marxists in the field of agricultural economics, and analogous divisions came to life everywhere. They reflected a contradiction in the polity of the 1920s. The new state sought to establish its legitimacy as the sole heir of the Russian revolution and the long-existing social quest for progress and modernity. Its propaganda apparatus mythologized the revolution's heroic years and promoted a militant class-struggle view of historical progress. It also promoted a youth cult, for the revolutionaries were young and the revolution reified the division between old and new worlds, a dismal past and a bright future. The Bolsheviks secured the future despite being thought reckless demagogues by their political rivals. Many young people could identify with this, and the party and the *komsomol* had no problem recruiting them. But the visionary militancy of the Bolsheviks' heroic days sat ill at ease with the managerial tasks of the NEP state. Young men who proved themselves to the party during the civil war were asked to help manage the NEP economy for the state and to act as watchdogs over 'bourgeois specialists'. Some of them learnt to think and act like managers, lawyers, civil servants, or whatever, while others were in their element only when they had an opportunity to use a 'class approach'. We noted in Chapter 5 that local party and government officials often acted arbitrarily against nepmen despite the official policies on trade, and the revelations of the 'Smolensk scandal' notwithstanding, rural officials often acted arbitrarily against the better-off peasants. Bukharin did his best to develop a Marxist theory that gave the NEP a positive place in socialist visions, but it was a complicated argument which was slow to impress militant minds. Without an appealing ideological bridge between Bolshevik revolution and NEP management, NEP and 'bourgeois specialist' professional hegemony always seemed to socialist visionaries an uncomfortable and temporary shackle on revolutionary progress. If the militants who had seen action in the civil war had a difficult role to play under the NEP, the party and *komsomol* members who came of age after the heroic days hardly had an outlet for their socialist militancy – until, that is, the campaigns of Stalin's 'left turn'.

As with the radical economists' ideas about the socialist superiority of a moneyless economy and the dynamic potential of unbalanced planning, the super-radicalism that emerged in other institutional spheres with the attack on 'bourgeois conservatism' marked the return of ideas and visions which had proliferated among left-wing Bolsheviks during the civil war. For example, visions of the 'withering away of the state' and radical Marxist critiques of 'bourgeois law', and the theoretical justifications of the Red Terror that had been formulated during the civil war, made a comeback in the field of jurisprudence. The established conceptions of the law and how justice should be served by the state judiciary were fundamentally flawed, it was now argued by a group of academics, because they had been developed under capitalism to safeguard the principles of private commodity exchange. The notion of 'equality before the law' was a bourgeois notion that served to obscure the fundamental inequality of class, and it would ill serve the tasks of transition to socialism. Judgements over alleged crimes and citizens' disputes should be made on the basis of 'social expediency' rather than literally interpreted laws. Socialist judges should not be limited to classifying as a crime only those acts which were already defined as such in the law books, and they should not be limited by any prescribed penalty scales in their sentencing decisions. Decisions should be based on assessing the social consequences of the acts in question and on who the perpetrator was as a 'social person' – where he or she stood in the class struggle. Most cases should be tried before lay 'comradely courts' in work places and neighbourhoods, while professional judges should specialize in arbitrating disputes between institutions. Like many of the other radical ideas that surfaced during this period, these proposals stirred up a heated polemic in their institutional sphere without actually becoming accepted as official policy by the party and government; but such were the times that there were judges who put them into practice, as was revealed by a marked increase in the already high number of judicial decisions that were overturned on appeal.

In the arts sphere, the 'proletarian culture' approach to aesthetics once more issued a challenge to the professional establishment, and academic élitism came under attack in schools and universities. Here the government was quick to throw its weight, as higher education courses were decreed to contract in length and entry qualifications for workers were reduced to completed primary schooling and apprenticeship training. Established values and hierarchies also came under pressure in the less intellectual spheres. *Komsomol* members demanded backing for their labour communes in which they experimented with collectivist ways of working and living, and production conferences on factory shopfloors enlivened as workers began to insist that management give them the right to vote foremen in and out of their jobs.

Additional platforms for militant left ideas were provided in 1929, by purges of party members and of government white-collar workers and officials. Neither of these campaigns was ostensibly directed against people who were pro-NEP; both tended to be conducted under procedures which supposedly allowed any member of a party cell or an employee of a government office to cite criticisms of a colleague. Special purge commissions would then call the named persons to account at general meetings. The purgees were allowed to defend themselves from inaccurate accusations, but they were also expected to come clean before the meetings with some heart-felt self-criticism. The meeting would then vote on its recommendations. Ten per cent of government officials lost their jobs in this way in 1929–30.

The resurgence of left-wing radicalism among young communists, the purge campaigns against 'party degeneracy' and 'bureaucratism', and the campaigns of class vigilance against the 'bourgeois specialists' created countless occasions on which pro-NEP or moderate views were lambasted as conservative and possibly expressive of their holders' corruption or class enmity. At the top of the party, Bukharin was voted out of the politburo in November 1929 and, in the following month, *Pravda* celebrated Stalin's fiftieth birthday by announcing a novel doctrine of party democracy: 'it is now completely clear that it is wrong to be for the party and against the *existing* Central Committee, to be for the Central Committee and against Stalin'.[1] The 'great breakthrough' was accomplished and there was no fortress the Bolsheviks would not storm, to paraphrase a favourite slogan of the times.

---

1 *Pravda*, 23 December 1929. Quoted in Davies, R. W. 1980: *The Socialist Offensive: The Collectivization of Soviet Agriculture, 1929–1930*. London: Macmillan, p. 175.

The 'Great Breakthrough' on the 'Grain Front', 1928–9

The Ural-Siberian method of grain collection was no longer simply recommended but decreed for countrywide application after the harvest of 1928. A hundred thousand urban officials and industrial workers were dispatched to the countryside to reinforce the local soviets and party authorities, or to bypass them if they appeared to be insufficiently enthusiastic about the grain-delivery quotas to be met in their localities. The urban plenipotentiaries organized village meetings where those who attended were cajoled and browbeaten into accepting an overall quota for the village, and individually specified targets for 'kulak' producers. Local soviets were empowered to punish failures to meet these targets and tax obligations by fines five times as high as the alleged debts; it was no longer necessary to have such penalties imposed by the courts. A failure to pay these fines became punishable by property confiscation and prison or exile. Coercive measures thus became applicable not only to the crime of hoarding grain with 'speculative' intent but also to simple failures in meeting the state-delivery quotas. We have seen in Chapter 3 that the village meetings that ratified the quotas were considered quorate if one-third of the *mir* members attended, and the authorities decreed that 'land society' (*mir*) membership was extended from landholding peasants to all village residents. It was thus possible for the quotas to be voted for without the consent of the households that were affected the most. This regime was imposed not only on the traditional grain-surplus areas but also on the rural districts of the central industrial region and the north, which had been net importers of grain.

Some positive incentives were involved in the campaign as well as threats. These incentives were mainly offered in the form of contracts with groups of households or whole villages whereby the grain-collection agencies undertook to supply high-quality seed, fertilizer, agricultural machinery, and consumer goods at low prices, and in some cases on credit. The flow of consumer goods from the industrial producers to the countryside indeed increased substantially in 1928–9 in comparison with previous years. But the effectiveness of this incentive was limited by the difference in size between the urban and rural parts of the economy. The diversion of consumer goods to the countryside was large enough to be felt negatively in the cities without being sufficient to cover the terms of all the grain-goods exchange contracts, which were then enforced one-sidedly; the peasants were held to their grain-delivery quotas regardless of whether the state agencies delivered their part of the bargain.

Besides, the differential between the state's grain prices and the prices prevalent on free markets became very wide – so wide that some farmers preferred to pay fines for shortfalls in state deliveries and spare some grain for free-market sales. Another ruse employed by the more productive farmers was to sell some of their surpluses to their poorer neighbours at discount prices, so that the poorer neighbours could make good profit by private resale; these arrangements, of course, served to strengthen the bonds of complicity between village neighbours and against the state's plenipotentiaries' efforts to get the poor peasant on their side against the 'kulak'. The authorities tried to stop the leakage of grain to free markets by imposing restrictions on its transportation by rail, although direct free marketing by peasants was still legal and, indeed, was depended upon by the populations of non-industrial towns as well as by the many rural dwellers who did not grow grain. However, the authorities were unable to stop night-time journeys on peasant carts and river barges. As during the civil war, state attempts to impose a grain-purchase monopoly turned into cat-and-mouse games where peasants hid the grain in camouflaged pits and the requisitioning agents had to meet their quotas by finding it. Violence, needless to say, was on an upward curve as the state's plenipotentiaries resorted to imposing their authority by more arrests and expropriations of the 'kulaks and their henchmen', and 'the class enemy' retaliated by more 'acts of terrorism' against the requisitioners.

Party and government policy-makers had always considered that the solution to the problem of fitting peasant agriculture into the state's economic plans would be found in collective farms. We saw in Chapter 3 that the 'bourgeois specialist' agronomists and land-consolidation experts occasionally succeeded in persuading the households involved in partial (group) consolidations of landholding to set themselves up as collective farms. But such collective farms tended to be small, and the main thrust of the agronomist short-term policy was to achieve land consolidation and farming improvements wherever and however this could be negotiated with the peasant landholders. The co-operative movement that was urged on peasant farms as immediately practical was to join trading co-operatives which would enable them to purchase quality fertilizer, seeds, and machines on a shared basis. The idea was that once the superior means of production were in place, further group land consolidation would follow as the part-owners or hirers of the machines would naturally not want the full utilization of their equipment to be impeded by interstripped land plots. Optimal-sized, consolidated landholdings under a co-operative enterprise management could then be envisaged as the culmination of a gradual voluntary process, since the trading co-operatives were proving popular and some land consolidation was taking place as well. However, everyone agreed that the process would take time. The formation of collective farms accelerated somewhat after 1926, when kulaks became subject to increasingly hefty taxation and some of them could see the advantages of becoming collective farmers instead. The proportion of peasant households in collective farms increased from less than one per cent in June 1927 to almost four per cent in June 1929.

By the beginning of 1929, however, the 'left turn' policies came to regard the formation of collective farms with an urgency born of the grain-requisitioning problems, and worries about the supposed domination of the peasantry by the 'kulak class'. Collectivization, it was now thought by the anti-NEP strand of socialist ideology, was too important to be left to a gradual process managed by 'bourgeois specialist' or 'neopopulist' agrarian reformers bent on piecemeal compromises with the peasant communes and with the better-off peasants in particular. It should be an active political campaign that appealed to the poor and 'middle' peasant, and it should be comprehensive (*sploshnaya*) – that is, aimed at the formation of large collective farms covering whole villages and districts, for only then could agricultural production be planned and 'petty bourgeois spontaneity' kept at bay. It was still to be a voluntary process, albeit one helped along by giving collective farms the advantage of the best land and exclusive rights of access to financial credit and industrial goods, which should take about 10 years to complete.

The grain-requisitioning plenipotentiaries and some regional party bosses tried to outdo each other in how quick a start they were capable of making on the road to comprehensive collectivization. The main argument that developed among them was what to do about the kulak: should he be allowed to join the collectives by contributing voluntarily his means of production, or should he be excluded? And if so, should he be allowed to hold on to all his property? The dilemma resolved itself where the grain-requisitioning authorities felt able to evoke their punitive powers of property confiscation against the kulaks who had fallen foul of their 'state obligations'. But not all kulaks were as yet in that situation: many of them had an influential elder status in their villages, and some of them might be willing to negotiate a collectivization deal on a pragmatic basis. There was something to be said for letting the most successful farmers take part.

The dilemma was settled with the help of another well publicized affair of the 'Smolensk scandal' type. This time the subject was a large collective farm called the Red Land-Improver (*Krasnyi meliorator*), which had enjoyed much success and fame ever since its formation in the steppe of the lower Volga region in 1924. In 1929, however, it was investigated by the Workers' and Peasants' Inspectorate (*rabkrin*) and found to be dominated by a group of 'former people' who either used to belong to prerevolutionary privileged classes themselves or were related to them by descent; four of them were already officially disenfranchised by the state for this reason, two were former members of the Social Revolutionary Party, and several were still resident in the homes they had owned in the district town as local merchants and professionals. One of the top managers had been the manager of one of the large private farming estates in the region before the revolution and, needless to say, the core group of the farm membership also included a number of former kulaks and *khutor* (enclosed farm) owners. The investigation found that the prosperity of this 'pseudo-collective farm' (*lzhekolkhoz*) had been based on the seasonal exploitation of migrant wage labourers who were disguised in the records as collective-farm members who had joined and then left. The *rabkrin* findings were supported by the district party committee but contradicted by government agricultural administration. The dispute ended in an intensification of the general purge of 'class aliens' from collective farms and agricultural administration, and in a party decree banning all 'kulak infiltration' of the collectivization movement.

Crash Collectivization and a Retreat, 1929–30

A crash collectivization campaign became the centrepiece of party policy in November 1929. Comprehensive collectivization was to be accomplished countrywide by 1932, and in the main grain-surplus regions as soon as possible. The hundred thousand urban plenipotentiaries already active in the countryside were reinforced by a further mobilization, which brought their number up to a quarter of a million. While new recruitment was still in progress, in December 1929, Stalin announced a new policy on the kulak to a conference of agrarian Marxists: the kulak was to be 'liquidated as a class' and the collectivization campaign was to sweep through the countryside in tandem with a 'dekulakization' campaign.

Many of the new mobilized plenipotentiaries were army officers on secondment, and the army also played an important role in organizing quick induction courses for the campaigners. Other major sources of recruitment were the party and *komsomol* organizations in government and city soviet offices, in higher education institutes, and in factories. The recruitment of industrial workers included the so-called '25 000ers', who volunteered to go to the countryside not just for the campaigns but on a permanent basis to provide a working-class leadership core for the socialized peasantry. They were a carefully screened élite. Recruitment was centred on the big industrial cities and the metal industries, and recruitment was to provide only the 'most advanced' workers – that is, ones who were 'thoroughly urbanized' and without any personal links with the peasantry. They should have at least five years' shopfloor experience, preferably in skilled jobs, and a proven record of active support for the regime. More than 70 000 applied and 27 519 were selected (rather than 25 000 as planned) from the whole of the Soviet Union, two-thirds of them from the Russian Republic, mainly men in their twenties and thirties who were party members. Many had been Red Army soldiers during the civil war, and many had taken part in grain-requisitioning campaigns either during the civil war or more recently. Nearly a half had been industrial workers for more than 12 years.[2]

On arriving in their designated rural districts, the campaigners were based in special field-staff headquarters which included OGPU (state security police) officers who had armed troops under their command. The campaigners were also armed themselves. They worked in small groups, travelling from one village to the next to implement the campaign plans. The dekulakization and collectivization campaigns were regarded formally as separate from one another. The collectivization campaigns were timed supposedly to reach a village on the heels of the dekulakization campaigns, but there was a great deal of overlap in personnel. Both sets of campaigners were recommended to use the Urals-Siberian tactic of seeking to turn a village politically by first talking to small groups of likely supporters. The practice varied; some teams of collectivizers took weeks to persuade the majority of households to form a collective farm, while others claimed to do the job in a day. The political pressures from above were more for speed than for patience, and local progress was paced by the logistics of police support movements as much as by the agitators' initial intentions.

The dekulakization campaign was under way for several weeks by the time the central authorities issued a directive on its quotas and procedures at the end of January 1930. The directive made explicit the agrarian Marxist assumption that up to five per cent of peasant households belonged to the kulak class in the main grain-producing regions, and up to three per cent in other rural areas. It divided the kulak class into three categories: first, 'the

---

2 Viola, L. 1987: *The Best Sons of the Fatherland: Workers in the Vanguard of Soviet Collectivization*. New York: Oxford University Press, p. 45.

counter-revolutionary activist core'; secondly, 'the remaining elements of the kulak activist core'; and, thirdly, the kulaks who were relatively 'loyal to Soviet power'. Kulak households of the first category were to be listed by the OGPU, and the heads of these households were to be sentenced to imprisonment or death. The OGPU was given a quota for the first category: 63 000 for the USSR as a whole, of which 52 000 were to be found in the Russian Federal Republic. The lists of the other two categories were to be drawn up by district committees of the soviets on the basis of consultation with poor and landless peasants in the villages. Second-category kulaks were to be deported to special OGPU-controlled settlements in northern European Russia, Siberia, and central Asia, while third-category kulaks were to be evicted from their homes and allowed to resettle on inferior land somewhere outside their village, but within the same administrative district. Family members of first-category kulaks were to be given second-category treatment. The quota for category two was fixed as 112 000 families for the Russian Republic and 150 000 families for the USSR as a whole. It is not known if there was a quota fixed for category three; according to the best estimates, 656 000 families were treated as category three in the Russian Republic, 852 000 in the USSR.[3] First-category kulaks had all their property confiscated, category two were allowed to take small amounts of cash and basic necessities such as they could carry as personal luggage to the deportation trains, and category-three kulaks were allowed to keep some of their farming implements as well as basic household and personal necessities. Property that was confiscated was to be transferred to collective farms and to poor peasants. Families who had some of their members serving in the Red Army or working in the factories were to be kept off the kulak lists. The dekulakization process as a whole was targeted for completion by May.

The dekulakization practice was naturally much less orderly than the bureaucratic guidelines. Apart from the inherent difficulty of telling a kulak household from a 'middle peasant' one in the many villages where social inequalities were far from self-evident, some kulaks turned out to be related by family to the Red Army or the industrial working class, while the expediency of quelling resistance against collectivization dictated that dekulakization be extended to 'sub-kulaks': the peasants who seemed especially troublesome though not rich by any standards. There were districts where up to 15 per cent of the peasantry came under the sway of dekulakization, although they were denounced by the party leadership as undesirable extreme cases. Designated kulaks' property was often looted mercilessly by the dekulakization brigades without regard to any limiting guidelines. Not all the kulaks and the peasants expecting to be so classified sat still: about a quarter of the total effected their own 'self-dekulakization' – they joined the swelling streams of labour migration to the industrialization sites and the cities before the dekulakization brigades could reach them.

The collectivization campaign proceeded frantically on the heels of dekulakization, but without much in the way of clear guidelines. In the absence of such, the vision that drove the collectivizers was one of very large collective

---

3 Davies, *The Socialist Offensive*, p. 236.

farms, perhaps subsuming several villages each, in which not only the grain-growing fields surrounding the villages but also the livestock and perhaps even the vegetables grown on the household plots within the villages should have the benefits of a socialized division of labour and economies of scale. The collective farms, in other words, should be an agricultural version of socialist industry. It did not matter that the technology which might justify huge consolidated fields and the removal of animals and vegetables from individual household care was not available. Did Marx and Stalin not say that the large 'manufacture', with a high division of labour (albeit as yet a low level of mechanization), was a progressive intermediate step between the cottage workshop and the industrial factory? There was not much that could be done immediately with snow-bound household vegetable plots. The priority was the demarcation of consolidated grain-growing fields and seed collection for spring ploughing and sowing. But cows and poultry as well as horses could often be removed from individual household sheds into larger collective ones straight- away. Collectivization measures caused the greatest outrage and the bitterest resistance when they encroached on the household plot and cowshed; the way the women saw it, such measures were robbing their children of a milk-based diet. The collectivization campaign was also combined with a renewed attack on religion. The urban youths of the Militant Godless League carried out their own icon-burning agitation, the priests' land plots were collectivized, church bells were taken down and the buildings turned to secular use, and priests were deported along with the kulaks.

The arrival of the collectivization brigades was preceded by intense rumours about the coming of the anti-Christ, the sale of women to China in payment for the Manchurian railway, the slaughter of old people to reduce peasant food consumption, the use of old women to sit on eggs so that the hens could be sent to town kitchens, enforced communal living, all villagers having to sleep together under a single large blanket, children being taken from their parents into an institutional care, and women having to cut their hair because it was needed as an industrial raw material. The authorities dismissed the rumours as the product of fevered imaginations by the dark illiterate masses and their women folk in particular, or as malicious gossip spread by the kulaks. But some had a basis in what some of the collectivizers said and did. There was indeed much agitational talk about nurseries for children and the desirability of communal living, the henless hatching of eggs in incubators, the importance of supplying town kitchens with food, and of paying for the industrialization effort in sweat and blood. There were plenipotentiaries who requisitioned blankets for future communal living arrangements, and at least one who forced peasant women to cut their hair short to make them look urban.[4]

The rumours helped to mobilize outrage and protest action. Murders, lynchings, and arson were often reported in the press as examples of the lengths to which the kulak class would go in its retaliation against Soviet officials and their activist supporters. The incidence of 'terrorist acts' had been correlated with the state's grain-requisitioning activities, and there can be no

---

4 Viola, L. 1986: 'Bab'i Bunty and peasant women's protest during collectivization'. *The Russian Review*, xlv, pp. 23–42.

doubt that it increased further in the winter 1929–30. Occasionally the dekulakizers and collectivizers encountered open armed resistance and their work could not be done until OGPU troops secured their entry into a village. This could be difficult in regions such as the steppe areas of the south settled by Cossack peasants who lived in very large villages ('stations'), who had strong traditions of military self-government, and, during the civil war, had mainly supported the Whites. By and large, however, peasant protest was local and vocal rather than semi-military. Peasants would gather in front of their churches to protect them from atheist militants, in front of kulak houses to protect them from dekulakization brigades; they would mob the plenipotentiaries, turn collectivization meetings into riotous assemblies, and crowds would break into grain stores and collectivized cowsheds to take back what they thought was theirs. The ringing of church bells often signalled the start of such protests, thus providing an additional reason why the socialist campaigners wanted to take them down.

The village women were most often in the front line of overt protest. Perhaps they felt more strongly than the men about the attacks on the church and about the perceived or real intentions of the collectivizers in regard to the peasant woman's realm – the family, the household plot, and its livestock. The feminine front line, however, was also a good tactic: it had often been employed during the peasantry's attacks on gentry property in 1905–7. Like the old-regime policemen and army officers, the new-regime campaigners could be relied upon to be more reluctant to use punitive force against rebellious crowds if they were women. The class-war imagery the new campaigners thought they were fighting was a masculine one. The kulak enemy was surely male. The protesting women were not a class enemy so much as a particularly backward section of the 'dark and illiterate' mass, which was unfortunately manipulable by the crafty kulaks and priests and prone to outbursts of crowd hysteria. Besides, using force against women would only mobilize all the men to join the fight on the wrong side, for the cross-class demands of chivalry would give them no option. Retreating from the women's wrath, on the other hand, was something a socialist class warrior could occasionally do without an irretrievable loss of face; it could be done in the spirit of condescension, and the kulaks to blame could be found later. The collectivizers' recollections of their meetings with the reluctant collective farmers resound with the high-pitched voices of spontaneous women folk refusing to listen to the politically correct reason, and turning an august occasion into mayhem. Sullen silence was the other discomforting sound the collectivizers had to get used to hearing.

Another form of 'kulak sabotage' that was apparently widespread and frequently commented upon in the press was the slaughtering of livestock. Overall livestock counts had been falling since the summer of 1928, and they would keep on falling to a disastrous all-time low in 1933. The kulak was alleged to kill his horse, cows, and pigs rather than let the collective farm have them. But impetuous protest against collectivization was far from the only cause of livestock depletion, and probably not the main one. The problem was that the state's rapacity in requisitioning grain and the demands that ever more of it be grown was making animal husbandry increasingly difficult for collective farms and individual peasant households alike. The publicity given to anti-collectivization animal slaughter reflected a partial truth: peasants, and not only kulaks, were 'cashing in' their livestock investments out of bitterness and also out of economic necessity brought about by excessive grain requisitioning.

By the end of February 1930 the proportion of peasant households reported to have joined a collective farm reached almost 60 per cent in Russia proper as well as the USSR as a whole. But the countryside was far from peaceful and the party leaders became worried about the progress of spring sowing. On March 2, *Pravda* published an article bearing Stalin's signature and the title 'Giddy with success', which acknowledged that collectivization was not always as voluntary as it should be and duly condemned plenipotentiaries and officials who resorted to 'bureaucratic methods' or antagonized the peasantry by insisting on collectivizing their livestock as well as their grain lands. The arbitrary closure of churches without the consent of village majorities was also condemned. Party decrees issued during the following weeks called for purges of officials found guilty of excesses, and for the rehabilitation of peasants who had been 'dekulakized' unjustly. Some 10 per cent of the dekulakized peasants won their appeals in the following months, although it is not clear whether all of those who had been deported and subsequently rehabilitated were in the event able to return home.

Above all, however, the party leaders appeared to be resuscitating the voluntary principle of collectivization. The March 2 issue of *Pravda* was a sell-out, with copies trading at exuberant prices. 'Giddy with success' was read with encores in meetings, tea-rooms, and throngs, toasted in impromptu celeb-rations, and waved at officials' faces. Land surveyors had to work at a feverish pace yet again, this time to divide up the collectivized land as ever more peasants took up their right to leave their collective farms or had them proclaimed null and void. By the end of the summer the overall proportion of peasant households in collective farms was down to 20 per cent. In the Moscow region, the drop was from almost 75 per cent in March to seven per cent in September; in the central black earth, from 83 per cent in March to 15 per cent in September.[5]

The Resumption of Collectivization, the Famine, and its Aftermath

The climate was kind and the harvest was good in 1930. As soon as the grain was safely in state storage, the collectivization drive resumed. This time there were clearer guidelines to curb extremist zealotry among the 240 000 plenipotentiaries. Collective farmers were given the right to hold on to their household plots and to keep some livestock for private use. A statute issued in 1935 would specify the right of each *kolkhoz* household to a private plot of between one-quarter and one-half of a hectare, the traditional size of the plots that were immediately behind peasant cottages. Collectivization, in other words, in the event subsumed what used to be the communally held lands in the village surroundings while leaving alone the household plots adjacent to

---

5 Davies, *The Socialist Offensive*, pp. 442–3.

the peasants' dwellings. The statute would also enshrine the right of every household to keep privately one cow and its calves, one sow and its piglets, four sheep, unlimited poultry and rabbits, and some other animals, such as goats, in unspecified quantities. This level of household livestock-keeping was not far below what had been kept by many peasants in the pre-Soviet period, if we discount the fact that collective farmers could not keep horses privately, and if we take into account that the average household now consisted only of four people compared with the average of six in the late tsarist period. From May 1932, collective farmers had the right to sell their household plots' produce and their privately kept livestock in bazaars, at unregulated prices. A compromise with peasant traditions was also evident in the average size of the collective farms in the mid-1930s: some 70 households, which was close to what the average village commune had been before collectivization.

The lynchpin of the difference between peasant life before and after collectivization was that the collective farmer had no control over the grain and cash crops that were produced on the collectivized land. The main focus of the new system of grain sowing and requisitioning was the motor-tractor station (MTS), a state institution that hired out machinery to the collective farms under its administration, supplied the seed, collected the grain for the state in accordance with the planned procurement quotas, had the last word in deciding what residual the collective farms could keep for their own members' consumption, collected the money from the state for the grain, paid the taxes, and subtracted its own charges before paying any residual cash to the collective farms. Each MTS thus controlled about 40 collective farms. Each MTS's management had to include a deputy director charged with political rather than managerial responsibilities; in 1933–4, this post involved the running of a special 'political department' within the MTS, and it had to be occupied by an OGPU officer. The residual of grain and cash that was payable to collective farmers under this system was predictable only in so far as it was always small; a peasant did not need to be a 'kulak agitator' to view collectivization as re-enserfment.

Another difference made by collectivization was that artisan workshops, which had been an important part of peasant livelihood in the central industrial region in particular, were also appropriated by the collective farms. Thus the household plot, which had been a supplementary source of subsistence for the peasant family alongside grain-growing and/or artisan production, was now providing the collective-farm family with two-thirds of its cash income. As the income obtainable from work on collective-farm fields and property was small and unpredictable, motivating this work quickly became a major problem for collective-farm managers. The collective farmers naturally preferred to maximize their labour on their household plots where the returns were more certain; and they had to work harder on them than ever before, as keeping private livestock, in particular, was more difficult now that the state was taking away even that part of the grain from the collectivized fields that would have fed the livestock in the old days. The most effective part of the collective-farm system was the way in which it secured the priority claims of the fast-growing urban sector on grain production, while keeping the price of grain low. But the over-requisitioning thus made possible was not only starving the peasantry of their main source of livelihood – it was also starving the collectivized as well as the private livestock, and it was starving the collective-farm production of willing labour, driving it to concentrate on eking out a private living on the household plots instead.

The collectivization drive that resumed in the winter of 1930–1 proceeded apace. More than a half of peasant households and more than two-thirds of grain-growing fields were in collective farms by July 1931, and 93 per cent of the households and 99 per cent of the grain fields by July 1937. The compromise on the household plot was not in itself sufficient to make this a peaceful process. The GULAG (Chief Directorate of Camps, the branch of OGPU responsible for running forced-labour establishments) system of forced-labour concentration camps, special labour settlements, and labour colonies that had grown chaotically in 1929–30 in support of the initial dekulakization became itself an important institution of the industrialization campaign, with the OGPU being given a direct managerial responsibility for the expansion of mining and lumbering and for capital construction projects. Like other industrial-sector enterprises, it tended to respond to problems of production-quota fulfilment by wanting even more than the planned quotas of labourers. The GULAG system needed the supply of inmates to continue beyond the initial dekulakization plans, and the supply had to continue to come mainly from the peasantry – still by far the most numerous section of the population. At the 'labour-supply' end in the countryside, the authorities needed the coercive apparatus at least as much as the GULAG system needed its slave labourers: in 1931, to get collectivization going again, and from the end of 1931 until the end of 1933 to keep grain-requisitioning high even in the face of failed harvests.

In 1931 the harvest was about 14 per cent lower than in the previous year, and it was slightly lower still in 1932. This was for the USSR as a whole. The harvest was about 11 per cent lower in 1931 than in 1930 in the central black-earth and the Volga regions, 30 per cent lower in the Urals and Siberia, and over five per cent lower in the Ukraine and north Caucasus. In 1932, it was four per cent higher than in 1931 in the central black earth and the Volga, 18 per cent higher in the Urals and Siberia, but 27 per cent lower in the Ukraine and north Caucasus.[6] The causes of the low harvests in 1931 and 1932 were complex. The weather played a part, as did inept management and low labour motivation in the collective farms; in 1932, the average acre of collective-farm land provided no better harvest than the average acre of the peasants who were still outside the collectivized sector, although the collective farms had taken the best land. The most important single cause, however, was the fact that the supply of tractors to collective farms was insufficient to compensate for the loss of horses that had gone to the slaughter houses along with other livestock. There simply was not enough power available for pulling the ploughs and grain carts.

Be this as it may, the magnitude of the harvest shortfalls was not in itself as disastrous as previous famine years; 1922, for example, had been worse in this

---

6 Based on data provided by Wheatcroft, S. 1985: 'The Soviet economic crisis of 1932: the crisis in agriculture'. Paper presented to the Soviet Industrialization Project Seminar, University of Birmingham, January.

respect, especially on the Volga. The unprecedented fact for the peasantry was that grain requisitioning had been relentless since 1928, thus leaving no reserves in the rural stores, and the state's demands did not relax when the harvests worsened. The number of people in towns and the industrial sector who were entitled to and dependent upon the state's food rations increased by 54 per cent between 1930 and 1932, from 26 million to 40 million. The amount of grain taken out of the central black earth and the Volga regions in 1931–2 was somewhat lower than in the previous requisitioning season, but still 44 per cent higher than the amount taken in 1929–30, and 130 per cent higher than the amount taken in 1927–8. The amount of grain taken out of these regions in 1932–3 was 53 per cent higher than in 1929–30, and 158 per cent higher than in 1927–8. The Urals and Siberia were permitted to be slight net importers of grain in 1931–2, but the amount taken out in 1932–3 was twice as much as the amount taken out in 1929–30, and only 10 per cent short of what had been taken out in the Urals-Siberian campaign in 1927–8. The amount of grain taken out of the Ukraine and north Caucasus in 1931–2 was only very slightly lower than in the previous year, but still 52 per cent higher than the amount taken out in 1929–30, and 110 per cent higher than in 1927–8. In 1932–3, after the second consecutive (and especially precipitous) reduction in the harvest, the amount of grain taken out of these regions was 55 per cent of the amount taken out in 1929–30, and 75 per cent of the amount taken out in 1927–8.[7]

Behind these estimates there was a reality in which the peasants, whether collectivized or not, were left with paltry amounts of grain for their own consumption, such as could not last from one harvest to the next. Since the potato crop was also reduced by the inclement weather and livestock was down to one-half of the 1928 level by 1933, the grain requisitioning which always had been a zero-sum game between the peasantry and the state became, literally, a deadly struggle between the harvests of 1931 and 1933. The situation was most desperate in the normally fertile southern steppe regions, where the absence of forests made winter hunting impossible as an additional survival option, and where the requisitioning quotas assumed high harvest yields. Eye-witness reports of people dying of starvation, of whole hamlets and villages depopulated by death, deportations, and migration, of district border checkpoints where armed troops sought to prevent peasants from travelling to purchase food in better supplied districts, of bloodily suppressed riots, of peasant soup-pots filled with inedible ingredients and in some cases with human flesh, originate mainly from southern Ukraine and north Caucasus in the winter-spring of 1933. But hunger and the consequent susceptibility to disease were suffered everywhere during 1931–4. What varied from one rural district to the next was the length of time over which extreme shortages of food had to be endured before the authorities provided some emergency relief, or before something edible could be gathered from the land again.

Coercion was a major ingredient in the relationship between the state and the peasantry. It is doubtful that many of the original category-three kulaks escaped eventual deportation into forced-labour establishments as they fell short of meeting their delivery quotas and tax obligations. From 1931 until the

---

7 Based on Wheatcroft, 'The Soviet economic crisis,' p. 15.

end of the decade, the sustained collectivization trend was undoubtedly helped along by the deportation of non-kulak peasants, who chose to stay outside the collective farms and subsequently failed to meet their quotas and taxes. But collectivization in the context of famine made the collective farms themselves into a battlefield between the state and the peasantry. In August 1932, the government made even petty-scale thefts of 'socialist property' subject to long, forced-labour sentences or to death. This law was widely used against collective farmers accused of trying to harvest some of the collective-farm grain for their own use, as well as against employees of the food-processing and distribution networks. In January 1933, the government issued passports to urban residents but not to rural ones, and it carried out a campaign of evicting people from the cities who did not have passports. The campaign's ostensible purpose was to purge the cities of escaped kulaks and criminal elements, but the campaign was also aimed at stopping collective as well as individual farmers from trying to escape their predicament by city-bound migration.

The coercive campaigns, however, were not saving the collective farms from the devastation wrought by famine-time grain requisitioning. Some collective farms simply collapsed by depopulation as deaths, deportations, and escapes by migration took their toll. The great majority did not collapse but all faced a difficult managerial problem as the labour power available for cultivating the collective fields was weakened and demotivated. The collective farms and grain requisitioning thus became objects of chaotic struggles within the bureaucratic ranks as well as between peasants and officials. The plenipotentiaries who had come to socialize the countryside had been handpicked for their credentials as 'working-class cadres' with no peasant connections, who had a strong belief that the peasantry would become more productive once it was rid of the kulak and enlightened in the principles of socialist doctrine, economies of scale, division of labour, and the personal working virtues known under the heading of 'industrial production culture'. Some contrived to bring with them symbolic trappings of industrial modernity such as Tannoy systems and factory sirens, to promote the progressive virtues. Many came forearmed with a conviction that their own primary-school literacy, army or factory experience, and party political training added up to a great superiority of consciousness over 'the dark illiterate mass', and the conviction was promptly reinforced as the peasants insisted on countering visionary dogmas with local knowledge and empirical pragmatism, or with sullenness. Some plenipotentiaries simply came prepared to wield a 'Bolshevik iron fist' in the service of procuring grain. But they all faced an unexpected dilemma as the famine took hold. Neither the 'industrial production culture' nor the 'Bolshevik iron fist' could make starving collective farmers work hard enough to meet delivery quotas, which would have been too high even for well fed ones. The name of the managerial game was to reduce the quotas and to be seen to be doing something about returning some of the food to the farmers – to resist the top-down flow of rapacious demands as well as to fight the recalcitrant peasant.

The regional patchwork in the degree of suffering inflicted on the peasantry partly reflected the differential success of local officials in renegotiating the delivery quotas, finding ways of allowing some means of subsistence despite them, and in persuading the bureaucratic machinery to provide some emergency relief for a locality before it was too late. But it was a risky political game, for the central authorities feared the consequences even more if the famine were to get out of hand in the urban-industrial sector. The OGPU-run political departments of the MTS that were set up in January 1933 were busy not only with preventing rebellion and 'theft of socialist property' by peasants but also with purging collective-farm officials. One-third of *kolkhoz* store-keepers and one-quarter of bookkeepers lost their jobs under charges of negligence, corruption, or 'wrecking' in 1933 alone, in addition to an unknown proportion of the *kolkhoz* chairmen and higher rural administrators. The turnover of rural party officials and plenipotentiaries was high, although at this stage repostings rather than departures for the GULAG camps were involved; but violent score-settling among bureau protagonists within the political administration system would wait only until 1936–8.

Relief from the worst struggles for a crust of bread came in the autumn of 1933, when the harvest turned out to be almost as good as in 1930, which started an upward trend. The average grain harvest in 1933–8 was six per cent higher than the prewar average of 1909–13, and 14 per cent higher than the precollectivization average of 1925–9.[8] This level of improvement, however, had to feed an urban population that had resumed growth after stagnating in 1932–3, so that by 1939 it was more than twice as large as in 1926. This growth was brought about by a rural labour force whose numerical strength in 1939 was just over two-thirds of what it had been in 1926. The collective farmers had not achieved these improvements through better technology. The number of tractors supplied to the agricultural sector during the 1930s was large – so large in fact that it tied up a lion's share of industrialization investment; but it was not large enough to compensate for the reduction in the number of horses, as the total of mechanical and live traction power added together still amounted to less in 1939 than it had been in 1929.[9] The post-famine harvest increases were achieved with the help of factories, schools, offices, and the army supplying 'voluntary' auxiliary labour to the collective farms at harvest times. They were also achieved at the expense of oversowing, which encroached on the principles of crop rotation: the land cultivation improvements introduced during the 1920s at the behest of the 'neopopulist' agronomists – innovative three-field or four-field crop rotation – were undone. They were, furthermore, achieved with the help of the weather, which was much kinder in 1933–9 than it had been during the NEP period. But above all, increased production was achieved by the collective farmers working much longer hours than they had worked before collectivization.

This additional labour time was expended perhaps as much on the household plots as in the collectivized fields; the post-famine increase of food production from this source – fruit, vegetables, and poultry products – was more impressive than the grain-production record. As regards overall cattle-

---

8 Based on data provided by Wheatcroft S. G. *et al.* 1986: 'Soviet industrialization reconsidered: some preliminary conclusions about economic development between 1926 and 1941'. *The Economic History Review*, second series, xxxix, 2, p. 283.

9 Hunter, H. 1988: 'Soviet agriculture with and without collectivization, 1928–1940'. *Slavic Review*, xlvii, 2, pp. 203–16.

breeding, however, the total in collectivized herds and on private household plots taken together, it took until 1938 to recover from the slaughter of 1928–32.

In 1939 the party leaders decided that collectivized agriculture was not doing as well as it could have done because collective farmers were paying too much attention to their private household plots and not enough to the collectivized fields and cowsheds. To support the efforts of collective-farm chairmen who apparently had to walk from one cottage to the next to persuade, cajole, and do informal deals with their subordinates to gather sufficient labour together for the collective tasks, the government issued a decree that specified a minimum number of labour days that had to be spent by each adult member of every household in the collectivized fields before the household qualified for its share of the collective grain and cash income. In addition, the new decree imposed a gamut of new taxes and controls on household plot production and the associated bazaar trade, to prevent 'capitalist abuses'.

Further Reading

The revivalist ideological militancy of the 'left turn' in a wide range of institutional settings is discussed in S. Fitzpatrick (ed.), *Cultural Revolution in Russia, 1928–31* (Bloomington, Ind.: Indiana University Press, 1978). The two key episodes that marked the momentum towards crash collectivization are described in D. R. Bower, 'The Smolensk scandal and the end of NEP', *Slavic Review*, xlv, no. 4, pp. 689–706 and L. Viola, 'The case of Krasnyi Meliorator or how the kulak grows into socialism', *Soviet Studies*, xxxviii, 1986, no. 4, pp. 508–29.

The dekulakization campaign and the first wave of crash collectivization are discussed in detail by R. W. Davies in the first two volumes of *The Industrialization of Soviet Russia: Volume 1 – The Socialist Offensive: The Collectivization of Soviet Agriculture, 1929–30* (London: Macmillan, 1980) and *Volume 2 – The Soviet Collective Farm, 1929–30* (London: Macmillan, 1980). A less detailed but a vivid and insightful account written by a social historian is M. Lewin, *Russian Peasants and Soviet Power: A Study of Collectivization* (New York: Norton, 1975); and, also, M. Lewin, *The Making of the Soviet System: Essays in the Social History of Interwar Russia* (London: Methuen, 1985), Chaps 4–7. L. Viola, 'The campaign to eliminate the kulak as a class, winter 1929–1930: a reevaluation of the legislation', *Slavic Review*, xlv, 1986, no. 3, pp. 503–24, provides information which emphasizes the role of regional party bosses who sought to break peasant resistance to grain requisitioning. A valuable book on the motivations, recruitment, and experiences of the '25 000ers' among the collectivizers is L. Viola, *The Best Sons of the Fatherland: Workers in the Vanguard of Soviet Collectivization* (New York and Oxford: Oxford University Press, 1987). The patterns of peasant protest are discussed by L. Viola in 'Bab'i Bunty and peasant women's protest during collectivization', *The Russian Review*, xlv, 1986, pp. 23–42.

M. B. Tauper, 'The 1932 harvest and the famine of 1933', *Slavic Review*, l, 1991, no. 1, pp. 70–89, is a measured account of policies during the worst famine year. R. Conquest, *The Harvest of Sorrow: Famine in the Ukraine*

(London: Arrow, 1988) is a harrowing account which brings together a wide range of eye-witness atrocity reports. The reader should bear in mind, though, that Conquest's thesis that the famine policy was a deliberate attack on the Ukrainian nation in particular, and his statistical extrapolations concerning the total number of victims, remain a controversial issue dividing historians in the West as well as in the former Soviet Union.

V. Kravchenko, *I Chose Freedom* (London: Robert Hale Ltd, 1947) is an autobiography written by a Stalinist official after his defection to the West; it includes chapters describing the author's tours of plenipotentiary duty in the countryside.

7

Workers, Managers, and Industrialization, 1928–39

Industrialization by Mobilization

The advocates of the fortress-storming approach to industrial development realized that unbalanced plans would create bottlenecks in industrial as well as consumer supplies, but they believed the problems could be resolved by political will. The political will would prioritize crisis spots and mobilize mass effort and ingenuity such as would widen those bottlenecks that stood in the way of the most important development targets. Development breakthroughs in the industrial priority areas would then create new, more favourable conditions for rapid increases in other areas of production. The critical resource, the left-turn industrializers argued, was the 'creative potential of the masses' and the political will to mobilize it.

The logic of industrialization by political mobilization emphasized inspirational, grandiose goals, priority-enforcing centralized powers, and struggles for production achievements in the form of struggles against its enemies. The supposed enemies included 'bourgeois conservatism', 'bureaucratism', petty-bourgeois egotistical desires for a quiet and comfortable life (*obyvatel'shchina*), the peasant masses' backward habits and consciousness – their ignorance, 'individualism', and 'petty-bourgeois spontaneity' – and, also, class enemies and agents of foreign powers bent on bringing the Soviet state to its knees by deliberate sabotage or 'wrecking'. The rhetoric of industrialization by 'taut planning' was martially as well as socially militant: targets were 'stormed', 'vanguard brigades' and 'reinforcements' of 'shock-strike detachments' (*udarnye otryady*) were 'thrown' into this or that 'production battle'; industrial sectors and problems were 'battle fronts', in which some proved 'heroes' and others 'deserters'; and things were organized by 'field-staffs' (*shtaby*) and from 'commanding posts'. The rhetoric of the 'taut plans' strategy celebrated revolutionary optimism, political vigilance, do-or-die exertions, selfless enthusiasm, and discipline: the virtues of all-out mobilization.

The rhetoric had a symbolic support in the bold, landscape-transforming scale of the main construction projects. They included waterways that would connect the White Sea with the Baltic, and the Volga with the Don, huge hydro-power stations, whole conglomerates of blast furnaces and steel mills, and a great number of massive new engineering factories. The 'giants' (*giganty*) were designed on the basis of a generally accepted belief in economies of scale, but the projects also had an iconic life in the mobilization propaganda, in the pictures of man-dwarfing electric pylons, smokestacks and cooling-towers, lake-forming dams, and engineering shopfloors so large that the aisles separating the ranks of gleaming machines seemed like straight lines coming together at a distant point. The triumphs of industrialization seemed the greater and more tangible if they could be represented visually on a monumental scale.

The industrialization effort in fact consisted of expanding existing plants and productive capacities as well as of building the brand-new *giganty*. Throughout the economy, the grandiosity of the flagship construction projects was echoed in a grandiose approach to statistical figures and graphs representing 'taut plan' targets and the mobilization undertakings of their overfulfilment. Regardless of the conditions prevailing at any particular production unit, year-on-year percentage increases of its output had to be talked about in at least double figures. Industrialization by mass mobilization called for impressive gestures of commitment and for intolerance of 'demobilization tendencies'; it made mere single-figure percentage increases seem expressions of a treacherous lack of commitment. Eventually in 1931, Stalin would criticize 'boastful talkers' who sought their moments of glory by making bombastic promises which they did not know how to honour. But in 1929–30 a cavalier approach to statistical target-setting was encouraged by the 'techniques' of stage-managed 'planning from below' (*vstrechnye plany*), in which taut-plan targets for particular production units were made tauter still by declamatory resolutions at work place meetings. Everywhere the future had the shape of a sharply upward-sloping achievement curve drawn on the basis of resources that were promised but not in hand.

The fulfilment of such plans was of course another matter: they were a poor guide to what would be achieved by when and what new resources would thus be made available. They were also poor in predicting production costs and a weak restraint on their escalation, as gross output targets were emphasized over all the other aspects of planning and performance measurement. They were an unreliable yardstick for evaluating the gross output achievements as well, because there was no way of knowing for sure how feasible or otherwise a gross output target was in the first place. The idea of planning as a means of rational economic management was undermined by the regime of industrialization by mobilization. Hold-ups in the supplies of necessary resources soon made themselves felt in mines and transport depots, on construction sites and factory floors alike. The success of any particular production unit depended on a high-powered political patron using his clout to divert resources to it, inevitably at the expense of another production unit, and on the managers manipulating the authorities into supplying at least *something* in greater quantities than the bare minimum so that there was something to barter unofficially with other managers. The everyday politics of industrialization by mobilization was made up of myriad struggles between officials for scarce resources, permeating all levels of the power structure up to the very top. The political patrons of the heavy-industry undertakings had a bigger clout than the rest, but even they could not patronize any particular flagship project with effective consistency, for the supplies crises quickly proliferated everywhere.

On the ground, in almost every work place, there was chaos. Work was started and then stopped because a raw material ran out, or a machine broke down and there were no spare parts, or because the word came down to stop this and start that instead. Periods of confused idleness and make-do, *ad hoc* measures were punctuated by patently expensive bursts of 'storming' to make up for lost production time. On the ground there was plenty of what could look to workers and sundry inspectors like mismanagement, or perhaps even someone's deliberate wrecking. It would not have been easy, however, to convict a person or identify the main cause of any particular episode of wasteful or faltering work before an impartial jury. There were too many adverse factors affecting each individual work place that were beyond the control of its workers or managers. They could have been summarized as the consequence of industrialization by mobilization 'system'. But references to 'hostile uncles' (to adverse conditions beyond one's control) were discouraged by the political authorities; and general criticisms of the industrial campaign strategy were ruled out as politically treacherous. In any case, it would have been hard to deny that many of the things that were going wrong in the work place were also due to the people in them. Most workers and managers in most work places were new to their jobs, few had been adequately trained, inexperience was rife, and competence hard to prove beyond doubt where things were generally chaotic and the goal-posts mobile. Whether a production breakdown was due to an 'honest mistake' or 'enemy wrecking' could never have been obvious. But the belief in the presence of wreckers was promoted by show trials and mobilization calls to vigilance, and rendered plausible to many when things were going wrong in great and small ways almost daily.

The grandiose goals and momentous symbols of the industrialization campaign were in sharp contrast to the everyday realities of working, replete as these were with metaphorical (and literal) broken spades, jammed wheelbarrow wheels, lost screws, misplaced blueprints, machine tools with the tool bits missing, trucks without tyres, crossed wires, pencils without paper, many irritations, petty conflicts and mutual recriminations, and much confused waiting around. The heroic war metaphor was perhaps apt in a way in that in real war the grandiosity of the propaganda and of the great battle often contrasts with individual tales of lice-ridden waiting around and comedy-of-errors muddling through.

Everyday experiences belied the official idea that 'taut planning' co-ordinated efforts in the pursuit of clearly understood overall priorities. 'Taut planning' called for taut muscles and caused taut nerves, but it did away with neither energy-sapping struggles for scarce resources nor wasteful duplication of efforts. It provided a framework for the allocation of scarce resources through myriad incidents of personal string-pulling, political bluster and petitioning, bureaucratic tugs of war, and subterfuge. It was a framework in which political bosses exercised effective personal power in their trouble-shooting moments, sometimes at cross-purposes with one another despite the highly centralized hierarchy, and in which the party bureaux and the government tried to assert centralized control over the economy by issuing numerous decrees and directives which – succeeding one another with conflicting messages – added up to a stream of policy proclamations rather than to an effective, enforceable legislation. Effective power lay with the bosses and their patronage networks rather than with the bureaux of government legislation and control. A government decree was a dead letter when it was not supported by a 'flavour-of-the-month' implementation campaign. Economic political power was exercised by personal, on-the-spot dictats, always in the name of the 'general party line', of course, and usually in the name of a campaign against some undesirable phenomenon or an allegedly corrupt practice. It was not exercised by a coherent and clear legislation nor by an impersonal government bureaucracy. The efforts of industrialization by mobilization were co-ordinated, in the participants' experience by power acts the rationality of which was defined by particular, already biting crises of co-ordination. They were not co-ordinated by an institutional authority that could prevent the crises or make evident a dominance of reason over personal fiat in economic affairs. The propaganda justified political power in terms of social and economic rationality while, in the everyday world of work and its management, effective decisions and control appeared either as negotiable on an *ad hoc* basis or as subject to arbitrary impositions. That it was all adding up to a rational pursuit of public aims had to be an article of faith.

The 'Production Culture' Counterpoint

The practices of industrialization by mobilization contrasted uncomfortably not only with the supposed rationality of planning and centralized command but also with the machine-utopia imagery of the overall aim. It was this imagery of the future that put a spring into the great leap forward. The 'left turn' abandonment of the New Economic Policy (NEP) promised fast investment in new technology, and the engineers' liberation from the shackles of financial accountancy. The 'bourgeois specialist' engineers did not approve of the 'taut planning', but the idea that the historically progressive form of reason was represented by production engineers rather than by economists or book-keepers had a growing international currency, besides having strong continuity links with the Russian ideas of modernity. The industrialization campaign's propaganda initially inspired many young people, and some older ones too, by the promise that the mobilized efforts would bring in, within a decade or so, a socialist version of a prosperous America – the America of high technology and the mass production line. The industrialization campaign would fetch the machines and the know-how from the advanced West and build up the industrial infrastructure for them; it would also transform Russia culturally, by putting an advanced 'industrial production culture' in the place of the peasant's 'lack of culture'. The visionary propaganda of the industrialization campaign often referred to the factories as 'cauldrons for the transformation (*perevarenie*) of people': as cultural melting-pots.

There were two meanings in the 'factory cauldron' idea that themselves were not necessarily mutually exclusive. One was that the new workers joining the modern factory setting would become 'politically conscious', active and, conscientious supporters of the Bolshevik Party and its state. This evoked the old socialist belief, mentioned in Chapter 5, which held that working with modern technology in large industrial work collectives expanded the workers' minds and brought their cultural level up to a high quality of proletarian consciousness. The other meaning of 'advanced production culture' drew in part on the prerevolutionary intelligentsia's understandings of the dichotomy between the peasantry and the modern urban culture, and in part on the post-revolutionary ideas of machine utopia and Taylorism. 'Cultured workers' were the ones who cared for improving their skills and work performance, who shared with work-study engineers the belief that the efficiency of effort could be (and should be) maximized by routinizing the best methods, and who were thoroughly accustomed to the disciplines of punctuality and sustained working at a regular pace. This 'cultured work' perspective naturally also defined good, professional management. Management was supposed to strive for a 'scientific organization of labour' and conditions that would make the production stream flow at full capacity, regularly and without wasted efforts.

Here the 'mobilization' and the 'production-culture' aspects of the industrialization campaign clashed. At the rhetorical level, the 'fortress-storming' calls to heroic exertions coincided uneasily with the Taylorist emphasis on efficiency, methodicality, and clockwork regularity in the work process. The 'fortresses' that had to be 'stormed' often as not represented particular tasks that had to be accomplished 'at all costs' as it were, with all the stops pulled out and resources diverted to them to save the day to deliver something that was badly needed by yesterday. Heroism could be displayed in this context by bouts of selfless working throughout the night and without tea-breaks, at maximum effort such as could never have been sustained over an indefinite period. Such bouts of 'storming' may have had their *effectiveness* in so far as the tasks were done and the achievement of particular priority goals was helped. But 'production culture' cared for *efficiency* first and foremost, for ways that would deliver the goods on schedule reliably while minimizing their unit costs and any waste of effort and material. It saw these ways in a regular process of working, where effort should be exerted only at levels that could be sustained. In the 'production culture' perspective, bouts of sweaty labour heroism were too reminiscent of the cyclicity of peasant work seasons to be admired. In 'production culture', time was linear and not cyclical, and work was efficient as a matter of methodical routine. Any heroism consisted in the day-after-day self-discipline that this required rather than in spectacular one-off feats.

The Taylorist version of the 'production culture' assumed the economies of scale and specialization and the production flows that would not need frequent changes of schedules and set-ups. It required work places to have the benefit of stable relationships with their organizational environments and regular supplies and orderly customer queues so that organizational efforts could be concentrated on fine tuning the production process. But that was exactly what the work places were not receiving in the 'taut plans' context. Managers had to be flexible. Production schedules and set-ups often had to be changed at short notice, and the advantages of specialization had often to be foregone as officially unplanned secondary production lines had to be set up to produce in-house things that should have been supplied by another producer. This called for skilled labour when the labour-training strategy assumed that specialized production and Taylorist 'scientific organization of labour' would make a modest level of industrial skill sufficient, and when the provision of any training could not keep up with the fast expansion of the labour force. Taylorism was the dominant mode of thinking about what a 'cultured' work place should be like, and which informed strategic macro-level decisions about labour training and the choice of technological equipment; but it had to remain an elusive ideal as managers struggled to create some productive order out of the 'taut plans' chaos.

Labour Migration

To some extent it was generally understood that the machine-utopia ideals would not become a reality straightaway. The first five-year plan had new capital construction as its main theme, which meant at first a rapid expansion of such activities as building and lumbering, with the expansion of industrial production taking the form of a switch to two-shift and three-shift working, the reopening of plants that had been closed during the rationalization drives of the 1920s, and the piecemeal introduction into existing factories of newly purchased machines. It was the intention that, in the main, the new factories and production lines would come on stream from the end of the first five-year plan (i.e., from 1932) and it stood to reason that there would be initial teething troubles.

No one expected the escalation of demand for labour that occurred in the initial years, and the extent of labour mobility. The first five-year plan assumed that it would mop up existing urban unemployment by 1932, and that the rate of migration out of the agricultural sector would remain constant. But urban unemployment was brought to an end by 1930, although by that time urban women's full-time employment had again become standard, and migration from country to town was greatly accelerated as a consequence of collectivization. Managers were taking on greater amounts of labour than planned to give themselves spare capacity for dealing with the unpredictable demands on their production units. The rapidly expanding employment opportunities throughout the economy led to very high labour turnover as workers who were already employed looked to improve their wages and conditions by changing jobs. In 1930, the average annual rate of labour turnover exceeded 150 per cent.[1] The average worker had been in the same job for substantially less than one year, and many workers changed employment more than once in the course of that year. This was despite legislation, passed in 1929, which sought to discourage workers from quitting their jobs without their employers' consent.

The personnel turnover in managerial posts was also very high, as the political authorities were in the habit of transferring trusted communist managers to prioritized crisis spots, and the trusted managers then tried to take their own most trusted junior colleagues with them. In addition, the repressive campaign against 'wreckers' was in effect transferring large numbers of

---

1 Davies, R. W. 1989: *The Soviet Economy in Turmoil, 1929–1930*. London: Macmillan, p. 531.

'bourgeois specialist' engineers to forced-labour camps (where they often worked in their professional capacity).

The peak year for migration as well as for job-changing was 1931, when the urban population was increased by the arrival of more than four million immigrants from the countryside. Another seven million travelled from one temporary labouring job to the next on industrial construction sites, and on canal-digging, coal-digging, and lumbering outside the already-existing towns.[2] Urban population grew by 44 per cent during the first five-year plan (1928–32). The typical migrant route from village to town, however, was circuitous. During the first five-year plan, the fastest expanding employment sector was construction. The number of people employed on construction sites, the biggest of which were outside the already-existing towns, more than quadrupled between 1928 and 1932, while the industrial workforce 'only' doubled.[3] Since technological investment was concentrated on the priority manufacturing sectors, building-site labour remained under-equipped and construction-site managers were more than any other managers driven to substitute plentiful brawn for lack of technology. The Taylorist research institutes of NOT (Scientific Organization of Labour) tried to devise rationalized work methods for construction sites, but here the battles for an efficient 'production culture' were even more unrealistic than in the factories. The mobilization calls for do-or-die labour heroism were in a way suited to construction-site settings, although they jarred in machine factory contexts. However, they must have had a particularly mixed reception on the construction sites, where the multitudes of unskilled labourers included many peasants escaping the ravages of the collectivization campaign, prisoner labourers, and *komsomol*-organized brigades of (initially) enthusiastic urban youths. Ex-peasants often migrated to towns via construction sites, and the new industrial plants, conglomerates, and townships that were built as greenfield projects recruited a large proportion of their labour from the people who built them.

Crises and Policy Changes, 1931–4

The chaos and stoppages on construction sites and in the factories were recognized anxiously in government circles as adding up to an economic crisis as early as the summer of 1930, when gross output figures fell from the levels of the preceeding months. By this time the mobilization calls no longer drew much enthusiasm from the younger generation. Some party leaders advocated a revision of the first five-year plan to achieve a smoother, if less ambitious, progress, but they were purged as a 'left-right' opposition bloc. Growth in industrial output soon resumed again, but in the following year the party

---

2 Lewin, M. 1985: *The Making of the Soviet System: Essays in the Social History of Interwar Russia*. London: Methuen, pp. 219–20.
3 Depretto, J.-P. 1992: 'Construction workers in the 1930s'. In Lampert, N. and Rittersporn, G. (eds), *Stalinism: Its Nature and Aftermath*. London: Macmillan, p. 185; Andrle, V. 1988: *Workers in Stalin's Russia: Industrialization and Social Change in a Planned Economy*. Hemel Hempstead: Harvester-Wheatsheaf, p. 34.

leadership made a number of policy departures which reflected a recognition that there was a conflict between some of the mobilization methods and the goals of productive efficiency. At the beginning of 1931, construction-project managers were denied their demand for a mobilization transfer of skilled labour from industry to priority construction sites, and a series of party decrees were issued in an attempt to stop altogether such mobilization borrowings of labour. In addition, a two-year moratorium was placed on the recruitment of skilled industrial workers to political and administrative posts.

In June 1931, Stalin made a keynote speech, the so-called 'six conditions speech', which marked the end of the 'great breakthrough' period. It called for the use of wage differentials to motivate workers to increase their skills, and for organizational changes throughout industry such as would counter the tendency to chaos, inefficiency, and a lack of personal accountability by workers and managers for their work; it demanded that technical competence rather than party membership should be the main criterion in appointments to executive posts, and that skilled and educated people should be treated with 'attention and solicitude'; 'bourgeois specialists' should no longer be subject to class prejudice and indiscriminate 'specialist baiting'; and a system of cost accounting (*khozraschet*) should be introduced to encourage managers to increase production without making further claims on the supplies of labour and equipment.

The institution that had been particularly closely associated with the 'left-turn' campaigns, the Workers' and Peasants' Inspectorate, was subjected to a purge and, later, in 1934, abolished. Industrial wage tariffs were scheduled for differential-enhancing reforms and wage policies became subject to a sustained campaign against 'levelling' (*uravnilovka*). The campaign called for payment by individual piece-rates wherever possible, and for bonus payments to reward individual performance. Egalitarian forms of wage payment, including the so-called 'collective piece-rates' where workers' brigades received performance-related pay which they could divide among their own members by their own rules, became branded as 'petty bourgeois'. The production communes that had been instigated under *komsomol* auspices in 1929–30 were dissolved. The extremely egalitarian ones had been formed, it was now proclaimed, by 'leftist blockheads' who had mistaken peasant communal forms for socialism. The party leaders' turn against the brigades served to reinforce the hiearchical principles of managerial authority as well as the economic principles of anti-levelling. Managerial authority was also reinforced by the denunciation of 'specialist baiting', which diminished workers' ability to intimidate the 'bourgeois specialists' politically in the course of shopfloor bargaining.

The call of the 'six conditions speech' to a struggle against a chronic 'lack of personal responsibility' (*obezlichka*) was followed by the calling-off of experiments in keeping some factories in production without any closing days while their workers had every fifth day off. This uninterrupted production regime (*nepreryvka*) tended to make it logistically impossible for a worker to do the same job and work with the same equipment over a period of time. Hence it was impossible to pin down responsibility when things broke or went missing, and it was very difficult to weave regular machine maintenance into schedules. Besides, workers often added to organizational headaches by demanding changes in their own working cycles when they wanted to be off on the same day as their family and friends. Reverting to the standard practice of factory closing on every sixth day was a relief to workers, managers, and machines alike.

In 1932–3, the campaign against the lack of personal responsibility led to abandoning experiments with 'functionalist' divisions of labour and management. 'Functionalism' had been advocated by F. W. Taylor and then by A. Gastev, the Soviet visionary of machine utopia. It meant that jobs should be divided to maximize specialization, so that a number of workers would be attending a number of machines simultaneously, with each worker moving from one machine to another to do a particular operation on it. Management should also be specialized so that, say, machine maintenance, tool-setting, the moving of raw materials, the allocation of tasks to individual workers and machines, the setting of individual work norms and piece-rates, floor-cleaning, and the introduction of further rationalization measures might all be regarded as separate functions and organized by separate managerial hierarchies. Gastev's experiments with the *funktsional'ka* were carried out on a large scale in the textile industry, and less comprehensively in other industries as well. The result was that the managers who were in charge of particular shopfloors and work places had to trouble shoot when things went wrong, which they did often, without having any clear authority over any of the functions. Abandoning extreme 'functionalism' meant a return towards a system where a machine operator carried out the whole range of operations on a particular machine and where the manager of a particular work place managed the work of all the people working there.

The 'six conditions speech' did not prevent a major crisis in the industrialization programme. The supply problems were compounded when, towards the end of 1931, imports of new technology from the West had to be slowed down because of balance-of-payments problems, and some resources had to be diverted to the defence of Manchuria against Japan. In 1932 (the last year of the first five-year plan), uncompleted construction projects with no sign of activity on them became a common sight, and remained so for another year. The new factories that were completed had to open with major gaps in equipment. This was, of course, also the time of the grain famine. Workers in the priority industries were protected from the worst effects by rationing, but rations were lowered for everyone. The rations for non-priority categories of the urban population were reduced to a threshold of starvation, and employing institutions and state retail shops varied in the regularity with which they were able to honour the ration coupons. In the textile industry region of Ivanovo, there were major bread riots in April 1932.[4] But general unrest, intemperate shopfloor reactions to managerial demands, and a further deterioration of attendance discipline as workers had to queue for food in work time if they were to eat at all, were rife everywhere. There was little triumphant rejoicing when the first five-year plan came officially to a close at the end of the year.

---

4 Khlebnyuk, O. 1991: '30-e gody: krizisy, reformy, nasilie'. *Svobodnaya mysl'*, xxvii, pp. 75–87.

Not surprisingly, most of the industrial output targets of the first five-year plan were unfulfilled, even according to the exaggerated official statistics. But the delays in completion of construction projects notwithstanding, a major expansion in the industrial base was achieved. The number of industrial enterprises was rising from 9000 in 1929 to 45 000 in 1934 and 64 000 in 1938 in the USSR as a whole.[5] This rapid creation of a large and diversified industrial base in itself forced the system of macro-economic co-ordination back on the political agenda. Besides, by 1932 industrial output per worker actually dropped below the levels of 1928, despite the injections of new technology. The quality of output had also to be acknowledged as having dropped alarmingly, and there was worrying evidence of the speedy deterioration of expensive new machinery. The strategy of the industrialization campaign had to be revised to make it more compatible with efficiency. Industrial enterprises were banned from enlarging their workforces in 1933, partly to stop any further growth of the burden on the urban food-rationing system, and partly because consolidation and a search for efficiency had to be the new name of the game. In January 1933, Stalin told the central committee of the party that the 'thunderous speeds' of industrial construction had achieved the aim of acquiring a base for an advanced industry and defence capability. Now it was 'obviously' no longer necessary to continue 'to whip the country and drive it on'. The aim now was 'the mastery of technology'. The growth of industrial output should be allowed to drop to perhaps as little as 13 per cent per year, to allow workers and engineers to learn to use technology cost-effectively and with an emphasis on raising quality.

During 1932–3, the economic press published advocacies of industrial reforms which would legalize the practice of industrial enterprises, made necessary by the lack of input-output balances in official plans, to barter and negotiate their own supplier-customer relations outside the centralized command framework. This legalization of autonomous activity, which would return the industrial system to something reminiscent of the NEP, did not occur. However, the central authorities did impose budgetary discipline, reduce the amount of money in circulation during the crisis years, and until 1936, pursue economic policies designed to increase the role of money as an economic regulator and motivator. The idea of a substantial budget-holding enterprise autonomy was pursued on an experimental basis in one of the steel-making conglomerates until the beginning of 1937. During 1932–3, publicized rationalization initiatives in the factories included the formation of 'integral-process brigades' (*skvoznye brigady*) of workers who revised some of their individual output norms downwards to achieve more even production flows.

In the event, the second five-year plan, for 1933–7, which was approved at the party congress in February 1934, targeted average annual growth rates of 16.5 per cent for industrial output. These were more feasible and better balanced targets than those set in 1929. They also reflected some concern for raising living standards, by envisaging some investment for consumer-goods

---

5 Wheatcroft, S. 1982: 'Changes in the pattern of employment in the USSR, 1926–1939'. Unpublished paper presented to SSRC Conference on Soviet Economic Development in the 1930s, University of Birmingham, June, Appendix 3.

industries, food-processing, and housing as well as for heavy industry, although the house-construction plans still fell seriously short of the need created by the shift of population from country to town. Housing became more evident as a priority in the third five-year plan. But the fact that the heavy-industry plans were better balanced provided hope that subsequent emergency prioritizations would not sacrifice the consumer-sector plans to heavy-industry claims on scarce resources as much as during the first five-year plan.

The second five-year plan and the speeches at the 'congress of victors' reiterated the 'mastery of technology' slogan as the primary one for the coming period. Research had shown, it was claimed, that on most shopfloors only four or five hours out of the seven-hour working day were productively utilized. There was a great deal of scope for increasing industrial efficiency by improving skills and organization as well as by tightening labour discipline. Increasing labour productivity was of the utmost importance because the planned expansion of industrial output was to be achieved without draining labour from agriculture, and because the projected financial flows envisaged labour productivity as rising twice as quickly as wages. Concern for product quality was also voiced, and this was soon backed by legislation which made managers and quality inspectors liable to prosecution if they were found to be responsible for shoddy production.

The Administrative Command System

Changes in policy from the industrialization by mobilization of the 'great breakthrough' years did not amount to a fundamental change in the relationship between managers and the political authorities. The centralized economic plans were now more moderate and better balanced, but the new and still rapidly growing complexity of the industrial economy meant that the broad summary targets defined by the central planning office had to be divided between the industrial ministries and then between the enterprises. This could never be precise, and the plans received by any one of the tens of thousands of enterprises seldom turned up in the form of feasible equations between the promised supplies of resources and the demanded outputs. Neither could they anticipate everything that would be urgently needed throughout the system. Besides, the fulfilment of output targets, which was the main yardstick for judging an enterprise's performance, often had unintended consequences: if a target specified so many tons of nails, for example, this did not prevent the nail manufacturer fulfilling the target by producing a great many very large nails and no small ones. Had the production target for nails been specified in so many million pieces, only small nails and no large ones might have been the result. The crisis in the supplies of small (or large) nails would eventually become evident to the bureaucracy via thousands of distressed telegrammes and phone calls, and some manufacturer would then be asked, at a short notice, to suspend previous plans and concentrate on small (or large) nails instead. These changes in production targets had further knock-on effects and unintended consequences so that, throughout the system, all enterprises were subjected to frequent changes in plans and a stream of various requests and prohibitions from the administrative channels. The party authorities had to be involved as well as the industrial branch hierarchies because they had the power to arbitrate between conflicting priorities and to cut across the departmental boundaries of the state economic bureaucracy. The second five-year plan's moderation promised that the bottlenecks in supplies would be corrected by administrative interventions and by unofficial bartering among production units so that they would not result in a seizure of the economy as a whole. Moderation made the administrative command system feasible. It could not guarantee perfect plans such as would make corrective administrative commands and interventions by political authorities in industrial affairs unnecessary, but it promised that the administrative commands and political interventions would become less frequent and the organizational environment of the factories more stable so that managers would be more able to take care of improving 'production culture' and efficiency.

The administrative command system was incompatible with giving enterprises autonomy which would enable the managers to refuse commands legitimately by reference to their own decision-making rights defined by some stable and explicit rules of the game. If the central authorities had been disabled from being arbitrary towards the managers they would not have had the power to trouble shoot the unintended consequences of their earlier decisions. But in practice the managers had to exercise some autonomous initiative. They could not be successful simply by saying 'yes' to the authorities and concentrating on the technical aspects of production management. To be successful, they could not treat all the commands and requests with equal urgency; they had to cut corners across the rules that stood in the way of meeting the most important output targets; they had to be creative in their accounting of resource needs and production capacities; and they had to hoard resources and trade with them unofficially. Every manager had to be delinquent in some respects to achieve any positive results at all. His career success depended on scoring the points that mattered the most at any particular time, and on persuading the officials who were responsible for combating the delinquencies to look the other way. Cultivating high-positioned political patrons by loyally and flexibly co-operating with their projects was clearly important, but so was cultivating informal networks of personal understandings with a range of managers, rule-enforcement agents, and political bosses at a local level.

The centralized command in turn was liable to surges of paranoia about this tendency to 'localism' (*mestnichestvo*). Networks of personal understandings between local officials, after all, presented a danger that local coalitions might be able to implement central policies at their own convenience, which would deny implementation at the centre and thus exempt the coalition's executive decision-making from central controls. In the policy context of 'mastery of technology' and the establishment of an efficiency-oriented 'production culture', concerns about 'localism' testified to central authorities' fears that managers might allow below-capacity, wasteful, and low-quality work practices. The mobilization of industry campaign channelled much of its efforts into centrally instigated onslaughts against various work and management practices that were considered harmful. Political methods included ones designed to break the protective collusions of 'localism'. They included administrative pressures on supervisory organs (the procuracy, the OGPU, the party, and various specialized inspectorates) to heighten vigilance against a particular kind of executive delinquency and to find exemplary culprits. They also included the mobilization methods of 'control from below', which encouraged as many people as possible to 'send signals' about delinquency to the supervisory authorities and the press, or to highlight it in work place meetings.

Factory managers and party secretaries were obliged to report on a regular basis to the authorities on the progress that was being made towards the fulfilment of the annual plan targets, on what was being done about improving the workforce's skills, and what measures were being taken to improve product quality, increase labour productivity, and reduce all manner of costs. In addition, they were also obliged to report on the 'political work' in their factories. They had to show responsiveness to the centrally instigated mobilization campaigns, including their 'mass control from below' aspects. But this reporting was not sufficient to allay central authorities' anxieties about the collusive powers of 'localism' to divert the effects of the policy-enforcement campaigns to the small fry in the local ponds from the big fish. The campaigns' instigators saw their effectiveness blunted by the suspected or real sins of 'localism' combining with those of 'bureaucratism'. Until the 'six conditions speech', the rule-of-thumb about vigilance against industrial 'wreckers' tended to be simple: the 'bourgeois specialists' were assumed to be prone to 'wrecking' while communist managers from working-class backgrounds committed only 'honest mistakes' because they were new to industrial management and still had to learn. After the 'six conditions speech', suspicions of industrial sabotage were lessened to some extent, while the sins of 'bureaucratism' came to the fore. And 'bureaucratism' was thought to be afflicting the party's own cadres.

The sin of 'bureaucratism' had three different meanings. First, it meant the executives' tendency to evade personal responsibility for their decisions by spinning red tape and hiding behind it. Thus the 'functionalism' and the tendency of extreme Taylorist searches for 'production culture' were criticized for promoting paperwork-laden systems of production process control, too many management meetings, and too many opportunities for shopfloor managers to claim powerlessness when things went wrong. Secondly, 'bureaucratism' also meant executives becoming 'local grandees torn away from the masses' (*vel'mozha*). The *vel'mozha* were at risk of causing general popular disaffection and, in particular, they were discouraging the masses from taking part in the 'control from below' aspects of mobilization campaigns. Thirdly, 'bureaucratism' meant the tendency of local executives to 'formalize' mobilization campaigns – that is, to turn them into institutional routines which were good for statistical reporting of 'political work with the masses' but which diluted any effects that grass-roots initiatives and 'control from below' activities might have had on actual working practices.

The fact that the central party authorities continued to insist on leading industry by the political methods of mobilization campaigning, after acknowledging, before the end of the first five-year plan that brawny 'storming work' campaigns (*shturmovshchina*) where harmful to the goals of 'production culture', might be seen as a ritual assertion of political domination over a nascent managerial technocracy. But the mobilization campaigning continued because the system of political economy did not offer a clear functional substitute for the efficiency-motivating drive of market competition, or any simple and reliable ways of making managers accountable to the state. The party and the state were combined in a very centralized policy-making structure which perhaps induced the men at the top to feel certain that their policies were correct but uncertain that they could succeed if they were vulnerable to uneven, half-hearted, incompetent, or perhaps even corrupt implementation throughout the executive hierarchy. Thus they fought the growing complexity of their industrial state by multiplying implementation accountability channels, setting up institutional as well as *ad hoc* watchdogs to check on other watchdogs, calling for vigilance against wreckers, slackers, flounderers, incompetents and egotists, and for the activists of the party and other 'social organizations' at the base (*aktiv*) to shoot at suitable targets with some 'criticism from below'.

The official principle of 'one-man management' in industry (*edinonachalie*) was always ambiguous. It was first proclaimed by Lenin in the spring of 1918, when he fought against the (suspected or real) anarchic predilections of the workers' factory committees. In fact the factories became run by collegiate boards dominated by the threesome (*troika* – this word had the romantic connotation of an aristocratic carriage drawn by three thoroughbred horses) of the 'red director' (appointed by the party to wield authority over 'bourgeois specialist' managers), the secretary of the factory party organization (a full-time official on the party pay-roll), and the chairman of the trade-union branch (also a full-time official). The 'left turn' caused some downgrading of the trade-union chairman, as the trade unions were purged of 'right deviationists' and told not to obstruct 'the Bolshevik speeds' of production. Thereafter, the factories were still run by something akin to board meetings of senior managers and the 'social organization' officials, with the twosome of the director and the party secretary clearly dominant. When 'functionalism' came under criticism, calls for 'one-man management' meant giving line managers (from the foremen up) powers that were previously shared with 'functional' specialists. Some of the party leaders also came to exhort line managers from director to foreman to assert their 'one-man management' authority as strong bosses who could expect compliance when they took a decision, since managerial orders that were ignored, countermanded, or argued against were commonplace on the factory floors. 'One-man management' never meant freedom of managerial hierarchies from party interference. Party officials were from time to time upbraided in general terms by the central party authorities for meddling too much in the day-to-day operations of management. However, 'turning their back on the problems of production' and organizing the 'political work with the masses' so that it did not impinge on the practice of work and management was much more heinous in the scale of mobilization campaigning values.

Many managers of course resented 'social organizations' meddling in their business, and they saw the necessity of showing a positive response to every latest mobilization campaign as burdensome or disruptive. There was a fault line between the technocratic, professional conceptions of industrial authority and the mobilization, campaigning preoccupations of political authority. It was evident in the differences of editorial emphasis between propaganda organs. The ones published under the auspices of the heavy-industry commissariat promoted a 'production culture' conceived as the object of professional, engineering, and managerial (Taylorist NOT) know-how. The image of good management that came across had the shape of a technology-understanding and 'business-like' (*delovoi*) man who did not waste time in airy talk. Ideological campaigning was paid lip service in editorial comments, but otherwise left outside or on the margins of the contents. From time to time, the heavy-industry newspaper published stories critical of procuracy officials and judges who harassed managers by petty law enforcement. The heavy-industry commissar and party politburo member, Ordzhonikidze, was developing a reputation for protecting managers from the 'disorganizing' incursions of over-zealous inspectors and law-enforcers. Preoccupations with the 'political work with the masses', rule-enforcement campaigns, and 'mass control from below' were the speciality of other politicians and the propaganda organs of which they were patrons.

But the differences between technocratic management and mobilization campaigning approaches did not coincide very clearly with the division of functions between managers and political officials. The great majority of the factory directors were *praktiki* – men without technical qualifications who were appointed by political patronage. Many clearly did try to catch up on technical knowledge, and in so doing perhaps tended to identify with the engineering outlook on the world. But their success depended on their ability to make deals with the various players in their organizational environment – that is, on their ability to be both business-like and political. On the other hand, the people in charge of 'political work' in the factories were the party secretaries whose performance was also judged by production results as well as by displays of mobilization campaigning. If the fulfilment of output targets looked good, the political officials' mobilization work was less likely to come under a close critical scrutiny; if the responsiveness to political campaigning concerns also looked good, output achievements were less likely to come under the shadow of hostile investigations of the costs. Factory managers and party secretaries were well advised to treat each other's functions with pragmatic understanding. This was, of course, the essential basis for developing the wider interpersonal networks that were necessary for sustained enterprise success, although the central authorities feared them as 'localism'. The central authorities often combined their campaigns with breaking up the partnerships between the directors and party secretaries in some factories, by putting pressure on the party secretary to break ranks, or simply by transferring either him or the director to another post. Political conflicts among officialdom were the result of three different kinds of fault line: between central leaders and 'localist' alliances; between rival alliances of officials competing for scarce resources; and between technocratic and mobilization outlooks on industrial leadership.

Besides, there was the perennial problem of how taut the targets of productive achievement should be: naturally each enterprise wanted relatively easy targets for itself, but whenever it petitioned the central authorities for help with resource bottlenecks it was putting pressure on them to tighten other enterprises' plans. The central authorities were naturally suspicious that enterprise managements were slower in improving the efficiency and 'production culture' of their units than they could have been.

Bureaucratic Campaigns and Factory Floor Bargains

At the factory floor level, the mobilization campaigns for improving 'production culture' were numerous and varied. Some were not controversial in their aims, and were organized mainly as 'initiatives from below' by the 'social organizations' in the factories – the party, the *komsomol*, and the trade unions. These were usually one-off efforts to unclutter yards and gang-ways, to change blatantly wasteful or unsafe working practices, or to provide peripheral trappings of 'culture', such as hygienic changing rooms for workers. Other campaigns were likewise uncontentious but organized mainly through the administrative managerial channels: for example, the campaigns to expand training opportunities for workers to upgrade their skills. The campaigns that were contentious, in that they were potentially provocative of labour unrest, were those intended to have a direct and immediate effect on labour productivity: the campaigns to enforce labour discipline, the campaigns to increase workers' output norms and decrease piece-rates, and the 'socialist competition' campaigns. All three were established perennials on the agendas of industrial authorities and factory 'social organizations' by the end of the first five-year plan, and all three had their centrally instigated revivals which punctuated periods of bureaucratic routinization between the end of 1932 and the end of the decade.

The labour discipline issue was interesting in that the authorities' attitudes to it were divided by the ideological notion that the industrial proletariat constituted a superior social force. In 1905 and 1917, the Bolsheviks supported striking workers' demands that managers relinquish their powers to discipline labour by imposing fines and sackings. After 1917, they introduced strong labour-protection legislation which made it difficult for managers to initiate and carry out such punishments. During the 1920s it had to be acknowledged that labour discipline remained a problem, despite the advent of the 'proletarian state'. This was explained routinely by the supposed 'dilution of the working class' consequent upon the promotion of its leading cadres to administrative and political posts. Responsibility for improving labour discipline standards was mainly vested in the educational functions of the 'social organizations' in the factories, such as the 'production comradely courts' that dealt with errant workers by publicizing their misdemeanours at factory floor meetings.

Managers were given increased powers to impose fines and sack incorrigible workers by government decrees issued in 1929–30. But sacking ceased to be an effective deterrent when the economy heated up and new jobs became easy to find. Besides, the punishments still remained subject to appeal procedures both within the factory and outside; penalized workers could seek redress at the factory labour-conflict commissions, the Commissariat of Labour, the courts, and the procuracy. The situation was further complicated when the courts and the procuracy were exhorted to be vigilant against managerial abuses by 'bourgeois specialists'. Even after Stalin's denunciation of excessive 'specialist baiting' it was still possible for a sacked worker to turn the table on the manager who had sacked him. In summer 1932, for example, a manager who sacked a maintenance worker for causing substantial damage by refusing to carry out an order to repair a faulty machine was prosecuted for 'being a Ford and an oppressor of the working class', sentenced to three months of 'corrective labour at the place of employment', and fined 25 per cent of his salary over the three months; the fine was paid to the reinstated worker as a compensation.[6]

It was perhaps to protect managers from such outcomes that the central authorities initiated new campaigning against labour indiscipline by issuing, in November 1932, a decree which made it *mandatory* for managers to sack workers for a single day's absenteeism. In addition, the sacked workers were to be deprived of food rations, banned from other industrial employment for six months, and, if they were living in factory accommodation, evicted immediately. This was a draconian law indeed, at the time when rationing coupons were crucial for keeping starvation at bay and when even the most squalid and overcrowded accommodation was extremely difficult to find. Why such a punitive measure was aimed at absenteeism in particular is not clear. That many workers occasionally failed to turn up when they should have was clearly a problem for managers, but not necessarily the greatest. The most alarmist reports of deteriorating industrial discipline were based on examples of what workers did when they were at work. They told of workers turning up drunk, catching up on sleep at work time, walking around the shopfloors on social visits, causing damage to machinery, ignoring or arguing against managers' instructions, deliberately working at a slow-down pace, and at times being threatening and violent, turning parts of the factory into no-go areas for certain managers and norm-setters. Workers could ill afford to miss wages through wanton absenteeism. If the statistics of registered unauthorized absences were creeping up in 1932, the reasons were probably connected with the increasing difficulties of everyday survival; some workers missed work because they had to stand in long queues, try to hawk and barter things, catch their own fish out of polluted city rivers, breed their own poultry and rabbits in city yards and apartments, or grow their own vegetables on city-edge allotments. But the officially registered average of six days of unauthorized absence per worker in 1932 did not compare badly with eight days in 1925–6.[7] It is, of course, possible that the authorities feared a spread of strikes (which were euphemistically mentioned in the press as 'organized mass absences from work').

The officials who were required to publicize the decree at workers' meetings had an unenviable task, for many workers were still outspoken on such occasions, despite the presence of OGPU officers and informers in the factories. The organs of state security were still concerned mainly with 'wreckers', whom they expected to find in the managerial rather than proletarian ranks. The majority of ordinary workers were too young to have

6 Andrle, *Workers*, p. 144.
7 Andrle, *Workers*, p. 129.

been mixed up with the wrong people during the revolution and civil war, and only a small number could be accused of coming from the wrong class background. The new arrivals from the peasant countryside among them were considered a backward element but not a class enemy. Rowdily hostile responses to the announcements of such measures as production speed-ups had been commonplace at factory meetings since the start of the industrialization campaign, and it was no different with the announcement of the draconian anti-absenteeism law. Press reports told of meetings where 'backward' workers shouted their outrage at being subjected to such a law when they were hungry and inadequately clothed, and when going absent now and then was a necessity. 'You live well yourselves, yet you keep hassling workers to give more, more and more' they told the propagandists, and 'why don't you chain us to the production line, you might as well!'[8]

The campaigning press gave the fight against absenteeism pride of place for several months. However, it reported not a single case of an exemplary factory where the decree was used to the letter and the standards of labour discipline raised. A flurry of sackings of especially troublesome workers perhaps did occur, as it had done in 1929, but press accounts of the campaign told mainly of 'liberal-opportunistic sabotage' of the decree by managers who were afraid to 'damage relations with workers'. Factory floor time-clerks refrained from registering unauthorized absences as such; foremen issued retrospective permission to workers to be absent; and doctors issued more sick notes. Managers breached the letter of the decree by not sacking the workers whose unauthorized absences were registered, referring them instead to 'production comradely courts' (which had no power to dismiss anyone); by rehiring the workers they had dismissed; or by giving the workers they did dismiss a certificate that they were made redundant so as not to prejudice their chances of finding other employment. Factory housing wardens did nothing to evict dismissed workers, preferring instead to abide by an earlier protection-of-tenants law, and dismissed workers usually held on to their rationing coupons.

The pattern was repeated after the government issued another decree on absenteeism in December 1938, which made coming to work 20 minutes late punishable by instant dismissal, and managerial reluctance to enforce it liable to prosecution. In addition, workers were issued 'labour books' in which the details of their performance and misdemeanours could be recorded and made known to any future employer. But managers still connived with workers to evade the full force of the disciplining measures, although many of them were now purge-time promotees whose instincts could have been expected to be more conformist than benevolent.

Managers usually explained their reluctance to enforce the decree by citing the compassionate circumstances of the individual workers involved, or by stating that they needed to hold on to the workers they had. But melting a draconian government law in a benevolent management hand was also sound industrial relations. Generally, managers saw labour discipline as a serious problem, but they also saw that enforcement of the rules would be counter-productive if it was too literal. It would appear patently unreasonable in

---

8 Andrle, *Workers*, p. 131.

situations where production could not flow smoothly even when all workers behaved impeccably.

Managers were also often unable to provide everything the workers were entitled to under the rules; workers often had to be asked to work without the prescribed safety clothing and devices, to tolerate delays in the payment of wages, and to work at a hectic pace during the 'storming' periods. The workers were often required to try to fulfil their output norms despite inferior raw materials, machinery faults, and sudden make-do changes in work processes that disrupted their work rhythm. They often had to be asked to do overtime and to work on their free days at short notice. Flexible goodwill was needed to achieve production results at all. Productive management–labour relations required give and take in regard to the formal rules. Shopfloor managers' success depended on the development of standards of working behaviour such as seemed reasonable and appropriate in the conditions of their shopfloor; such standards could have been identical with bureaucratically defined formal rules only in a never-never machine-utopia land. In the real world, working standards were created and sustained by continuous processes of informal, tacit bargaining over conditions and rewards. The collusive bending of formal rules was a part of this process. Not only did production depend on this but also the workers' practical acceptance of the political structures, for the managerial authority they encountered at work was also a major part of their contact with authority in general. Communists as well as non-communists were reported to be involved in ostracizing activists who went over the top in trying to make their mark as 'uncompromising fighters for labour discipline'.

Workers were, of course, disabled by the repressive powers of the state from explicit collective bargaining over their wages and conditions. Bargaining had to be tacit and localized within the contexts of particular factory floors. One form of such bargaining was provided by the demand for labour. It was not difficult to find another job, especially for workers with some skills. The government tried to play its part in reducing labour turnover by introducing industry-wide wage-scales related to grades of skill. If wages for comparable workers were made comparable between different places of work, then there would be less incentive for workers to improve their living standards by a search for greener pastures. This could never have been a completely successful measure for preventing voluntary movement between jobs because it could not anticipate the ways in which workers experienced the local conditions of a work place, and how hard a job was for the wages it gave. Besides, managers competed with one another for the better quality workers, and there were always ways of outbidding a competitor by offering a higher skill-grading, better welfare provision, and more agreeable working conditions.

Another complicating factor in the government's search for a labour-stabilizing wage policy was the post-1931 commitment to the strategy of motivating labour by performance-related pay. Managers were under pressure to maximize the proportion of workers paid on a piece-rate basis. The tariffs of hourly pay, which were differentiated by the payee's skill-grading, therefore had to be translated into piece-rates related to particular kinds of individual output. Here the lynchpin was the daily or hourly output norm for the job. A 100 per cent fulfilment of the norm should yield the wages specified in the tariff, but the worker could earn more or less than that depending on how his or her actual output compared with the norm. The Taylorist machine utopia envisaged output norms set for each job by professional 'norm-setters' on the basis of a scientific measurement of the time, motion, and energy required by the most efficient working method. In the real world the norms had to be set by a combination of actual performance statistics, guesswork about what was feasible, some experimental observation with stopwatches (with guesswork about whether the observed worker was showing a 'normal' speed), and by trial and error. Workers who found a new norm too difficult complained to the foreman, demonstrated their reasons for doing so, and, if they won the argument, the foreman went to argue with the norm-setter. Much of the wage bargaining thus took the form of arguments over the correctness of the norms, and the ways in which norm-fulfilment rates were calculated – for example, whether non-productive time should be included in the calculations when a stoppage was due to circumstances beyond the worker's control. Corollary arguments contested the rates of pay at stoppage times. The government tried to limit this to two-thirds of the basic hourly rate, but many managements paid out more.

After 1933 the expansion of the industrial labour force resumed, and so did rural-urban migration. The rates of labour turnover, however, fell markedly from the chaos-reflecting heights of the first five-year plan. They were still high by international standards, but the relative stability was indicative of the fact that, overall, living standards had started to recover from the drop of the crisis years, that more workers were experiencing improvements without having to change jobs, and fewer workers were driven to change jobs through feeling unjustly treated. Whether workers felt on the whole justly treated depended in large part on whether the conditions of work and pay allowed them fairly regular and predictable earnings, at a level currently thought appropriate to their skills and type of work, without having to work harder for it than their colleagues. As in other work places across the industrial world, a feeling of justice depended on the sense that one's effort was not being undervalued. The minimization of such a sense of injustice was a necessary everyday goal of factory floor management, for too many chronically aggrieved workers spelt poor work morale and unpredictable performance in the work place, and it was an outcome of tacit local bargaining processes over particular conditions of work and pay. The arguments with norm-setters mentioned above, in which the foremen often took the workers' side, were an important part of this process. Another part was the allocation of jobs among workers, since the outcome of norm-setting inevitably led to some jobs becoming known locally as subject to norms that were not particularly difficult to fulfil while others were; a sense of justice depended on workers feeling that, over time, they had a fair mix of both kinds of jobs. A corollary to this was a fair distribution of the effects of supplies shortages – a worker who was always on piece-rated jobs which were subject to stoppages because the materials were running out and the equipment breaking down clearly had a cause to feel aggrieved. Where it was not possible to spread the effects of the 'organizational breakdowns', managers were under pressure from workers to break the government rules concerning wage payment for stoppage times. Finally, the achievement of work place stability depended on shopfloor managers knowing when to turn a blind eye to production workers making their earnings with the help of breaking various rules; the piece-rate workers often misreported the times at which they started and ended particular job batches, they held on to instruments which they should have returned to the store-room, they tinkered with machine set-ups to make them work faster (possibly at a cost to the machines and the product quality), sometimes they cheated or intimidated quality inspectors, or they found ways of jumping queues for assistance by auxilliary workers, maintenance workers, store-room clerks, and machine fitters.

The collusive practices of shopfloor managers and groups of workers were an essential ingredient of the moral economy that kept production going in difficult organizational environments. The central authorities, however, suspected them of harbouring slack standards and putting a brake on the desired progress towards industrial efficiency. This was analogous to the central authorities' suspicions of 'bureaucratism' and 'localism' in executive ranks. In the factory floor context, the sin was referred to as 'the appeasement of grabbing tendencies on the part of unconscious workers', and 'the subversion of material incentives by levelling'. The principal administrative instrument of forcing efficiency drives from above was to require the factories to carry out, periodically, a wholesale tightening of the individual output norms. It was probably understood by the central authorities that norm-tightening was bound to cause much anger on the factory floors, but the hope was that this would help concentrate managers' minds on organizational and technical innovation that would enable workers to improve their earnings despite the increased norms. Until 1934, the timings and details of the norm-revision drives varied between factories; from 1935, the drives were conducted annually as centralized, high-profile government campaigns, with decrees specifying implementation deadlines and average percentages by which the norms should be increased in each branch of industry. Only in 1938 did no such campaign take place.

Factory statistics of production workers' norm fulfilment duly showed lower rates in the immediate aftermath of each norm-revision campaign. This did not necessarily mean that many workers' earnings dropped, because the revision campaigns were usually accompanied by some increases in wage tariffs, and sometimes also by promoting some workers to higher skill-grades. In the months that followed, increasing proportions of the workers were recorded as overfulfilling their norms. Overall output per factory worker, however, was not rising as quickly as could be expected from the statistics of norm-tightening and norm-fulfilment. This was due to factories hiring additional auxilliary labour to assist the production workers, norm-setters loosening tightened norms on appeal, and shopfloor managements modifying the ways in which norm-fulfilment rates were calculated. The annual cycle was completed by a new wave of allegations in the campaigning press that there were still too many outdated, slack norms, and an announcement of the next norm-revision round.

Shock Workers and Stakhanovites

Another kind of campaigning on the 'labour productivity front' took the form of 'socialist competition' activities. This was the principal form of the 'political work with the masses' demanded by the mobilization approach to industrialization in the factories. In 1929, the *komsomol* encouraged its members in the factories to make their input into meetings discussing the business of making the taut plans tauter. They declared themselves to be 'shock work brigades' ready to show up the 'technological conservatism' of 'bourgeois specialists' and other opponents of 'Bolshevik speeds'. The 'shock work brigades' undertook to overfulfil the output norms by hefty margins, to prove that there was enough spare capacity to make the tautest of production plans possible. Another occasion on which the brigades declared themselves were the 'storming' campaigns which 'saved the plans' by bouts of heroic exertion to catch up on deadlines. A celebratory gathering in the Kremlin in November marked the turning of the movement into an institution. Henceforth, 'social organizations' in the factories, and the trade unions in particular, were expected to turn out regular statistical reports showing how many workers were registered as participants in socialist competition, and how many achieved the honourable status of 'shock worker'. In 1931 shock workers were issued with cards which entitled them to various privileges, including extra rationing coupons.

The initial wave of the shock work movement was supported by the organs of class vigilance. Workers who showed their displeasure with the activists by beating them up were not punished simply for violent behaviour; they were charged with the much more serious, political crime of 'wrecking', especially if they could be shown to have come from families of kulaks, priests, or other kinds of 'class enemy'. More numerous and more telling were the charges of 'wrecking' levelled against managers and clerks who were denounced for crossing the shock work brigades. Foremen might be charged with 'wrecking the shock work movement' when they failed to guarantee the supplies the shock workers needed for their production feats, when they allocated inferior raw material and machines to the shock workers, when they gave shock workers mainly tight-norm jobs, or when they took their promises at face value and reduced the number of workers in the relevant section. Wage-clerks might be charged with wrecking if they reduced the piece-rates on the overfulfilled norms; quality inspectors if they checked the shock workers' products too meticulously; and time-clerks if they recorded their tardiness. In other words, 'wrecking' might occur when shock workers were denied privileged allocations, or when they were excluded from the benevolent aspects of shopfloor custom and practice, or simply ignored and ostracized.

Many of the initial shock brigade activists were probably genuine ideological enthusiasts. But they were mainly young urban men and women fresh from schools. As newcomers, they had a junior status in the unofficial stratification systems on the factory floors. They might have believed genuinely that if they made managers fix unfaltering supplies for their production feats, then eventually the managers would learn to organize unfaltering supplies to everyone. But the managers and the more experienced workers knew this would not be possible. Allocations that enabled fast, high-earning work without stoppages would always remain a privilege. On factory floors with an egalitarian ethos, such privilege belonged to no one in particular and problems with supplies were expected to be distributed evenly. In less egalitarian work places, allocations reflected seniority status; the earning capacity of the longer-serving, skilled workers was looked after first, that of the new workers last. The *komsomol* activist youth, however, were explicit in demanding privileged treatment in allocations. It was a standard part of the shock brigade declarations to make their undertakings on the condition that the management support them. Some shock brigades embarrassed managers and supplies-allocation clerks by inviting them to join them as members; and some attempted to claim direct authority over supplies. In addition, the shock brigades that also declared themselves to be 'living labour communes' tried to jump queues for housing by claiming that their wish to live together in communes deserved political support. Shared housing was of course the only kind available in any case.

The initial shock brigades thus upset managers and senior workers by inviting tauter plan targets, and they upset everyone by demanding privileged treatment in return for rate-busting. Their initiatives were resisted, and eventually neutralized by the collusive arts of 'bureaucratic formalism'. This was undoubtedly helped by the fact that many of the zealots were soon transferred from the factory floors to political posts and higher education courses. The 'shock workers' who gathered at the November congress were mainly ones who were senior by conventional standards; nearly one-half had been workers for more than 10 years – that is, unlikely to have been among the *komsomol* youth that started the movement. Henceforth, the ranks of the workers officially registered as taking part in the movement grew while the practical meaning of it diminished. Almost two-thirds of all industrial workers were counted as being involved in socialist competition in 1931, three-quarters by 1935. By 1935, almost a half of all industrial workers were issued with shock worker identity cards. Being issued with the card became an almost automatic rite of passage in a worker's progression from junior to senior status on the shopfloor. Nearly all skilled workers, a good proportion of semi-skilled machine operatives, and very few unskilled auxilliary labourers had it. More men had it than women. One's chances of receiving it increased with years in employment. The rules prevented workers from receiving it if they had been in their factory for less than a year. Rate-busting achievements were not necessary for becoming a shock worker; moderate overfulfilment of the norms on a regular basis and a reasonably clean discipline record were often as not all that were required of the workers with the higher skill-grades. Junior workers might enhance their chances of gaining the status early by participation in the various 'social work' activities organized by the party and trade unions, or by doing a course at a night school.

That the bureaucratic routinization disarmed the shock-work movement from causing shake-ups of established working practices did not escape political mobilizers' notice. The campaigning press often told tales of 'phoney shock work' (*lzheudarnichestvo*) in factories where workers did not even know that they were registered as taking part in a socialist competition, and where shock workers' standards of work and discipline were no better than the generally prevalent ones. From 1931 to 1935, a number of additional 'movements' of socialist competition were started with spurts of publicity, but none of these appeared to repeat the initial shock work campaign in the pressure they put on managers and shopfloor relations.

These pressures returned with the political mobilizers' new offensive 'on the production front', which gathered quick momentum after a miner called Alexei Stakhanov dug a multiple of his shift-quota of coal in August 1935. The Stakhanovite campaign started amid criticisms of the ways in which the implementation of the government-decreed norm-revision campaign of the spring and summer of 1935 was bringing about only limited productivity improvements. The blame for this was put on 'office methods' in norm-setting, the 'technological conservatism' of engineers and technicians who did their work in isolation from the best shopfloor workers, and collusive shopfloor practices and hierarchies that kept innovative and energetic workers from reaching their full productive potential. The Stakhanovite publicity soon included not just a celebration of particular production feats and descriptions of successful innovative measures but also reports of struggles between Stakhanovite militants and their enemies in the factories, and of 'proletarian justice' punishments meted out to the enemies. The content and flavour of the reports was strongly reminiscent of the 'shock work movement' reports in 1929. 'Class enemies' who had managed to infiltrate the working class were intimidating the Stakhanovites by physical violence or ostracism while managers, engineers, norm-setters, quality inspectors, foremen, and 'bureaucrats' in social organizations were 'wrecking' the movement by colluding in a refusal to lavish privileged allocations and care on Stakhanovite initiatives. In November, the movement and its struggles received a high-profile ceremonial endorsement at a congress of Stakhanovites in the Kremlin, where the new breed of labour heroes told Stalin and his politburo colleagues of their struggles and triumphs, and received the heady VIP treatment of a social élite to whom belonged a radiant future. By that time, every factory was scrambling to arrange a world production record. In December, the customary month of 'storming' on the annual production targets, the Stakhanovite record mania reached its high point.

By spring 1936, however, the record mania came under public criticism if it consisted of little more than spectacular production feats specially arranged as one-off publicity stunts. The true Stakhanovite spirit, it was now argued, was about managers, engineers, and workers constantly searching together for innovative ways of raising efficiency standards which could be sustained. The Stakhanovite competition should now take the form of five-day, ten-day, and monthly periods over which whole shopfloors or factories should experiment with speedier and more efficient production methods. These calls implied that concerns for achieving smoothly co-ordinated production flows should outweigh concerns for conjuring up spectacular speed-ups. The managers should lead the Stakhanovite movement, said the Heavy Industry Commissar, Ordzhonikidze, to a conference of managers, by which he meant that they should not be giving up responsibility for a sustainable, efficient organization of their factories in the face of pressures to create individual Stakhanovite heroes. He also reassured his audience that he believed 'the vast majority' of managers were not wreckers; many lacked experience and had much to learn, and some had forgotten that much could be learnt from the best workers; but they were honest patriots with an important job to do, which, he implied, was not reducible to letting 'mass mobilization' agitators always have their way.

By late spring 1936, criticisms also appeared in the press of factories where care for Stakhanovites led to a neglect of shock workers. This was a euphemism for criticizing the divisive nature of lavishing allocations and rewards on a privileged minority. By this time, many managements indeed anticipated these criticisms by discontinuing the practice of contriving to let their Stakhanovites earn a multiple of average wages. Top Stakhanovite earnings started to come down after reaching their peak in the winter months, while average earnings continued to rise. And, as Stakhanovite privileges diminished, the proportion of workers who were officially designated Stakhanovites grew. For example, in a large Moscow machine-tool factory, one-third of all workers were officially designated 'Stakhanovites' by the end of 1936, including one-half of the production-line workers in the highest skill categories but very few unskilled workers. The difference between the recorded norm-fulfilment rates of the 'Stakhanovites' and the rest were nowhere near to what they had been in the previous winter; it appeared that earning the title became a part of an orderly progression of workers towards seniority status – it was no longer the result of extraordinary innovation or rate-busting. The moral economy of factory floor custom and practice was reasserting itself – both in the ways in which managers allocated jobs, equipment, raw material, and auxiliary assistance to production workers on piece-rates, and in the ways in which 'social organizations' went about proving on paper that all was well with their 'work with the masses'. Some of the early Stakhanovites bemoaned the fact that they were no longer guaranteed what they needed for full-capacity performance and earnings, but there were not many left in that position, as many were promoted to management, seconded to higher education, or appointed to technical-instructor posts. Those who remained on the shop-floors and insisted on privileged treatment too vociferously could be again browbeaten by their foremen as 'speculators' and transferred to more difficult and less lucrative work.

There were similarities between the shock work and Stakhanovite campaigns in the ways in which they waxed and waned as an assertion of political mobilization methods against industrial working relations that supposedly harboured slack productivity standards. Both movements were started under the ideological banner of a creative working-class challenge to allegedly conservative aspects of technocratic authority, and by an alliance of political organizers in the factories with workers who felt thwarted in their ambitions by the established allocative practices in their work places. Many of these workers were relatively junior in the informal hierarchies of shopfloor seniority. The militants of both movements were resisted as upstart rate-busters disrupting peaceful working relations by making unfair claims on scarce resources for themselves. But political backing gave them a chance of rapid elevation to senior skilled status or a promotion to non-manual posts. Both movements became subject to a kind of bureaucratic routinization in the course of which their controversial edge was eventually blunted, managerial authority reaffirmed against the 'excesses' of 'control from below', and the informal shopfloor ways of maintaining working peace re-established.

But the Stakhanovite campaign was also the product of its own time rather than a mere repetition of the earlier cycle of 'socialist competition' campaigning. First, the Stakhanovite campaign still bore the hallmarks of the 'technological mastery' slogan that had been proclaimed for the second five-year plan, although it implied that this goal was no longer best served by an emphasis on managerial controls and 'technological discipline'. The campaign started on the sound premiss that many workers who were operating machines on piece-rates were already doing clandestine experiments with machine set-ups and production processes such as enabled them to work quickly when this was advantageous to their earnings. It enticed workers to divulge their speed-up secrets to engineers who were encouraged to learn from the most inventive workers and support the innovations by designing special devices, with the help of which the speedier work could carry on without overloading the machines or jeopardizing product quality. In practice, the record mania often did lead to speed-ups which were detrimental to both the quality and the equipment. But it also increased the production of simple and effective add-ons to machines which enhanced their capacity and made production more efficient.

The campaign was also accompanied by a fast expansion of training opportunities for workers. Again, the emphasis on quantity often devalued the quality of the training provision, but skill levels undoubtedly improved overall during the second half of the decade. Furthermore, the campaign's propaganda gave a new voice to the old 'production culture' themes, in that it publicized the benefits of efficient, methodical, time-oriented and technically knowledgeable work habits and self-improvement efforts to the workers themselves as well as to the economy as a whole; for example, it publicized research findings which claimed that Stakhanovite workers were healthier and less fatigued than the rest because of their 'cultured' ways of working. The Stakhanovite campaign was an attempt to synthesize the heroic themes of industrialization by mass mobilization with the modernization themes of 'production culture'. Finally, the campaign arguably supported the 'technological mastery' slogan in that it attacked those aspects of Taylorism which emphasized the role of theory and theory-based management while assuming that manual labour need be disciplined but not especially skilled. Stakhanovite propaganda modified the vision of progress towards machine-utopia by infusing it with the notion that manual work should be done by increasingly skilled and technically educated workers who would eventually break down the divisions between manual and mental labour.

The second distinctive characteristic of the Stakhanovite campaign was that it represented an escalation of the 'anti-levelling' policies that had been announced four years earlier. The shock workers' brigades of 1929–30 pressed demands for privileged allocations at work, and in some cases for special housing, but they put into effect egalitarian principles of wage distribution among their own members. The Stakhanovite campaign, on the other hand, glorified individual stars making extraordinary earnings on individual piece-rates during the winter of 1935–6. In February the earnings of top Stakhanovites were reported in the region of 800 roubles, while the average industrial wages were only just creeping up to 250 roubles. In addition, the trade unions and the distributive bureaucracies were exhorted to lavish special care on the

Stakhanovites. Many of the initial hatch of Stakhanovite heroes were awarded the unheard-of luxury of self-contained family apartments in city centres, in which they lived as neighbours to high-ranking managers and officials. The Stakhanovites also joined the élite categories of people for whom special shops were set up in which they could spend their money, without queueing, on quality food, clothing, and consumer goods that were unavailable to ordinary mortals. Some were given interest-free loans for the purchase of expensive items, which enabled several Stakhanovites to be among the first private car-owners in the Soviet era. 'Cadres decide everything', said Stalin in a well publicized speech to military academy graduates in May 1935, and 'care for living people' was what was needed to shift the industrialization drive into a higher gear. The Stakhanovite campaign translated the policy into highly publicized acts of special care for the needs of a hastily created cadre of working-class 'technology masters'.

There was an interesting corollary to the propaganda surrounding the élite performance-related earnings and special privileges: the idea that good industrial work need be motivated by prospects of private luxury consumption, and that 'cultured living' involved not just work-oriented self-improvement, good works in spare time, and edifying leisure pursuits but also private affluence. 'Life has become better, comrades, life has become easier', said Stalin to the excited Stakhanovites at the Kremlin gathering, and they responded by telling tales of their struggles on the factory floors – and also of their pleasure in the goods they bought for their augmented wages. Suits and ties, silk blouses, leather shoes, furcoats, home furnishings, radio receivers, bicycles, and sometimes cars were celebrated as just rewards to those who truly 'harnessed technology', as symbols of their personal progress from humble beginnings to élite status, and as the promise of affluence that industrialization held to everyone prepared to work for it. The industrial work ethic promoted by the propaganda media was no longer couched in the rhetoric of revolutionary asceticism alone.

The third distinctive characteristic of the Stakhanovite campaign was that it marked a revision of official attitudes to ex-peasant workers. Until then, attitudes were exemplified by the following report published in the industrial newspaper in February 1931:

> A lathe turner is stooping over a gleaming, gently turning shaft. His jacket is covered in steel dust and flooded with sparks. His face is tense, streams of sweat are mixing with grime and grease. It is difficult to put a finger on it, but there is something distinctively peasant about him. It could be the squat posture, or perhaps the way his elbows wave about when his fingers are at work, and his nose sort of twitches – devil knows what it is![9]

The fact that the growing industrial workforce consisted largely of recent arrivals from the peasant countryside was routinely cited as a major problem. The peasants were thought to be burdened with an uncultured background and their 'influx' into the factories was blamed for poor work discipline, shoddy products, breakage of equipment, and low productivity standards. It would take time and much socializing effort in the 'factory cauldrons' for the 'raw

---

9 Andrle, *Workers*, p. 101.

workforce' to become imbued with the refinements of high 'production culture'. The contrast between the 'gleaming, gently turning shaft' and a grimy, elbow-waving, squat person in the description above sought to illustrate the point that even well meaning and trained machine operators remained clumsy and error-prone until the passage of time washed the peasant rawness from their souls. On the factory floors, ex-peasants naturally had a junior status in the unofficial hierarchies, marked not only by allocative practices but also symbolically by the array of abusive terms for peasants with which the more urbanized senior workers and foremen addressed the new arrivals whenever they did anything wrong.

But the junior workers whom the Stakhanovite campaign promoted to rate bust the established hegemonies of shopfloor working customs included many immigrants from the country-cousin mass. This inclusion of ex-peasants in the political mobilizers' visions of a new working-class élite was presaged by Stalin's 'cadres decide everything' speech. The speech, which asserted the case for 'taut planning' and insinuated that calls for moderation in the industrialization drive had been coming from the ranks of enemy plotters, was spiked with metaphors and analogies from peasant environments. Technology would have to be 'harnessed' (instead of 'mastered') and managers whose visions of progress were fixated on machines in disregard for the creative potential of the workers who operated them were akin to the country-estate bosses of the old days 'who valued horses above people'. The Stakhanovite campaign subsequently created and celebrated many a tale of fast social mobility by ambitious and energetic individuals from a bewildered migrant mass to a new élite of technology-harnessers. It did not make the peasantry respectable, but it drove underground the time-honoured notion that peasant backgrounds constituted a heavy ballast on cultural development. The Stakhanovite propaganda lambasted foreign experts who had designed production processes on the assumption of an unskilled, inferior workforce. Stalin's industrial achievers were inferior to no one, it claimed, even if some of them had only recently arrived with country mud on their boots, because their future was stronger than their past.

Finally, the 'cadres decide everything' speech made a point of attacking 'soulless bureaucrats' and the militant phase of the Stakhanovite campaign was accompanied by strident rhetorical attacks on the sins of 'bureaucratism'. The enemy were no longer just people from 'class enemy' backgrounds who 'wormed their way' into Soviet institutions, but also officials from impeccable 'proletarian' backgrounds who became imbued with 'bureaucratism', in any of the three forms discussed earlier in this chapter, in their practice of holding office. As the militant edge of the Stakhanovite campaign became blunted by the practices of routinization in the spring–summer of 1936, industrial commissar and politburo member, Ordzhonikidze, appeared to try to reassure his managerial cadre that they were not political suspects, and that they had the right and duty to uphold the principles of rational management against the disruptive excesses of 'mass mobilization' initiatives. But in 1936 there occurred the trial of Zinoviev, Kamenev, and several other former Bolshevik leaders charged with political conspiracies that had allegedly led to the assassination (in December 1934) of the Leningrad Party boss, Kirov. Then the OGPU received a new boss, Yezhov, and extended its search for political enemies within. In February 1937, Ordzhonikidze suddenly died (in somewhat mysterious circumstances), industrial managers lost their strongest patron in the party politburo, and the search for the enemy within swept through their ranks. The beginning of this process coincided with calls to a Stakhanovite revival in the industrial press.

The Stakhanovite revival calls, however, were only discernible as a distinctive message in the rising din of 'criticism and self-criticism' for a few weeks. After that, the denuciatory frenzy that filled the communication channels conveyed little in the way of a coherent message on industrial policy. The things for which managers and other officials were denounced belonged to either side of any conceivable definition of practical decision-making alternatives. To some extent they reflected the fault lines of the new industrial system discussed earlier in this chapter: the conflicts between the principles of centralism and the tendencies to 'localism', the conflicts between rival cliques of office holders for scarce resources, between the technocratic and mobilization approaches to industrialization, and the conflicts of opinion between those who thought that industrial targets should be moderated in the interests of overall co-ordination and those who thought that the plans should be tauter. But this no longer had much to do with the Stakhanovite campaign as such. Even if there had been a high-powered central policy on rescuing Stakhanovism from the inevitabilities of 'bureaucratic formalism', the executive structure was not up to a sustained implementation of it on the factory floors. Managers, industrial party secretaries, and all the other kinds of official were busy denouncing each other and defending themselves from denunciations at party meetings and in OGPU interrogation cells, and they kept suddenly disappearing from their posts.

The purges were called off at the end of 1938. Yezhov went down the well trodden path to execution cells and the people who were now occupying the offices of industrial management and 'social organizations' were told by Stalin that they could be trusted. They were after all the truly Stalinist generation of executives, the young men who had received their qualifications and career opportunities since the 'great breakthrough', the fast-promotion beneficiaries of the purges. The new decrees on labour discipline and output-norm revision, however, became subject to the same patterns of implementation as had been evident at least since 1933–5. Custom and practice, the informal manager–worker bargains of the factory floor moral economy, remained an important fact of factory life; here was an element of continuity with both established working-class traditions and the kinds of response to managerial controls that occur in industries throughout the world.

Output-norm reviews, searches for more effective performance-related pay-schemes, tinkerings with administrative organization, 'socialist competition' revivals, labour-discipline drives, promotions of 'scientific organization of labour', provision of technical education at all levels, and 'production culture' propaganda became established as the durable routines of productivity campaigning in Soviet industry. Political campaigns against 'bureaucratism' and 'localism' too, although they would never again escalate into a repetition of Yezhov's purges.

Further Reading

The content of this chapter is derived mainly from V. Andrle, *Workers in Stalin's Russia: Industrialization and Social change in a Planned Economy* (Hemel Hempstead: Harvester-Wheatsheaf, 1988). But the available literature on the complexities of the industrialization campaign is quite extensive and varied. A brief introductory overview that remains a classic can be found in M. Lewin, *The Making of the Soviet System: Essays in the Social History of Interwar Russia* (London: Methuen, 1985), Chap. 10. A good, detailed account of industrial policies and their effects on the working class (especially the alienative effects) is offered by D. A. Filtzer, *Soviet Workers and Stalinist Industrialization: The Formation of Modern Soviet Production Relations, 1928–41* (London: Pluto Press, 1986). An even more detailed and painstaking account of industrial policy during the five-year plan period is in H. Kuromiya, *Stalin's Industrial Revolution: Politics and Workers, 1928–1932* (Cambridge: Cambridge University Press, 1988), although the analyses and interpretations of this book tend to take at face value some of the ideological notions about the working class that permeated Stalinist policy-making and propaganda. Dealing also with the early period of the industrialization drive is a history of one of the grand construction projects: A. D. Rassweiler, *The Generation of Power: The History of Dneprostroi* (New York: Oxford University Press, 1988). As regards understanding the developments in industrial policies and relations in the second half of the 1930s, much can be gained from this careful study of the Stakhanovite campaign: L. H. Siegelbaum, *Stakhanovism and the Politics of Productivity in the USSR, 1935–1941* (Cambridge: Cambridge University Press, 1988).

There is a good review article dealing with the above publications by L. Vanrossum in *International Review of Social History*, xxxv, 1990, pp. 433–53.

A study of factory floor relations is well served by paying close analytical attention to the role and practices of the foreman; this is provided by L. H. Siegelbaum, 'Masters of the shop floor: foremen and Soviet industrialisation', in N. Lampert and G. Rittersporn (eds), *Stalinism: Its Nature and Aftermath* (London: Macmillan, 1992), pp. 127–56.

On the relations between industrial managers and political authorities, a concise but insightful account is provided by M. B. Beissinger, *Scientific Management, Socialist Discipline, and Soviet Power* (London: Tauris & Co, 1988), Chaps 3–4.

There is an older book on management structures and practices that remains a classic: J. S. Berliner, *Factory and Manager in the USSR* (Cambridge, Mass.: Harvard University Press, 1957).

A succinct evaluation of the economic achievements of the industrialization campaign is in S. G. Wheatcroft, R. W. Davies, and J. M. Cooper, 'Soviet industrialization reconsidered: some preliminary conclusions about economic development between 1926 and 1941', *The Economic History Review*, Second Series, xxxix, 1986, no. 2, pp. 264–94. The standard economic history of the industrialization drive is gradually being provided by R. W. Davies, in his series of volumes on *The Industrialisation of Soviet Russia* (London: Macmillan).

Finally, of the memoir material available in English two books in particular provide good insider information relevant to the themes of this chapter: J. Scott, *Behind the Urals* (Bloomington, Ind.: Indiana University Press, 1973) is by an American who spent a number of years as a worker in Magnitogorsk; and V. Kravchenko, *I Chose Freedom: The Personal and Political Life of a Soviet Official* (London: Readers' Union and Hale, 1949) is by one of the Stalinist generation of industrial managers who rose up the hierarchy during the 1930s before defecting to the West.

8

Stalinism and Society, 1929–53

From his fiftieth birthday in 1929, when newspaper editorials proclaimed that unswerving loyalty to him was a necessary condition of party discipline, until his death in March 1953, Stalin's autocratic rule over the Soviet empire equalled any tsar's in Russian history. He was feared, adulated, and deified. From the mid-1930s, it was customary for newspapers to print *STALIN* in italicized, all-capital letters, as if to make sure that print fonts do not put a sacred concept on a level with profane realities. Cracking a joke about him could be enough for a one-way ticket to a prison camp. The dominance of his 'personality cult', as the phenomenon would be called later, over the symbols and messages of public life assumed truly bizarre dimensions. History was rewritten in its service while other Bolshevik politicians who might have had a claim to a place in the pantheon of revolutionary mythology were redefined into villains, expunged from the pictures which had shown them by Lenin's side, and hounded to ignominious deaths. During and after the war, the countless stories of wartime patriotism put out by the culture industry were not complete without a hero going to his death with the Leader's name on his lips.

It is impossible to make a quantitative assessment of how the public devotions shaped individuals' private opinions. Eye-witness reports from the forced-labour camps tell of prisoners who exempted the autocrat from personal blame for their misfortune, in a manner reminiscent of old peasant folklore in which the tsar was always good though some of his minions were bad. But they also tell of prisoners who greeted the news of the dictator's death by throwing their hats towards the sky in exuberant joy. As for the majority of civilians and war veterans who were not in the camps, their feelings were a mixture of relief and a sense of loss.

The crowds the funeral procession in central Moscow drew were so large that over a hundred people were crushed to death. The war with Germany (June 1941–May 1945) had been fought against an invader whose victory plans had spelt extinction or slavery to the Slavic and non-ayrian races of the Soviet Union, and Stalin had emerged from it widely accepted as the architect of successful patriotic self-defence. At the early stages of the war, however, when the Wehrmacht was making fast progress towards Moscow, popular disaffection with the Soviet regime and civil disobedience had been in evidence both in the capital city and in the industrial regions (including Ivanovo again) where workers protested against evacuation to eastern parts of the country.

The historic era that passed with the forming of a clot on the dictator's brain was one of mass mobilization in the name of social progress and the defence of the state. The collectivization assault on the 'petty bourgeois' peasantry and the industralization campaign were the first mass mobilizations. Then came the mobilizations of the war: industrial plants, their workers, and some of the civilian population were transferred from the western territories to the Urals and beyond – up to 25 million people were involved in these eastward movements, while 30 million were called to the army during 1939–45, as military strategy was of the sort that cost dear in troops' lives. The civilian populations of several large cities had to be hastily mobilized to build fortifications. Industry, one-half of whose total wartime output was for direct military use, was in a constant need of mobilizing labour for round-the-clock exertions to keep supplies to the fronts going. The labour mobilization had to continue after the war to rebuild the cities, industries, and infrastructure that had been reduced to rubble by military bombardments and scorched-earth retreats. In 1940, leaving employment against the management's wishes became an offence punishable by several months in a labour camp. During the war, the sentences were lengthened to up to eight years and the population often found itself under virtual martial law.

The Stalin era was one of brutal repressions and large-scale deportations to prison camps and exile settlements. After the terror campaigns against the 'bourgeois specialists' (1928–31), the peasantry (1929–33), and the political-administrative, managerial and military officer corps (1936–8) came the campaigns against other categories of the population that were suspected of disloyalty. The intellectual élites of the Polish and Baltic nations were purged after the annexation of their lands to the Soviet Union in 1940. The Volga Germans were deported *en masse* to Kazakhstan and central Asia in 1941, the Crimean Tartars and other ethnic groups from Crimea and the north Caucasus in 1943–5. Other populations that had spent time living under German occupation during the war were subjected to mass screening in special filtration camps from where those unable to dispel suspicions of collaboration were dispatched to prison camps and eastern exile settlements. Ethnic non-Russians again bore the brunt of these policies, concentrated as they had been in the territories held by the Wehrmacht during 1941–4. Many Ukrainians were caught on the wrong side of the loyalty tests in the post-war filtration camps, as some of them had greeted the invading Germans as liberators from the state that had subjected them to the famine of 1932–3. This motive for collaboration had also been evident in the north Caucasus, where the policy of the German Army had been to take advantage of it, in contrast to the German occupation regimes in the Ukraine. Poles and the Baltic nationalities continued to be treated as suspect groups after the war, along with the inhabitants of the other annexed lands, Moldova and Bukovina. In addition, most Soviet troops who had been taken prisoner by the Germans and survived were deported to Siberian prison camps in 1945–6. At the same time, the range of the ethnic categories subjected to xenophobic vigilance was extended to include Jews. Just before Stalin's death, a group of prominent doctors with Jewish names were charged with plotting medical murders of party leaders.

The language in which the indictment were publicized indicated that a wave of purges reminiscent of 1936–8 might be about to gather momentum.

The 'Totalitarian State' Thesis and its Revisions

The activities of Stalin's state, then, were largely defined by mobilizing people: in the physical sense of moving them about in large organized numbers from their homes to construction projects, to the army, or to eastern hinterlands as evacuees, deportees, or prisoners; and in the social sense of seeking to change their behaviourial patterns by a mixture of coercion, manipulation, and propaganda aimed at integrating disparate masses into a singular movement against the enemy – the capitalist powers abroad, 'the wreckers' at home, and the ideologically unsound instincts in the soul. 'A mobilization regime' is thus one of the labels under which the activities, structure, and ideology of the Soviet state have been summarized by Western political scientists, and Stalin's period in power was the one during which the regime was particularly true to its type.

Another label that has been widely used is 'the totalitarian state' because the mass-mobilization ideology envisaged societies as systemic totalities and the function of communist political organization as no less than the transformation of one social totality into another. The state thus sought to substitute its own organizations and controls for all social institutions, and its own claims on personal loyalties and morals for all social bonds. It was a telling phenomenon of the 1930s that a number of Stalin's colleagues in the top offices of the party and the state apparently concurred with having their close relatives sent to concentration camps for alleged political misdemeanours, and that literary fiction created a much celebrated hero in Pavka Morozov, a country child who denounced his kulak father and fell victim to his relatives' revenge. The state used terror and propaganda to guarantee its monopoly of the public sphere of life and, at the same time, to extend this sphere into the spaces previously regarded as personal, private, or apolitical. What Lenin had started by the Red Terror campaign during the civil war, which destroyed the nuclei of a civil society, Stalin completed by his terror campaigns, which destroyed the peasant commune and any remaining sense of personal inviolability among the urban population as well – the state's own officials included. The appropriation of the individual, communities, and society by the organized powers of a political dictatorship thus became total, argues the 'totalitarian state' thesis, and that was the main difference that separated the communist dictatorship from other kinds of authoritarian state, including the tsarist autocracy.

Unlike the 'mobilization regime' label, which has an easily demonstrable and direct relationship with the empirical realities of the Stalin era, the 'totalitarian state' is more like one of Max Weber's sociological 'ideal types' where the logical coherence of its generalizations is tidier than historical realities can ever be. The justification of such analytical models is that they afford an orderly and illuminating comparisons with empirical realities, but the danger in them is that their closed logic makes them into suggestive substitutes for the latter, turning attention away from the elements that do not fit easily. The cult of the leader, the one-party state with its mass organizations, the comprehensive ideology masquerading as an invincible science, its disdain for 'petty bourgeois' notions of individual inviolability, the centrally controlled use of mass propaganda, the intolerant rhetoric of a state under siege from all-comer enemies and, above all, the ubiquitous state security police with its means of mass terror – all these phenomena fit together as a neat singular package in the theory of the 'totalitarian state'. It is a package representing a nightmarish logical opposite to the ideals of individualistic humanism and democratic polity, a state behemoth reducing nations into atomized 'masses' and ruling them by fear, for its leader's absolute-power ends and in the name of a communalist utopia.

In one way of reading it, the 'totalitarian state' theory spells an end to social history. If the state substituted its own organizational controls for all social relations, there were no autonomous social movements or trends in patterns of social interaction for a history to describe. There was only the state left as a historical subject – in particular its repressive actions against the population, the will-to-power machinations of the leader and his lieutenants, and occasionally perhaps the heroic stand of political dissenters. But this extreme reading of the 'totalitarian state' theory relies on an acceptance of three assumptions. First, that the state actually did succeed in putting all social life under its control. Secondly, that it remained itself a monolithic, single-mind, and co-ordinated-body sort of power structure while extending the scope of its controls. And thirdly, that it controlled its population so effectively that the outcomes of its policies corresponded closely to the policy intentions. The discussion of the industrialization campaign in Chapter 7, however, shows that none of these three assumptions was entirely true. The state did not succeed in putting industrial relations under its control, for example, and as for labour migration, until 1940 it stopped short of even trying to control it, in that it did not take the rights of movement between jobs from workers, although labour turnover was always perceived as a serious problem. In putting the economy under its command, the state became a complex bureaucracy in which the unison acclamations of 'the general line' disguised conflicts over interpretation of what it meant in practice: deal-making, struggles for scarce resources, the making of self-protective alliances, and the varied collusive arts of bureau-cratic politicking in general. And the policies whose outcomes turned out to be different from the intentions were legion – labour productivity rose slower than wages, for example, and the factory floor culture that emerged was not the 'production culture' that was intended, etc.

In fact, far from succeeding in breaking down the boundaries between public and private lives, the state unintentionally encouraged their renewal. Cer-tainly, the great majority of individuals became exposed to the rhetoric of public life, and well advised to master the language. But they lived in situations in which they could not help knowing that things were otherwise: where there was said to be a plan, chaos was the experience; when a grand public achievement was celebrated, a new tractor factory, for example, the know-ledge intruded of dispatch yards full of rusting products sitting on wheel-less axles; when the government issued a new decree, the smart executive knew that the thing to do was to consult the grapevine, or just wait and see, before taking it literally; when a new state shop was opened, the consumer soon learnt that this was not necessarily the place where the goods could be bought; when a newsreel showed collective farmers in joyous harvest-gathering, many a viewer must have remembered different news from a desperate country relative; when a newspaper published a picture of a socialist building-site busy at work, many a reader had cause to wonder if this was where a prisoner relative might be. The situations in which individuals lived were hardly conducive to an unvaried, naive hearing of public messages. They encouraged individuals to become fine judges of when they needed to speak the language of public life and espouse official truths as if they were their own; and to value the making of personal contacts, the process of self-integration into networks of acquaintances, allies, and friends, in which language could be inflected to serve differentiated, more individual understandings and ends. The police terror tried to protect the state interests by breaking private loyalties. But it could never be entirely successful because the state was a large and complicated bureaucracy in which the pulling of strings, the making of collusive nods and winks, exchanging favours, and the proferring of 'can I speak frankly to you' moments were integral to how things worked – for the public goals as well as for individual satisfactions.

It is possible for the 'totalitarian state' theory to accommodate these observations. But once it is accepted that the state was not monolithic in its practices of policy implementation, that it struggled to control the population with only a mixed success, and that its policies were replete with unintended effects, then the history of the Stalin era is no longer adequately represented by the study of the political dictatorship, its ideology, and power apparatus alone. This is the plank of the 'revisionist' historians of Stalinism, who advocate the study of 'from below' pressures on the dictatorship, and the ways in which political rule relied not on terror and ideological dogma alone but also on processes which involved an element of pragmatic solicitation of support from various sections of the population. There is a place for a 'social history' of the Stalin era after all, argue the 'revisionists'; the population was differentiated in its patterns of experience and in its preoccupations, and 'social conditions' – both the phenomena bequeathed by the past and those created as an unintended consequence of regime policies – limited and shaped the exertions of political power. In this respects, the Stalinist state was not altogether unlike any other. It had to interact with its society. Admittedly, 'society' no longer existed as the *obshchestvo* of the late tsarist times, as social movements and organizations existing outside of the state bureaucracy and presenting an articulate public counterpart to it; it was not a 'civil society'. But there were patterns and trends of social life outside the offices of the state, and inside as well, in the habits of mind and the customary practices brought in from the outside, and also those grown as inside adaptations to bureaucratic controls and performance indicators.

The revisionist project of focusing on the interactions between the state and society implies a relationship which was not simply one of oppressor and victim. The people, it implies, may have good reasons to fear the repressive machinery of the state, but the fear did not stop them from participating in the public as well as private spheres of life as individuals with their own interests; and their perceptions of the various acts of the state encompassed the whole range, including approval, just as their individual encounters with the authorities varied in how agreeable they were. This kind of imagery of the state–society interchange has provoked much wrath from some advocates of the 'totalitarian' version of the Stalin era. It sanitizes the Stalinist regime, the anti-revisionists argue, by highlighting the 'trivial' elements of everyday life and government social policy at the expense of what was its truly unique feature – the atrocities committed on countless innocent citizens, and the crippling damage done to a nation that was robbed of liberal freedoms and endowed instead with the GULAG (Chief Directorate of Camps), the system of forced-labour camps, colonies, and exile settlements under secret-police administration. To this the 'social historians' may retort that understanding how people lived with the regime that committed the atrocities is an important part of inquiry into what made the atrocities possible, which in itself neither trivializes what happened nor denies Stalin's responsibility for the regime's policies.

There is in fact some common ground between the totalitarian and revisionist approaches to the Stalin era. First, the totalitarian model can be qualified to relax somewhat the assumptions that were mentioned above as empirically dubious in their extreme form, and to acknowledge that the regime did not control everything even if it wanted to. It was the intention to control, and the apparatus for it, that defined the character of the state as 'totalitarian', not the accomplishment of a complete control. And secondly, one of the principal formulators of the totalitarian thesis, Hannah Arendt, herself pointed out that totalitarianism thrives in chaotic social conditions. When social expectations are in flux and the mode of living tends towards anarchy, the ideologically motivated state can fill an organizational vacuum with its own apparatus of control and its leader cult. And social uprooting, migration, rapid social mobility, and the prevalence of situations to which everyone was new, was indeed a major characteristic of civilian life throughout the 1930s, a compelling starting point for any empirical investigation of social conditions.

Social Conditions in the Towns

We saw in the last chapter that the expansion of urban-sector employment and migration from villages to construction projects and to towns exceeded the intentions of the first five-year plan, amounting to a shocking migration rate in 1930–1. The trains were crowded with people with one-way tickets, and railway stations with arrivees staying there among the few possessions they could carry until they found their first employer and another overcrowded temporary accommodation. Migration continued after the initial deluge at a high rate throughout the decade. Russia's cities had always been largely occupied by migrants, but the patterns of movement tended to be set by traditional links between employers and villages. This was until the 1920s when, for the first time, it was typical for migrants to bring their families into the towns for permanent residence. The 1930s migrants also came to the towns with the intention of settling permanently, but the deluge created a housing crisis on an unprecedented scale, condemning the vast majority to periods of time in makeshift and extremely overcrowded accommodation that made family life virtually impossible. Success in settling down, finding a combination of employer and housing which was conducive to staying put, could take a very long time of 'flitting' – wandering from one employer to the next on the basis of hearsay about better chances.

This was not an administratively controlled migration. The big cities as well as the numerous new industrial frontier settlements were full of people on the run from something or after something. In 1932–3, the issue of passports to urban residents (with the associated screening of the population for 'anti-social elements' to be expelled from the cities in a vulnerable passportless state) was hurried, because of fear that the urban food-rationing system might collapse if the city populations were not reduced or at least kept from increasing while the famine lasted. But the cities and the new urban settlements also needed a system of personal identification for the citizenry because of mundane law-and-order problems. Crime was rife. Some factories had to adopt special measures to enable their workers to reach their homes on paydays before dark. Reports in the trade-union press told of certain housing estates being veritable ganglands into which the militia (the regular police force) would only dare go when an inert body had to be collected. At the non-violent end of the crime scale were numerous cases of workers disappearing into the mass of 'flitters' the moment they received a works' issue of boots or safety clothing, or after they managed to steal something. Petty offenders often found it easy to escape justice even if they were caught in the first place. They tended to be sentenced by 'people's courts' to terms of 'corrective labour', either at their place of work (which in practice meant the docking of a quarter of their wages) or in forced-labour colonies (a different regime from the GULAG labour camps) if they did not have a steady job. In 1932, however, a survey of 6000 such sentences pronounced by the Moscow courts found that only 2273 were being served, as the rest of the offenders had left fictitious names and addresses behind when released from police custody. By that time, the Moscow 'bureau of forced labour', the body responsible for administering the sentences in the city, had 6600 names on its evasive persons' list.[1]

The fact that, in 1933, the non-agricultural population supposedly became passport bearers with officially registered places of residence was clearly a step forward in the state's efforts to put its mobile citizenry under administrative tabs. But it did not limit the adoption of fictitious identities to individuals in the seriously criminal fraternity. False and stolen passports were available through the *blat* networks, along with party cards, trade-union cards, ration coupons, and residence warrants.

Blat was the generic name for the all-pervasive activities whereby people met their needs through unofficial channels. Personal documents of dubious origin were but a small part of the goods and services that were traded or exchanged *po blatu*. Black-market trading and the corruption of officials by straightforward bribery was a part of what *blat* was about, but a much larger part was made up of the myriad ways in which people cultivated and used personal connections to circumvent bureaucratic controls over scarce resources. Involvement in *blat* was a necessity for almost everyone and almost a sport for some. A sturdy pair of shoes, a meal in a restricted-access canteen, a

---

1 Andrle, V. 1988: *Workers in Stalin's Russia*. Hemel Hempstead: Harvester-Wheatsheaf, p. 60.

holiday in a sanatorium, a place on a higher education course, a joyride in an official limousine, a jump forward in a housing queue – everything that was obtainable under administrative auspices was also obtainable, and generally believed to be often obtained, by the manipulation of personal connections. It is difficult for a person who had some kind of official authority or a physical access to a scarce resource to refuse personal consideration of friends and acquaintances. To refuse to be *blatnyi* carried the risk of social ostracism or indeed victimization in a world in which playing only by the official rules was seldom a practical proposition. The patterns of rule-bending connivance described as part of work relations in the last chapter spilled over to blend with the patterns of social life outside work. Who was anonymously denounced to the authorities for breaking some rule of discipline or official propriety? Often someone who had made an enemy by refusing to give a personal consideration. The belief that the world moved by personal string-pulling was widespread, and the incentives to try it strong, as were the incentives to exaggerate to one's friends and acquaintances the extent and fixing powers of one's connections. *Blat* was a prominent, inescapable aspect of social life under the auspices of the all-administering state. For the immigrant, the process of settling down in a new locale was as much about becoming a part of a network of useful contacts as about becoming a new entry in official files as an employee, a resident, and a member of edifying 'social organizations'.

That social life included unofficial circulations of goods and services, and searches for personal string-pulling opportunities was not in itself remarkable – a successful substitution for it of a smoothly functioning and truly impersonal, uncorrupt bureaucracy would have been much more remarkable. More peculiar was the fact that there was a single and widely used name, *blat*, to cover the whole range of unofficial dealings, from clear-cut crime at one extreme to an innocuously mundane efforts to meet one's needs and wants at the other. The word had a connotation of illegitimacy, but comments on it in everyday conversations reflected a general recognition of a phenomenon that few individuals could claim to manage to avoid. A popular saying such as *blat vyshe Stalina* ('*blat* is higher than Stalin') could be understood in a spirit of regret, that one would rather have had one's needs met on the basis of entitlement, without having to scrape and hustle. It could be also understood as a humorous spirit of anarchic welcome to the fact that hierarchical authority was no match to its subjects' wits. An element of hypocrisy was common in the comments on *blat*, where one's own involvement and the actions of friends were judged differently from those of strangers and enemies.

The belief that the world moved by personal connections, string-pulling, and cliquish fixing meant that the individual was liable to perceive his or her own hardships as the result of corrupt others' actions. A shop assistant who said that there was no bread left was often suspected of keeping some under the counter for someone else, and this kind of suspicion attached to anyone who could not be trusted on a personal basis and who said '*niet*'. Official anti-corruption drives and purges, therefore, could be quite popular. The trade unions apparently had no shortage of voluntary helpers when they organized workers' brigades of spot-check inspectors of retail outlets, and purge commissions as well as the whole range of other authorities had no shortage of letters, usually anonymous ones, naming individuals who should be investigated. Draconian laws, such as the famine-time August 1932 decree under which many a baker, canteen cook, and shop assistant were sentenced to long years in the camps on the evidence of no more than petty theft from food stocks, could be deemed appropriate by many who believed their hunger was in part caused by venal food-handlers. A general centralization and streamlining of authority would be craved, for example, by the family who had to defend its corner of an apartment from a group of invading youths who claimed their right of residence by waving a warrant signed by an obliging *komsomol* official; the family had to hold fort physically until the wife managed to persuade the director of the factory in which she worked to intervene. A state power that purged, punished, and centralized could be applauded and abetted by people who felt themselves vulnerable to anarchy. A state official would be perceived as good when he helped someone and bad when he did not. And the conspiracy theories, in which the prosecutors framed the defendants as well as world politics at the political show trials, could seem plausible to people who perceived their own world as given to cliquish struggles.

Social dislocation, imperfect bureaucracy, law-and-order problems, the differentiation of the private from the public spheres of life, the *blat*, and the belief in personal patronage, corruption, and conspiracies both fed and thwarted the Stalinist political regime. Poverty was another inescapable fact of life. City apartments were bursting at the seams, with families who were strangers to one another sharing rooms, and with additional tenants occupying floor space in the kitchens and corridors. More people than ever lived in hastily erected, bug-ridden barrack dormitories, while some of the construction-site workers had to live in flimsily roofed dug-outs. Some workers had to work barefoot where sturdy boots were prescribed by the safety rules; some had no clothes to change into when they clocked out of hot and dirty factory floors or muddy building sites. Many people had to make ends meet by holding casual labouring jobs on top of their normal ones – 16 per cent of the total money paid out by state enterprises in wages was officially accounted as paid out to moonlighters in 1936, evidently a smaller proportion than in earlier years.[2] City residents kept poultry and rabbits or tilled city-edge vegetable allotments to supplement their diet. Rickets and other diseases of poverty were common, and epidemics of infectious disease raged through the housing squalor. To their credit, factory trade unions operated relief funds to alleviate the worst cases of hardship among their members, on which they spent much more of their funds than on special additional rewards to élite workers, even during the Stakhanovite-time anti-levelling campaigns. But it was the relatively privileged part of the population that worked in places where there was a trade union with a sizeable relief fund to dispense. Real wages were rising and basic necessities were becoming less scarce from 1934 until the war, but the improvements were not quick enough to remove the general population from the precarious margins of subsistence before the war inflicted extreme hardships again. Housing construction only began to enlarge the average per capita floor space slightly (the average was equivalent to a narrow bed with one

2 Andrle, *Workers*, p. 45.

or two small bits of furniture right next to it) during the last pre-war years, under the third five-year plan.

The general observation that living standards were low does not necessarily imply a mass disaffection with the state on the part of the urban population. Such connections between economics and attitudes depend on the perceptions of causes of poverty and the prospects for improvement. At the beginning of the industrialization campaign, many people were willing to accept some belt-tightening as a price worth paying for a modernizing investment. Besides, the decline of the average real wage during the first five-year plan did not necessarily mean that the majority of individuals in the urban-industrial sector felt it personally. The worst hardships tended to be suffered by new immigrants, while the relatively longer-settled workers made their personal climbs up the wage scales. The famine years of 1932–3 were the crisis ones, as they came after the initial enthusiasm about the industrialization had worn out. They inflicted acute survival problems on almost everyone. It was the failures of the authorities to honour bread rations that caused the most serious disturbances, and the authorities' fear that the situation might get out of hand among the working class goes a long way to explaining the ruthlessness with which famine relief was denied to the peasantry. The improvements in living standards after the famine years gave grounds for optimism among the urban population, whom the party leaders encouraged further by the publicity surrounding 'the care for cadres' slogan and the Stakhanovite consumer-spending sprees. The latter half of the 1930s, we shall see, was also a period when the authorities took additional measures to encourage the sense that puritan revolutionary austerity no longer had to be the sum of legitimate individual aspirations. The war hardships were endured by the population as a necessity, often with patriotic pride, while the war victory could do no harm to the optimism with which the population set about the business of post-war reconstruction.

Social-Stability Concerns and Ideological Modifications

After the famine years, the propaganda themes and various socio-cultural policies were modified, with an eye to popular appeal. The cinema is a good example of this. In 1940, the average man, women, and infant in the Soviet Union visited a cinema five times as a paying customer.[3] The industry had grown to become a major provider of popular entertainment in the 1920s, but its offerings were divided between avant-garde productions with strongly ideological themes that not many people paid to watch, and commercial productions, both foreign and home-made, that had few edifying pretentions. This duality ended with the 'left turn', when a single state monopoly was established. This had the injunction to produce films that would serve the

---

3 Thurston, R. W. 1991: 'Social dimensions of Stalinist rule: humour and terror in the USSR, 1935–1941'. *Journal of Social History*, xxiv, no. 3, p. 551. Thurston cites the amount of tickets sold as one billion.

propaganda aims by being accessible and entertaining to mass audiences. Thus 'socialist realism' emerged as the ruling doctrine. In the cinema, the doctrine turned out to mean not simply a limitation of subject matter to ideologically correct themes, although films were duly produced about happy collective farmers and optimistic worker heroes: above all, it put an end to modernist experiments with plotless image montage and impersonal Taylorist method-acting. Instead, it concentrated its resources on films with strong story lines and character development using professional actors. Films about the civil war became a popular genre reminiscent of the Hollywood westerns, but the repertoire of box-office hits also included musicals, comedies, and fairytales. 'Socialist realism', in other words, meant the adoption of classical narrative forms with unambiguous content and morals. The requirement was that the message should be optimistic and supportive of approved social aims, but that it should be conveyed through characters with whom many cinema-goers could identify. The comedies also provided characters the audience loved to see lampooned, including stuck-up local bureaucrats and compulsive denouncers.

Sport was another example of the ways in which ideological searches for a specifically socialist form of mass edification were suspended in the interests of popular appeal. In the 1920s, sports organizations had tended to favour non-competitive physical education and participation in favour of watching. In the 1930s, however, huge stadiums were built in the cities (the one in Leningrad accommodating 150 000 spectators), and the whole range of sports previously regarded as 'bourgeois' were organized in clubs and competitive leagues at all levels, creating a large participation base, a professional élite of sports stars, and a major form of spectator entertainment. The range of spectator sports even included horse-racing with gambling facilities. In practice, sport was developed in ways that were not altogether unlike the developments that had taken place in Western countries during their industrializations, replacing older forms of popular entertainment, such as gambling on fist fights in taverns, with organized activities that had standard rules, that offered a ladder of recognized achievement, that channelled energies into a disciplined self-improvement, and that created appreciative audiences who could award fame.

There were also ways in which the policies of the latter half of the 1930s expressed their concerns for creating a settled, urban society. We noted in the last chapter that the publicity surrounding the Stakhanovite movement included the celebration of consumer goods, nice clothes, and comfortably furnished self-contained apartments, as the artefacts of modern cultured living achievable by cultured working. In May 1936, the concern for cultured living received new impetus when Stalin, Ordzhonikidze, and other luminaries attended a conference of the wives of senior managers in heavy industry. The wives, it transpired, had a special role: they should lead a voluntary social movement for cultured living because they were 'developed' people who were already imbued with it, and because they were in a position to persuade their husbands to secure the necessary resources and co-operation from the factories. They could organize the tidying of public places, the provision of clean metal cutlery and tablecloths in works' canteens, the planting of trees, they could create clean washrooms with mirrors and soap, visit problem families, organize courses for women workers to teach them how to keep nice homes, and a whole host of other activities that a pre-revolutionary generation of professional men's wives might have thought of in the course of their voluntary work to help improve living standards. A special magazine was published to support this female social activism from that year until the outbreak of the war, alongside with the magazines published for women workers and women peasants. Cultured living (*kul'turnyi byt*), in other words, re-emerged under the auspices of the Stalinist state as an image of middle-class urban life for the 'backward' immigrant masses to aspire to.

The fact that a conference of *wives* was convened in the Kremlin was something of an aberration. By 1939, less than a quarter of adult working-age women were still outside the official employment sector, and the dominant ideology regarded women who were not employed as socially unprogressive. Some of the women at the conference, however, were clearly housewives – after all, their men were of the small privileged minority whose incomes were large enough to sustain a whole family in comfort – and those who were employed were considered, by implication, as having less time-consuming jobs than their husbands. The conference, however, coincided with the adoption of pro-family social policies, which was prompted in part by alarm about the scale of law-and-order problems, but in particular by falling birth rates. The average rural family had by now 4.3 members and the average urban family 3.6 members. Two-thirds of all families had four or fewer members.[4] The very liberal procedures for divorce that had been in force since the early 1920s were revised. A fee now had to be paid for a divorce, and divorcee status was recorded in passports. Evading alimony payments was also made more difficult, and abortion was outlawed. The party leaders looked to the family as a positive social institution worthy of support – contrary to the earlier Bolshevik tendency to view it as a private enclave that discouraged people from devoted work for public causes. The *Pavlik Morozov* story received a new twist when it was retold in later editions: the father who was denounced by his son to the authorities, was no longer defined primarily as a member of the kulak class but as a morally degenerate drunkard and a bad family man. With the rehabilitation of family values came a partial rehabilitation of traditional conceptions of gender differences and roles. In the publicity surrounding the industrialists' wives gathering, women were presented as having a positive social role to play by applying their supposed feminine qualities of caring for personal morals, communal uplift, and harmonious homes. The creation of a new cult of motherhood soon followed. Patriotic posters adopted the image of a woman with a baby in her protective arms as the symbol of the motherland that had to be defended from foreign enemies, and women who gave birth to large families became publicized recipients of state honours.

The propaganda upgrading of family life, wifely supportiveness, and devoted motherhood should not be taken as evidence of a clear-cut U-turn from mobilization militancy to social conservatism. The women who received medals for producing many babies were just one of the many kinds of people to whose chests the state pinned medals. Alongside them were the increasing numbers of women who were receiving their medals for the same reasons as

4 Thurston, R. W. 1991: 'The Soviet family during the Greaet Terror, 1935–1941'. *Soviet Studies*, xliii, no. 3, p. 554.

male achievers: because they were highly productive workers, devoted social activists, or top performers in the arts and sports. The expectation that women should work, strive for excellence in their jobs, further their education, and take a full part in public life was not relaxed. Women who had to tame or divorce traditionalist husbands in their bid to take a full part in public life were just as often celebrated in the propaganda as the women achievers who delighted the journalists by showing them that they also managed to keep their homes and children. State institutions sponsored a women's soccer league as well as women's magazines with crotchet patterns and child-care hints, and the propaganda about cultured living was mixed in with sarcastic attacks on people who cared about their living (*byt*) more than about their contribution to the public good. The propaganda messages were becoming more complex and contradictory as the party leaders' worries came to encompass social stability as well as political mobilization.

The proliferation of state honours and fame-making publicity that was heaped on achievers, from fertile mothers to super-athletes and arctic-flying pilots, was an extention of the anti-levelling philosophy the Stalinist regime favoured from 1931 onwards. From the end of the 1930s until the end of Stalin's rule, officially quantifiable inequalities in earnings stretched to higher ratios than ever before or since. Occupational wage-scales lengthened, and the differentials between priority sectors and the rest increased, as did the differentials between professional and manual jobs. The individuals who received state honours for their achievements often as not also received large cash awards and self-contained apartments. The new social élite were often people who rose high quickly from humble origins, a fact the publicity never failed to highlight. The anti-levelling state created long ladders with many rungs on offer to individuals who wanted to climb. The purges, of course, added snakes to the ladders, and climbing to the heavens without sliding to the pits required shrewdness and luck in the use of political patronage. But meritocracy became the name of the game, and the acquisition of academic qualifications and measurable achievement records were an important part of many a successful climb. The heroic publicity given to award-winning individuals also fitted with the promotion of the personality cult. Heroes and heroines were made in many walks of life, to serve as role-models whom many others could aspire to follow; and the role-models never omitted to put on record that Stalin was their hero.

The meritocratic invitations to upward social mobility did not mean that the criteria of merit were free of political ties. We saw in the last chapter that Stakhanovite heroes were made as much by factory floor politicking as by the energetic ambitions of the rate-busters themselves, and that plan-fulfilment records could never be accepted as objective criteria of managers' perform-ances. The institutional ranks in the non-industrial spheres were no more purely meritocratic than the industry could be purely technocratic. In science and academia, for example, the principles of meritorious hierarchy were restored in the mid-1930s in so far as courses were lengthened and the academic content of the curricula strengthened. Professorial authority over students and the junior faculty was re-established, and the students' progress from course entry to graduation was determined by examinations. The Academy of Sciences was re-established as an élite institution with hierarchical ranks reminiscent of the prerevolutionary academy. Some of its luminaries who were lionized by Stalin as national heroes were indeed professors who had already belonged to the scientific élite in the tsarist state, and who never bothered to acquire any ideological credentials (e.g., the psychologist Pavlov). But it was a Stalinist bureaucracy nevertheless. Scientific disputes were allowed to continue only as long as no side succeeded in obtaining political backing by declaring its own theory as the truth, and for monopolizing the research resources and publication rights. In some disciplines the infighting was bitter to the end. In biology, for example, genetics was defeated for generations. Its principal professorial opponent, Lysenko, persuaded Stalin that all the resources should back his theory because this was more in tune with historical materialism and it also promised rich rewards in the form of environmentally adaptive agricultural crops. In the post-war period, Stalin himself sorted out the fields of linguistics and political economy by publishing pamphlets on the subjects under his own name.

The creation of a radiant social élite of loyal achievers on a hierarchical servitor-state basis was buttressed by nationalist as well as socialist rhetoric. The Stakhanovite worker stars were celebrated for their contribution to socialist construction and also for putting their country on a supposed world map of production records. The Soviet radio listener, of course, did not know that, when a newscaster broke into the airwaves with the triumphant announcement that, say, a Soviet miner had broken a world coal-digging record previously held by a German miner, there really was no German public hearing the news on their radios, or indeed no world audience that cared, and no world-shared record book of this kind. But the implication that there was a world audience to take note of new world records achieved by Soviet workers enhanced the pangs of national pride such news could induce. Soviet athletes, too, were in the news from time to time for breaking world records, although they were still outside the international framework of official record-keepers. The arctic explorer heroes were making an entry into a field contested by several foreign powers, and no Soviet citizen would miss their triumphant return. Soviet mountaineers scaled peaks previously untouched by human foot – ones as high and difficult as any that the best foreign mountaineers had adorned with their national flags. The achiever stars were part of a new nation-building process.

Another part of this process was the way in which the galaxy of stars celebrated in the media was extended to include Russian historical figures. The centenary of the poet Pushkin in 1937 was commemorated not as a literary event but a veritable state occasion. In this respect the state perhaps only amplified the long-existing tendencies of the Russian intelligentsia to promote its nineteenth-century classical culture as an icon for patriotic worship (see Chapters 1 and 4). However, not only were the leading figures of Russian high culture and science now celebrated. Contrary to the traditions of the Russian intelligentsia, the state now celebrated some of the Russian princes, tsars, and military leaders who were involved in Russian wars from the thirteenth century until the triumph over Napoleon at the beginning of the nineteenth. During 1937–46, the film industry produced epics about Alexander Nevsky, Peter I, Ivan IV, and the generals, Kutuzov and Suvorov. The intensely anti-German wartime output of the culture industry also resuscitated the pan-Slav themes of the nineteenth-century Russian nationalism – the idea that the Russian state should have the mission of unifying the nationalist aspirations of all European Slavs from the Balkans to Poland. Another ideological shift by which the Stalinist state sought to rally its citizenry at the beginning of the war was a new agreement with the Orthodox Church. The Church was allowed to appoint its patriarch and to expand its activities as a legitimate institution in return for enjoining its believers to a wholehearted support of the war effort. The orthodoxy of official Marxism was shelved during the war.

Social Stratification

In 1936 the new state constitution that proclaimed the USSR to be socialist was introduced with a relaxation of the authorities' tendency (prominent since the revolution) to discriminate between individual citizens on the basis of their 'social origins'. The son of a kulak was not responsible for the sins of his father, proclaimed Stalin. The old classes were defeated and all citizens were expected to take part in the 'mass democracy' process by attending meetings about the new constitution. They were told that class exploitation was no more and everyone would be rewarded according to their contribution. There were now only two friendly classes in the official picture of society – the collectivized peasantry and the working class – and there was also 'a stratum', the intelligentsia and non-manual employees, who served society by their brains. Propaganda tended to portray the technology-wielding industrial worker and the professional engineer who had acquired his qualifications in the new era as the epitome of Soviet progress in the non-agricultural sector.

The industrialization campaign had changed the social structure, but not quite to the extent advertised by 'socialist realism'. In the USSR as a whole, the proportion of the population classified as resident in rural areas dropped from 82 per cent in 1926 to 67 per cent in 1939, and 57 per cent in 1953. The absolute number of urban residents more than doubled between the censuses of 1926 and 1939, while the number of people earning their livings in the non-agricultural sectors of the economy more than trebled; the number of rural residents, on the other hand, declined slightly, and the number of people of normal working age who were engaged in farming declined by a third. The manual workforce of large-scale manufacturing quadrupled, but in 1939 is still constituted less than half the 20 million manual workers in the non-agricultural sphere of 'material production'. When the fact that the factories in all probability employed as many auxiliary labourers for heaving materials about as machine operators for applying technological processes to them is taken into account, the great majority of the 'material production' jobs created by the industrialization campaign were of a labouring rather than machine-wielding kind. Moreover, the 'material production' occupations were not the only ones that had increased by the industrialization campaign. The numbers of 'junior service personnel' (ranging from doormen and watchmen to cleaners and cooks) grew just as quickly, reaching almost six million by 1939.[5] Thus for

---

5 Wheatcroft, S. G. 1982: 'Changes in the pattern of employment in the USSR, 1926–1939'. Unpublished paper presented at CREES, University of Birmingham, June.

every worker who epitomized progress by obtaining a technology-related job there were several more who joined a variety of occupations that had been known to the non-agricultural poor of earlier eras. The disparate nature of the new 'working class' was evident but understated in the official census data which, for example, recorded no domestic servants at all, although advertisements seeking and offering positions for live-in domestics were appearing in the local press at the time.

The 1939 census counted almost 12 million people in the 'intelligentsia and non-manual employees' category. This category, however, encompassed a very varied range – anything from party bosses to university professors, to telephonists to the grossly underpaid and generally abused shop assistants. Fewer than a million were higher education graduates, and just under a third of them were in an engineering speciality, although engineering courses were the fastest-growing type of higher education.[6] The production of a new, educated élite lagged behind the speed with which the industrialization campaign created jobs for specialists, managers, and administrators. For every graduate there were one or two *praktiki* (usually men), with no more than rudimentary educational qualifications who occupied posts that were thought to require a high standard of education. Many of the *praktiki* sought to enhance their credibility by enrolling on evening or correspondence courses. Evening study at all levels was a widespread phenomenon, among ambitious factory workers as well as among officials and white-collar employees. An urban society with a large component of Soviet-educated professionals, however, was still in the future.

The published statistical analyses of the 1939 census gave no information about the number of people held prisoner in forced-labour establishments. The size of this during the Stalin era has been subject to wide-ranging estimates in Western publications, based on various kinds of fragmentary data and extrapolation methods. Since the late 1980s, some historians have been granted access to previously closed archival records from which it is possible to calculate the number of people incarcerated in penal establishments by less speculative means. Uncertainties, however, remain because the records give rise to an element of confusion about the definition of the prisoner categories that were counted, and there is doubt they are accurate and comprehensive. They show that the number of people held in labour camps, labour colonies, and exile labour settlements rose from two million in 1935 to 2.6 million in 1939, and to over three million in 1941. During the war it decreased as almost a million male prisoners were drafted into the army; as a result, the proportion of women in the incarcerated convict population rose from seven per cent in 1941 to 26 per cent in 1944. After the war the ranks of forced labourers grew again, reaching 4.7 million by 1949. The figure of 2.6 million given for 1939 (the year of a general census) represents three per cent of the total employed population (and close to six per cent of the adult male population). These levels are substantially lower than the estimates made earlier by Western

---

6 Bailes, K. E. 1978: *Technology and Society under Lenin and Stalin: Origins of the Soviet Technical Intelligentsia, 1917–1941.* Princeton, NJ: Princeton University Press, p. 219.

situations may yet prove appropriate to revise them upwards as more historians gain access to further archival data.[7] However, given the fact that a percentage of the prisoners died every year and others came to the end of their sentences or escaped, the proportion of the total population passing through adulthood in the Stalin era that experienced arrest, deportation, and forced labour was much higher than the proportion of prisoners in the population total on census day.

Counting Those Who Did Not Survive

Counting the people who died prematurely during the Stalin era is even more hazardous than determining the size of the forced-labour system at any particular point of time, although more archival data is now becoming available relating to the census which was carried out but suppressed in 1937. This census evidently found the all-USSR population as totalling just over 162 million, which was over six million fewer than had been expected by the statisticians. The census of 1939, which stated the all-USSR population as being 170.6 million, exaggerated the total by between 1.8 and 3.3 million, presumably to mitigate the impression the campaigns of the 1930s had taken on the population. The detailed demographic data on the years between the censuses of 1926 and 1939 are as yet unknown, and they never will be complete because, as the statisticians acknowledged in the documents recently made public, the system of registering births and deaths broke down in the worst-hit areas during the 1932–3 famine. It is likewise doubtful that full documentation will ever be found concerning the 'dekulakized' peasants who failed to survive the unspeakable conditions in which they were transported to the exile settlements. A Russian historian estimates (on the basis of recently discovered archival documents – demographers' opinions put on record in 1937 and other pieces of evidence) that, by 1937, two million people (mainly central Asians during the collectivization campaign) fled across the borders, and 6.6 million people died as a result of the famine or imprisonment. By January 1939, the same historian (Tsaplin) concludes that the death toll rose to eight million. In the purge year of 1937, 353 074 people were shot by order of NKVD (People's Commissariat of Internal Affairs – succeeded OGPU as the institution charged with state-security police functions in 1934) special tribunals alone.[8] The figures for summary death sentences during the other frantic purge year, 1938, are still unknown. Tsaplin's figure of eight million victims during 1930–8 appears low in the light of other evidence – for example, a calculation that indicates that eight million more people died during the famine year 1933 than

---

7 For a more detailed and precise discussion of these statistics, see Bacon, E. 1992: 'Glasnost and the gulag: new information on Soviet forced labour around World War II'. *Soviet Studies*, xliv, no. 6.

8 Nove, A. 1990: 'How many victims in the 1930s?' *Soviet Studies*, xlii, no. 2, pp. 369–73.

in the year that followed,[9] which implies that the famine toll was substantially higher than the 5.1 million estimated by Tsaplin.

The majority of the millions who paid for the campaigns of the 1930s with their lives were ordinary peasants who were left to starve by drought-time grain-requisitioning, and 'dekulakized' peasants who died of hunger, cold, and maltreatment in captivity. Ukrainians bore a much heavier toll of the famine (and in all probability of dekulakization as well) than Russians. In 1933, more than half of all deaths that occurred in the USSR occurred in the Ukraine, where only a fifth of all Soviet citizens lived.[10] The nomadic tribes of Kazakhstan and the Cossacks, as well as the small ethnic groups resident in the steppes of European Russia's south-east and north Caucasus, likewise bore a disproportionately large death toll. There is little evidence as yet, however, that the deadly confrontations between the state and the peasantry correlated with ethnic differences as a matter of deliberate policy. The prejudices mobilized by the campaigning rhetoric of the early 1930s were class related rather than ethnic. It was only in 1945 that Stalin put on record his belief that the Russian nation had a leading role to play in the march of the Soviet peoples towards progress.

The war with Germany in 1941–5 exacted a massive casualty toll from Russians and non-Russians alike. About nine million soldiers died, perhaps half of them in German captivity, and 19 million civilians. Some of the civilians fell victim to bombs and atrocities, but the majority to hunger, cold, disease, and exhaustion. One million died in Leningrad alone (40 per cent of the city's eve-of-war population) while the city was under Wehrmacht siege in 1941–3. In the camps, one-fifth of the prisoners died in 1942, and another fifth in the following year. About a million Jews died in the German-occupied territories.[11] Overall the Soviet mortality rate was 24 per 1000 in the dark year of 1942, compared to 18 per 1000 in 1940 and nine per 1000 in 1945. The death rates were higher among the urban population than in rural areas.

The increase in the number of deportees and prisoners in 1946–53 certainly added further premature deaths to those inflicted in the 1930s and in wartime. Many of the new labour camps were set up to mine minerals in the most inhospitable regions of north-east Siberia and, as always, lack of food must have been particularly severe in the labour camps after a drought resulted in a poor harvest in 1947.

The census of 1959 shows the imprint of the war and the Stalin-era campaigns on the population's demographic profile. It found 56 per cent of the population to be under 30 years of age and, within this group (none of whose members had reached adulthood until after the war), the sex ratio was more or less balanced. But the war and the Stalin-era campaigns had been more life-threatening to males than females, thus accelerating markedly the natural tendency of male populations to decrease more quickly with age than female

---

9 Conquest, R. 1991: 'Excess deaths and camp numbers: some comments'. *Soviet Studies*, xliii, no. 5, pp. 949–52.

10 Nove, 'How many?', pp. 369–73.

11 Barber, J. and Harrison, M. 1991: *The Soviet Home Front 1941–1945: A Social and Economic History of the USSR in World War II*. London: Longman, pp. 41–2.

populations. The census found only 83 men for every 100 women in the 30–5 age-group, 64 men for every 100 women in the 35–9 age-group, and the ratio went down to 50 men per 100 women in the 55–9 age-group. The people who had lived through the Stalin era were a marked generation – those who mourned the dictator's passing as well as those who felt relief.

Further Reading

C. Ward, *Stalin's Russia* (London: Edward Arnold, 1992) is a slim and useful introduction to Stalinism and Russia in the 1930s. The literature which addresses 'Stalinism' as a political system and history is huge and widely listed in the many available textbooks on Soviet politics. The details and merits of the totalitarian model constitute a large part of its content. In this chapter I have made special reference to H. Arendt, *The Origins of Totalitarianism*, revised edition (New York: Harcourt, Brace, & World, 1966); this extensive work on political philosophy and historical observation was perhaps the first scholarly articulation of what Hitler's and Stalin's states brought to the twentieth century.

In the early post-war years, a group of Harvard sociologists carried out a large-scale questionnaire and interviews project with former Soviet citizens who found themselves in Western refugee camps after the war. The data are analysed in A. Inkeles and R. A. Bauer, *The Soviet Citizen: Daily Life in a Totalitarian Society* (Cambridge, Mass.: Harvard University Press, 1959) and R. A. Bauer, A. Inkeles and C. Kluckhohn, *How the Soviet System Works* (Cambridge, Mass.: Harvard University Press, 1956).

In the 1960s and 1970s, much of the debate among Anglo-American experts on the Soviet Union turned on the issue of continuity or discontinuity between the 1920s and 1930s. A useful compilation on this is R. C. Tucker (ed.), *Stalinism: Essays in Historical Interpretation* (New York: W. W. Norton, 1977). Also see M. Lewin, *The Making of the Soviet System: Essays in the Social History of Interwar Russia* (London: Methuen, 1985), Chaps 8–9 and 11–12.

A more recent polemic about the 'totalitarian', 'social-historical', and 'revisionist' approaches to the Stalin era can be tasted by reading the articles by S. Fitzpatrick, S. F. Cohen, G. Eley, P. Kenez, and A. G. Meyer in *Russian Review*, xlv, 1986), pp. 357–413. An interpretative analysis of the polemic is offered by V. Andrle, 'Demons and devil's advocates: problems in historical writing on the Stalin era', in N. Lampert and G. Rittersporn (eds), *Stalinism: Its Nature and Aftermath* (London: Macmillan, 1992), pp. 25–47.

In the Lampert and Rittersporn, *Stalinism*, three essays discuss or present alternative perspectives: M. Perrie, 'The tsar, the emperor, the leader: Ivan the Terrible, Peter the Great and Anatolii Rybakov's Stalin', pp. 77–100; G. T. Rittersporn, 'The omnipresent conspiracy: on Soviet imagery of politics and social relations in the 1930s', pp. 101–20; and H.-H. Schroeder, 'Urban social mobility and mass repression: Communist Party and Soviet society', pp. 157–83.

For examples of 'revisionist' renderings of politics and terror in the 1930s, see J. A. Getty, *Origins of the Great Purges: The Soviet Communist Party*

Reconsidered, 1933–1938 (Cambridge: Cambridge University Press, 1985); J. A. Getty, 'State and society under Stalin: constitutions and elections in the 1930s', *Slavic Review*, l, 1991, no. 1, pp. 18–35; G. T. Rittersporn, *Simplifications staliniennes et complications politiques* (Montreux: Gordon and Beach Science Publishers, 1988); G. T. Rittersporn, 'Soviet politics in the 1930s', *Studies in Comparative Communism*, 1986, no. 2; R. W. Thurston, 'Fear and belief in the USSR's "Great Terror": response to arrest, 1935–1939', *Slavic Review*, xlv, 1986, no. 2, pp. 213–34; R. W. Thurston, 'The Soviet family during the "Great Terror", 1935–1941', *Soviet Studies*, xliii, 1991, no. 3, pp. 553–74; R. W. Thurston, 'Social dimensions of Stalinist rule: humour and terror in the USSR, 1935–1941', *Journal of Social History*, xxiv, 1991, no. 3, pp. 541–62; and R. T. Manning, 'Government in the Soviet countryside the Stalinist thirties: the case of the Belyi Raion in 1937', *Carl Beck Papers in Russian and East European Studies* (Pittsburgh, Pa., n.d.). Much of the content of these studies is engaged with the most detailed history of Stalinist repressions written in the classical 'totalitarian' mould. This has recently been republished in an updated version: R. Conquest, *The Great Terror: A Reassessment* (New York: Oxford University Press, 1990).

For admirably clear analyses of the recently released data that have relevance to the difficult task of counting the casualties of the Stalin era, see A. Nove, 'How many victims in the 1930s?', *Soviet Studies*, xlii, 1990, no. 2, pp. 369–73, and 'How many victims? – II', *Soviet Studies*, xlii, no. 4, pp. 811–14; E. Bacon, 'Glasnost and the gulag: new information on Soviet forced labour around World War II', *Soviet Studies*, xliv, 1992, no. 6, pp. 1069–86. But see also R. Conquest, 'Excess deaths and camp numbers: some comments', *Soviet Studies*, xliii, 1991, no. 5, pp. 949–52.

An interesting article on social stratification which corrects the tendency to view this in terms of the large class categories defined by official Soviet sociology is by S. Fitzpatrick, 'After NEP: the fate of NEP entrepreneurs, traders, and artisans in "Socialist Russia" of the 1930s', *Russian History*, xiii, 1986, nos 2–3, pp. 187–234. For a discussion of the promotion of 'cultured living' values, see S. Fitzpatrick, ' "Middle-class values" and Soviet life in the 1930s', in T. L. Thompson and R. Sheldon (eds), *Soviet Society and Culture* (Boulder, Colo.: Westview Press, 1988). My comments in this chapter concerning the changes in the provision of mass entertainment by the film industry and the sports system have drawn on R. Taylor, 'Ideology and mass entertainment: Boris Shumyatsky and Soviet cinema in the 1930s', in R. Taylor and I. Christie (eds), *Inside the Film factory: New Approaches to Russian and Soviet Cinema* (London: Routledge, 1991); and J. Riordan, *Sport in Soviet Society* (Cambridge: Cambridge University Press, 1977). For another insight into the changes of social policy in the 1930s, see E. Walters, 'The modernization of Russian motherhood, 1917–1937', *Soviet Studies*, xliv, 1992, no. 1, pp. 123–35.

There is now a concise account of wartime mobilizations and social conditions: J. Barber and M. Harrison, *The Soviet Home Front 1941–1945: A Social and Economic History of the USSR in World War II* (London: Longman, 1991).

9

De-Stalinization and the Reborn Intelligentsia, 1953–64

Stalin left no instructions behind as to who should succeed him. The men who presided over the funeral ceremonies had been members of his politburo and trusted lieutenants since the 1930s. The contest for the top position of power took place in ways that were reminiscent of the years following Lenin's death. The main contestants were people capable of claiming close association with the former leader. They sought to form factions within the 'collective leadership' to isolate rivals who would be charged by a majority politburo vote with past errors as well as present misconduct. These charges were subsequently made known to the public, perhaps giving the victims a chance to recant but not dispute their fairness. The politics of succession also involved contestants building up their power bases outside the politburo through patronage, and cultivating a political constituency which would readily identify with their public pronouncements. The contest also involved policy issues, but a leader falling from the 'collective leadership' did not necessarily mean the fall of his preferred policies as some of the fallen leader's ideas might subsequently be adopted by the victorious faction – albeit without due acknowledgement. Stalin, of course, was the supreme master of this game, to which he eventually added the final stroke: the security police's involvement in the elimination of potential rivals. The lieutenants he left behind as the 'collective leadership' had learnt their politics in the Stalin school, the only one their careers had exposed them to. Those closest to Stalin in his final years were Beria, Molotov, Malenkov, and Khrushchev. Beria was the security police chief, and so he was seen by the others as the most dangerous. The first factional conspiracy was therefore against Beria. This enlisted the help of a military chief, Zhukov, who was not a politburo member. Three months after Stalin's death, Beria was put under arrest during a politburo meeting and executed shortly afterwards as 'a British spy'. This was the last cloak-and-dagger conspiracy.

Molotov was the most experienced and prestigious of the remaining three. He adopted a conservative position on most policy issues. Malenkov, on the other hand, wanted a crackdown on the corruptions of 'bureaucratism', and he supported a relaxation of ideological controls over the cultural establishment and academia. He also supported a supremacy of technical rationalism and efficiency orientation over political-mobilization methods in the running of the economy, a stronger emphasis on legal codes and the due process of law, and a shift of investment priorities from the heavy-industry sector to consumer-goods production and housing. Advocating economic shift also implied a change in foreign policy such as could facilitate a reduction in the defence burden. Malenkov had become chairman of the Council of Ministers when Stalin died, which gave him the opportunity to cultivate a power base in state structures rather than in the party apparatus. Khrushchev was also quick to associate himself with the idea that new policy departures were needed, urging that something needed be done quickly about agricultural problems. His personal style carried the promise of change, for he often travelled to the provinces where he liked to show the common touch by engaging ordinary people as well as local officials in lively, impromptu debates about practical problems. He became the first secretary of the party, and immediately busied himself with building up a wider power base by promoting a younger generation to party posts (as Stalin had done in the 1920s). Khrushchev and Malenkov were the dominant two. In 1955, however, Khrushchev helped to form a politburo majority which relieved Malenkov of his government chair, though not as yet his politburo membership. Khrushchev accused him of too much bias against heavy industry, and an intention to make the offices of state dominant over the party. With Malenkov out of serious contention, Khrushchev assumed the mantel of the prime reformer.

It should not have been surprising, perhaps, that Stalin's most trusted protégés created a sense of division between their reformist and conservative tendencies. The dictator's death undoubtedly created a strong shared sense that an era was at an end, and of what the new era should be made of. After the mobilization campaigns of crash industrialization, the war, and post-war reconstruction, the population was ready for a period of rising living standards and civilian normality. The vast majority still lived in squalid subsistence, the economy having become more complex but still mean in its delivery of basic comforts. Besides, the world had changed. The USSR was now a nuclear power (having tested its first atomic bomb in 1949 and a hydrogen bomb in 1953), locked in a bitter cold war with an economically much stronger antagonist. The 'socialist camp' had been enlarged by China and North Korea as well as the European satellites, but Moscow had lost its ideological hegemony over the international communist movement: there was now a significant communist state in Europe, Yugoslavia, which presented an alternative to the Stalinist version of Marxism by asserting its independence. Finally, at home there was a fast-growing and, therefore, largely youthful stratum of university-educated professionals; the population as a whole was completely literate; and the younger generation was the beneficiary of an education system in which schooling up to 14 was the basic minimum. Growth in general education had extended the sphere of influence for the élite of culture and science, and this élite was smarting from the reimposition by the party of crude Marxist orthodoxy in the immediate post-war period, when prominent intellectuals who strayed from the straight and narrow of 'socialist realism' or 'historical materialism' were shunted to low-level jobs.

In 1954 the publication of the novel *The Thaw* by Ilya Erenburg gave a new name to the hopes for change and it crystallized the collective conscience of the liberal intelligentsia. The book treated with irony the single-minded, ruthless pursuit of production quotas by a metal-industry factory director, and it counterposed this to the spiritual need for artistic values and freedoms expressed through the character of the director's wife, a teacher. Another literary landmark of the 'thaw' was published in 1956. *Not by Bread Alone*, by Vladimir Dudintsev, was an instant bestseller made even more famous when Khrushchev rebuked it for going too far. Written as a 'socialist-realist' epic of struggle for technological progress, the novel pitted its hero (an individualist but socially responsible and determined engineer-innovator) against industrial managers, government officials, party secretaries, and establishment academicians. In a way, the novel's negative characters represented the sins of 'bureaucratism', and in that sense a target for criticism which had an established legitimacy. But these characters seemed to be not so much individually corrupt or malevolent as simply typical of the system which gave them their position: although they were eventually defeated when the innovator-hero was helped by a good party official, there was a hint that their actions and outlooks were those of a new Soviet boss class. The literary 'thaw' was bringing an aspect of Stalin's legacy under public discussion and thus defining a division between orthodox and reformist attitudes.

In 1956 Khrushchev dropped a bombshell when he treated a closed session of the twentieth party congress to a critical examination of Stalin's record. The speech defaced the Stalin icon by telling the shocked delegates about the hitherto suppressed 'Lenin testament' which warned of Stalin's predilection for 'administrative methods' and intolerance of those party comrades who crossed him. In Khrushchev's analysis, Lenin's warning had proved true after the seventeenth party congress in 1934, which showed Kirov to be more popular with the delegates than Stalin. Until then, Stalin's policies – the industrialization and collectivization campaigns and the defeats of the 'left' and 'right' oppositions that preceded them – had been correct, Khrushchev asserted. But from 1934 Stalin had committed numerous crimes by using terror against good communists and by setting his 'personality cult' above party rules. Khrushchev named a number of prominent Bolsheviks who had perished in the purges brought about by Stalin's orders, and concluded that it was imperative to make sure that the 'Leninist norms of party life', the principles of 'collective leadership', and 'socialist legality' were never again perverted.

The speech was supposed to be privileged information for the assembled delegates, but its contents were widely leaked and avidly circulated. It had an even more dramatic and immediate effect in Poland and Hungary, where it stimulated uprisings. In Poland, the situation was contained by a Soviet-approved call to power by Gomulka, a communist politician who had been imprisoned by the regime during its witch-hunt of the pro-Yugoslav heresy. Gomulka immediately set a reformist course by, among other things, allowing agriculture to return to private farming. The Hungarian uprising became more violent and radical, threatening a total overthrow of the communist state and the country's withdrawal from the newly formed Warsaw Pact. The uprising was quelled by Soviet tanks, but the party leader who was thus installed, Kadar, also set out on a cautiously reformist course after suppressing the insurgents. The insurgents, however, included workers seeking to substitute a government by workers' councils for the Communist Party regime, and their repression caused a major crisis of conscience in the international socialist movement. The Soviet Communist Party lost its moral hold on the radical left-wing movements of the West. These developments added to the pressure on Khrushchev from his politburo colleagues, for they proved that revelations about Stalin were a threat to political stability. Uprisings were unlikely in Russia, but the effects on the population of taking down an icon who had symbolized the regime and its power for so long were difficult to fathom. Khrushchev's response to the conservatives was, on occasions, to blow with them – after Hungary, for example, he blew a chill wind on the literary thaw. However, his main strategy was to keep the policy-making initiative. A reformist momentum had started the previous year when the party ideologues proclaimed Yugoslavia a socialist country after all, and Khrushchev made a public apology to Tito for Stalin's intolerance of different 'roads to socialism'. Now there were two more countries, Hungary and Poland, whose ruling communist parties sponsored their own searches for economic reforms and a broadened Marxist framework for their intellectuals. This helped to revitalize the ideology and policy-making Khrushchev was seeking to stimulate and channel within his own party under the banner of de-Stalinization.

At the beginning of 1957, Khrushchev's politburo colleagues formed a majority that was preparing to vote him out of office. He prevented them, however, by using his power as the first secretary to convene a special plenary session of the central committee, the body to which the politburo was formally answerable between party congresses. The delegates, many of whom were brought from the provinces in military aircraft, were, in the main, of the younger generation of officials who were rising under Khrushchev's auspices. They voted the 'anti-party faction', including Malenkov, Molotov, and Kaganovich, out of the politburo, thus leaving Khrushchev to preside over a 'collective leadership' which was more of his choosing than before. The newly confirmed party leader was free to escalate his programme of reforms and dominate the political stage by his energetic persona. He soon enlarged his formal status by becoming chairman of the council of ministers in addition to being the first party secretary. In 1959 the twenty-first party congress radiated a feeling that the party was no longer under the shadow of a Stalin personality cult because it now had a Khrushchev cult instead. The contradictions of Khrushchev's de-Stalinization reforms are discussed in more detail later in this chapter but, for the moment, it is worth noting that the downfall of the 'anti-party faction' was a downfall into a materially comfortable oblivion, despite the strong language of the accusations. When Khrushchev himself eventually fell victim to an ouster vote by a politburo majority in 1964, he too, lived his remaining years in personal comfort – as was generally expected. He was even able to write a voluminous memoir for publication in the capitalist West. Political play within the establishment was no longer life-threatening and, in that sense at least, post-1934 Stalinism became a thing of the past.

Changes in Ideology

The new party leader's reputation and personal style was of the salt-of-the-earth type, a zestful solver of practical problems rather than a purveyor of fine words. By the twenty-second party congress of 1961, however, the expansive think-tanks of his administration made a range of pronouncements on ideological doctrine and a new version of the party programme. Perhaps the first ideological revision was the explicit abandonment of the Stalinist doctrine that the Marxist laws of class struggle were making inevitable a war between the 'camps' of capitalism and socialism. The even older Bolshevik doctrine, according to which socialist revolutions would overthrow rather than work through the parliamentary institutions of 'bourgeois democracies', was also dropped. Peaceful coexistence with the capitalist powers was thus possible and indeed necessary in view of the globally destructive potential of armed conflict in the age of nuclear weapons; and Western communist parties were entitled to follow their own 'roads to socialism', which did not exclude the possibility of working in parliaments as loyal oppositions or government coalition partners. This ideological revision was clearly meant to reassure Western partners that the USSR was genuinely interested in *détente*.

The ideological pronouncements relevant to domestic policies and reforms, however, had a strong visionary component. Historical progress was now at a stage where socialism was accomplished, and the party's main task was to lead the country to communism. The year 1981 was boldly announced as the year in which 'to catch up and surpass' should become a reality – the slogan first proclaimed in the 1930s as an injunction to catch up economically with the most advanced Western countries. After that, fully fledged communism, the system in which every citizen would be materially provided for according to individual need rather than according to the value of his or her particular contribution to the productive process, should be achieved for the youngest generation to enjoy in its own lifetime. Building communism was to be a classless process – the party and the state were 'all-people's' rather than class-based institutions. Building communism was to involve a devolution of administrative functions from the state to 'social organizations' because, as both Marx and Lenin had said, the state would become gradually redundant in administering social processes once there were no class antagonisms to be kept under coercive control. This meant an increasing rather than diminishing role for the party, however. The bold pursuit of the communist goal in domestic policies would fit in well with a foreign policy of peaceful coexistence, Khrushchev thought, because the relaxation of cold-war tensions would enable the 'construction of communism' to progress faster if it had a lighter defence burden. And accelerated socio-economic progress at home would prove to the electorates of 'bourgeois democracies' and to the nationalist movements of the decolonized developing countries that socialism was superior to capitalism both morally and materially.

The de-emphasis on class-struggle militancy, the vision of the socialist state as gradually losing its functions to 'social organizations', and the belief in the possibility of peaceful coexistence with capitalist states marked a departure from the doctrines associated with Stalin's rule. In other respects the Khrushchevian ideological revisions did not break the established mould.

First, the principle that progress in all walks of life should be directed under the authoritative guidance of an official Marxist-Leninist ideology remained in place, and the ideology underwent little more than slight changes of emphases on some points. The dimensions of permissable debate about public issues were broadening, but the need to demonstrate the legitimacy of an opinion by citing either Lenin or a recent high-level pronouncement (or both) was not relaxed. The regime supported its ideology by a new offensive against religion. Secondly, the ideology remained productivist in its emphasis. It confirmed the industrialization of the 1930s as a socialist triumph, and fast-rising labour productivity as the key task for the future as well. The 'construction of communism' remained primarily a matter of economic planning, science, and technology, the extension of industrial methods to agriculture, 'scientific organization of labour', educational improvements and skills training, a strong work ethic, the right kind of material motivation for the workers, and mobilization activism to combat inefficiencies and slack standards: in other words, industrially minded continuity with the Stalinist development strategy.

Thirdly, setting visionary goals for the lifetime of the post-war generation, and of very ambitious targets for new lines of production (particularly in the chemical industry), was a testimony to the traditions of a mobilization regime. Khrushchev's first policy on taking the office of first party secretary was in fact a spectacular mobilization campaign, the virgin-lands (*tseliny*) project, in the course of which hundreds of thousands urban *komsomol* volunteers went to convert the arid steppes of south-east European Russia, the north Caucasus, northern Kazakhstan, and western Siberia into large-scale grain farming. This venture helped the new party leader in his ascendancy, confirmed the mobilization role of the party within the economy, and its success was duly hailed at the de-Stalinizing party congress of 1956. Henceforth, de-Stalinization was in large part about catching the upcoming generation's imagination and creating an optimistic new-era atmosphere such as the party needed if it were to generate an energetic following for its programme without the use of terror. Khrushchev himself was of the generation of party activists who had been brought into the regime's service on the wave of the 'socialist construction' optimism at the start of Stalin's industrialization campaign, and now he needed to breathe new life into the party's 'leading role', which he saw as necessary for the 'communist construction'. As in the first five-year plan, visionary goals and bold projects carried the risk of later disillusionment, but they were stirring mobilization symbols when announced. In contrast to the first five-year plan, the mobilization targets did not now include class enemies; but, thought Khrushchev, changes in organization and working practice were needed in many spheres, and they needed plenty of revitalized 'party spirit' to carry them out against conservative resistance. As in the late 1920s, fomenting a new-era optimism was the order of the day.

After the initial success of the virgin-lands campaign, the credibility of the Khrushchevian propaganda was boosted by the impressive advent of the space programme. The year 1957, in which Khrushchev dismissed the 'anti-party faction' and escalated his reformist programme, also happened to be the year in which the first Soviet sputnik went into the Earth's orbit. In 1961, the year in which Khrushchev announced a further de-Stalinization of the party and country at the twenty-second party congress, was also the year in which the first cosmonaut did an orbit round the Earth. Gagarin's youthful, smiling face was doing for Khrushchev's new-era promise what the arctic-flying pilot Chkalov had done for Stalin's in the 1930s. By 1963 there was also the first woman cosmonaut, Tereshkova, to symbolize progress. 'To catch up and surpass' the best of the West did not seem a far-fetched target when Soviet space technology already looked ahead of the Americans'. But the cosmonautic 'firsts' could not in themselves provide lasting credibility for high-profile mobilization propaganda. The credibility in no small part depended on the popularity and success of specific policies and on the ability of the policy-initiating party leader to keep disgruntled voices muffled when success was mixed, and the means of muffling limited by his own de-Stalinization stance.

Foreign and Defence Policy

Soon after Stalin's death, a three-year-old war in Korea was quickly settled and Soviet foreign policy moved towards relaxing the cold war. In 1955 Khrushchev met President Eisenhower in Geneva. There was much talk in the world press of the 'Geneva spirit', but in the USSR the fact that a summit meeting took place at all and that further meetings were on the cards in themselves contributed to the climate of 'thaw'. In 1956 Khrushchev visited Britain and, in 1959, he led a large high-ranking delegation on a tour of the USA, which included extensive talks with President Eisenhower at Camp David. The president was to return the visit in 1960.

Perhaps the most powerful evidence of the seriousness of Khrushchev's intentions of *détente* with the West was the fact that he was willing to sacrifice the established alliance with that other great communist power, China. Mao-Tse-Tung was an outspoken critic of the *détente* policy, and his displeasure with it grew when 'the Geneva spirit' led to the USSR withdrawing aid to the Chinese nuclear programme and staying neutral during China's disputes with Taiwan and India. By 1960 the two powers were at veritable loggerheads, with Mao slagging Khrushchev off for 'revisionism' and being branded with 'dogmatism' in return. The split with China, in combination with Khrushchev's reconciliation with Yugoslavia, was also an encouraging confirmation of de-Stalinization to the newly reborn Russian intelligentsia.

In 1960–2, however, the cold war triumphed over any *détente* intentions in Soviet–Western relations. The incidents that marked this increase in tensions included, in 1960, protests and denials concerning US spy airplanes; the shooting down of one of these airplanes over the Urals and putting of the captured pilot on show to the world's media; Khrushchev walking out of a summit meeting in Paris; the cancellation of Eisenhower's visit to Moscow; Khrushchev's interrupting a speech in the UN by banging a shoe on the table; in 1961, a meeting in Vienna with President Kennedy which yielded no substantive agreement; the building of the Berlin wall; the resumption of on-the-ground testing of nuclear warheads; and, in 1962, the Soviet attempt to install nuclear missiles in Cuba, an American blocade of the island, and several days of fingers-on-buttons until the Cuba-bound cargoes of Soviet missiles turned back for home. Germany was the main bone of contention throughout. Khrushchev wanted the Western powers to recognize East Germany and take

NATO forces out of Berlin. They would not do that. The Cuban adventure was an attempt to alter the balance of power quickly and cheaply, since the strategic status quo was proving unconducive to Western concessions on Germany.

Khrushchev failed in his main foreign-policy goal – to reduce the defence burden on the economy and, at the same time, to secure the strategic position that had been won by the costly Second World War victory. When he announced his 'peaceful coexistence' doctrine, he also put on record an intention to reduce substantially the size of the Soviet army and the spending on conventional arms. After the failure of the negotiations on Germany and the Cuban gamble, maintaining global power status appeared bereft of cheap options. Henceforth, defence policy was to continue building the arsenal of expensive long-range nuclear missiles *and* the strength of the conventional army. The difference of opinion between Khrushchev and the army generals on the projected defence cuts was never a secret, and in the event it was the military that had its way.

'Peaceful coexistence' with the West thus turned out to be about managing the cold war without the repeat of Cuban-style brinkmanship rather than about creating a wide freedom of manoeuvre for redistributing resources in the economy. Khrushchev's plans to widen this freedom by securing Western aid to develop the chemical industry did not work out either. On the other hand, a limited *détente* became a reality again. In 1963 a treaty was signed with the USA banning on-the-ground tests of nuclear warheads, which was perhaps a small token in itself, but useful for the management of nuclear umbrella relations in that it set a precedent for arms-limitations talks. New training institutions were set up to put foreign policy and diplomacy on a professional footing. Agreements with Western countries on scientific and cultural exchanges, first started in the mid-1950s, provided narrowly circumscribed but highly prized opportunities of Western contact for some members of the establishment intelligentsia. Some wheat was purchased from the USA in 1963. These were small changes in themselves, but they added up to the sense, at least among the intelligentsia, that de-Stalinization was making a third world war less likely and total isolation from the West a thing of the past.

Agricultural Policies and Reforms

The new party leader was a zealous mobilization campaigner in the agricultural sphere. He committed the party to making its leading role felt in the virgin-lands campaign and, especially after his return from the USA, in a campaign to persuade the peasantry in the traditional wheat-and-rye zones to grow maize to feed to livestock so that there would be 'meat, butter, and milk for everyone'. In the longer term, Khrushchev saw progress in terms of narrowing the differences between town and country. Collective farms should be gradually replaced by very large state farms specializing in a particular product and including food-processing factories. Eventually, the state farms should form larger complexes by mergers, and 'agritowns' would be built in which the workers could enjoy the facilities for cultured leisure after their normal hours of mechanized work instead of spending all their spare time on private plots.

This long-term vision, of course, had been around at the inception of the collectivization campaign, and Khrushchev resuscitated it while Stalin was still alive. The idea that state farms were a higher form than collective farms was old doctrine. The practical message in putting it on the agenda again was that agriculture was underinvested and due to be made a development priority so that it could move towards the higher forms. It was state farms rather than collective farms that the virgin-lands pioneers formed. State farm workers enjoyed the security of wage-scales and pension entitlements, but they were given smaller private plots than the average collective-farm household.

The virgin-lands campaign succeeded in that the motorized ploughing-up of the boundless steppes immediately provided a substantial increase in total grain sown and harvested. But the success peaked early. From 1957 on, the crash methods of the preceeding four years produced soil erosion. The quota-busting ploughing had been done regardless of whether irrigation work was lagging behind and whether there was enough fertilizer, while the sowing quotas were chased at the expense of careful crop rotation. The soil was disappearing into dust storms and, by the drought year of 1963, the campaign's early triumph was too damaged by soil erosion to forestall an overall harvest disaster that would have caused a famine of earlier proportions had the state not made its first wheat-import deal with American farmers. Besides, the campaign ran into problems with its own foot soldiers even before the dust storms. Most of the young volunteers intended to do no more than temporary stints that would look good on their career profiles, and some of them cut their stays short rather than put up with inadequate conditions. Some of those who originally meant to stay permanently also left in disillusionment. In northern Kazakhstan the settlers found a less than enthusiastic welcome from the local authorities as well as the native population, who were not too pleased to see the steppes colonized by the Slavs, let alone by industrial centres. The campaign was true to its mass mobilization form in achieving a contradiction between propaganda and eye-witness tales.

The maize-and-meat campaign also gathered ill repute for its excesses. Collective farm chairmen, who wanted to curry favour with the party bosses by busting a meat-delivery quota, sometimes did so by adopting a slaughter-this-year strategy that left insufficient livestock for breeding in the following year. *Kukuruza*, the Russian word for maize, became a popular nickname for Khrushchev. It was used none too affectionately in the many areas of the country where the crop had to be planted against the peasants' better judgement, and the soil and climate duly proved inhospitable to the party leader's yellow-cobbed dream. Party officials' claims that the sorry-looking fields represented progress was unconvincing.

There were also some policies that helped the collective farm peasantry. Soon after Stalin's death the moneys payable by the state for delivery quotas were increased, and taxes on market sales from private plots decreased. After 1958 came a more substantial reform of the *kolkhoz* system: the MTSs (Machinery and Tractor Stations) were abolished, and with them the system which had been keeping the collective farm revenues down to small and unpredictable residuals. Henceforth, the collective farms would be able to share with other state institutions the ability to pay their workers regular basic wages, even if this meant a budget deficit. This was a considerable relief although it was marred by the fact that the reform obliged the collective farms to pay the state for the machines that were transferred into their ownership after the liquidation of the MTSs. Overall, however, the countryside was benefiting from the changes in the terms of economic exchange with the towns. It was not a costless policy. The burgeoning urban sector was accustomed to decreases in the prices of basic foods. In 1962, however, the prices increased and the range of responses to the news included a mass uprising in the south-Russian town of Novocherkassk, where the timing of the news coincided with industrial workers facing a norm-tightening campaign.

Khrushchev was much exercised by the fact that *kolkhoz* farmers were more motivated to work on their private household plots than in the collectivized fields. The reforms associated with the abolition of the MTSs were aimed at providing stronger incentives for the collective work. The longer-term strategy of turning the *kolkhoz* farms into state farms was also in part about reducing the size of the private plots and the peasants' economic dependence on them. In the short run, after reducing the taxes on sales from the private plots, the party leader tried to instigate a policy of reducing the size of the *kolkhoz* farmers' household plots, and to lower the limits on private livestock ownership. Here he was trying to claw back the concession Stalin had made in the 1930s. Khrushchev's strategy was to reactivate party interference in rural management, but encroaching on the private plot-holding was a more delicate and complicated matter than planting maize in the collectivized fields. Some local party authorities tried it by permitting the construction of new housing only if the housing departed from established village tradition by clustering residential dwellings (as in the envisioned agritowns) and the villagers' private allotments on separate pieces of land. Such policies, however, did not survive their unpopularity. The typical *kolkhoz* house remained attached to 0.3 or so private hectares,[1] the traditional plot size enshrined in the statute of 1935.

Industrial Policies

The 1938–40 and wartime decrees which had criminalized work truancy and job-quitting were defunct – at least since a secret Supreme Court instruction put their use on ice in 1951. From 1956, the spirit of de-Stalinization was evident in further amendments to the laws that restored the degree of labour protection to the level it had been in the 1920s. These laws made only 'systematic' infractions of discipline by manual workers punishable by sacking, and that only after due process involving three prior warnings, a hearing of the culprit's explanations, and a chance for the factory trade-union committee to veto the dismissal. The dismissed workers had a right of appeal to the courts. A lack of formal qualifications did not count as sufficient grounds for a worker to be dismissed for incompetence. The laws also limited the managers' rights to make workers do other work other than that specified by their job titles. Temporary transfers to lower-grade jobs were possible as a punishment (after

---

1 Shinn, W. T. jr 1987: *The Decline of the Russian Peasant Household*. New York: Praeger, The Washington Papers/124.

due disciplinary hearings) or as a response to emergency, subject to approval by the trade-union committee. Managers' rights to request overtime work was similarly limited. The standard working hours were reduced to seven a day (six in underground mining and heavy metallurgy), with a half-day on Saturday and a free Sunday. Labour disputes commissions, consisting of equal numbers of managerial and trade-union representatives, were set up at shopfloor level to resolve conflicts between individual workers and managers, their decisions being subject to appeal to the factory trade-union committee. From 1958, unilateral job-quitting by workers no longer incurred a risk of reduction in pensionable years if another state employment was entered within a month. Interestingly, however, the amended labour code was not quite as strong in protecting the rights of managerial and professional-technical staff (ITR), who could still in principle be dismissed or transferred without trade-union approval and without prior official warnings, and who could appeal such decisions only to the enterprise director's superiors in the industrial bureaucracy.

The removal of Stalin's coercive decrees on labour discipline from the statute books did not make a substantial difference to management–worker relations because, as we saw in Chapter 7, managers rarely saw a literal or zealous enforcement of the decrees as of practical advantage to them. But the repeal of draconian laws was an essential part of a de-Stalinization in general and, in this particular instance, integral to the new party leader's hopes that de-Stalinization could be an industrial morale-raiser.

Industrial policy and practice, however, remained true to the patterns that emerged in the 1930s. The immediate policy goal was to set labour productivity on a sharper upward slope than wages, and output-norm revisions, performance-related pay, and the enlistment of 'mass mobilization' activism the strategy. A large-scale norm-revision campaign was announced under the banner of a wage reform. This reform streamlined the system of skill-gradings and wage tariffs, shortened somewhat the basic wage-scales, set a minimum wage, reduced the proportion of jobs payable by individual piece-rates to some 60 per cent (the level of the 1930s), and introduced new bonus payments. The skill-regradings, the raising of the money payable for a 100 per cent fulfilment of the piecework norms, and the payment of bonuses were linked to the introduction of 'technical norms' in place of the majority of the norms that were by now regularly overfulfilled by very substantial margins. The new structure of wage tariffs and skill-grading looked similar to the one established in the mid-1930s, before the subsequent refinements of it under the proliferating industrial ministries made it more complicated. As for the norm-revision campaign, its implementation in the factories was no different from the informal wage-productivity bargaining patterns that became customary in the 1930s (see Chapter 7).

The workers' ability to persuade management to implement the norm-revision campaign in unhurtful ways as always depended on local conditions and, in particular, on the managers' powers to negotiate large wage budgets with the planning authorities or to get away with overspending the budgets. As before, heavy industries on the whole tended to enjoy more of these powers than light industries. Khrushchev tried to reduce the dominance of heavy-industry interests over the economy, but only with slight and patchy success.

The patches where the effort worked included, for example, non-defence-related engineering in Leningrad, where the norm-tightening consequently hurt machine operators in particular. A well-publicized labour shortage resulted from the spate of job-quitting by the aggrieved workers.

The overall pattern of outcomes of campaign incidentally reinforced the already existing post-war trend of increasing income differentiation between male and female workers. In the light industries, for example, the bosses had relatively lesser power to negotiate budget-slacks and the sexual nature of the division of labour, where the machine operatives and menial auxiliaries were female while the skilled machine setters, maintenance workers, foremen, etc., were male. This discouraged the cross-occupational solidarity needed for the informal shopfloor custom and practice that drew the teeth out of norm-tightening in other industries. In industries where sexual job demarcation was not so clear, this sometimes became more so after the jobs that had suffered a norm-tightening excess were vacated by the workers who could find better jobs elsewhere, for these jobs were eventually filled by females.

The policies of the Khrushchev administration to revitalize the 'social organizations' in the factories never included a repeat of the militant shake-ups of the shock-worker campaign in 1929 or the Stakhanovite campaign in 1935–6. Otherwise, however, their form and substance was true to the traditions started in the 1920s and 1930s. Propagandist efforts were expended on collective agreements meant to produce local deals where workers would co-operate with efficiency measures in return for management undertakings to invest in workers' housing, better canteens, kindergartens, clubs, holiday homes, summer camps for children, etc. Production conferences at shopfloor and factory levels were elected from the ranks of workers and engineering-technical staff (ITR) to help organize innovation measures and hear reports from the management on their implementation. Various 'bureaux' with worker representation on them were set up to generate rationalization and norm-revision proposals. Activist 'raids' did on-the-spot investigations to highlight underused equipment, slack work discipline, various inefficiencies, and the costs of catching up on production plans by 'storming'. 'Comradely courts' held meetings to shame delinquent workers and 'worker' correspondents' supplied information on problems to the campaigning press. 'Socialist competition' was organized and honorary titles, such as 'communist labour brigades', awarded. All this 'mass work' activism in the factories was carefully controlled and kept within the bounds of acceptability to management by the party organizers and by the long-established methods ritually criticized in the press as 'bureaucratic formalism'.

The Khrushchevite policy was not intended to pit political methods of mass mobilization against managerial professionalism; rather, it was to revitalize the 'mass activist' aspect of factory life by giving it a technically qualified leadership. Party organizers in industry and regional party officials were increasingly recruited from the ranks of engineering graduates of the post-war generation whose careers were to combine party posts with management ones. As before, the role of party-led activism in industry was to keep managers from succumbing to the temptations of 'bureaucratic conservatism', to keep them searching for efficiency improvements, but this was now to be done by the authority of technical expertise rather than by ideological bluster. The party was to lead industry by being the main agent of productivity-enhancing reforms, but it was to do it by creating pro-reform consensus among managers and workers rather than by a political exploitation of conflicts of interest within industrial organizations. De-Stalinization philosophy regarded class-warrior rhetoric and demagoguery as out of date in industry as well as all other spheres of public life. The revitalization of party activism in industry, however, presupposed a strong work ethic among 'the masses' and practical situations where bad management, slack labour discipline, and lazy performance standards were all that stood in the way of successful innovation. These presuppositions were not much more realistic than before; existing industrial practice was entrenched in the broader framework of economic organization that had given rise to it and that remained in place. Appointing engineering graduates to party posts could not rescue the 'mass mobilization' activism from being little more than a matter of ritual affirmation of the party's 'leading role', and an opportunity for ambitious people to be listed in the party's 'cadre reserves' – the registers of suitable candidates for the 'responsible' posts, appointments to which were subject to party control under the *nomenklatura* system (see Chapter 10).

Khrushchev's industrial policies did address the broader problem. In 1957, the industrial branch principle of centralized economic control, under which a factory's main production line defined the ministry to which the factory belonged, was replaced by a territorial structure. The industrial ministries were abolished and all the factories located in a certain region were placed under the command of the regional economic council (*sovnarkhoz* or SNKh); the regions were in turn under the centralized command of the supreme economic council (VSNKh). The regional councils were not free to allocate resources among the industrial branches under their control as they saw fit – the gamut of planning quotas and allocations was still set for each branch of industry centrally by the state planning office, the Gosplan. The aim of the reorganization was to bring the main intermediate tier of administrative co-ordination nearer to where the plants were located and to do away with the problem of 'departmentalism' (*vedomstvennost'*), the ministries' tendency to maximize their resources by, for example, blocking the release of equipment known to have been hoarded by one of their plants to a neighbouring plant if the neighbour belonged to another ministry. The reform, however, reduced the 'departmentalism' problem by magnifying the problem of 'localism' (*mestnichestvo*); the regions now looked after their own, inhibiting co-operation between same-industry or complementary production plants if they were situated across the regional boundaries. 'Localism', of course, was also considered a problem under the old system, as we saw in Chapter 7, since administrative localities with their party officials, procuracy officials, and economic bosses of various kinds were always productive of informal networks for mutual protection and wheeler-dealing. The institutional framework became more comfortable for this process when ministerial interference was removed and the boundaries of economic administration coincided with the political regions.

Without the ministries, the main burden of making sure that central policies were not thwarted by conniving implementation in the regions fell on the party, and in particular on the regional (*oblast'*) party secretaries. This was in line with Khrushchev's aim of making the party the backbone of the overall structure of power and policy administration. The new economic structure also enhanced the regional party secretary's role in co-ordinating the practical measures that were needed to overcome faults in industrial planning. The *oblast'* party officials were in effect confirmed as the principal brokers between central powers and regional economic interests. In 1962 a reorganization of the party apparatus emphasized its functions in the productive sphere by creating provincial party bureaux for transport and industry, on the one hand, and agriculture on the other. This new-look structure to the party bureaucracy in the provinces increased the demand for technically qualified staff and activists without doing much for career opportunities of provincial 'ideological work' experts. In fact, the intention was to reduce the full-time staff overall and to let volunteer activists and people on temporary secondment from other careers do more of the work. New party rules adopted by the twenty-second party congress in 1961 also made appointments to lower-level party posts subject to confirmation by members' ballot and limited the number of terms a low-level party official could stay in the same post. In the earlier drafts of the new rules, this 'rotation of cadres' principle had been applied to all levels of the hiearchy, but the final version related only to the tiers below the *oblast'* level. The reformist proposals whittled down by conservative opposition aimed for a measure of 'democratization', but also for accelerating the replacement of old-style party careerists with people ready to carry through a more substantial reform of the economic management structure.

It was not clear whether the changes in the industrial administrative structure and the party bore benefits that outweighed the disruptive effects of reorganization. The unpopularity of the policies with many of the administrators, however, could not be in doubt. They were particularly displeasing to the industrial ministry officials who had to move from Moscow to the provinces as a result of the *sovnarkhoz* reform, and to the lower-level party officials who had to play musical chairs with their posts to meet the 'rotation of cadres' requirements. Inside the factories, the Khrushchev years brought another spate of administrative pressures to renegotiate wage-effort bargains – never a popular policy in itself. The failure to shift the balance of investments from heavy to consumer industries frustrated the expectations of very rapid rises in living standards, and the Novocherkassk riots were a reminder of the working-class discontent that loomed should agricultural problems compound the industrial ones. Nevertheless, industry was doing well enough in most branches to keep living standards lifting from the post-war low. Housing construction in particular expanded substantially thanks to the arrival of prefabricated-panels technology: 22.7 million new flats were built in 1956–65, providing accommodation for 84 million people, 40 per cent of the total population.[2] But the achievements seemed to beg rather than answer the question of how the advances could be sustained.

---

2 Filtzer, D. 1992: *Soviet Workers and De-Stalinization*. Cambridge: Cambridge University Press, p. 51.

The Debate on Economic Reforms

Khrushchev criticized the Academy of Sciences for neglecting economics, and new institutes were set up for generating ideas on more fundamental economic reforms. Advocacies of linking the management of state enterprises to overall economic plans by profit incentives rather than by administrative commands and quotas first appeared in the press in 1956; arguments by a Polish economist (W. Brus) about combining centralized planning for strategic products with market mechanisms for the rest were published in 1961; and in the following year, an article in *Pravda* by Professor Liberman under the title 'Plan, profit and bonus' started a busy period of public debate. The economy became the main battlefield between reformers and conservatives. Ideas favouring a capitalist market economy remained out of bounds, and it is doubtful they had many genuine adherents. The reformist economists and their supporters among the educated public remained true to the Russian intelligentsia's socialist traditions. In any case, opening channels of contact with Western ideas reinforced rather than undermined the socialist commitment, for the ideas that were then gaining dominance in Western social science were those of 'convergence theory'. These saw the course of Western progress as led by technocratic corporate managers, planners, public-sector agencies, and welfare-orientated governments rather than by private-owning entrepreneurs. The reformist inspiration was coming from Soviet history – the economic philosophies of the New Economic Policy (NEP) period and the ideas that enjoyed some temporary political patronage during the crisis of 1932–3. The NEP inspiration could not be articulated publicly, however, because the collectivization of farming was declared unambiguously by the party leadership as essentially a positive heritage.

The debate brought into the open all the problems of the existing system of planning and administrative command discussed in Chapter 7. The particular problems (supplies bottlenecks, hoarding of resources, low-quality production, 'storming', irresponsiveness to consumer demand, the wasteful absurdities caused by clumsy performance indicators, lack of innovation, the thwarting of government orders by executive subterfuge, and a lack of reliable criteria for evaluating investment options) had been no state secret in any case, but they were now analysed as the result of the system itself rather than of incompetent or corrupt practice by the people in it. The way forward, the reformists argued, was for central government to regulate the work of productive enterprises indirectly by 'economic mechanisms' rather than by the direct methods of setting volume targets with a plethora of supplementary performance indicators and directives. Enterprise managements should be, above all, motivated to maximize the difference between the value of output and inputs, and they should be given sufficient autonomy to innovate for this purpose, although they should not be free to set their own product prices or change the main use of their plants. The price structure should be reformed, however, so that price relativities reflected market scarcities and government priorities. The reforms should aim to achieve a system where the central planners concentrate on development strategy and inter-sectoral balance while being able to leave more detailed decision-making to the levels at which the relevant information for it was readily available. Budgets and prices should become the main instruments of government control, and profits the main motive force of managerial strategies at the enterprise level. Enterprises should be free to make their own customer-supplier agreements where possible. This was to be a socialist economy in that the government would still be in charge of planning and the means of production would remain in state ownership; but it would share with market economies the advantages of automatic self-regulation and inbuilt pressures to innovate. Some of the reformers also argued that the 'economic mechanism' should not be devoid of a competitive element, although they stopped short of advocating the free-market penalties of bankruptcy and unemployment for failing competitors.

The conservatives countered these ideas by scepticism that the prevalence of state interests over private speculative intent on the part of individual enterprises could be guaranteed if direct administrative controls were relinquished. Here was a weakness in the reformist argument. This was based on promising the central authorities a more effective instrument for controlling the economy than they already had; no one was arguing that the state interests ought not to be guaranteed prevalence over individual self-interests, but the advocacy of suspending administrative command was based on a theoretical model which was, by definition, untested in practice. The Yugoslav version of 'market socialism' and 'self-management' was mentioned occasionally but generally not as a proven package suitable for Soviet importation. In the eyes of the broadening public, in front of whom the arguments were rehearsed, however, the conservatives spoiled their case by mainly relying on Marxist political-economy formulae taken straight out of orthodox Stalinist texts. The reformist arguments sounded rational, scientific, and practical by comparison, and the critique of the status quo on which they were based was undisputably empirical. The claim that they offered a better, more modern version of socialism rather than a slide into capitalist anarchy therefore seemed doubtful only to the Stalinist 'dogmatists'.

The debate was quickly extended beyond the technically economic. Some of the commentaries in the press attacked the one-man-management principle which, in the words of an engineer writing in the economic weekly, had made the 'cult of office' common and the managers always '*ex officio* right', although the 'collective competence (of employees) is often greater than that of a competent manager'.[3] Factories should be run by a collegiate authority of senior technical specialists, or by elected committees of workers and ITR, or by democratically elected directors. The fictional writings that followed the path beaten by Dudintsev's *Not by Bread Alone*, some of which were published while others were circulated informally having been refused publication, focused even more strongly on the authoritarian nature of the status quo – a system in which bosses ruled their subordinates by arbitrary fiat, surrounded themselves by yesmen, and deferred irresponsibly to the views of their own bosses. A system, in other words, which ran roughshod over both workers' welfare and the rational advice of technically qualified employees, and which corrupted morals by forcing executives, specialists, and workers to

---

3 *Ekonomicheskaya gazeta*, ix, 1963, p. 35; quoted in Andrle, V. 1976: *Managerial Power in the Soviet Union*. Farnborough: Saxon House, p. 67.

do wasteful things against their better judgement. The broader themes of de-Stalinization and 'the thaw' were thus aligned with the issue of economic rationality and efficiency.

The fictional writings created a picture of the Stalinist boss in industry who was in his element when there was an emergency, for then his forceful way of taking charge could be seen by all to have validity. But he was given to exercising his authority by bluster rather than by rational persuasion just as much in normal times. The de-Stalinization discourse in the press as well as in fiction thus resuscitated an old modernization theme, that of 'cultured' management of the production process and the human relations within it. In the Stalin era, public discourse on management was consistent in its stress on 'production culture', but it was equivocal on the human-relations aspect in that it celebrated single-minded task-masters as well as attacking 'soulless bureaucrats' for being rude to workers. From the late nineteenth century right through to the 1920s, however, crude rank-pulling by managers was constantly anathemized in the discourse on backwardness and modernity. 'Dignity issues', after all, were often evident in workers' expressions of grievance, during the 1930s as well as in the preceeding five decades. Now the de-Stalinization discourse took them up again, and associated the anathema with the character of the Stalinist boss, who had been given licence to be 'uncultured' by the system that had made the fulfilment of production quotas and rushed priorities an over-riding higher cause that justified everything. Khrushchev himself advised managers that civility was good industrial practice, in contrast to his ousted ex-colleague Kaganovich who, in his days as the heavy-industry commissar twenty years earlier, advised the 'one-man' managers that the earth should tremble when they did their shopfloor walkabouts. The contributors to the economic-reform debate who advocated some kind of work place democracy in place of the 'one-man-management' (*edinonachalie*) prerogative in the event did not get their way, but de-Stalinization restated the contrast between 'cultured' and authoritarian leadership styles and marginalized the authoritarian, at least in theory.

'Socialist Legality' Policies

De-Stalinization produced some swift effects in the legal area. The KGB (Committee of State Security) that was formed in place of the MVD (Ministry of Internal Affairs renamed from NKVD after the war) did not inherit from its predecessor the power to try suspects before its own collegia. The judiciary thus having its monopoly restored over custodial sentencing, criminal law was overhauled in 1955–8. People could be held under police arrest only for a short initial period, after that only if the procurator decided there was a likely case to prosecute. Limits were also set on the length of time suspects could be held in procuracy custody. Defence was given access to the prosecution case at the preliminary court hearing at the latest, before the panel of judges decided whether the indictment prepared by the procuracy was sound enough to go for trial. The charges had to relate specifically to offences defined in the criminal law – it became impossible to try a person for an act which was merely 'analogous' to an existing offence definition. A person could be tried only for an offence that was actually committed and not for one that was merely intended. Confessions had to be corroborated by additional evidence, and torturing suspects to obtain confessions or evidence was confirmed as illegal. Vague offences, such as 'counter-revolutionary activity' or 'being an enemy of the people', were removed from the statute books. The death penalty was abolished for all crimes with the exception of treason, although in 1961 it was restored for large-scale black-market operations and, after Khrushchev's ouster, it would be restored for murder. Custodial sentences were limited to 10 years.

Against the general liberalizing grain of the reforms was the inclusion (in 1957) of a vaguely worded crime of 'parasitism' in the statute books, which made a labour-camp term a possibility for anyone who did not have a steady job. Incorrect political activity remained punishable as the crime of 'anti-Soviet agitation'. Law enforcement and judicial proceedings were still subject to interference from the political authorities, and the KGB still went about protecting the state by its own methods, whose innovations now included the enlistment of 'hooligans' to disrupt poetry readings and of psychiatrists to put determined sticklers for civil rights under debilitating drug treatment in mental asylums. The principle that new laws should not be retrospective was violated at Khrushchev's own public insistence when the restoration of death penalty for black-market traders was applied to several convicts already serving their custodial terms under the pre-1961 law. The cases of people who had fallen victim to the 'proletarian justice' of the Stalin era were reviewed by a process that was grudgingly slow, secretive, and selective.

The propaganda campaign promoted by the regime under the 'socialist legality' slogan was at least as much about teaching the 'masses' to be law-abiding as teaching them their legal rights. It also brought the legalist reformism that aimed to minimize miscarriages of justice by strengthening the due process of the law (the rules of procedure guaranteeing the rights of defensive advocacy and the 'innocent until proven guilty' presumption, and limiting the criteria on which a guilty verdict could be made) into conflict with the resuscitation of 'comradely courts'. These were set up in residential districts as well as in work places to try petty offences and disputes at staged meetings geared more to mobilizing opinion against delinquency than to scruple about giving the defendants a fair hearing. 'The comradely courts' could impose only non-custodial sentences, and they dealt only with cases that otherwise might have been heard before the 'people's courts' – the lowest level of the state judiciary. Trials at the 'people's courts' also tended to be conducted in ways that were only loosely bound by legalistic formalities, with the defendant's character being subjected to a wide-ranging discussion as well as the evidence relating specifically to the indictment, people talking over one another to make counter-accusations, special pleadings and hear-say statements that would have been ruled as irrelevant in Western courts, and the judges doing their summing up in teacherish admonitory tones. The 'comradely courts' were thus only a small step further away than the 'people's courts' from the legalistic ideals of procedure-based guarantees of fairness. The substantive justice of the decisions reached by the 'people's courts' generally was not an issue for the reformist wing of the legal profession, though the 'comradely courts' were criticized for being prone to errors. The reformist wing of the legal profession, however, wanted the judicial process at all levels to become more 'legally cultured' – that is, more scrupulous about procedural formality, more professional, and less populist.

The conflict over whether 'socialist legality' should mean primarily 'socialist' forms of control over deviants or 'legal' ones thus brought back a modernization issue that had exercised the intelligentsia and government reformers in tsarist times. Was progress compatible with the social pragmatism of popular customary justice, or was it predicated upon the 'legal state' that made justice a matter of formal laws and procedures that would safeguard the universal applicability of the law to all citizens and the rationality of judicial decision-making? For the legal professionals and the newly born Western-oriented intelligentsia, de-Stalinization was about dissolving the arbitrary, irrational powers of autocracy by advancing the 'legal state'. For Khrushchev, on the other hand, de-Stalinization was also about having 'the people' (*narod*) participate in, and give legitimacy to, public affairs by the party-controlled forms of 'mass democracy'.

Reforms in Education

It was in the educational sphere, however, that Khrushchev's populist attitudes came into the most clear-cut conflict with the intelligentsia. Khrushchev was worried that the school system was too academic, defining success in terms of progress towards higher education, associating manual labour with intellectual failure, enhancing class divisions by making success easier for children from educated backgrounds, and supplying the manual labour market with reluctant, troublesome, and unskilled adolescents. In short, he saw the existing system as one in which the desirable expansion of secondary-level education had the undesirable cost of turning whole generations of youth into *beloruchki* ('whitehands' – the contemptuous term by which the working class referred to intellectuals and white-collar workers in tsarist times). The answer lay, Khrushchev thought, in making general education 'polytechnical'; here he drew on some of the educational ideas popular among the Bolsheviks in the 1920s, although the reform announced in 1958 was not nearly as visionary or radical as the earlier 'polytechnical' philosophies and experiments.

The reform imposed an obligation on general secondary schools to provide training in a manual skill and regular work experience in nearby factories or farms in addition to the academic curriculum. The lower tier of the secondary school was extended from three to four years to accommodate the enlarged curriculum, and it was made compulsory. Until then, only the four-year primary school had been compulsory, although the great majority of the children in urban and less remote rural areas (and some three-quarters in the USSR as a whole by 1958[4]) were already staying in school up to the completion of the lower secondary tier. The higher tier of the secondary school, however, remained three years long as before, although the new curriculum required a

---

4 Matthews, M. 1982: *Education in the Soviet Union: Policies and Institutions since Stalin*. London: Allen & Unwin, p. 7.

work placement in a factory or farm of up to 12 hours per week at term time, in addition to several weeks of vacation work. The option of staying on in full-time general education for the upper three years was being taken up by an increasing minority (about one-third in the USSR as a whole by 1958), but the thrust of the new policy was to render this option relatively less attractive, thus encouraging 15-year-olds to enter employment instead and complete their secondary education in part-time evening courses, or otherwise to opt for full-time education in technical schools geared to vocational rather than university-entry qualifications. The imposition of the manual-skills curriculum on the full-time general secondary schools inevitably reduced the hours available for academic subject teaching and homework, thus lowering academic standards towards the levels attainable in evening courses or in vocational schools. At the same time, universities were obliged to change their admissions policies; instead of filling all their places by competitive entrance examinations, they had to set aside up to 60 per cent of their admissions quotas for applicants who had at least two years of employment behind them and a recommendation from their work place 'social organizations'.

As a palliative to the charge that the higher-education sector was being set back by these policies because they reduced the academic standard of entrants, the reform allowed for an expansion of the élite minority of special secondary schools for gifted children, which were exempt from the manual-skills requirement to allow the teaching of a foreign language, an art, maths, or a science to a very high standard. But this provision was only relevant to a very small minority of highly talented or highly connected children, and to the most select of the higher education establishments to which the graduates of these schools invariably proceeded.

The 'polytechnization' reform quickly proved a shambles. Few schools managed to secure such a liaison with a nearby factory or farm to facilitate skills-training and work placements for the pupils that could be of interest to them. The compulsory exposure to manual work did nothing to reduce the prevalent aspiration of the secondary-school pupils to join the ranks of the intelligentsia by securing a place on a full-time higher education course. The reform did not reduce the influence of social class on the chances of success in this respect either: the children of educated parents were still receiving substantially more than their 'fair share' of university places relative to the children of workers or peasants, although some of them had to take the circuitous route of acquiring 'worker' status first by a two-year spell in employment. Neither was the reform solving the problem of skilled-labour shortage. Few school-leavers took jobs in the manual trades they supposedly learnt in school, and those who took manual employment did so mainly as a temporary expedient. As for the pupils who did their days of work experience in the factories, organizing them to do something useful was more trouble than it was worth to managers.

The 'polytechnization' reform was always known to be unpopular with the teachers, the academically able pupils and their parents, the administrators and managers who had to implement it, and with the universities. Its abandonment was already signalled in summer 1964, just before Khrushchev was ousted from power. The senior tier of the general secondary school was reduced to two years and the curriculum of both tiers was largely freed of the manual-skills training and in-term work-placement obligations. Full-time students were allowed to outnumber part-time students, and the universities were again allowed to select their students mainly by competitive entrance examinations, as the quotas set aside for 'candidates from production' were reduced to 23 per cent of the total intake.[5]

The Campaign against Religion

The last five years of Khrushchev's rule saw an intense regime against religion. Students and members of the intelligentsia were encouraged to do their voluntary 'social work' by joining the Knowledge Society, a mass organization devoted to promoting 'scientific atheism' among the populations still considered vulnerable to the appeal of 'religious superstitions'. This was the campaign's benign face. Other measures were directly repressive and in breach of Stalin's wartime concordat with the churches as well as of the constitutional principles, first proclaimed by Lenin, of separation of church and state affairs and the individual's rights of religious conscience and worship. Parish priests were excluded from the committees running the affairs of state-registered churches, and appointments to the priestless committees became subject to interference from the party and KGB. In addition, special commissions were set up for the supervision of church activities, and the churches were obliged to register with the state authorities all the baptisms, weddings, and other rites carried out for the benefit of individual believers. Some of the top Russian orthodox dignitaries were forced into retirement, and those who resisted the new offensive were put on trial. There were also several well publicized trials of low-level priests, on charges ranging from tax evasion to indulging in 'barbaric' rites. Unauthorized religious activities were made a criminal offence punishable by up to five years in camps or exile. Unauthorized activities were, of course, encouraged by the way the state-registered churches were forced to comply with the anti-religious campaign. The Russian Orthodox Church alone closed some 10 000 of its parish churches, thus reducing the total number by half, and the majority of its remaining monasteries and theological seminaries, reducing their number to single figures.[6] The closure of the monasteries was 'justified' by their depopulation, as many of the monks and seminary students were drafted to the army. These measures produced something of a schism within the Russian Orthodox Church, as the leading dignitaries who opposed them proclaimed the Patriarchate and the Church Council so compliant with the atheist authorities as to no longer having a valid claim to represent Christian authority. A similar schism occurred in the Baptist Church, where the state-registered council was opposed by a well organized and militant evangelical movement, the so-called *initsiativniki*. Besides, the Soviet authorities estimated that there were some 400 sects and cults. After Khrushchev was removed from power, the state authorities would try to diffuse the under-

---

5 Matthews, *Education*, p. 157.
6 Bordeaux, M. 1968: *Religious Ferment in Russia*. London: Macmillan, p. 14.

ground movements by giving concessions to the state-registered churches (e.g., by allowing them to publish more of their own literature) and by supporting their fight against the schismatics.

It is not known how many people were sent to labour camps, deported to remote areas, or incarcerated in mental hospitals for their religious beliefs. The well organized *initsiativniki* compiled a victim list of their own members that went into hundreds. The closure of the orthodox churches was often opposed by their congregations and enforced by deliberately provocative methods that must have resulted in numerous arrests and prosecutions. Physical provocations were also the order of the day against believers who went on pilgrimages to the closed monasteries. The criminal code was used against people who organized religious instruction or services in their homes. Legal repressions apart, the local commissions supervising religious activities organized visits to known believers to harangue them. The children of believers were sent to boarding schools where they were forced to join the pioneers or *komsomol*.

The anti-religious campaign gave rise to a dissident movement with its leaders, martyrs, and circulation networks of *samizdat* bulletins. The evangelical underground was mainly working class in its composition, and particularly militant in that it opposed laws which banned the spread of 'religious propaganda'. The orthodox dissidents, on the other hand, protested against the violations by the authorities of the laws that supposedly guaranteed freedom of religious belief and worship. In this sense, they fought a common cause with the rising intelligentsia dissident movement, whose strategy also consisted of highlighting the ways in which the authorities violated 'socialist legality' and the constitution in their use of repressive powers. Some of the writers who led the dissident wing of the intelligentsia, such as Solzhenitsyn and Sinyavsky, would indeed soon ally themselves in particular with the view that the freedom of the Russian Orthodox Belief was vital not only as a matter of civil rights but also because it was central to the culture and identity of the Russian people. In tsarist times, the Russian intelligentsia had a radical wing which was mainly atheist and generally saw the church as associated with the twin enemies of popular backwardness and political autocracy. Now the intelligentsia had a growing dissident wing whose range of anti-political autocracy attitudes included, for the first time, respect for the premodern association of Russian nationhood with orthodox Christianity, and the church now had articulate ecclesiastical spokesmen with an affinity for the modern concerns of citizenship and human rights (although Father Gapon of the 1904–05 labour movement perhaps also belonged to this category).

The New Intelligentsia

Urbanization resumed its rapid progress after the war. By 1959, urban residents made up 52 per cent of the population of the Russian Federated Republic, Moscow had over six million inhabitants, and Leningrad over 3.3 million. The proportion of the working population engaged in agriculture was edging down to below 40 per cent. Of the non-agricultural sector, just over two-thirds were in manual or menial service jobs, and this proportion was on a slight upward trend. Although not as quickly as the manual urban-sector ranks, the non-manual sector was nevertheless growing, and the component of 'specialists' within it particularly so. Career opportunities for higher-education graduates were further enhanced by the fact that many of the jobs classified as requiring graduate qualifications were still occupied by the *praktiki*, the people appointed to them during the 1930s when educational provision could not keep up with the very fast expansion of the managerial, administrative, and 'specialist' occupations. Many *praktiki* were now approaching retirement, and some were demoted to lower-level posts. Khrushchev's concerns about the 'whitehands' (*beloruchki*) did not extend to challenging the assumption that the elimination of the *praktiki* route to authoritative and professional jobs was a necessary part of progress, and that formal education should thus constitute the main route. The only hesitation in this respect was evident during three or four years prior to 1958, when year-on-year increases in the intake of students to higher-education courses were halted in preference to expanding vocational secondary-level schools. But in 1958 the higher education sector resumed its steady and substantial growth. If in 1953 admissions to higher-education courses amounted to about one-twentieth of the number of 18-year-olds in the country, the resumption of expansion in 1958, coinciding as it did with the demographic dip occasioned by the low wartime birth-rate, resulted in admissions growing to about one-ninth of the number of 18-year-olds in the early 1960s. This upward trend would be sustained even as the larger post-war cohort reached the student age, so that by the 1970s undergraduate admissions would be amounting to about one-eighth of all 18-year-olds.[7] By 1959, the number of higher-education graduates was more than three times larger than in 1939, making up 3.3 per cent of the total labour force[8] and 18 per cent of the people in non-manual occupations (compared to eight per cent in 1939). The graduate contingent was especially high in Moscow, Leningrad, and several other centres of scientific and technological research, such as the newly built Akademgorod near Novosibirsk. Somewhat uneven though it may have been in its geographical spread, its expansion was such that very soon those who had gained their education in the post-Stalin years predominated numerically over their Stalin-era elders everywhere.

Secondary-school children's ambition to proceed to higher education (so lamented by Khrushchev) was confirmed by sociological research. In a country whose official ideology had been celebrating the industrial working class for 40 years, and when the difference in earnings between the average manual worker and the average professional employee was narrowing, this ambition seems surprising. (In industry, average ITR pay was 2.1 times higher than the average manual workers' pay in 1940, 1.5 times higher in 1960, and 1.4 times higher in 1970.[9]) Some 80 per cent of the growing proportion of youth that stayed on in school to complete the secondary level wished to proceed to higher education. Secondary-school pupils consistently ranked professional

7 Matthews, *Education*, p. 103.
8 Ryan, M. and Prentice, R. 1987: *Social Trends in the USSR from 1950*. London: Macmillan, p. 72.
9 Lane, D. 1992: *Soviet Society under Perestroika*. London: Routledge, p. 168.

occupations, such as 'mathematician', 'physicist', 'scientific worker', 'radio engineer', and 'physician', as the most desirable and commanding the highest social prestige; but they took any higher education places they could get, even if their interest in the course was less than avid, since they considered any graduate qualification better than a non-graduate alternative. For men, the attractiveness of full-time higher education was undoubtedly enhanced by the fact that the military training they received as students exempted them from having to do military service proper (two to three years). But higher education was also aspired to by women, the student body having had only a slight male majority since the war. Soon it became slightly more female than male. Skilled manual jobs in industry, such as afforded relatively high earnings, appeared heavily male biased in recruitment, which left the graduate professions as the only route to reasonable levels of pay for women.

The emphasis on formal qualifications in the recruitment to 'specialist' and authoritative non-manual posts cut off the opportunities for manual workers to move from factory floor to office desk, which had been ample between the revolution and the war. A study of social mobility carried out in two provincial towns (Ufa and Orenburg) found 91 per cent of the people who had manual jobs in 1950 and did not retire during the next 15 years still doing manual work in 1965; and only about three per cent could be considered to have moved further away from the bench than the lowest non-manual ranks.[10] But reserving 'specialist' and 'responsible' jobs for people with educational qualifications had its effects on the pattern of social mobility between generations. The tendency for educational attainment to run in families was marked even in the 1920s and the 1930s, when the children of educated parents were finding their way to higher education despite the regime's discriminatory measures in favour of working-class youth. This tendency also survived Khrushchev's short-lived attempt to change it. In 1938, the proportion of the student body claiming a working-class background was roughly the same as the proportion of non-agricultural manual workers in the working population, while the children of white-collar parents were substantially over-represented in the student body and the children of collective farmers very substantially under-represented. In the 1960s, the gap between the educational chances bequeathed by agricultural and urban-manual backgrounds was reduced; both were under-represented in the student body to a similar degree, which was not nearly as high as the under-representation of peasant-background children before the war. Children from white-collar backgrounds made up more than a half of the student body, however, a proportion which was more than double that of white-collar employees in the working population; this degree of over-representation was in line with that of the late 1930s, though perhaps slightly lesser than that of the early 1950s.[11]

The general category of 'employee' (non-manual) backgrounds was of course very heterogeneous, and its use for measuring the student body's social composition disguised rather than revealed the strength of the correlation

10 Yanowitch, M. 1977: *Social and Economic Inequality in the Soviet Union*. London: Martin Robertson, p. 128.
11 Matthews, *Education*, p. 159.

between the educational attainment of parents and children. A large-scale study carried out later, in the early 1970s, provided a better illustration when it found that 32 per cent of the fathers and 27 per cent of the mothers of first-year students on higher education courses were themselves graduates.[12] At that time, graduates made up six or seven per cent of the total working population,[13] and an even smaller proportion of the parental age-group. In short, the educational system was expanding quickly enough to provide an opportunity of passage to 'responsible' and 'specialist' jobs for a minority of the children born to uneducated parents; but it was also a system in which being born to educated parents was an advantage. It was unusual for a child born to a white-collar family to end up in manual work, and the growing ranks of 'specialists' had an increasing contingent of second-generation members.

The second-generation contingent particularly dominated the occupations that were considered the most desirable by secondary-school leavers. The secondary schools were expanding faster than tertiary ones. In the early 1950s, the number of students admitted to higher education amounted to some two-thirds of the number of secondary-school leavers; by the early 1960s, the proportion was down to one-third and dropping towards one-fifth by the early 1970s. The increasing rate of failure by school-leavers to secure a place in higher education was mainly borne by the first-generation aspirants to educated careers. Moreover, the great majority of the higher-education institutes (VUZy) were smallish establishments providing vocationally orientated courses for teachers, engineers of various kinds, agronomists, economists, medical doctors, lawyers, etc. Fewer than 10 per cent of the student body were actually in universities, doing pure sciences or humanities. The large universities of Moscow and Leningrad (with the addition of Novosibirsk university), and several of the specialized VUZy situated mainly in the capital cities, however, constituted the academic élite and the recruitment ground for the careers that were considered the most desirable and prestigious by secondary-school leavers, such as the careers subsumable under the occupational category of 'scientific worker'. Students from uneducated families were numerically dominant only in the vocational and provincial VUZy, while the sons and daughters of educated parents were a clear majority in the universities and in the most prestigious VUZy. A sociological survey of young graduate specialists in the early 1970s found that whereas of those working as 'managerial-technical staff' (ITR) in the factories, 37 per cent had come from specialist home backgrounds and the vast majority were vocational VUZy graduates, of those employed as 'scientific workers' by the Academy of Sciences, 70 per cent had come from specialist home backgrounds and 59 per cent received their degrees in the universities.[14]

These patterns were reflected in the differences between the social profiles of the professional strata in the provinces and the main cities. The provincial urban areas were acquiring a sizeable 'intelligentsia' class, mainly thanks to the growth of large-scale industry. Here there were still many *praktiki*, the

---

12 Kneen, P. 1984: *Soviet Scientists and the State*. London: Macmillan, p. 25.
13 Ryan and Prentice, *Social Trends*, p. 72.
14 Kneen, *Soviet Scientists*, p. 27.

majority of graduates received their education in the common run of VUZy, and they were the first generation to have left their labouring-class backgrounds. In the main cities, on the other hand, career possibilities for graduates varied from industrial ITR to élite academy institutes, and in Moscow to government bureaucracy and central-committee think-tanks; the *praktiki* were disappearing quickly, and the graduates tended to come from the more select places of learning and educated or non-manual home backgrounds.

The late 1950s and 1960s were years of growth in the ranks of 'scientific workers' holding jobs in research institutes. Most worked on technological research and development under industrial ministries, while a minority (under 10 per cent) worked on 'fundamental' research under the Academy of Sciences, and some were in research posts attached to the universities and VUZy. A minority (about one-fifth) worked in the humanities and the social sciences, including the new fields of economics and sociology created by de-Stalinization, while the rest were natural scientists and applied-science specialists. Natural scientists made up some 60 per cent of the Academy of Sciences' staff. The number of scientific workers almost trebled between 1955 and 1965, reaching nearly 665 000 by 1965 in the USSR as a whole.[15] These numbers made up less than one-tenth of the total of graduates working in the economy, but the 'scientific worker' profession is of interest because careers within it were prestigious and sought after, and because the profession had its own Academy of Sciences' élite including both people who had access to the political power centre and people who became leading reformists or were about to become leading dissidents. The nature of the profession, after all, was such as to predispose its members towards the liberal values of unrestricted information, sceptical thought, internationalism, collegiality, and self-directed work, putting them at odds with the political system. Science held a greater promise than ever to the political leaders and the general population at the time of the first space shots; the political leaders did not hesitate to commit ever greater sums of money to it, and Khrushchev's de-Stalinization measures allowed it more diversity and less party tutelage.

In tsarist times, as we saw in Chapter 1, the social and political modernization movements created a 'civil society' (*obshchestvo*) with its self-conscious nucleus: the intelligentsia committed to the Enlightenment values of high secular culture, science, technological progress, and rationality in the ordering of public affairs in the service of 'the people'. The intelligentsia had its reformist wing that strove to modernize the tsarist state from within and its revolutionary underground trying to overthrow it, with many people in between. It had its own institutions – the cultural salons under noble patronage, the 'thick' literary journals that were vehicles for social and political debate as well as for cultured entertainment, the theatres, and the enclaves within academia and state bureaucracy that afforded protection for independent opinion makers – to name just the above-ground ones. The intelligentsia had its venerated leaders and heroes, and an ongoing history of

15 Kneen, *Soviet Scientists*, p. 13.

brushes with state authorities which confirmed them in the intelligentsia's eyes as capricious, irrational, inefficient, unenlightened, uncultured, and bureaucratic. The intelligentsia thus defined itself *vis-à-vis* the autocracy and, in addition, *vis-à-vis* 'the people' whom it wanted to help out of 'darkness'.

The intelligentsia was decimated by the Bolshevik hijack of the revolution, cast by political force into two categories of public servants, 'the bourgeois specialists' and the Bolsheviks' own agitprop cadres, although the regime reflected the fact that the revolutionary movement that created it had its own origins in the inteligentsia by incorporating the latter's culturist and industrialist visions of modernity into its own philosophy. It provided patronage and institutions for the *élites* of culture and science, and committed resources to the spread of education. At the same time, however, during the Stalin era in particular it prevented the intelligentsia from being what it had been under the tsars, the creator of a public counterpart to the state, a 'civil society' nucleus.

This changed somewhat with Khrushchev's de-Stalinization, which created a public sense of a duality between reformism and conservatism in politics. Reformist politicians in the Kremlin recruited their own teams of advisers from a post-Stalin generation of graduate high-fliers, and this enlarged wing of the top political establishment provided political patronage for cultural and scholarly figures, who quickly made the cause of de-Stalinization their own. 'Thick' literary journals such as *Novyi mir* and *Yunost'*, theatres such as the Taganka in Moscow, the newly established academy institutes for sociology, economics, and mathematical economics, and several academy institutes and university departments of law became known publicly as liberal and reformist, while other institutions – the literary journals *Literatura i zhizn'* and *Oktyabr*, and the old-established institutes of economics, for example, became widely known as conservative. This duality allowed people to express their allegiances by what they read, at which theatre they queued for tickets, or which authorities they cited in their conversations about economic reforms. The Taganka, university, and public lectures given by academics known to have taken an 'anti-dogmatic' stand, public readings by such poets as Yevtushenko and Voznesensky, were packed with students of all subjects and with the post-Stalin generation of professional people. Cultural establishments of conservative repute were mainly attended by organized parties of visitors from the provinces, conservative writers' and scholars' public lectures by 'responsible' officials. Thus there were liberal gatherings and the rest, and the liberal gatherings were enthusiastic, packed, youthful, and educated. Reading and attending the events of 'the thaw' was an expression of a liberal political allegiance and, at the same time, a mark of belonging to an educated, cultured, and progressive social group, an intelligentsia. Whereas in Stalin's times the 'intelligentsia' was more a statistical category of official sociology than a distinctive social body providing a critical public to the men of state, de-Stalinization gave a rebirth to the social body.

The new intelligentsia was not the same as the old. It was massive by comparison, its networks were not nearly as closely knit, its bloodlines were varied and plebeian, its careers wedded to technology and the state, and its experiences devoid of foreign travel. This intelligentsia was less moved by the idea of a potent marriage with 'the people', considering it as consummated in the birth of the Soviet state and perhaps overworked in the state's own rhetoric. It had no revolutionary underground, and it was of the new mass-media age where independence of mind from the state could be expressed in the privacy of one's home by trying to tune the radio to the BBC or Radio Liberty Russian-language news bulletins.

The new intelligentsia, however, had its radical leaders and their *cause célèbre* confrontations with the authorities. The writer, Boris Pasternak, was harassed to his premature death after his *Dr Zhivago* was published in the West and awarded the Nobel Prize; his funeral in 1960 turned into a public demonstration. Other *cause célèbre* events included the KGB attacks on poetry readings at Mayakovsky Square, the prosecution of the poet Brodsky under the new-fangled 'parasitism' law, and the occasion where Khrushchev swept with his entourage into an exhibition of modern art to lambast the artists, but one of them, the sculptor Neizvestny, talked back.

These confrontations over artistic freedom also involved wider issues, such as anti-semitism. In the immediate post-war years, during his spell as the party boss of the Ukrainian Republic, Khrushchev had put a stop to plans to build a memorial in Babi Yar, the ravine in the outskirts of Kiev where some 20 000 of the city's residents had perished in mass executions during the German occupation. At least 90 000 of them were Jews, the victims of a systematic genocide campaign carried out in the first three months of the occupation, the implementation of which was not without some Ukrainian support and involvement. This was an awkward fact to commemorate in the post-war years when 'Zionists' and 'cosmopolitans' were the new enemies in Stalinist political visions. The killing ground remained uncommemorated, and it was redeveloped by a large-scale construction project featuring a dam. The 'thaw' that followed Stalin's death allowed calls for a Babi Yar monument to be heard again, but Khrushchev reiterated his stance against. In 1961 the dam burst, the deluge and landslide killing over a hundred Kievans. The whole story was told by Yevtushenko in a harrowing epic poem that indicted the anti-semitism of both the Nazis who perpetrated the mass atrocity and the Stalinists who built the ill-fated dam. After the first readings by the poet to student assemblies, a publication in the *Literaturnaya gazeta* weekly and a concert where the poem was recited to music composed by Shostakovich, Khrushchev had one of his outbursts against the 'bourgeois' leanings of the creative intelligentsia. Yevtushenko was forced to change the poem, the conservative press went on an offensive against 'cosmopolitans' as well as 'bourgeois liberals', and Babi Yar was put under concrete again, though eventually also adorned by a monument which, however, did not acknowledge the Jewish holocaust aspect of the event.

Leading scientists also played their part in resuscitating some of the old intelligentsia traditions of political engagement, by petitioning the party authorities on the issue of atmospheric testing of nuclear warheads, for example. The radical activists from the élites of arts and science who embarrassed the political authorities by raising issues of moral principle were, of course, no more but a tiny minority of the new intelligentsia, but their names and actions became fairly widely known through foreign broadcasts as well as through metropolitan grapevines and the growing circulations of *samizdat* reading matter.

That the intelligentsia began to form something like a broader social public producing its own pressures on the political system was, however, abundantly evident in the official media in the contexts of debates concerning de-Stalinization and the Khrushchevite reforms. The 'polytechnization' aspect of the education reforms was widely acknowledged in the press as problematic and controversial – and the opposition to it won through. The 'parasitism' law was contested publicly by the legal profession, and when it was forced on to the statute book, the judiciary drew the sting out of it by overthrowing a large number of the convictions at the appeal courts on various legal technicality grounds. We saw in the discussion of economic reforms how the agenda was broadened to create a discourse in which economic inefficiencies were associated with the political faults of bureaucratic centralism. The literary fiction that grew alongside this debate defined a contrast of values between intelligentsia heroes and bureaucratic villains. 'A bureaucrat is someone who used to be a lazy never-do-well at school when he was a boy', observed the hero of a novel serialized in *Novyi mir*, a scientist-engineer who was glad to be sacked from a managerial post because that enabled him to do 'the real work' of a committed professional.[16] De-Stalinization politics became infused with the values of the intelligentsia's social identity.

The reborn intelligentsia was less influenced than its tsarist-times predecessor by the radical populist project of incorporating 'the people' into the movement against political autocracy. It did, however, reflect the old themes of concern about the material and cultural condition of the working classes. Stalinist industrial bosses were portrayed in the new fiction as hypocrites using an ideological vernacular to disguise their indifference or callousness towards their workers. The renaissance of social science produced statistical measurements highlighting how far the economy still had to go to lift the masses from precarious levels of subsistence. Surveys and analyses of family budgets, for example, defined the monthly minimum *per capita* income needed by urban residents to keep them above the 'underprovisioned' (*maloobespechennye*) levels of life as just over 50 roubles, and found one-third of urban workers' families still below that level in the mid-1960s.[17]

The Russian intelligentsia's time-honoured preoccupations with the cultural level of the masses were expressed through sociological 'time-budget' surveys which, like the family-budget investigations, drew on methodologies developed in the 1920s. These surveys duly found that educated people owned more books and spent more of their non-working time than their blue-collar cousins in 'cultured recreation', 'social work' activities, and educational self-improvement. They also discovered, however, that all classes still favoured the traditional leisure patterns based on the apparently aimless spontaneity of having a good time with family and friends, and that the gains in free time afforded by the shortening of work hours were not really given over to more edifying pursuits. The expert commentaries that followed decried both the traditional leisure patterns and the newly spreading popular pastime of TV-watching from a standpoint that approved only of high culture and organized

---

16 Davydova, N. 1960: 'Lyubov' inzhenera Izotova'. *Novyi mir*, i–iii.
17 McAuley, A. 1979: *Economic Welfare in the Soviet Union: Poverty, Living Standards, and Inequality*. London: Allen & Unwin, p. 83.

'active leisure' as good for 'the development of the human spirit'. Alcohol consumption was singled out for particular disapproval as a symptom of the 'uncultured' popular traditions surviving in the new urban environments, and as the principal cause of social ills ranging from indisciplined work behaviour to crime and rising divorce rates. The growing sociological writing was in many ways continuous with the themes dating from the beginning of the century, which identified social progress with more people having longer book shelves in their homes and lesser preference for frivolous entertainment.

These themes ran through the policies and rhetoric of the Soviet regime as well as the prerevolutionary, intelligentsia-dominated modernization movement. Until the mid-1930s, however, they had to coexist with the militant rhetoric of the 'workers' state', in which idealized 'proletarian' virtues were seen as contrasting to 'bourgeois' vices. Stalin 'resolved' this conundrum in the 1930s by replacing both the revolutionary intellectual avant-garde and the 'bourgeois specialists'. The new generation of professionals were educated for technical service to the state, the arts were channelled into accessible classical and 'socialist realist' forms of edifying entertainment, and 'culture' was promoted as 'production culture' – the virtues of efficient, skilled, and self-disciplined work. Upward mobility was on offer as a reward to self-improving workers, and also the promise of a 'living (*bytovaya*) culture' – the sober and urbane enjoyment of the material comforts that a general economic growth and individual work success might bring. The Stalinist state gave 'responsible' positions to its educated 'cadres' and perhaps allowed them a shared sense of social superiority over the 'masses' who had yet to acquire 'culture'; but it did not allow them to express any other collective identity than that which it defined for them.

By the beginning of the Khrushchev period, extra-educational channels for workers' upward mobility were blocked, and the growing educated core was at least second generation, and separated from the less educated by 'cultured' backgrounds as well as individual success. The new sociology counted workers' leisure preferences only to find them still wanting in 'culture' The school-leavers' occupational aspirations were found to fall into a hierarchy, with the better educated jobs at the top. Both of these findings reinforced the educated readers' sense of social superiority. Besides, de-Stalinization now made it possible for the educated to acquire a collective identity which naturally overlapped with the identities defined by positions in the administrative structures of the state, but which was also separate and more general. 'Culture' began to acquire its less accessible, avant-garde layers again (abstract art, non-realist literature) and its politically controversial flowerings; and it was produced for a public that 'understood' rather than for the state.

Khrushchev's de-Stalinization was in a sense a restorative policy intended to revitalize the 'leading role' of the party by a return to 'the Leninist norms'. It neither sought nor caused a substantial change in the structure of political power and its philosophy. The political establishment remained centralized and authoritarian, the careers within it shaped by personal patronage, and the hierarchy of party and state workers buttressed by a rank-graded system for the dispensation of privilege. The regime 'merely' became less life-threatening, more civilian than militant, and it allowed itself to be seen to be searching for some new policies. Many of the policies the leader identified with were known to be disapproved of by various people, and many were seen to fail. This was not an unimportant change, for it led to a new configuration in the relationship between state and society. In the Stalin era, as we saw in the last chapter, what might be seen as the social realm, the sphere of life that was not directly organized by the political regime, was limited to the interstices of the bureaucracy itself and a residual semi-private sphere: a question of informal patterns of adaptation that were the unintended consequence of the regime's policies or outside the range of political concerns. Under Khrushchev, the state–society duality became more public and under the influence of something that was almost like a social class differentiated from both 'the people' and the state, and capable of drawing on its own historic traditions. The intelligentsia's rebirth was perhaps an unintended consequence of Khrushchev's de-Staliniza-tion, but it was its most important legacy.

Further Reading

An insider view of de-Stalinization politics at the high establishment level is offered by F. Burlatsky, *Khrushchev and the First Russian Spring* (London: Weidenfeld & Nicolson, 1991). The author was one of the young men recruited almost straight from university to work for two politburo members in succession, Kuusinen and Andropov, as a speech-writer and a member of policy-making teams. He was also on the staff that accompanied Khrushchev on some of his foreign travels. He lost his power-centre job after Khrushchev's removal, but remained a part of the intellectual establishment as a political journalist, biographer, and theorist – one of the circle that eventually resurfaced to political prominence with Gorbachev's *perestroika*. Burlatsky's highly readable book provides an insight not only into the Khrushchevite political spirit but also more generally into the political class way of life.

The Further Reading section of the last chapter mentioned a split between 'totalitarian' and 'revisionist' schools of thought among (mainly American) Western historians of the Stalin period. That was in fact the second wave of revisionist challenge to the totalitarian model, which occurred in the 1980s. The first wave occurred in the 1960s as a reflection of Khrushchev's de-Stalinization, and it was driven by political scientists rather than historians. If the post-Stalin system no longer had terror at the centre of its workings, then perhaps it was appropriate to view it as in some ways comparable rather than just contrasting with Western political systems; for example, the post-Stalin version of communist rule could be seen as involving processes in which something like interest groups make themselves felt and party officials function in part as brokers between conflicting interests. The books that were particularly influential in this context were G. Skilling and F. Griffiths (eds), *Interest Groups in Soviet Politics* (Princeton, NJ: Princeton University Press, 1971) and J. Hough, *The Soviet Prefects: The Local Party Organs in Industrial Decision-Making* (Cambridge, Mass.: Harvard University Press, 1969). The former includes articles by R. Judy on the economists, E. Simmons on the writers, and D. Barry and H. Berman on the jurists, which provide some of the information on which I have drawn in this chapter. C. Linden, *Khrushchev and the Soviet Leadership 1957–1964* (Baltimore, Md: Johns Hopkins University

Press, 1966) also makes a case for a 'conflict model' of Soviet politics and, at the same time, provides a useful summary of political events. Another good political account is R. and Z. Medvedev, *Khrushchev: The Years in Power* (Oxford: Oxford University Press, 1977). A. Nove, *Stalinism and After* (London: George Allen & Unwin 1975) is still a very useful and readable introductory essay on the post-Stalin era.

M. Lewin, *Political Undercurrents in Soviet Economic Debates* (Princeton, NJ: Princeton University Press, 1984) is full of insight into the relationship between economic and political reformism and its historical continuities, with a particular emphasis on the legacy of the ideas that had been developed under Bukharin's patronage prior to Stalin's defeat of the 'right opposition'. Other books that provide fuller accounts of the topics touched on in this chapter include M. Matthews, *Education in the Soviet Union: Policies and Institutions since Stalin* (London: Allen & Unwin, 1982); B. Bociurkiw and J. Strong, *Religion and Atheism in the USSR and Eastern Europe* (London: Macmillan, 1975), Chaps 3–4; M. Bordeaux, *Religious Ferment in Russia: Protestant Opposition to Soviet Religious Policy* (London: Macmillan, 1968) and *Patriarch and Prophets: Persecution of the Russian Orthodox Church Today* (London: Macmillan, 1969); D. Filtzer, *Soviet Workers and De-Stalinization* (Cambridge: Cambridge University Press, 1992); M. McAuley, *Labour Disputes in Soviet Russia, 1957–1965* (Oxford: Oxford University Press, 1969); and M. McCauley, *Khrushchev and the Development of Soviet Agriculture: the Virgin Lands Programme, 1953–64* (London: Macmillan, 1976).

T. L. Thompson and R. Sheldon (eds), *Soviet Society and Culture* (Boulder, Colo. and London, Westview Press, 1988) is again useful; the chapter by J. Bushnell on 'Urban leisure culture' summarizes the Soviet sociologists' research on the subject and throws into relief the culturist assumptions of both Soviet and Western commentators on such matters; and a chapter by R. Sheldon tells the Babi Yar story. A range of Soviet sociological research on social mobility, occupational prestige, etc., is given, for example, in M. Yanowitch and W. Fisher (eds), *Social Stratification and Mobility in the USSR* (White Plains, NY: International Arts and Sciences Press, 1973) and M. Yanowitch (ed.), *Social and Economic Inequality in the Soviet Union* (London: Martin Robertson, 1977).

10

State and Society in the Last Soviet Decades, 1964–89

Khrushchev was not a popular figure when his politburo recalled him from holiday to vote him into retirement. He had offended the intelligentsia by his outbursts against the arts, his education policies, and by the 'uncultured', folksy style in which he presented himself on television. He had offended industrial workers by his productivity campaigns and rising food prices, and collective farmers by his intentions to reduce household plots. He also offended the establishment: the army officer corps by his attempts to reduce defence spending, the economic officialdom by forcing many of them to move from Moscow to the provinces as a result of the *sovnarkhoz* reform, and party *apparatchiki* by his 'circulation of cadres' policies and by the splitting of the apparatus into industrial and agricultural hierarchies. Although his sudden retirement was ostensibly due to advancing years and failing health, press commentaries and the oral briefings made to rank-and-file party meetings throughout the land made it clear that the party wanted no more 'voluntarism', the faulty leadership style that caused chaos by well intentioned but high-handed reform campaigns. The new leadership promised a consultative style and policy-making based on professional expertise.

The politburo thus ushered in a 20-year period during which piecemeal reforms were never off the agenda while the dominant political tune was increasingly one of devotion to the virtues of continuity and stability. The main discontinuity consisted in the fact that, as we shall see below, ideological justification of party rule ceased to draw on the idea that the party was there to use politics for a revolutionary transformation of society. This was not a great break with traditions, for the *realpolitik* of managing society had been a part of what the party was about ever since Lenin came to power; but a break it was nevertheless, for it was only after Khrushchev's fall that the managing became unaccompanied by utopian visions. The nature of this regime, its strategies of social control and the social trends and movements that interacted with it, will be explored below, after a summary of the policies that were not directly concerned with the management of domestic stability but nevertheless contributed to the overall climate.

Policies of the Brezhnev Regime, 1964–82

The politburo that voted Khrushchev out of power installed Brezhnev as the party first secretary and Kosygin as the Council of Ministers chairman. But this time there was no question as to which of these functions was on top. The man who headed the party apparatus also chaired the party politburo, and that this was the cabinet of central rule was now an established principle. As formerly, the initial post-succession phase was marked by proclamations that the politburo constituted a 'collective leadership'; and as before, the first secretary (soon renamed 'general secretary', the title Stalin had held) duly rose to a clear top oligarch status. New legislation made the Council of Ministers an explicitly subordinate body to the Supreme Soviet as well as the party, and in 1977 Brezhnev became chairman of the Supreme Soviet (i.e., the head of state) in addition to his party office. He also became a Marshal of the Soviet Union and the Chairman of the Defence Council, the supreme commander of the armed forces.

In the 1970s, the Brezhnev regime brought Russian imperial power to its historical zenith. Unlike Khrushchev, Brezhnev backed his foreign policy by a clear commitment to increasing military strength. The 1970s were a decade of an unprecedented arms build-up combined with 'relaxation of tensions' exchanges of presidential visits and agreements with the West that did no harm to the Soviet global position. The USSR supported the winning side in the Vietnam war, the conclusion of which was followed by a swell of pro-*détente* electoral pressures on Western leaders. By the middle of the decade Russia had the agreement it wanted on East German borders, good terms for repeated and substantial imports of American grain, a substantial German investment in the construction of a pipeline to convey Siberian gas for export to central Europe, a major joint venture with Fiat to build a mass-production car plant, etc. At the same time, it extended substantially its sphere of influence in Africa by backing 'national liberation struggles' there, most notably by supporting the extensive involvement of Cuban military in Angola, and also in south-east Asia, most notably by supporting a Vietnamese occupation of Cambodia.

China, however, remained a thorn in the flesh. There were armed clashes on the border with Manchuria in 1969, the tensions remained unresolved, and Russian global diplomacy failed in its efforts to prevent China from making its own *détente* agreements with the USA and Japan at the end of the decade. Soviet domestic propaganda preached that the Western governments were but reluctant partners to the USSR in the making of the 'relaxation of tensions' agreements, forced to them by Soviet strength and popular peace movements against resistance from the war-mongering tendencies of capitalist imperialism. This was standard propaganda fare which many took with a pinch of salt. The 'Chinese threat', however, was felt readily and widely among the Russian population.

Soviet relations with Western Europe were if anything better than with the USA, and they received an important symbolic landmark in the signing of the multinational Helsinki agreement in 1975. This agreement had an impact on the domestic political scene in that it included clauses on human rights, giving a fresh boost to the dissident movement, and forcing the regime to relax its restrictions on the emigration of Jews and ethnic Germans.

Another foreign-affairs event that had an impact on domestic politics had been the Prague Spring and the invasion of Czechoslovakia in 1968. This caused only a minor setback to Russian diplomacy *vis-à-vis* Western powers, however, because the West regarded it as a matter internal to the Eastern bloc. The doctrine of 'proletarian internationalism' which Brezhnev announced to justify the invasion reversed Khrushchev's policy of tolerance towards 'different roads to socialism'. Unlike the Hungarian uprising in 1956, the Prague Spring was a peaceful liberalization process which was giving the Czech Communist Party an unprecedented popularity. Neither a capitalist restoration nor a withdrawal from the Warsaw Pact were on the agenda, and the invasion was in fact timed to prevent a legitimately convened party congress from taking place. The Brezhnev doctrine in effect arrogated to the Kremlin the right to use force against allied communist states to prevent any autonomous developments. Domestically, the doctrine was reflected in a marked narrowing of the limits of permissable debate and in the tightening of political controls over the intelligentsia to keep its dissident and reformist wings at bay. The jamming of Western radio broadcasts was renewed, and the country's political atmosphere became one which the liberal intelligentsia perceived as 're-Stalinization'.

In 1980 the Soviet army invaded Afghanistan under the auspices of Brezhnev's 'proletarian internationalism' doctrine, embroiling itself in a war against Islamic insurgents that proved unwinnable. Some 140 000 conscripts took part by the time the Gorbachev regime withdrew the army from the country in 1989, almost 14 000 losing their lives and another 30 000 returning home with serious injuries.[1] The end of the Brezhnev regime was thus marred by an exposure of a weakness in imperial armour and a freeze in the relations with the West. This was symbolized by a Western boycott of the Moscow Olympics in 1980 and the subsequent Soviet boycott of the next games in Los Angeles. More ominously for a country whose economy was by then all too evidently straining under the defence burden, the Reagan administration in the USA suspended a commitment to the *détente* type of cold-war management in favour of threatening to take the arms race to a new and very expensive 'star wars' stage.

In agriculture, the Brezhnev regime abandoned Khrushchev's maize-planting as one of the fallen leader's 'hare-brained schemes', but otherwise kept continuity with the already established principles. The strategic goal remained the creation of an agri-industry with a high degree of specialization, mechanization, and economies of scale. Collective farms were merged and many of the resulting large units were converted to single-product state farms. There was a sustained growth in agricultural investment, increasing the provision of chemical fertilizers, machinery, storage facilities, and food-processing plants. Dairy farming remained a particular growth priority, while grain-harvest shortfalls were made good by American imports. The regime also took measures to slow down the drain of labour from farming to towns by

---

1 Lane, D. 1992: *Soviet Society under Perestroika*. London: Routledge, p. 280.

reducing the economic disadvantages of staying in the countryside. Collective farmers as well as state farm workers became entitled to state pensions and protected by minimum-wage legislation. New statutes also reaffirmed the rights of collective farmers to their household plots and private-produce trade. At the end of the 1970s, these rights received a further boost when the government decreed that industry should add machines for small-plot cultivation in its plans, to be made available for purchase by private individuals. Overall, agriculture remained vulnerable to the vagaries of weather and its efficiency remained well behind Western standards. It was still making available less meat and fewer dairy products than the amount required by official dietary standards. But the average citizen's food consumption was becoming less starchy and the improvement in the towns was not at the expense of making things worse for the rural population.

In industry, the Brezhnev era started with a reorganization which did away with the territorial, *sovnarkhoz* structure of command introduced by Khrushchev. It re-established the traditional, industrial branch system of control through Moscow-based ministries. The new leadership evidently decided that the tendencies of 'departmentalism' (*vedomstvennost'*) were a more containable problem than 'localism' (*mestnichestvo*). In the years that followed there were further reorganizations, concerned mainly with merging enterprises into large conglomerates (*obyedineniya*) including research-and-development institutes as well as manufacturing subsidiaries, so that the *obyedinenie* managements in effect became a new kind of intermediate level of command between ministry and factory. These searches for organizational improvements that could enable the central authorities to keep 50 000 factories under effective control had to remain on the agenda because the new leadership decided against taking the risk of a more substantial economic reform.

The statute on industrial enterprise that accompanied the re-establishment of the ministerial structure ostensibly granted more autonomy to factory managers. The number of performance indicators was reduced, and the main one was defined in terms of the rouble value of the principal lines of output rather than in tonnes or pieces. Enterprises were free to spend a part of their profits on bonus payments, welfare facilities, and secondary production investments, and apparently also to negotiate some of their own customer-supplier relationships. But prices were set by the state, the principal production targets were defined by the centralized planning authorities, and an increasing range of raw materials was under the monopoly control of the state office governing the distribution of supplies. Furthermore, the rights of decision-making that the statute defined for enterprise management were always qualified by the rights of the 'higher organs' to intervene on behalf of the interests of state. This was not the 'market socialism' charter the radical economists had advocated; it was a reaffirmation of the traditional centralized system with some nods in the direction of the idea that decentralized, enterprise-level initiative deserved encouragement as long as it did not conflict with the central authorities' goals.

The nods were sufficient to keep the reformist–conservative debate going for a while, as a contest of views concerning the spirit in which the statute should be implemented. After the Czech invasion, however, the media became closed to the bolder expressions of pro-market, decentralist arguments for economic reforms. They remained open, on the other hand, to celebrations of the promise that new computer technology held for rationalizing the economic system. Computerization would allow the central planners to process more detailed information into better input–output-balanced plans, and the science of 'cybernetics' to devise sophisticated information flows and rational organization structures. The information flows, it was argued, could even simulate the messages that a market would have given about consumer preferences without incurring the costs of *ex-post facto* adjustments to market demands. Although the original mathematical economists had been decentralizers in the early 1960s, their ideas were now being incorporated into a new version of planned-economy centralism.

The channels of public discourse also remained open to a debate on managerial professionalism. We saw in the last chapter that the de-Stalinization movement under Khrushchev often typecast the factory director as an uncultured bureaucrat. The fact that senior management ranks were steadily becoming saturated with engineering graduates was slow to correct their status incongruity. Jobs in industrial management were known to bestow money and power but not much prestige. Sociological surveys showed that they were the desired destination for only 10 per cent of engineering students, a minority undistinguished in its academic quality and deviant from the majority by expressing a 'careerist' orientation to work in which monetary rewards were considered more important than 'creative content'.[2] Industrial executives, in other words, were widely considered by the intelligentsia to be bureaucratic politicians rather than professional 'specialists'. The enterprise statute advertised the idea that the road to industrial efficiency lay in giving enterprise management greater scope for independent decision-making, and in so doing gave concerns about the calibre of the managerial 'cadre' official currency. Policies for improving it appeared on the politburo agenda, and tens of thousands of executives were put through management retraining schemes in the 1970s.

The management educational provision became the subject of a continuous debate, the topics of which included the merits of regarding managerial expertise as cross-applicable between specific branches of industry, and developing a specialist education for a professional élite of 'generalist managers'. Here was a conduit for a new wave of Western influence, as the professionalization of management had been a strong trend in the USA during the previous two decades, which was marked by the rise to prominence of élite academic centres such as the Harvard Business School. The Soviet debate included explicit advocacies of this, though they were not unopposed by ideological objections to 'managerialism' and pragmatic scepticism about the applicability of capitalist business-school knowledge to socialist conditions. New courses, textbooks, and even computerized business games were nevertheless being developed under the influence of Western management schools, or indeed with their participation under the auspices of the *détente*

---

2 Beissinger, M. R. 1988: *Scientific Managmeent, Socialist Discipline, and Soviet Power*. London: Tauris & Co., p. 210.

agreements on scientific-cultural exchange. The debate surrounding the adoption of Western management theories and methods even included calls for modernizing the *nomenklatura* system of party control over executive appointments, by having the party-held files on potential executive appointees ('the cadre reserves') include management-training records and the results of 'objective' personal-ability tests rather than just the confidential testimonies written by personnel officers, senior managers, and party secretaries.

In practice, the Brezhnev period was an era in which the system we described in Chapter 7 as emerging from Stalin's industrialization drive attained its peak of routinization. It was worked by an unspoken consensual acknowledgement that informal negotiations and wheeler-dealing at all levels of the command hierarchy were a necessary supplement of formal rules and directives. Unlike in the 1930s and the late 1950s, the managers of large enterprises and the officials they dealt with were not subject to sudden demotions, promotions, or transfers to other localities. Careers were steady and informal networks of barter and pragmatically negotiated understandings were seldom disrupted. Executives at all levels knew what to expect from their decision-making environments, and how to achieve moderate success without an undue toll in stomach ulcers and heart-attacks. Planning was in effect 'from achieved levels'; managers knew that their targets were subject to annual increases, but they were party to explicit and implicit negotiations which kept the margins within reasonable bounds from their point of view. Creative accounting (*pripiski*), resource-hoarding, and some extra-plan trading were a part of the game; the higher authorities did not try to eliminate these practices by disciplinary clampdowns, being content with keeping them from escalating into major fraud scandals. On the whole, only the low-powered managers of small enterprises were vulnerable to zealous inspections. The executive bigger-fry also did not need to fear dynamic inputs from the party authorities. Reversing the bifurcation of the party apparatus into industrial and agricultural branches was the very first act of the Brezhnev regime, and the Khrushchevite intention to use the party's own industrial experts for an initiation of reformist shake-ups was also annulled. The party authorities would carry on with helping to co-ordinate economic affairs where necessary, but interference with managerial processes would not be their main function. In any case, important managers had *ex officio* seats on party committees at all levels.

The routinized ways of the economic bureaucracy made up a system with the same kind of endemic problems as those described in Chapter 7. Only the extremes were missing – production flows were much less prone to acute crises and chaotic extemporizations. The system was allowed to settle into its *modus operandi*, to benefit from accumulated expertise and rising levels of education and skill, and it was pressured into no more than gradual improvements on specific problems of quality and efficiency. It was not entirely inert, but it was not dynamic either. It made substantial changes seem risky in their disruptive effects on the negotiated order, and their benefits not so urgent.

The radical experiment of the Brezhnev period was the one named Shchekino after the locale of the factory where it was first promoted. This was about giving factories the incentive of keeping the cost-savings that could be had from substantial staff reductions. The original experiment was hailed as a great success, with the factory making impressive strides in labour productivity and all the laid-off employees finding jobs elsewhere. But as was the way with such trail-blazing experiments, generalizing them into the economy as a whole was a process that withered. Few of the 50 000 industrial establishments were able to obtain the political support they needed to survive without hoarded labour and place the laid-off staff in alternative employment. A more widespread emulation would have required an economic context characterized by a buyers' market for production materials and permission to make people unemployed. Neither was forthcoming: excess of supply over demand was contrary to both the tendencies of the system and the prevalent philosophy that considered it a phenomenon of wasteful overproduction; and the political regime was not about to risk the consequences of giving up its legitimacy trump-card – a commitment to full employment.

The bureaucratic routinization of the economic system was evident on factory floors as well as in offices. Management was benevolent rather than driving, allowing standards of discipline that gave workers a leeway for personal errands during working hours, and a possibility to take some factory goods for personal use or to use factory machinery and materials for some artisan repairs or manufacture of their own. The most notable innovation of the Brezhnev era on the factory floors was the promotion of the 'brigade' system of labour organization. Until then the ruling philosophy of 'scientific organization of labour' was a strongly Taylorist one, but it always tended to be corrupted in practice by informal work-group customs. The brigade system made shopfloor autonomy *de jure*. It had a pre-Taylorist precedent in labour gangs that worked without direct interference after negotiating terms for their collective performance, contemporary examples in post-Taylorist Western approaches to labour management that similarly favoured the advantages of flexible teamwork over rigid division-of-labour prescriptions, and an intellectual justification in the 'human relations' school of Western organization theory which emphasized the functionality of informal work-group practices. It also had a Soviet precedent in the 'communist labour brigades' of 1929, the 'integral process' (*skvoznye*) and 'autonomous budget' (*khozraschet*) brigades that were the celebrated innovations in 1932–4, and the 'collective piece-rate' incentive schemes that many managers preferred throughout the 1930s. That industrial workers were now becoming a well educated social group was an additional reason for entrusting them with an element of collective self-management, although the strategies that factory managements could in fact try under the newly fashionable 'brigade system' were, as always, variable.

The Brezhnev administration was ideologically tolerant or indeed supportive of rising consumerist aspirations, but it refrained from making any major commitments to transfer the balance of investments from heavy to light industries. Its policy was not to threaten the priority-hogging status of the metal-working, machine-building, and defence-production enterprises, but to give them incentives to develop secondary production lines for the consumer sector. Overall, the production of consumer durables appeared to expand commensurably with the overall industrial growth during the first 10 years of the Brezhnev regime. While the tonnes of annually produced iron and steel (the traditional index of industrial growth) increased by 55 per cent between 1965 and 1975, the annual production of cars increased sixfold, TV sets almost doubled, and refrigerators more than trebled.[3] The relatively large increase in car production was due to the opening of the Fiat-built plant in the early 1970s; this event marked the beginning of private car-owning on any scale, as the industry had previously been making passenger cars only for institutional vehicle pools and taxi fleets. In the latter half of the 1970s, however, the rate of overall industrial growth decreased substantially, and with it the rates of growth in both investment and consumer-goods production. Pent-up consumer demand was noted in official statistics by a fast rise in the excess of total cash savings held by individuals in their bank accounts over the rouble value of consumer goods in stock. Moreover, problems with the assortment and quality of the Soviet-made goods were not disappearing; resources were still being wasted on the production of things that people were not buying and random spot-checks found that between 25 and 40 per cent of the household appliances passing through the shops were defective.[4] Increased imports of more desirable (and expensive) products from east Europe paid for by exports of oil and Siberian gas, could offer no more than a partial solution to the growing magnitude of the consumer frustration problem.

The Brezhnevite 'Well Ordered State'

One of the vast array of political jokes that percolated society said that Brezhnev's bushy eyebrows were in fact Stalin's moustache on a higher level. The liberal intelligentsia in particular had reason to allege that the politics of the Brezhnev regime amounted to 're-Stalinization'. One year after Khrushchev's demise, the writers Daniel and Sinyavsky were arrested and put on trial for publishing their works abroad. The invasion of Czechoslovakia was followed by a purge of liberal editorial offices and sociological institutes. Khrushchevite criticisms of Stalin were quietly discontinued. Khrushchev rather than Stalin was upbraided for the 'cult of personality' and an autocratic style of rule ('voluntarism') in party education sessions, and the work of the commission set up by Khrushchev to make further investigation of Stalin's crimes was suspended. Brezhnev's politburo restored *ex officio* seats to KGB and army chiefs. It also reversed Khrushchev's pledge to demilitarize society by giving the army a high profile on public occasions and Brezhnev the supreme military rank, and by boosting the cultural output and propaganda themes devoted to war heroism and Great Russian nationalism. The Brezhnev regime annulled Khrushchev's party reforms; it did away with the industrial-agricultural bifurcation of the apparatus, cancelled the limitations on party-office tenures, and repeatedly emphasized the importance of the party's 'ideological work'. It also lifted the Khrushchevite restraints on the 'cult of personality' by allowing local authorities to build monuments to living leaders

---

3 See Smith, A. H. 1983: 'Soviet economic prospects: can the Soviet economic system survive?' In M. McCauley (ed.), *The Soviet Union after Brezhnev*. New York: Homes & Meier, p. 77.
4 Shapiro, J. P. 1980: 'Soviet consumer policy in the 1970s: plan and performance'. In D. R. Kelley (ed.), *Soviet Politics in the Brezhnev Era*. New York: Praeger, p. 117.

and name streets and buildings after them. Brezhnev's cult waxed. The leader became the bearer of the highest war-hero medals and the Lenin Peace Prize, to which the Lenin Prize for Literature was added when he published his memoirs.

'Re-Stalinization', however, is not a very precise concept. It tends to imply that Khrushchev's 'de-Stalinization' had gone far in transforming the political system in the first place, and that Brezhnev was restoring the whole status quo from before Khrushchev. Both these propositions are questionable. Brezhnev did not restore the threat of terror over the bureaucratic establishment and, unlike Khrushchev or Stalin, he did not try to instigate radical changes by political-mobilization methods, allowing instead the campaigning aspect of party heritage to be confined within the phenomenon of bureaucratic ritualism. Brezhnev's was no mobilization regime. Its continuities with Stalin were most clear in regard to the policies concerned with consolidation and a stable urban society based on a well organized, hierarchical servitor state: the policies of 1934–6 perhaps, but without the Stakhanovite and post-Kirov militancies; the policies of giving the state a constitution, the economy a technocratic management, and self-improving people a promise of 'cultured living'.

The Brezhnevite ideologues quietly dropped the Khrushchevite tidings of soon-to-come communism and concentrated their efforts on celebrating the presence of 'developed socialism'. The achievement of communism was still an ultimate goal, but it was not subject to specific time schedules. The task at hand was 'to perfect' the socialist organization of life in a context where human needs as well as the economy were rightfully becoming more complex. The socio-political revolution was accomplished. Further transformation would be a matter of 'scientific-technological revolution'. Itself the beneficiary of new developments in science and technology, socialist planning would enable science to deliver the general satisfaction of material needs and the removal of social inequalities between town, country, manual, and mental work – eventually. In the meantime, progress was a matter of gradual improvements in welfare provision and living standards affording the spread of *Sovetsky byt* ('Soviet lifestyle') based on economic security, a comfortable family life, and personal self-realization through work, voluntary 'social work', and edifying leisure. The social division of labour was affirmed as making some inequalities of rewards a continuing necessity for an unspecified period. Propaganda on 'developed socialism' and *Sovetsky byt* also acknowledged that it was no longer realistic to offer a promise of personal social mobility to every ambitious individual. It was inevitable that an educational meritocracy should tend to make class membership hereditary between generations. The best manual workers should be encouraged to find their self-realization within their own vocation just as the best chess-players realize their talents as chess-masters; and the propaganda included the celebration of 'working-class dynasties' – the growing number of skilled workers who were second or third generation.

The Brezhnev regime also quietly dropped the Khrushchevite ideas about the functions of the state devolving on voluntary activists in 'social organiza-tions'. It preferred the *Rechtsstaat* ideals of modern civilization based on professional administrators and a strong element of legal regulation. In 1977, after a long consultative process between legal experts, party authorities, and the representatives of various institutions, it enshrined the 'developed socialism' doctrine in a new state constitution. This was a much lengthier, more elaborate, and comprehensive document than the one it replaced. It defined the mutual rights and duties of state and citizen and the functions of the whole range of state and social institutions, not neglecting the 'guiding function' of the party, and it codified the principles of long-term policy-making. As could be expected from a constitution that was adopted in the wake of the Helsinki agreement, it gave a detailed treatment to human rights, albeit one balanced by the listing of duties to the state and qualified by catch-all phrases about over-riding general interest. The constitution and a number of laws and decrees that followed it specified the channels of redress a private citizen might follow against abuses of office by administrators. It stopped short, however, of making political power hostage to a constitutionalist rule of law. Not unlike the tsarist state in its mature years, the 'developed socialist state' reflected the principles of a *Polizeistaat* (well ordered police state) tempered by *Rechtsstaat* (legal state) trimmings.

Political power remained based on the administration of privilege. The system had a history of continuous development right from the beginning of the Soviet era. Its backbone was the *nomenklatura*, the listings of all posts of authority or social influence in party secretariats from district to the central-committee level, depending on their importance, appointments to which were subject to the rights of veto by the party, and the party-held files on the 'cadre reserves' deemed suitable for such appointments. The population was thus in effect divided between a non-nomenclatured majority and a nomenclatured minority, the minority being ranked from the district-level *nomenklatura* to the central-committee listed élite. It was not necessary for a person to be a party member to obtain *nomenklatura* rank, but it was necessary to be recommended by a party member of an appropriate standing. Aligned to this system was a privileged distribution network administered by a special council of ministers office. Here the central committee-level *nomenklatura* posts were further classified by sector and rank to determine their precise range of entitlements, and priority supplies were organized for shops, canteens, holiday resorts, sanatoria, health clinics, hospitals, housing construction, and *dacha* building reserved for meeting of these entitlements. Some privileged access provision was organized at more local levels for the regional-level *nomenklatura*. The system of privileged distribution for the official ranks was not limited to material goods. Information was also part of it. While the proverbial man in the street received his news of the world from the mass media, some of the ranked categories of citizen could receive theirs from press-agency bulletins of restricted circulation. Privileged information was also the currency of oral briefings by party propaganda activists. While ordinary workers had to listen to low-level activists repeating newspaper commentaries, the *nomenklatura* occasionally went to talks given by bright young men from central committee departments empowered to impart interesting 'for your ears only' titbits. Thus a sense of identification with one's rank and the regime that bestowed it was forged. Brezhnev was true to his promise of a consultative leadership style. New policies took shape by a slow process involving the representatives of vested interests in the guise of expert commissions and working parties, and if there were irreconcilable conflicts that necessitated some reshuffling of high-level personnel, the losers were spared a drop in rank and entitlements. The top boss was not making enemies, and the emulation of his style throughout the establishment meant that the privileged distribution network had to cater for a growing number of people with entitlements. A proliferation of officers with the rank of general in the armed forces exemplified the trend. At the same time, however, the rarity of downranking was limiting the chances of younger officials to move up.

The system of privileged distribution was not limited to the nomenclatured officialdom. It applied also to enterprises. Beyond the traditional prioritization of heavy over light industry, there were the 'secrecy regime' enterprises whose workers as well as white-collar staff were subject to personal security vetting, the requirement to sign away some of their legal labour-protection rights, and the obligation to treat their work as a state secret. But they had a priority claim on supplies and high-technology equipment, and their employees enjoyed substantially higher earnings, better welfare provision, and special entitlements such as advanced placings in waiting lists for the purchase of private cars or building materials for *dachas*. Initially only important defence-industry plants were in this category, but their number increased substantially in the 1970s in response to requests by the managers who sought the advantages of priority status as much as by the military authorities.

Cities, too, were ranked and the state shops in them supplied accordingly. Moscow was naturally at the top of this particular hierarchy, followed by Leningrad, Novosibirsk (and outside Russia the republican capitals), then the larger provincial centres. Residence in these cities was not legal without a permit recorded in the inhabitants' passports. Those who grew up there obtained permits automatically, but would-be immigrants had to gain them either by marriage or by an application supported by employers. Moscow employers, however, were not supposed to employ people who were not already legal residents. The fact that the city's population nevertheless continued to grow with immigrants contributing a lion's share of the annual increment testified to much busy string-pulling. In 1977, for example, Moscow grew by 91 000 inhabitants while the excess of births over deaths in the city amounted to 12 000.[5]

Social mobility was thus a matter of not just educational attainment and devotion to doing a job well but also a matter of negotiating the crossing of administrative status boundaries. A manual worker could leap forward in his living standards by obtaining a clearance for employment in the 'secrecy regime' sector; a provincial town-dweller achieved an elevation for himself and his family when he gained a capital-city residence permit; a specialist or manager when he advanced into a higher *nomenklatura* listing; a collective farmer when he or she received a passport without which moving out would be impossible (collective-farm dwellers were still the only citizens not issued with passports automatically on reaching the age of 14). The administrative categories into which the state divided its citizens influenced the citizens' life chances and social identities, and set the hurdles to be negotiated with the

---

5 *Moskva v tsifrakh v 1980 godu* (Moscow: izd. 'Finansy i statistika', 1981), p. 7.

authorities in the course of personal self-advancement. They also provided the regime with a facility for a divide-and-rule approach to the management of discontent. Muscovites were encouraged to believe that the problems they had in obtaining things in their shops were the result of illegal residents in their midst and provincial tourists who sought things to buy rather than cultural monuments to admire. They could be also encouraged to blame law-and-order problems on the underclass of *limitchiki*, the immigrants issued with temporary residence permits to do the dirty jobs Muscovites would not do, and who lived in crowded hostels like the migrant labourers of yesteryear. Some of the educated Russians aspiring to the coveted research institute careers may have had some satisfaction when the government imposed quota limits on the appointment of Jews in the early 1970s. One's ethnicity was a matter of inherited status for ever recorded in one's passport – only the children of mixed marriages had a choice of which 'nationality' they were – and the use of ethnic quotas in élite recruitment was a growing trend.

The Brezhnev administration adopted a complex policy towards the intelligentsia. It resisted calls for reducing admissions to higher education, which were prompted by signs that there were more graduate specialists trained than needed. Restricting admissions would have either further decreased intergenerational social mobility as more selectivity would have accentuated the educational advantages of intelligentsia children, or it would have required a return to the Khrushchevite positive discrimination policies that had proven so unpopular with the intelligentsia. Higher education thus continued expanding and all graduates continued to be guaranteed work in the specialist occupations for which they were trained, albeit at the expense of an increasing proportion of them finding the jobs more routinely clerical than specialist professional. At the same time, there was an increasing overlap between manual and intelligentsia occupations in the range of earnings. In industry, the average professional-technical worker (ITR) was earning only 10 per cent more than the average manual worker by the early 1980s (while clerical staff were earning 20 per cent less). Scientific workers' pay-scales were similar to the industrial ITR, and the pay-scales of other graduate professions were lower. This equalization of incomes between the intelligentsia and the manual working class hid substantial pay differentials within each category; the skill-graded wage-scales of manual workers made the highest incomes about three times as large as the lowest, while the senior élite of the graduate professions earnt perhaps as much as 10 times more than the junior group of freshly graduated engineers, medical practitioners, or research workers. But a specialist's progression from junior status towards the high-earning élite was of course a matter of getting into the *nomenklatura* at some point.

The Brezhnev regime made it a priority to recruit graduates into party membership. In the Khrushchev era, the working class had been a particular recruitment target and the party membership total had grown by 70 per cent. In the Brezhnev era, the party grew by 60 per cent and the proportion of graduates within it increased from 15 per cent to 30 per cent (while the proportion of graduates in the total adult population increased roughly from five to 10 per cent). By the second half of the 1970s there was a better than 50/50 chance that any male graduate passed the age of 30 was a party member.

For women the chance was much lower – only about 15 per cent of female graduates aged 30 or above were party members.[6] The party was recruiting the graduates who looked like advancing in their professional careers – it was not insisting on ideological enthusiasm, a willingness not to rock the political boat was enough. Its policy was to co-opt if possible the people who commanded the respect of their employers and professional peers, and to make them subject to the rules of party discipline. At the same time, the party increased its emphasis on 'ideological work' among scientists and professionals. Academy of Sciences' workers in all fields of scholarship were expected to attend seminars on Marxist philosophy, for example. The content of these discussions varied to include topics that were not narrowly doctrinaire; they were occasions for circulating Western philosophy-of-science ideas, perhaps, albeit with a ritual element of putting 'bourgeois philosophy' under a critical light. Natural scientists were not under any pressure to give their research methodologies or theory-building any particular philosophical trimmings; they were simply expected not to quarrel with the axiom that there was no contradiction between scientific methodology and the precepts of 'dialectical materialism'. They were under pressure to do some applied research, and to work according to plan; but the process of research work-planning was such that it allowed the more senior scientists to shape their plans themselves. Historical and social-science research, however, was subject to tighter controls. Party policies *vis-à-vis* the professions were primarily about separating the two trends that had formed a unity in the Khrushchev era, the re-emergence of the intelligentsia's class identity and political liberalism.

The Brezhnev regime tried to offer something for everyone. It countered the critics of the command economy by promising greater efficiency in the shape of computer-wielding, professionally trained managers and planners. It offered the citizens more protection from the arbitrary powers of officials by an increasing emphasis on the legal regulation of decision-making; the collective farmers rights to welfare benefits as well as to private trade (by 1980 the average rural savings account was slightly higher than the average urban account); the skilled industrial workers more autonomy on the job and earnings that were higher than the white-collar average; and the brightest graduates a continuous expansion of employment in research institutes. Everyone was promised employment security, stable prices, better welfare provision, more consumer goods and family housing in self-contained apartments. The lowest-paid benefited from periodic increases in the legal wage minimum (from 50 to 80 rubles per month), and almost everyone from the reduction of standard working week to five days. High earners had legal opportunities to shorten their wait for housing by buying membership in apartment-building co-operatives, and to become private owners of *dachas* to drive to at weekends in their cars.

---

6 Hough, J. 1977: *The Soviet Union and Social Science Theory*. (Cambridge, Mass.: Harvard University Press, pp. 131–3.

Social Movements and Trends in the Brezhnev Era

The dissident movement started with a collection of signatures in protest against Sinyavsky's and Daniel's trial. Human-rights issues, solidarity campaigns against the victimization of activists, and the use of Western media for putting pressure on the *détente*-seeking regime remained the common denominator of what was otherwise ideologically an increasingly diverse movement. Liberal activists organized a network of committees for the defence of civil rights, Amnesty International branches, and the regular *samizdat* publication of *Chronicle of Current Events* in the late 1960s, and, after the government signed the Helsinki agreement in 1975, Helsinki-implementation watch groups. An essay written as an open letter to Brezhnev by academicians, Sakharov, Turchin, and Roy Medvedev, just after the dismissal of Alexander Tvardovsky from the editorship of *Novyi mir* in 1970, articulated something like a manifesto of the liberal, Western-oriented intelligentsia, advocating as it did the indivisibility of intellectual freedoms, civil rights, détente, and economic progress. The majority of public protest gatherings, however, were organized by religious and ethnic groups, although they were supported by the liberal human-rights activists. In the republics outside Russia, the main thrust of dissident political activism was nationalist. In Russia proper the dissident groups and ideologies mushroomed to include Russian nationalism, free trade unionism, and, eventually, feminism and environmentalism.

Jews and ethnic Germans won a qualified right to emigrate. In the late 1960s and early 1970, the Jewish emigration movement was mainly outside Russia proper, in the areas of the empire that had been the Jewish Pale in tsarist times. It was religious and Zionist in its orientation, and most of the emigration was to Israel. In the 1970s, however, it became easier for Soviet Jewish emigrants to settle in the USA and other Western countries, and the majority of the applicants as well as the people granted permission to leave were from Russia's heartlands. These were mainly secular people from the professional classes who would have been Russians if they had not had a Jewish identity stamped in their passports. Some wanted to leave because they faced increasing discrimination in their careers, other simply because they hoped to find a better life in the West; indeed, there were not a few Russians who tried to join the exodus on the basis of spurious claims to Jewishness. The annual outflow was increasing in the 1970s, peaking at 50 000 by the end of the decade. The numbers applying nevertheless always exceeded those granted a leave. The refused applicants formed a *refuzenik* movement to publicize their plight, their declared wish to emigrate having exposed them to discriminatory sanctions by the authorities. After the invasion of Afghanistan the authorities reduced emigration to a trickle. By this time about 260 000 Jews and 70 000 ethnic Germans had emigrated.

In the 1970s the emigration movement gave the regime an opportunity to counter political dissidence by sending its leaders abroad. In addition to the actual deportation in 1974 of the most prominent opposition figure, Alexander Solzhenitsyn, a good number of the dissidents who enjoyed an international reputation were given the choice of leaving the country after they served a term in labour camps or, indeed, before they were charged with any criminal offence. The police repression of dissidence was by no means consistently harsh. The people arrested at protest rallies were often as not released after a warning, and most of those who were tried received light sentences. It was mainly the hard-core activist organizers the KGB harrassed, framed for criminal prosecutions, or, most frighteningly of all, pushed into the hands of regime psychiatrists. The internationally famous Sakharov (who received Nobel Peace Prize in 1975) was allowed to remain a prominent figure in Moscow until he was exiled from the city in 1980. Many of the intellectual élite of the Khrushchev-era thaws and de-Stalinization were allowed to work in their professional capacities although their access to the official media and corridors of power was made conditional on how they behaved.

There were some clampdowns on the more political *samizdat* publishing in the early 1970s and then again in the early 1980s. On the whole, however, the regime refrained from trying to stop people circulating among their friends *samizdat*, *magnetizdat* (unofficially recorded audiotapes), and *tamizdat* (Russian reading matter published by the growing émigré community in the West). These semi-clandestine forms of intellectual and cultural life flourished and allowed individuals to assert their autonomy from officially approved views with different degrees of commitment. It was possible for academics to indicate their liberality to one another by passing copies of Sakharov's letter to Brezhnev under the table during their official philosophy seminars, without actually sticking their necks out by disrupting the proceedings. The regime seemed satisfied if people affirmed its legitimacy by taking part in its public rituals; as long as they kept public expressions of their views within a permissible range, it did not matter if they strayed in their private debates. The majority acknowledged this *modus vivendi*. The hard core of dissidents who kept asserting their moral conscience in head-on collisions with the authorities were admired as heroes by some of their informal public. Party propagandists, however, were not altogether unsuccessful in planting the thought among the intelligentsia that the hard-core dissidents were peculiar individuals who were driven by either a psychological need for martyrdom or a desire for profitable Western fame.

Besides, the radical liberal ideas received increasing competition in the semi-clandestine circulation from extreme Russian nationalist views, not excluding anti-semitism, racist concerns with the 'yellow peril' represented by China and the high birth-rates among the natives of Soviet Asian republics, and attacks on the economic costs of aid to third-world countries. Russian nationalist revivalism did not need to be confined to *samizdat* publications. Its expressions were on a continuum with officially promoted patriotism, just as many of the liberal views were on a continuum with official commitments to constitution and legalism, science, culture, economic growth, and *détente*. Russian nationalist revival took place in the increasing membership of local ethnographic societies, pressure groups for the preservation of national monuments, and informal hobby networks devoted to collecting icons. The Brezhnev regime did not campaign against religion with the same zeal as its predecessor, and the increasing popularity of acknowledging the orthodox-church roots in the Russian identity was rumoured to be shared in high political circles. The KGB chief and politburo member, Yury Andropov, was said to be an avid collector of icons as well as modern jazz records, for example.

It is questionable that the majority of the printed matter and tape-recordings in unofficial circulation was a phenomenon of political dissent. It was political in the limited sense that its producers and consumers were bypassing official channels, and that the Western commentators on 'uncensored Russia' mirrored their official Soviet counterparts in tending to frame their interpretative comments in political terms. But much of the material was cultural rather than particularly ideological, concerned with a variety of personal experiences. And there was no clear dichotomy of content between unofficial and official cultural productions. Each official production involved a negotiation with the authorities and therefore a degree of self-censorship and compromise, but the results were neither uniform nor such as to appeal only to audiences with politically correct attitudes. Existential angst, urban man's romantic nostalgia for a bucolic soul, wryly realistic portrayals of everyday life, the individual's alienation from collective pressures, complex explorations of moral conflict, satires, comedies, and tragedies dealing with corruption and other symptoms of social *malaise* – all these themes found their way into the output of a vast cultural industry along with the ones expressive of patriotism and socialist optimism. Many official productions were successful with their audiences, and they encompassed the whole range from high brow to middle brow and mass entertainment. There were guitar poets such as Alexander Galich, who crossed the line from the cultural establishment to a protest underground (and eventually to emigration), and others such as Vladimir Vysotsky, who straddled both worlds as a popular film actor, Taganka Theatre artist, and an underground singing and dancing beat poet. There were also jazz and rock musicians who went the other way, starting off in venues organized locally under the cover of *komsomol* or trade-union clubs, who were co-opted into the mass-entertainment world of TV appearances, state recording-studios, and nationwide tours. Some 1500 rock and pop groups were estimated to ply their trade in the Moscow region alone in venues and events of differing shades on the spectrum, from defiantly underground to officially sponsored.[7] The political underground, in other words, was a small section of the activities that grew from below, through the spaces made by the informally bendable rules of bureaucracy, and also into the spaces that the officialdom reserved for what was popular and co-optable. And the public controversies about the increasingly varied strands of popular culture cut across political dividing lines, for the bone of contention was the traditional culturist one of high-brow contempt for the less refined forms of entertainment.

This was also a question of generations. The dissidents who went to protest rallies were mainly men and women in their thirties or older, and their leaders were of statesman age. The flourishing rock-music underground was young. The young expressed their authenticity by turning their backs on politics, and by embracing the global youth-culture of fads, pop-idols, style-statements, and

---

7 Stites, R. 1992: *Russian Popular Culture: Entertainment and Society since 1900.* Cambridge: Cambridge University Press, p. 161.

consumerist hedonism without ideological pieties. There had always been street gangs of youths for, after all, self-entertainment in public places has always been a favoured form of leisure. But now there were hippies with their networks of hang-out places and crash-pads, 'pacifists' and punks, as well as working-class gangs of more traditional hues who liked to bash the hippies or fly football-club colours and fight on match days. The subcultures were varied and linked to one another at the same time through the ease of travel that tape-recorders gave to musical styles. The Brezhnev regime eventually became worried by the 'nihilism' of the youth subcultures. In the late 1970s, it repeated the Khrushchevite 1950s attempt to offer the young an opportunity for pioneer romance. This time the big campaign youth project was not the virgin lands but the construction of a new railway in the Siberian far east. Its youth-edification value, however, proved just as mixed and many who went did so for the high wages that were offered.

Another social trend was the ubiquitous search for consumer prosperity through the informal offices of *blat*. We saw in Chapter 8 the importance of this phenomenon during the formative 1930s. It was an integral part of economic shortage under never-perfect bureaucratic controls, and it did not wane. Khrushchev's keenness on the 'anti-parasite' laws and on the death penalty for serious 'economic crimes' signalled an intention to combat it, but this was never followed by a clampdown of the scale and intensity that would have been needed to make an impact. Under Brezhnev, the regime's attitude to the myriad of daily transactions in which individuals found the goods and services they wanted *po blatu* or *nalevo* ('on the left') was analogous to the tolerance of the benevolent patterns of formal-rule enforcement in work places. The Brezhnev regime was ideologically tolerant or indeed supportive of rising consumerist aspirations, and generally tended to rest its legitimacy on 'never had it so good' messages about the Soviet *byt* (lifestyle). There was a continuity here with the celebrations of the non-puritan, individual-prosperity rewards of progress that made up a theme of Stalinist propaganda about *kul'turnyi byt* ('cultured living') and social mobility in the later 1930s. Then, of course, *kul'turnyi byt* was a realistic prospect for only a tiny élite which was provided with its privileges by the state. The *blat* dealings were in the main something the non-élite majority had to engage in to obtain the dire necessities and perhaps the occasional petty luxury. During the first 10 years of the Brezhnev regime, living standards rose and consumerist aspirations to obtain things that were more than necessities spread. *Na levo* dealings became not just about the basic necessities of living but also about the consumerist pleasures in things that were novelties, markers of taste, and status symbols. These pleasures became unobtainable almost by definition through what was routinely provided by general state distribution networks. The people in the provinces prized possessions that could normally be obtained only in Moscow, and Muscovites prized the things that could normally be obtained in élite closed shops or abroad. That which was easily acquired with no interesting tale to tell about the process of acquisition was believed to be inferior.

Na levo wheeler-dealings were made the more necessary as more things were owned because the official economy was the most deficient in the service sector; having TV set repaired, apartment fittings and fixtures done, or a newly purchased piece of furniture moved to one's home would have been impossible otherwise. The benevolent pattern of management in the state's work places made possible private moonlighting with the state's materials and equipment, and petty and not-so-petty frauds and thefts that siphoned state property off for private use or black-market trade. Items in unofficial circulation included closed-shop vouchers, Western currencies, consumer goods brought in from east Europe, and even winning state-lottery tickets because they had a black-market value as legitimate cover for clandestinely acquired cash hoards. The legal twilight zone of the unofficial economy boomed, and people of all classes and age-groups were involved. It provided a partial compensation for the regime's unwillingness or inability to restructure the economy for a consumerist era, and opportunities for many people to augment their incomes. Ever more people sought these opportunities because black-market prices were high. Corruption was spreading and with it the belief in the venality of everyone. If the health service, for example, was on the whole working by professional ethics in the 1960s, by the end of the 1970s patients tended to expect that the undivided attention of their doctors had a price.

In the 1960s and early 1970s there were several incidents of working-class disquiet in provincial industrial centres (including the textile city of Ivanovo again, the place with a labour-unrest record in every era since 1905) – usually walk-outs and street demonstrations precipitated by severe shortages in the shops. But these incidents became no more frequent or larger in scale after the early 1970s. The intelligentsia was optimistic about economic prospects during the Khrushchev period, but became markedly pessimistic during the second half of the 1970s. The mid-decade slow-down in the officially counted growth-rates was widely regarded among the educated classes as chronic rather than temporary. The slow-down in housing construction was felt immediately by the younger generation in the lengthening waiting lists for apartments. Among the younger intelligentsia, the sense of grievance was compounded by an awareness that their incomes were often lower and less augmentable by unofficial-economy activities than manual workers'. In addition, there was an increasing awareness of middle-class living standards in the West and, even more to the point, that the USSR remained a poor country relative to the socialist satellites behind her Western borders. By the mid-1970s perhaps 12–15 million Soviet citizens had travelled to east Europe bringing back with them prized consumer acquisitions to bear witness to the Soviet economic lag.[8] The Soviet economy was closing the prosperity gap with neither the West nor the better-off socialist countries, and the intelligentsia perceived this fact more acutely than the improvements that had occurred since the mid-1950s. In the early 1980s the regime's propaganda tried to counter the disenchantment by claiming that a socialist economy deserved to be judged by other than consumerist yardsticks, and by publicizing tales of woe from emigrants who wanted to return.

But by this time ideological appeals elicited little besides cynical thoughts. Among the intelligentsia, party membership was generally regarded as an

---

8 Bushnell, J. 1980: 'The "new Soviet man" turns pessimist'. In Cohen, S. F. *et al.* (eds), *The Soviet Union since Stalin*. London: Macmillan, p. 192.

artefact of career moves rather than ideological belief; and among the young, the ideological discourse tended to be heard as a symptom of an ageing and corrupt establishment's pomposity. 'The young neither fight against communism, argue against it, nor curse it; something much worse has happened to communism: they laugh at it', wrote a contributor to an émigré journal who contrasted this observation with the three previous generations among whom he believed a faith in communist ideals had been quite common.[9] A joke in semi-clandestine circulation summed up the contemporary Soviet *byt* as one of six paradoxes:

(1) there's no unemployment, but no one works;
(2) no one works, but productivity goes up;
(3) productivity goes up, but there is nothing in the stores;
(4) there's nothing in the stores, but at home there's everything;
(5) at home there's everything, but no one is satisfied;
(6) no one is satisfied, but everyone votes yes.[10]

By the end of the 1970s the ideological spirit was believed to be extinct within the political establishment itself, and the regime also to be failing in the technocratic foundations of its legitimacy. The political atmosphere was one of wait and see what changes happen when the septuagenarian General Secretary, President, and Marshal dies.

By the time of Brezhnev's death in 1982 Russia was by all criteria an urban society: 71 per cent of the population lived in cities and towns, and of the working population between three-quarters and four-fifths earnt their living outside agriculture. In the non-agricultural sector, the ratio of manual and menial-service workers to white-collar employees was now two:one, roughly the same as in 1960 but slightly smaller than in 1970. Higher education graduates now made up over 10 per cent of all employed people and 35 per cent of all white-collar employees.[11] Moscow now had 8.2 million inhabitants, Leningrad over 4.5 million (in 1959 the respective populations had been six million and 3.3 million). In addition, there were now 10 other cities in the Russian Federal Republic with populations of more than a million.

Just over one-half of all living space in Moscow was in buildings constructed during the Brezhnev era, and only 14 per cent was in buildings of pre-1956 vintage. The vast level of overcrowding that was such an overwhelming characteristic of Moscow in the 1930s came down to a level comparable to the last tsarist years by the early 1960s. Henceforth, the provision of living space grew very slightly more quickly than the population, and the privacy of accommodation a little more markedly. The big jump in this respect occurred in the Khrushchev era, when the building of communal apartments was abandoned in favour of small family apartments. In 1980 Moscow had more

9 Levitin-Krasnov, A. 1976: 'Pis'ma o russkoi molodezhi'. In Belotserkovskii, V. (ed.), *SSSR, Demokraticheskie alternativy*. Achberg: Achberger Verlangstalt. Quoted in Zaslavsky V. 1982: *The Neo-Stalinist State*. New York: M E Sharpe Inc., p. 15.
10 Medish, V. 1987: *The Soviet Union*. Englewood Cliffs, NJ: Prentice-Hall, p. 298.
11 *RSFSR v tsifrakh v 1981 godu*. Moskva, izd. 'Finansy i statistika', 1982, pp. 5, 55, 57, 71, 73.

than five times more residents than it had in 1913, but over eight-times more accommodation space and almost 14 times more apartments.[12] By official statistics there were 3.2 persons per apartment, the average Russian urban family size (average rural family size was 3.4); and the living area per person was on average about 15 square metres. It is possible that in reality living was rather more crowded than these figures suggest, as the statistics counted only legal residents and perhaps included some dwellings that were only completed on paper. The averages also hid the number of young families who were obliged to live in parental homes while waiting to be allocated apartments of their own. The average size of the families who were allocated newly constructed urban apartments in the Russian republic was 3.6 in the 1960s and 3.5 in the 1970s.[13] In other words, new apartments tended to be allocated to married couples who already had children and/or other relatives living with them.

The repeatedly proclaimed goal of housing policy was to provide an apartment for every family, thus assuming and reinforcing family life as the norm. Only 13 per cent of the population lived as single persons or apart from their families, a similar proportion to what it had been already by the late 1950s. However, 63 per cent of the families had fewer than four members and only five per cent had six or more members. About two-thirds of the families were nuclear, 12 per cent were lone parent, and 20 per cent were various other kinship combinations. In the latter an elderly female relative often featured, for more than one-third of the women aged 50–9 and almost three-quarters of those aged 60 or more were widowed, divorced, or single. People were married quite early and the average age of newly-weds was on a slightly downward trend. In 1979, 38 per cent of the men and 60 per cent of the women aged 20–4 were married; and 79 per cent of the men and 81 per cent of the women aged 25–9. Divorce rates, however, had been on an upward trend for some time, from seven per 1000 married couples in 1959 to 13 in 1970 and 18 in 1979.[14] By the latter date the authorities were registering one divorce for every three weddings.

About two-thirds of the divorces were initiated by the wives. Working-class women in particular often cited the husband's excessive drinking as the motive for their petition, but sociologists found a host of other sources of family stress. Almost all women were in full-time employment, and the vast majority found themselves doing twice or three times as much housework as their husbands. Time-budget surveys found that for the woman who was a mother as well as a wife, the 'second shift' of domestic chores amounted to almost four-fifths of the time spent in paid employment. Women bore the brunt of the economy's shortcomings. Consumer-goods industries were providing almost every household with a TV set but not with automatic washing-machines, freezers, and

12 *Moskva v tsifrakh v 1981 godu*. Moskva, izd. 'Finansy i statistika', 1982, pp. 7–9, 155–6.
13 *RSFSR v tsifrakh*, p. 79.
14 Ryan, M. and Prentice, R. 1987: *Social Trends in the Soviet Union from 1950*. London: Macmillan, pp. 49–59.

vacuum cleaners. Daily shopping remained a time-consuming business, and what could be bought did not include precooked meals. The lag in the provision of things and services that would have made the household division of labour a less contentious issue was acknowledged often enough as a problem in the media and official government pronouncements, but the balance of the economy did not shift to help. Conflicts over the sharing of family chores loomed large among the things that soured marriages, especially among the younger generation whose women were less resigned than their mothers to the inequities of the domestic burden.

Sociologists and media moralists did not omit to lament the Russian husband's traditional resistance to 'women's work' in the home. Such comments however, were firmly embedded in psychological viewpoints that saw home-making and child-care as a natural feminine virtue and the mother as the heart of family life. The moralists in fact blamed a wide range of factors for the high divorce rates and low birth-rates. Couples wedded before they knew each other sufficiently well, very often in a hurry because the bride was pregnant, and they put consumerist prosperity above having more than one or two children. Many couples ran into strain because the women were highly educated, often better educated than their men, and professionally rather than domestically oriented. Social tolerance of extra-marital sex was also cited. Men were thought to be resentful domestic partners because their childhood had been dominated by female authority at home and school. The more liberal commentators saw the rising divorce rates as a legitimate part of urban social progress, which had given women economic and personal independence. The family stability and low-natality problems, an increasing number of commentators thought, could be solved if further economic progress made it possible for some women to work part time or not at all while they raised their children.

The low birth-rate was a serious problem. It was going to reduce the labour force and army conscriptions, and bequeath a top-heavy age structure on society. The trend towards an Asian majority in the empire's racial mix was also a concern to some, and there were pundits who worried about how many children were being raised without siblings. But the pro-natalist voices were singularly ineffective. Contraceptives being among the things in short supply, the average woman underwent several abortions to keep her family manageably small. The annual number of the legally performed abortions counted in official statistics amounted to over 12 per cent of the total female population aged 15–49.[15] (The outright ban on abortions imposed in the 1930s was lifted soon after Stalin's death.)

Women were supposedly equal partners in marriage (the constitution said so), but they were the bearers of domestic burdens. In employment they were also men's equals in law, but their average earnings were about 70 per cent of men's. Among the manual classes, the gap was because the more feminized a sector of employment was, the lower were its basic wage-scales. Light industries were feminine and low paid, heavy industries were masculine and

---

15 Buckley, M. 1990: 'Glasnost and the woman question'. In Edmondson, L. (ed.), *Women and Society in Russia and the Soviet Union*. Cambridge: Cambridge University Press, p. 212.

high paid. In industries intermediate on this scale, such as engineering industries, women were well represented among the machine operatives but not among the highest skill-grades. Apprenticeships and training schemes for the high-graded jobs were largely a male concern. Worker recruitment to the higher-paid 'secrecy regime' enterprises was also male biased, possibly because military service counted as a relevant qualification for security clearance. Outside industry a service sector, such as transport, was largely male and high paid, while retail and other services were female and very low paid. In agriculture the better paid jobs were held by mechanics and drivers, a masculine enclave. The gender segregation of industrial sectors, occupations, and jobs was, if anything, stronger now than in the immediate pre-war and post-war periods.

Women were becoming the majority sex among higher education graduates and professional employees by the early 1980s. There were some very feminized occupations such as doctors, teachers, accountants, and lawyers, but women were well represented also among engineers and scientific workers. They remained under-represented in senior and executive posts, however. Well over two-thirds of medical doctors were women, but just over one-half of the 'chief physicians'; almost three-quarters of teachers were women, but only just over one-third of secondary-school directors.[16] Over 40 per cent of scientific workers were women, but under 30 per cent of candidates of science and heads of laboratories and departments, 14 per cent of doctors of Science, and three per cent of the members of the Academy of Sciences.[17] Over one-half of the engineers employed in industry were women, but less than one-tenth of the senior enterprise managers. The female minority among industrial managers was concentrated in the highly feminized low-priority industries.

In professional sectors, such as scientific research and academia, the diminishing proportion of women further up the hierarchy was partly explicable by the age factor: the senior élite were senior in age, of a generation that had started their careers when women were still a minority among higher education graduates. It was, however, acknowledged that among recent graduates relatively more men than women were advancing above the junior 'scientific worker' ranks, because motherhood was a strong brake on one's personal career progress in a way that fatherhood was not. In industry it was often acknowledged that employers were reluctant to appoint women to important posts because they feared maternity-leave complications. The *nomenklatura* system also played its part in keeping executive careers masculine. The party was a male institution, with women making up a quarter of the total membership: three per cent of the central-committee members and a single-figure percentage of the first secretaries of district and regional committees. Getting into the *nomenklatura* files as a suitable candidate for power-grooming was a matter of personal recommendation by senior party members, who were exposed to few pressures to revise the traditional masculine image of what a potential high-flyer looked like.

While the rising divorce rates and low birth-rates testified to an increasing

16 Lane, *Soviet Society*, p. 258.
17 Kneen, P. 1984: *Soviet Scientists and the State*. London: Macmillan, p. 28.

proportion of women refusing to be long-suffering drudges in their homes, there is little evidence of widespread resentment of the gender-segregation aspects of employment and power hierarchies. Even among the women who emigrated during the 1970s there were relatively few who reported professional career frustrations as important draw-backs to their Soviet experience. Most professional women wanted to be mothers as well, and they accepted motherhood as incompatible with a single-minded devotion to promotion ladder-climbing; it seemed natural that more men than women should be making the climb. Working-class women did not object on principle to the segregation of jobs between men and women. If the conditions of women's work made it easier to combine the job with feminine domestic roles (good nurseries, no pressures to do overtime, ease of leave-taking when a child was sick, not much hard or dirty physical labour), it did not seem to matter so much if the wages were lower than in men's jobs. Dissatisfaction arose when these conditions were not met. A substantial minority of women workers did do jobs that involved hard physical labour, and putting up with heat, noise, and dust was the lot of many textile-industry workers. But disgruntlement at harsh working conditions was localized and seldom articulated as a demand that a textile worker should be rewarded as well as a heavy-industry one. Protesting against the gendered nature of manual jobs *per se* would have evoked memories of wartime hardships – the image of large peasant women in unshapely clothes working as building-site labourers. Feminism was a small part in the growing variety of discontents voiced in the *samizdat* pamphlets and underground popular culture; not all of it questioned the assumption that men and women had different capacities and needs, and it did not address the gender bar that operated within the manual sector to keep women out of the skilled and best paid jobs.

From Anti-Corruption to *Perestroika*

Within days of Brezhnev's death in November 1982, Yuri Andropov, until recently the KGB chief, became the General Secretary. Then new leader's first priority was to start a campaign against bureaucratic corruption and slack labour discipline. The police were made busy with the novel task of doing spot-checks on people in the streets, shops, bath-houses, and restaurants to report those who were there instead of at work to their employers. The procuracy, courts, state inspectorates, and the press were made busy with clamping down on bribe-taking, fraudulent book-keeping, statistical misreporting, and general rule-bending by administrators. For the first time since Khrushchev's times, industrial workers were subjected to a strong norm-raising campaign. And there was a new public-order campaign against drunkenness. These measures did have a short-term beneficial effect on the economy, in that output and labour-productivity statistics registered a slight increase after several flat years. But the discipline drive was not easy to sustain, although Andropov took care to install hundreds of new brooms in the top layers of the party and the state, a task in which he was helped considerably by the fact that so many incumbent oligarchs were close to retirement age. The discipline drive in fact had a discernible ebb and flow, which coincided with the leader's periods of illness and health. Sociological surveys indicated what it was up against: only a small minority of citizens were in favour of petty briberies, frauds, and thefts at work to be treated as punishable offences, and agreement with punitive measures was less than unanimous even in regard to large-scale embezzlement by store managers. Besides, Andropov did not have unanimous backing in the politburo for a severe shake-up of the administrative apparatus. His rival in the succession process, Konstantin Chernenko, became known as giving protection to senior officials who were under cloud of corrupt-practice allegations, and senior procuracy officials alluded to the Stalinist precedent as a good reason for keeping at bay the temptation to struggle against bureaucratic corruption with too much punitive zeal. Somewhat incongruously with the campaign to keep executive practices under a stricter supervision, Andropov also put some decentralizing economic reforms back on the agenda. But he died only 15 months after taking the top office.

The ageing Chernenko became General Secretary. He died after 13 months in office, to be succeeded by the youngest politburo member and Andropov's protégé, Michail Gorbachev. In 1985–6 the new leader's domestic policy had many of the hallmarks of Andropov's. The process of retiring Brezhnevite time-servers from the party and state-executive posts was restarted with new vigour, and so were the anti-corruption, labour-discipline, and anti-alcohol campaigns. The new leader's ideologues stressed the crisis proportions of the economic stagnation and social *malaise* that had occurred under Brezhnev. The phrase 'developed socialism' was modified to 'developing socialism' to drive the point against complacency, and 'speed-up' (*uskorenie*) was urged on the country. Economic reform was back on the public agenda, and the terms of the debate about it were immediately widened to include proposals that were more radical than those mooted under Andropov's patronage.

People who had been the young generation of radical reformers in Khrushchev's time resurfaced into prominence. Gorbachev himself started his career in the heady days of Khrushchevite thaw and de-Stalinization. Like Khrushchev, he sought a revitalization of party and society, travelled a great deal, used the media to show him persuading ordinary people to join the movement against bureaucratic inertia, and engaged in a diplomatic peace offensive *vis-à-vis* the West that promised a lessening of the military burden on the economy. 'Dogmatism' was again the body-politic illness named by the promotional rhetoric of the new thaw. But Gorbachev did not share Khrushchev's populist ambivalence towards the pro-Western, liberal intelligentsia. The professional intelligentsia had been the fast-growing class of recent urbanization decades, and Gorbachevite reformism was quite clear in regarding it as its natural social constituency. The Brezhnev regime was blamed in the revitalized reformist discourse for creating the boundaries between official and dissident politics. *Novyi mir* and other journals became easily identifiable again as the centres of liberal thought, and quickly increased their circulation by publishing works that had been previously denied publication. Leading liberal dissidents such as Sakharov were allowed back into the mainstream of public life, and the Gorbachevite reformers drew on their ideas.

The key words of the reforms were *perestroika* ('restructuring' or 'reconstruction'), *glasnost'* ('openness' or 'giving voice to public concerns'), the 'socialist legal state', 'socialist pluralism', and 'democratization'. Exactly what these terms should mean in practice was an issue of contention in an unfolding discourse in which, as per political tradition, all the participants claimed to be in agreement with the party leader's promotion of the terms but in disagreement with other people's misinterpretations of them.

'Restructuring' originally signified that the overcoming of 'stagnation' required a change in attitudes so that people became responsible rather than alienated or corrupt participants in the economy, and that this change needed to be supported by a reform of the institutional structures in which they worked. The diagnosis of the 'administrative system' that was holding the economy back was similar to the ideas of Khrushchev-time advocates of 'market socialism'. The previous wave of pro-market reformism, however, floundered because of bureaucratic vested interest, the reformers now argued; a successful economic reform needed the *perestroika* to extend into political structures so that these no longer gave bureaucratic conservatives protection from the social forces of change. A more rational economic framework needed a new kind of partnership between political institutions and 'civil society' (*obshchestvo*), and a legal framework that would encourage people to do what was not forbidden rather than just what was specifically authorized. With an eye perhaps on the New Economic Policy (NEP) precedent (Bukharin was officially rehabilitated by 1988), new decrees and laws gave legitimacy to much of the informal economy; they encouraged self-employment in the service and artisan sectors, the formation of enterprise co-operatives in these spheres, and the leasing of some state property to the co-operatives and self-employed tradespeople.

State enterprises were given wider powers to control their budgets, encouraged to put an increasing part of their production plans on the basis of 'horizontally' negotiated agreements with customers, and to devolve more of their internal management to the factory floor brigades. By late 1980s they were also encouraged to experiment with making chief executives subject to election by workers. But the complicated matter of who had what rights in the management of state property and how planning should be combined with market relations was not receiving clear resolution. Planning authorities and ministries continued their work, although the republican-level authorities were being put in control of industries that were previously under all-union ministries, and although they exercised their control more as privileged 'customers' with a right to place priority 'state orders' than as superior organs imposing plan targets. Most product prices in the state sector remained controlled by the central authorities. Strategies for a more fundamental restructuring of the economy were under debate, but in practice the huge state sector (the non-agricultural co-operatives and self-employed people were still amounting to only about five per cent of the total labour force by 1989) continued to be managed through the formal and informal networks of enterprise directors and officials within which production and the movement of the products were negotiated.

Most participants in public debates agreed that an element of market discipline was needed to reduce state-industry overstaffing (which was estimated to be up to 20 per cent of the labour force) and to make production more responsive to customers' demand. Prices would have to be freed and state subsidies reduced to enable decentralized decision-makers to see where investment should go, argued the reform-minded economists. The question was how quickly or gradually should the reforms be carried out, and how far they should go in pushing back the province of state planning to make room for market-oriented activity. The regime's spokesmen were still insisting that the result of the *perestroika* should be a market socialism, which they envisaged as a mixture of different types of ownership and a system in which the decentralized decision-makers' profit orientation would not be allowed to jeopardize the interests of society as a whole. But many of the Western-oriented liberal economists were now influenced by economic philosophies which stressed the importance of market competition, sound money, and free trade against the mixed-economy ideals that had been dominant in the West in the 1960s. The drift of their logic was stretching the spectrum of opinions into the realm of pro-capitalist viewpoints. The divisions between Western-oriented and Russophile intellectuals had a long tradition; but if frankly pro-capitalist voices celebrating the virtues of business culture and equating socialism with bureaucracy had been relatively weak among the Westernizers let alone the Russophiles of tsarist times, they became quite distinct at the end of the 1980s. The professional intelligentsia Gorbachev regarded as his natural constituency at the beginning of his reign was becoming increasingly divided in its attitudes and opinions. As for the general population, opinion surveys carried out in the early 1990s were still showing only a small minority in favour of privatizing heavy industries; and as the co-operatives were finding to their cost, many people (including those in militia uniforms) assumed that entrepreneurial prosperity equalled anti-social profiteering and crime.

Glasnost' initially meant the media's participation in the campaign to highlight corrupt bureaucratic practices. This was not in itself new. Making revelations about the shortcomings of a previous regime and publicity campaigns against 'bureaucratism' belonged to the traditions of political life. The new regime wanted the media to be less formulaic, more factual and argumentative, but it still expected them to support the party programme. The links between political patrons and editorial offices were not dissolved. Journalists were used to the political patrons wanting them to show initiative but not irresponsibility, and editors did not rush to test if the Gorbachevite call for 'openness' meant a real press freedom. But when the press kept the population uninformed about the nuclear power-station accident in Chernobyl until several days after the event, the lapse in *glasnost'* became a public scandal. From 1986 onwards, protecting the population from disturbing news was considered a bad old habit and the openness of the public channels of communication increased to an unprecedented degree, effectively transforming the social and political climate. Only conservative and frankly Stalinist views were denied access. When, in 1988, a newspaper published an article by a technical college lecturer who criticized what was going wrong in the country from a conservative standpoint, the event was widely understood to signal an impending anti-*perestroika* change in party leadership. Gorbachev supporters closed ranks and the newspaper (*Sovetskaya Rossiya*) was forced to print an editorial apology for its irresponsibility. All the readers' letters that were subsequently published in the press attacked the article and the author (Nina

Andreyeva) had to use an Italian journal to let the world know that she received thousands of letters in support.

The 'socialist legal state' was a phrase of the Gorbachevite ideological output that initially had the connotation of a clampdown on bureaucratic corruption. It also signalled a contrast from the Khrushchevite idea of devolving administrative functions from state institutions to the party and other 'social organizations', and a commitment to making rule of law a dominant principle over the rights of administrative command. It pleased the liberal reformers who wanted people to be able to do whatever was not forbidden rather than just what some authority prescribed, and also the less liberal intellectuals whose vision of progress had the shape of a strong, rationally organized, and legitimate state capable of keeping law and order over a population they considered naturally predisposed towards an anarchic lack of discipline. The renewed commitment to the *Rechtsstaat* ideal, however, put the party's 'leading role' under further pressure. Until the late 1980s, Gorbachev's view was that the party should retain its 'leading role' as the only political party. In 1989 he was elected Chair of the Supreme Soviet, however, and unlike his predecessors in this office, he set about shifting the centre of power to it from the party central committee and politburo. The party renounced its monopoly on political organization in the following year.

'Socialist pluralism' was a corollary of the *perestroika* ideology which signalled a clear departure from Stalinist orthodoxy. It reflected the idea that diverse preferences and conflicts of interest were a necessary characteristic of any society which was modern and therefore complex. Marxist supporters of liberal reforms argued that no social system could be entirely harmonious and without contradictions, that without contradictions there could have been no social change, and that Stalinist ideologues parted ways with Marxism when they assumed socialism to be exempt from these maxims. Gorbachev and his supporters also believed that open contests between different viewpoints were necessary for distinguishing falsehoods from truth, a process on which the basis of wide consensus and popular participation in public life could eventually take place. By the end of the decade, however, radical liberals began to argue for 'socialist pluralism' in terms of Western social science in which the function of politics was to broker conflicting interests and achieve social stability based on the acceptance of diversity and a political culture geared to a peaceful conflict management. The 'socialist pluralism' arguments implied that there was a legitimate role for interest pressure groups in public life and that if, say, strikes occurred in the course of industrial restructuring, this would neither prove the reforms wrong nor pose a threat of social disintegration. Without 'socialist pluralism' there could be no growth of 'civil society', no breaching of the hypocritical barriers between public and private, formal and informal spheres of life, and no cultivation of the individual's sense of social responsibility.

At the practical level Gorbachev's acceptance of these arguments was most clearly manifested by his encouragement of the local authorities not to stand in the way of 'informal organizations', to rent space to them for offices and meetings, and to start a system of official registration of them such as would give them rights of regular access to public decision-makers and in some cases to public funds. In 1989 the number of above-ground 'informal groups' was estimated as 30 000 and in 1990 as 60 000. Their activities ranged from leisure pursuits to organizing improved welfare provision for various disadvantaged groups, to publicity and political campaigning on particular issues. Environmentalist groups grew especially quickly in response to *glasnost'* revelations concerning health statistics (life expectancy started to fall in the 1970s) and the extent of industrial pollution. They were credited with some impressive victories, for example, the government's decision to suspend work on diverting southwards the flow of Siberian rivers.

Gorbachev initially drew a line between 'socialist' and 'political' pluralism. 'Democratization' meant giving voters a choice of candidates in elections to the soviets, and making it possible for the most important of the registered 'informal groups' to put up their own candidates. Within the party, 'democratization' meant renouncing the old principles of 'democratic centralism' in favour of electing officials by secret ballot and allowing them to express their different viewpoints when they stood as candidates for party office. The general idea was to stimulate popular participation in political affairs but not to let 'democratization' go as far as a multiparty political system. But Gorbachev underestimated how far the legitimacy of the Communist Party was eroded by the time he took power, and how quickly it would crumble altogether under the weight of *glasnost'* reporting on the state of the country. When he jettisoned the one-party principle in 1990, he acted under pressure of events that had gathered a momentum he did not control. The coalescing of some of the more politically minded 'informal organizations' into embryonic parties started in 1988. By 1990 there were about 20 self-proclaimed political parties. They reflected a wide range of ideologies, but much of their membership was made up of people who left the Communist Party and the people who used to be dissidents; the vast majority of the population refrained from joining organized politics.

The lifting of official restraints on cultural life, informal groups, and the media made the plurality of subcultures that had grown during the Brezhnev regime even greater and more spectacular. The underground youth-culture themes of alienation and spiritual authenticity filled the airways along with many other forms of popular entertainment, social reporting and personal viewpoints. Spiritual healers, disaffected veterans of the Afghan war, orthodox priests, gulag survivors, hippies, pacifists, fascist hoodlums, descendants of tsarist-time nobles, health victims of pollution, 'metalists' (heavy-metal rockers revelling in the irony of sharing a name with the heroic proletarians of Bolshevik mythology), slum-living *limitchiki* and illegal residents, prostitutes, beauty queens, officials made to look shifty under investigative interviewing, serious *perestroika* propagandists – they and many other types were passing across the television screens. Russian society was presenting itself to its members in an image that was a mêlée compared to the categorical ordering of public messages in the past.

Of the established institutions, only the Orthodox Church was a beneficiary of the discernible trends; unsurprisingly, because by the end of the Brezhnev period sociological surveys had found those who believed in God (20 per cent of the total) outnumbering atheists (15 per cent). The agnostic majority was there to be attracted by an institution that offered a Russian and non-communist identity. The Church was a thousand years old in 1988, and it celebrated the anniversary in the knowledge that it was now gaining the respect of the young and educated such as it had not had since the dawn of this century.

The Communist Party was the greatest loser. Its ideology and symbols were the butt of the iconoclasm of the underground cultures that sprang on to the platforms of decontrolled commercial entertainment. The failures of its long years in power became an inescapable matter of public knowledge as well as of privately shared perceptions, and so did the furtive but thoroughly institution-alized inequities represented by the *nomenklatura*-linked privileged distribu-tion networks. Television pictures had a strong impact on their viewers when they showed a factory making quality sausage for the closed shops and canteens under the guise of making dietary foods for hospitals, or a car crashed by a provincial official to have its boot full of otherwise seldom-seen groceries. Party officials pleaded that such publicity sensationalized the degree of privilege that their special shops and canteens were in fact providing, but nobody believed them. Privileged supplies were a sore point because goods shortages in state shops were becoming worse in many places.

This was the result of political-decentralization pressures. The Gorbachev leadership wanted the party apparatus to reduce its involvement in the day-to-day functioning of the economy, and the central co-ordination powers of the ministerial institutions were weakened by confusing tugs-of-war over jurisdic-tion between all-union and republican authorities. Devolution of executive powers on to the republics was accelerated by the nationalist independence movements which Gorbachev tried to diffuse by offering more autonomy to the republican governments. The rifts in the political structures added to the processes of realignment in the networks of producers and suppliers, which were also on the cards as a result of the fact that enterprises were able to claim the right to choose their own customers. More goods were finding their way into the co-operative and private-trading sector where prices were de-controlled, and the goods that remained in the state sector had their particular destinations changed as new political patrons and considerations entered into the processes of administrative negotiation. The *perestroika* idea was that decentralization should put enterprises under market competition pressures to increase their efficiency in general and output of the products for which there was the most demand in particular. But this was not happening. As before, the competition was between buyers rather than sellers, and which buyers had priority was a matter for political-administrative negotiations. Until 1988, overall production was rising slightly while the supply-network realignments occasioned some redistribution of shortages within the state retail networks, and between the state sector and the growing non-state trading (co-operatives, private bazaars, black markets). But by the end of the decade the supply-network realignments began to cause problems to the manufacturing enter-prises. By 1990, many of them experienced disruption of raw-material supplies, production stoppages for this reason multiplied, total output and labour productivity started to fall, and inflationary pressures grew. The weakening and splitting of centralized political authority in a context where the invisible co-ordinating hand of competitive markets was still far from becoming real was sending the economy on a downward spiral.

Gorbachev's *perestroika* rhetoric was falling into disrepute among the general population as the economy was failing to deliver better living standards. Besides, the Soviet empire was cracking at the seams, with events in east Europe adding their impetus to separatist movements in the republics. In 1989, the process of 'restructuring' was heading for a precipitous stage. Strikes involving some 500 000 miners in the coalfields of Siberia and eastern Ukraine dominated home affairs in the summer months. Gorbachev as well as the politicians who were putting him under pressure from both conservative and radical ends of the spectrum were claiming that it was proving their point. For the first time in the Soviet era, strikes were made legal by new laws. But they did not catch on. Russia was a different country from what it had been in the last years of the tsarist empire, and the labour movement was not to have the historical importance it had then, at least not yet. The momentum for change that was gathering was in the political sphere, the structures of the state. Time will tell what social forces emerge to provide stable constituencies for the political players of the post-communist age.

Further Reading

The number of books that provide information on the period covered in this chapter is enormous. In writing on Brezhnev government policies I have drawn on D. R. Kelley (ed.), *Soviet Politics in the Brezhnev Era* (New York: Praeger, 1980). For the relationship between the Brezhenvite state and its society, on V. Zaslavsky, *The Neo-Stalinist State: Class, Ethnicity, and Consensus in Soviet Society* (New York: M. E. Sharpe Inc., 1982); T. L. Thompson and R. Sheldon (eds), *Soviet Society and Culture* (Boulder, Colo.: Westview press, 1988); and S. F. Cohen *et al.* (eds), *The Soviet Union since Stalin* (London: Macmillan, 1980). M. R. Beissinger, *Scientific Management, Socialist Discipline, and Soviet Power* (London: Tauris & Co., 1988), Chaps 6–8, provides a fine account of developments in the management world; and R. Stites, *Russian Popular Culture: Entertainment and Society since 1900* (Cambridge: Cambridge University Press, 1992), Chaps 6–7, is an indispensable source of social insights.

L. Attwood, *The New Soviet Man and Woman: Sex-Role Socialization in the USSR* (London: Macmillan, 1990) is a thorough examination of the ways in which gender differences have been conceptualized in Soviet academic theories, journalism, and policy-making. The gender theme in the developments of Soviet official ideology is also well presented in M. Buckley, *Women and Ideology in the Soviet Union* (New York: Harvester Wheatsheaf, 1989). G. W. Lapidus (ed.), *Women, Work, and the Family in the Soviet Union* (New York: M. E. Sharpe, 1982), is a wide ranging compilation of short empirical studies by Soviet social scientists. S. Bridger, *Women in the Soviet Countryside* (Cambridge: Cambridge University Press, 1987) is a valuable monograph on the sexual inequality problematic that at the same time provides a rare sociological focus on rural life. In L. Edmondson (ed.), *Women and Society in Russia and the Soviet Union* (Cambridge: Cambridge University Press, 1992), the articles by Bridger and Buckley offer succinct critical examination of the effects of *perestroika* on the position of women. A. McAuley, *Women's Work and Wages in the Soviet Union* (London: Allen & Unwin, 1981) is a summary and analysis of the quantitative data concerning gender inequalities in the labour markets.

D. Lane, *Soviet Society under Perestroika* (London: Routledge, 1992), is a useful textbook with a focus on Gorbachev-time developmkents. Other convenient sources of a good range of information on *perestroika* include J. Bloomfield (ed.), *The Soviet Revolution: Perestroika and the Remaking of Socialism* (London: Lawrence & Wishart, 1989) and S. Bialer (ed.), *Politics, Society, and Nationality Inside Gorbachev's Russia* (Boulder, Colo.: Westview Press, 1989). A stimulating essay on the historical causes of *perestroika*, written from a modernizing perspective, is M. Lewin, *The Gorbachev Phenomenon: A Hisorical Interpretation* (Los Angeles, Calif.: University of California, 1988).

On corruption and corruption campaigns, see L. Holmes, *The End of Communist Power: Anti-Corruption Campaigns and Legitimation Crisis* (Cambridge: Polity Press, 1993). On informal groups, see G. Hosking, J. Aves, and P. Duncan, *The Road to Post-Communism* (London: Pinter, 1993).

An insightful analysis of the effects of economic reform on industry in the early 1990s, which is based on a factory floor study and characterizes the effects as a transition to 'merchant capitalism', is offered by M. Burawoy and P. Krotov, 'The Soviet transition from socialism to capitalism: worker control and economic bargaining in the wood industry', *American Sociological Review* lvii, 1992, pp. 16–38. P. Rutland, 'Labour unrest and movements in 1989 and 1990', *Soviet Economy*, vi, 1990, no. 3, pp. 345–84, gives a detailed analytical account of the miners' strike.

H. Smith, *The Russians* (New York: Ballantine Books, 1976) is a highly readable and insightful report on everyday life in the 1970s written by an American journalist who had been based in Moscow as a correspondent over a long period. A more recent collection of sketches of Russian characters and their everyday lives is S. Richards, *Epics of Everyday Life* (Harmondsworth: Penguin Books, 1991). V. Voinovich, *The Ivankiad or the Tale of the Writer Voinovich's Installation in his New Apartment* (London: Jonathan Cape, 1978) is a superb account of the relations between individual and bureaucracy. For Russian women's perceptions of their worlds and responses to Western feminist ideas, see C. Hansson and K. Liden, *Moscow Women: Thirteen Interviews* (London: Allison & Busby, 1984); T. Mamonova (ed.), *Women and Russia* (Oxford: Basil Blackwell, 1984); and the translation of a *samizdat*, 'Almanach for women about women', December 1979, *Women and Russia* (London: Sheba Feminist Publishers, 1980).

Finally, the reader who is interested in the developments of the early 1990s, which are not covered in this book, will be well served by R. Sakwa, *Russian Politics and Society* (London: Routledge, 1993).

Postscript

The period of history covered in this book includes famines, wars and revolutions, slides to anarchy and dictatorial repressions, and processes of social change associated with industrialization and urbanization. A focus on political events and regimes reveals the replacement of the tsarist state by a communist one in 1917 as the towering historical landmark, and somewhat more tentatively perhaps, the formation of a postcommunist Russian state in the early 1990s. A focus on social order and change, the worlds in which people live their everyday lives, highlights different historical turning points. 1917 and its aftermath descended into anarchy and an economic crisis in which day-to-day survival meant relying on primitive political and economic organization; it was a world in which the peasantry produced the means of subsistence and men on horseback raided their grain stores for their clients. This kind of ancient social order had the temporary nature of an emergency situation, and there was ambiguity surrounding its significance for longer-term developments. From this perspective, the historical landmarks of social change can be seen in the years around 1905, in the 1930s, and the 1960s.

Prior to 1905, 'society' consisted of small if self-consciously progressive communities of educated Russians; then there was the tsarist monarchy with its ways of administering the populace as a set of 'social estates', the Orthodox Church, and a huge hinterland of peasant communities. The events of 1905 highlighted a profound shift in the relationship between state and society. 'Society' came to mean something similar to what 'civil society' meant in the West during the late nineteenth century. The social estates declined in their importance for government administration and people's identities. The Church lost its hold on the nation, the tsarist autocracy its popular mystique. Noble landholders lost their hold in the countryside. Modern social ideologies dictated the terms of public discourse. Education accelerated its advancement into the hinterland, the main cities changed their appearance, their life became animated by new civic movements and popular culture. New professions proliferated. Issues of industrial relations came to the fore in the growing factories and rail and telegraph transformed communications. In 1905, longer-term developments fused with a political crisis to create a moment of transformation.

In the civil society that grew to put tsarist autocracy under pressure, however, the intelligentsia rather than an entrepreneurial bourgeoisie defined the values of progress. Within the intelligentsia, neither Westernizers nor Slavophiles had allowed much space for the expression of strongly pro-business views. After 1905 such views gained their articulate proponents but remained on the margins of mainstream social opinion. In this respect there was an affinity between the state bureaucracy and its critics. The tsarist state had never accepted the view that its main role should be to provide a congenial home for free capitalist enterprise. The Stolypin reforms did not change that: technical modernization rather than individual ownership rights became their dominant goal, negotiating with rather than destroying the powers of communal control their method. The tsarist state took it upon itself to lead industrialization and keep it under control, and its policies included those for which the epithet 'police socialism' was quite fitting.

The Bolsheviks hijacked the revolution in 1917, but they were not the only ones to reject the values of capitalist individualism. Their rivals for power in the revolutionary republic tended to admire German organization of wartime economy more than Anglo-Saxon celebrations of free trade, and many of them favoured socialist ideologies. Self-confessed idealists rejected the cash-nexus materialism of market economy on moral grounds, while self-confessed materialists saw markets as anarchic obstacles to the development of a rational, scientific and technological civilization. The Bolsheviks were able to play propaganda tunes that included evocations of widely-shared beliefs in socialist, cultural and scientific-technological progress. The political culture and revolutionary institutions in which they played for power between February and October 1917 had their precedent in 1905. The October outcome was not inevitable – history is full of might-have-beens – but the communist regime was a child from a home that became evident on the historical landscape in 1905.

In the 1930s the communist regime forced a social transformation that turned the worlds of all sectors of the population. It put a brutal end to the established peasant order in the countryside, carried out an industrialization drive, precipitated a huge wave of migration from village to town, gave the country a new bureaucracy and social structure, police terror with labour camps, a new culture and national identity. The campaigns of the Stalin's 'revolution from above' left a huge historical legacy at all levels – political, social, cultural and economic. Much more than the transitions of 1905 and 1917, their effects on the population were immediate, radical, lasting, and no individual could retreat from them.

The 1960s are a landmark in Russian social history for quite a different reason. The country had entered the post-Stalin era, and the relationship between state and society was changed. The main reason, however, was that longer-term processes of urbanization began to reach their culmination. Urban dwellers were a rapidly increasing majority, and for the first time, housing construction began to catch up with the urban population growth; even starting to provide families with the privacy of self-contained apartments. Until the 1920s, most metropolitan residents were migrant labourers living away from their families. In the Stalin era, migrants were coming to towns for good and lived there with their own families, but in multioccupied as well as overcrowded accommodation. In the 1960s urban living began to lose its makeshift character. At the same time, state welfare provision was extended to collective farmers, and the gap between urban and rural living standards began to close. Radio and TV in the homes, a high educational profile of both male and female population, falling birth-rate and rising divorce-rate, consumerist aspirations – features of a new, urban and industrial society were coming to the fore and, Russia's political regime stopped being bent on militant mobilizations.

But the regime decayed and failed in its attempt to renew itself. Russia is in turmoil again. As I write these lines (March 1994), the news on Western television screens is of spies, resurgent imperial ambitions, backtracking on economic reforms, alliance of communists and nationalists in the parliament, crime and corruption, soaring infant mortality, President Yeltsin's failing health, the disenchantment of Russians with the West. It is too early to see what such fragments represent of the transformations that are under way.

A transition to capitalism was never going to be an easy item on the Russian political agenda, especially if the goal is defined in the somewhat idealized terms of perfect market competition and a limitation of state involvement to guaranteeing rights of private property, anti-trust legislation and the management of money supply. The economic theory that envisions entrepreneurial citizens creating a prosperous and peaceful society without a reliance on politicians and bureaucracies forgets that Western economies themselves, being the result of their own historical developments, are not always true to it. Tsarist Russia was certainly not true to it; and, the Soviet era has bequeathed a huge, complex industrial economy with its own culture. In the Russian context, rolling back the boundaries of the state is prone to create anarchy – or more precisely, a commercial sector in which protection rackets run by the criminal fraternity and former policemen play a prominent role. This sector is growing amongst large corporate islands in which production and the flow of goods is managed through networks established under the old planning system. Neither the new commercial sector nor the corporations, freed though they have been of state planners and party authorities, look like forming the kind of capitalism that radical reformers want.

Among the corporate managerial networks, mutual loyalties play a larger role in decision-making than profit maximization. Insiders maintain each other's supplies at cost-plus price and perhaps on credit, while buyers from outside the networks get only what is left, at a premium charge. Mutual loyalties have been always the important means of achieving stability in a potentially fickle environment. The industrial managers are just as before concerned above all to maintain production, that is, to assure the reliability of supplies, and to keep their workforce stable. They maintain welfare provision for their employees despite escalating costs, and in some cases enlarge it, for example by bartering factory products for food which they sell to employees at cheaper prices than those charged at normal shops. Many corporate managers take a special pride in their paternal care for their 'collectives'. The importance of the factories as centres of welfare provision in times of economic crisis has a long historical tradition. The managers' strategies amount to a resistance against radical reformist policies, because they only increase market segmentation, do not release capital resources for new investment, and do not reduce public spending. The reformers have been unable so far to get the national bank to counter the resistance by imposing strict budget constraints on the corporations.

To many Russians, the industrial managers appear as the respectable part of the economic sector, for they can explain much of what they do as being based on the social responsibility they have as employers of large numbers of people.

The new entrepreneurs, on the other hand, appear to many as 'parasitic', in that they trade rather than produce, and as people whose money-making is based on greed, sharp practice, and probably some involvement in crime. This is a difficult conundrum for marketization policies.

Another political difficulty has been the fact that, in the inflationary crisis that followed the deregulation of prices, access to dollars has a lot to do with the chances of an entrepreneurial institution or individual to do well. There is an interesting social history to be written on the patterns of interaction between Westerners and Russians at all levels of society, from government and large corporations to street tourist trade, that have emerged since Russia opened herself to the West. In Russia, the pros and cons of openness or closure to the West have divided attitudes for centuries. Openness now is not just a question of abstract opinion; it is a new reality and a new source of social differentiation. It deals dollars to some and devalued roubles to others, positive experiences to some and negative to others. There is enough of the latter about to give fresh resonance to the nationalist rhetoric of hurt pride.

On the other hand, capitalism is on the agenda now as it never was before. New departures do happen in history. Withdrawal into militarily guarded insulation from the world and continued feeding of industrial dinosaurs, after all, hardly presents an attractive alternative to marketization. Time will tell what kind of state and society emerge from the 1990s.

Index